Family Law and the Pursuit of Intimacy

Family Law and the Pursuit of Intimacy

Milton C. Regan, Jr.

NEW YORK UNIVERSITY PRESS
New York and London

NEW YORK UNIVERSITY PRESS
New York and London

Library of Congress Cataloging-in-Publication Data
Regan, Milton C.
Family law and the pursuit of intimacy / Milton C. Regan, Jr.
p.   cm.
Includes bibliographical references and index.
ISBN 0-8147-7430-X (cloth : alk. paper)
 1. Domestic relations—United States.   2. Husband and wife—
United States.   3. Intimacy (Psychology)   I. Title.
KF505.R43   1993
346.7301'5—dc20
[347.30615]   92-38948
                        CIP

New York University Press Books are printed on acid-free paper,
and their binding materials are chosen for strength and durability.

Manufactured in the United States of America

c 10 9 8 7 6 5 4 3 2 1

To Nancy, Rebecca, and Benjamin

Contents

Acknowledgments

I've benefited greatly from the generosity and insight of many people in writing this book. Mark Tushnet and Mary Ann Glendon read an early draft of the entire manuscript and offered both comments and encouragement. Judy Areen, William Galston, Steve Goldberg, Martha Minow, Nancy Sachs, Carl Schneider, and Gerry Spann also read drafts of the full manuscript and provided helpful criticism and suggestions. In addition, Gerry graciously took time away from work on his own book to lead me through many of the intricacies of modern word processing. Several other persons read selected portions of the book and helped me sharpen or rethink my treatment of many issues: Gregg Bloche, Peter Byrne, Richard Chused, Dan Ernst, Bill Eskridge, Jim Feinerman, Chai Feldblum, Hendrik Hartog, Vicki Jackson, Laura Macklin, Jane Stromseth, Robin West, and Steve Winter. I'm also grateful to participants in the Georgetown University Law Center Faculty Workshop and Carl Schneider's Family Law Seminar at the University of Michigan Law School for their helpful comments. Numerous conversations with Carl also have provided enjoyable opportunities to test and refine my ideas. In addition, I appreciate the careful review and constructive suggestions that Steven Mintz offered as a reader for New York University Press, which have greatly improved this work. Dean Judy Areen and Associate Dean Wendy Williams at Georgetown have provided important writer's grant funds for my work on the book. Jeffrey Orchard, Ronnit Rhojany, and Julie Uebler furnished very able and indispensable research assistance. Finally, my wife, Nancy Sachs, continues to offer rich intellectual and personal insights into the ways in which an intimate relationship can transform daily life into a common journey.

Family Law and the Pursuit of Intimacy

Introduction

The middle distance fell away, so the grids (from small to large) that had sup-
ported the middle distance fell into disuse and ceased to be understandable. Two
grids remained. The grid of two hundred million and the grid of intimacy.
                    —George W. S. Trow, *Within the Context of No Context*

Family may be the vessel that holds our deepest longing for connection
with others. In a recent survey of American family life by Mass Mutual
Insurance Company, people expressed intense devotion to the idea of the
family as a realm of unselfish commitment and unconditional acceptance.
The words "caring" and "loving" were most often used to describe the
family.[1] Researchers report, "This is a primary function of family: caring,
nurturing, and loving."[2] The idea of family thus has powerful resonance
as a "middle distance" between isolated individuals on the one hand and
mass society on the other, a realm in which we can cultivate the social
dimension of the self in recognizable form.

Yet, as the same survey indicates, family life often disappoints us,
seems to fall short of the hopes that we project onto it. "Interestingly,"
researchers note, "respondents are less inclined to believe that their families provide emotional support, are close, or communicate well."[3] While
the idea of family evokes emotions of care and love, "many do not report
the actions that are associated with these emotions."[4] As a result, the
survey concludes: "It would seem that in many families members have
positive feelings but lack the skills to express them to each other."[5]

Family life in the last decade of the twentieth century thus seems to
provoke both longing and disillusionment, an acute sense that the intimacy we pursue too often eludes us. In this book, I will argue that much
of modern family law reinforces this condition. This is because the prem-

I

ise of family law increasingly is that the vessel of family shouldn't be filled with substantive moral content, but should be left empty so that individuals can use it for their own purposes. On this view, family law, like other modern liberal institutions, should remain neutral among visions of the good life, intervening only when necessary to prevent one individual from harming another.[6]

The expression of this outlook in family law is rejection of status in favor of contract as the governing legal principle of family life. While status purports to bestow standard rights and obligations on all who have legal identities, such as husband, wife, or parent, contract insists that individuals themselves should determine the terms of their intimate relationships. A contractual approach is skeptical of the notion that the family should be regarded as a social institution amenable to being shaped by collective ends.[7] Instead, it asserts that the family is fundamentally a zone of private choice, in which the individual seeks to cultivate an authentic sense of self through intimacy with others. On this view, contract is the rule; "harm" is the only exception that justifies collective nullification of private choices. The result is that consent, rather than communal expectation, becomes the touchstone of obligation within the family.

In the pages that follow, I explore the implicit vision of intimacy that underlies this commitment to contract, or private ordering, as the governing principle of family law. This vision of intimacy is premised on what I call the model of the *acontextual* self—a belief in the existence of an authentic self who stands apart from any social relationship in which he or she is involved. On this view, being a husband, for instance, is a role that I play, not part of who I am in any fundamental way. I am truly myself insofar as I am free to choose which role to play, not insofar as I carry out the prescriptions of any one of them. For the acontextual self, "I am what I choose to be. I can always, if I wish to, put in question what are taken to be the merely contingent social features of my existence."[8] Under the tenets of what I call modernism, social progress is achieved by treating more and more of my social features as contingent rather than constitutive. Freed of the distortions of "external" social convention, individuals can then fashion intimate relationships on terms that they choose, in accordance with their deepest needs and desires.

The promise of the modernist vision therefore is that family life will be a haven of genuine intimacy among authentic individuals. Yet there is reason to question whether this vision is being realized. A recent review of research on the family, for instance, describes "a renewed and growing concern, perhaps even a greater sense of urgency" in the last decade that marriage and family are being "severely weakened and threatened under the press of accelerated and pervasive social change."[9] Recent projections are that as many as two-thirds of marriages will face disruption through separation and divorce,[10] and people now spend a smaller percentage of their lives in a family setting than ever before.[11] The Mass Mutual survey that I described earlier indicated that 62 percent of all Americans believe that family values have weakened in recent years, while only 14 percent believe that they have gotten stronger.[12] Almost three out of five respondents rated the quality of family life negatively, and almost 40 percent who rated it positively expected to rate it negatively ten years from now.[13] The perception of crisis is not new to our age; the latter half of the nineteenth century, for instance, was marked by acute anxiety about family stability.[14] Nonetheless, contemporary life seems particularly haunted by a sense that the family is less and less able to offer a safe harbor from the relentless tides of social fragmentation.

One response is to insist that the modernist project is incomplete—that true intimacy will be achieved only when we are fully liberated from the collective demands that constrain our individuality. On this view, commitment to contract in family law is a vehicle for eliminating what may be the last obstacle to the modernist dream of individual emancipation. I will argue, however, that a better response is to question the premises of the modernist project. Those premises, I argue, ignore the social context in which individual identity emerges and in which intimacy is sustained.[15] They foster the view that "private" life is preeminently the domain of the individual, who may draw upon intimate relationships as a resource in pursuing a genuine self, but whose authentic identity depends upon never being defined in terms of any given relationship.

These assumptions ironically undermine the quest for identity and intimacy that is the rationale for a regime of contract in family law, because they neglect the communal preconditions of that quest. This critique suggests that commitment to contract is problematic not simply when the "harm" exception applies, but more generally because its vision of the self is fundamentally asocial. Rather than endorse a legal regime in which contract is the rule and harm the exception, we may do better if we strive to sustain an equilibrium in which both contract and status play important roles. Appreciation of the limitations of private ordering should lead us to ask whether a new model of status, shorn of its traditionally sexist assumptions, might serve an important function in family law.

In order to explore the contribution that a new model of status might make, we need to examine the era in which family law first emerged as a distinct body of law—the Victorian age. Much of modern family law's rejection of status is based on aversion to the gender roles that Victorian legal status reinforced. This aversion is eminently justified. Yet we may still be able to learn something from the Victorians if we appreciate that they were the first to confront the widespread influence of modernism. Recent scholarship suggests that this confrontation provoked a fear that rising individualism would dissolve any sense of self that was rooted in communal responsibility. A conception of the family as a network of interdependent roles, and the reinforcement of those roles through legal status, was one response to this concern. Status thus offered a way to foster a sense of individual identity that drew in part on social expectations. Indeed, it was during the Victorian era that the family achieved broad cultural significance as a model of what I call *relational* identity— a sense of oneself as defined in part by relationships with others.

This suggests that the use of status in family law may still have value for us today, even as we reject the gendered form that it took in the Victorian era. Specifically, status can express social commitment to the view that relationships of interdependence can give rise to responsibility in ways that a purely voluntary conception of obligation can't fully capture.[16] This affirms that family life is not simply a private sphere, but a realm of important public concern. The family is our first and most intense experience of sociality, a form of life in which we learn enduring lessons about self in relationship with others. If we are truly concerned about the formation of individual identity and the attainment of intimacy, then, we can't afford to be neutral about the terms on which family life is lived. We need to attend to the desire for greater equality and the fact of more diversity in family life—benefits largely attributable to a contractual outlook. At the same time, however, we need to retain a communitarian perspective that recognizes the importance of the family as a model of relational identity.

This implies that the function of family law should not be simply to provide a neutral framework for private ordering, qualified only by the need to prevent harm to others. Family law also should promote a substantive moral vision of commitment and responsibility. My argument is not that status should be the governing legal principle of family life. Neither status nor contract should be dominant, because individuals possess dimensions of both solitude and connection that require attention. Rather, my aim is to promote a restoration of balance by providing a contemporary justification for the continuing relevance of status.

I will pursue these themes, first, by comparing the ways in which the family law of the Victorian era and the late twentieth century reflect distinct conceptions of identity and intimacy. I examine Victorian family law and family life in chapter 1, arguing that the Victorians sought to preserve a relational sense of self by promoting what I call "role identification." The use of status in family law was one part of this effort to promote a vision of the self as realized through the performance of social roles. In chapter 2, I explore contemporary family law and family life, suggesting that the current age is characterized by what might be called "role distance."[7] This attitude reflects the view that self-realization occurs in opposition to the demands of social role, and thus places a premium on private ordering of family life. In chapter 3, I discuss what some observers have described as the postmodern fragmentation of identity, in which it becomes harder to sustain a unified sense of the self over time. I argue that this condition can be seen as the logical culmination of insistence on the acontextual self, an insistence that renders not only identity problematic but intimacy as well. In chapter 4, I suggest that legal status, typically viewed as antithetical to genuine intimacy, may in fact promote it. It can do so both by protecting emotional reliance in intimate relationships and by fostering a coherent sense of identity that is necessary for the capacity to make intimate commitments. In chapter 5, I explore how a new model of status might inform our consideration of several family law issues. Finally, in chapter 6 I address objections to a reinvigoration of status in family law.

I must confess that being a father has been perhaps as important an impetus for this book as being a scholar. While the model of the acontextual self has wide appeal, it is men traditionally who have been socialized most vigorously in its image. This creates the risk that the advent of fatherhood will be experienced by many men as an occasion of loss—the loss of a self who can pursue his life's mission without constraint. In a world in which men are surrounded by ideals of unfettered autonomy and individual fulfillment, fatherhood may come to seem an impediment to self-realization. Too often, the result may be that the distance of the acontextual self from its roles is played out in the emotional distance of men from their families. A relational sense of self can offer a way out of this impasse, a perspective from which a child's call for assistance can seem less an intrusion on the project of the self, and more a way of realizing it. Such an understanding requires cultural support if it is to flourish. To the extent that we model family law primarily on the image of the acontextual self, however, we risk losing a language that can provide this support. This book, then, is a small step in an effort to preserve and strengthen such a language, one in which "we could all, men and women, see that dependence and independence are deeply related, and that we can be independent persons without denying that we need one another."[18]

1. The Victorian Construction of Intimacy

Family law first achieved widespread acceptance as a discrete and self-conscious field of law in the Victorian era, which roughly corresponds to the latter two-thirds of the nineteenth century.[1] The basic organizing principle of this body of law was status, the notion that family members had specific legal identities that were the source of relatively fixed rights and obligations. This principle reflected an idea of the family as an institution comprised of individuals who performed specific interrelated roles. Those roles, of course, were based on the assumption that men and women by nature were fit for certain distinct pursuits, an assumption with which modern society takes issue.

In this chapter, I want to argue that the Victorian use of status in family law contains the kernel of a vision that we may want to salvage, even as we reject its gendered manifestation during the Victorian era itself. That vision is of the self as relational— as constituted in part by the relationships in which it is involved. We can appreciate this understanding of identity by attending to scholarship that suggests that the Victorians were the first to confront directly the forces of modernization and the modernist sensibility that accompanied them. From this perspective, it is possible to see Victorian emphasis on family roles, and the system of family law that reinforced those roles, as an effort to provide a model of how the pursuit of individual satisfaction might be tempered by shared norms of responsibility. It is this distinct construction of intimacy, and the legal regime associated with it, that I want to explore in this chapter.

A few caveats are in order at this point. First, any effort to discuss the Victorian era must contend with Lytton Strachey's comment that "[t]he history of the Victorian Age will never be written; we know too much about it."[2] As Strachey's remark suggests, the wealth of available contemporaneous material from the nineteenth century can't help but impress upon us the multiple strands of Victorian thought and orientation. It was an age that, broadly defined, encompassed both Shelley's exaltation of free love[3] and Tennyson's dark warning that adultery inexorably leads to the corruption and downfall of any civilized society.[4] Anyone must be cautious, therefore, in attempting to draw conclusions about the sensibilities of the age. This is especially true when focusing on one aspect of Victorian culture, in a schematic fashion that can't fully convey the rich texture of social experience. Any such effort necessarily risks neglecting important qualifications and counterexamples.

My hope nonetheless is to contribute to a more complex understanding of the family law of the period by challenging the popular perception that the phrase "Victorian intimacy" is an oxymoron. The influential image of Victorian life as sexually repressed, emotionally remote, and hypocritical[5] is one reason that the use of status in family law now tends to be regarded as antithetical to the promotion of intimacy. By offering a different image, I aim to promote a more balanced dialogue about the functions that status might serve in a modern family law regime.

A second caveat is that the Victorian middle class that most faithfully embraced the ideals that I will discuss was a minority.[6] Indeed, the gravity and tenacity with which it clung to its ethic in part reflected nervous uncertainty about the survival of the middle class itself.[7] Yet despite its minority status, the earnest middle class made up in influence what it lacked in numbers.[8] Its power rested not simply on privileged economic status but also in part on the emergence in the United States of a national culture that drew sustenance from dissemination of the printed word.[9] Its influence was also derived from the zealous sense of mission that animated aggressive efforts to inculcate nonbelievers with the Victorian ethic. As Elaine May notes, "Victorians waged a vigorous campaign to bring outsiders into the fold. They used every means of persuasion or coercion within their power to encourage, or even force, conformity to the code."[10]

Next, one may question the wisdom of attempting to extract some saving elements from a Victorian regime so permeated with gendered assumptions. Victorian family law and social life, one might argue, promoted a relational sense of self far more vigorously for women than for men—so much so that it's unwarranted to impute to the era a belief in the reciprocal family duties of both women and men. Furthermore, even if there were proclamations of this belief, these can be seen as the ideological veneer of a system of gender privilege.

There is no doubt that gender was deeply implicated in Victorian family law and family life, which fact should cut short any inclination to idealize the Victorian family as a paragon of communal devotion. Yet recent scholarship suggests that the impulses that underlay construction of the Victorian family were more complex than a simple desire to perpetuate male domination. By attending to this complexity, we may be able to recognize ways in which concepts of family status and family roles were responsive to concerns that remain relevant in our own day. If so, we may be able to discern a general value in Victorian notions of identity and intimacy that transcends their specific Victorian embodiments.

This leads to a final point. My argument is that Victorian reliance on status in family law was part of an effort to preserve a relational sense of self in the face of perceived atomizing tendencies of modernization. Despite scholarly support for this interpretation, there is room for argument that the Victorians themselves didn't consciously see their enterprise in such terms, or that this purpose was dwarfed by others that were more significant. I regard my analysis, however, as an exercise in what Druscilla Cornell calls "recollective imagination,"[11] which seeks to extract from past practice a normative vision that can inform a critical understanding of both the past and the future. Specifically, I maintain that the model of the relational self latent in Victorian status contains such a vision. That vision provides a vantage point from which to criticize the gendered form that Victorian status took, in light of what "might have been" had the vision been fully realized.[12] At the same time, this process offers a glimpse of what future social life "should be" if we take the precepts of that vision seriously.[13] My discussion of the conceptual underpinnings of the tradition of status in family law, therefore, is a plea for us to "tell a 'new' story and to project the stories we read into the tradition as constitutive of that tradition, as well as regulative of who we might become."[14]

Victorian Family Law

In the mid-Victorian period, Henry Maine noted a movement from status to contract in Western law, suggesting that the progress of civilization was marked by such an evolution.[15] Maine's focus was on the diminishing role of the family as a source of legal identity, as the individual emerged in civil society as the locus of legal capacity. Within the family itself, however, status continued to order relationships for perhaps as long as a century after Maine's observations.

In discussing Victorian family law's reliance on status, it will be useful to discuss the concept of "role" as well as "status." Role focuses on "behaviors that are characteristic of persons in a context."[16] The context is defined by a pattern of "positions"[17] that are related "through reciprocal ties, through rights and duties binding on the incumbents."[18] A role, then, "consists of the activity the incumbent would engage in were he to act solely in terms of the normative demands upon someone in his position."[19] As a general matter, those demands or expectations are impersonal, in that they apply to whoever occupies that position, regardless of her personal characteristics or preferences.[20] Thus, we expect certain kinds of behavior from people such as parents, judges, teachers, or bank tellers when they're performing their roles as such.

By "status" I mean a legal identity that is subject to a set of publicly imposed expectations largely independent of the preferences of the person who holds that status.[21] Put another way, status is the formal expression of the behavior expected of a role occupant. Status was a crucial component of Victorian family law in the sense that a person's identity as husband, wife, father, or mother was intended to be a significant determinant of that person's conduct within the family. Family law during this era thus fostered a vision of the family as a set of reciprocal roles in which proper individual conduct was determined by the individual's relationship to others in the family. Such an orientation evinced relatively little formal solicitude for private ordering in most aspects of family life.

I must hasten to add that I am speaking only about the broad outline of nineteenth-century family law. I don't mean to suggest that the law was either monolithic or static during this period; indeed, family law during the era was marked by great ferment.[22] Nor do I mean to suggest that the predominance of status was uncontested. The issue of divorce, for instance, was a source of much contention during the century, with an ebb and flow of liberal and restrictive legislation that reflected views about the relative "public" and "private" elements of marriage.[23] Furthermore, as Martha Minow has pointed out, women sometimes used their roles and status to expand the range of permissible behavior, thus actively reshaping the expectations associated with these concepts.[24] The law on the books thus cannot be taken as the only indication of the prevalence or influence of certain ideals.

With these caveats in mind, my point is a fairly simple one: as a whole, Victorian family law reflected a relatively strong sense that men and women within the family should act in accordance with certain standard expectations that flowed from their statuses as husbands, wives, fathers, and mothers. I focus on this aspect of the law in particular because I see it as one of the features that distinguishes Victorian family law from family law late in our own century.

Nineteenth-century judges and scholars were explicit in emphasizing that marriage was a status rather than simply a contract. As the Supreme Court stated in *Maynard v. Hill*,

Marriage is more than a mere contract. The consent of the parties is of course essential to its existence, but when the contract to marry is executed by the marriage, a relation is created between the parties which they cannot change.[25]

Similarly, Joel Bishop, author of an influential family law treatise, noted in his 1891 edition that courts generally had abandoned their careless use of contract rhetoric since the time of his first treatise in 1852. The law was currently much clearer, he wrote, that, while husband and wife had consented to marry, their promise to marry constituted consent to assume the marital status.[26] The clear message of nineteenth-century law was that marriage was not simply a private matter primarily of concern to the parties involved.

As a status, marriage involved certain standard rights and duties. As Bishop expressed it, "marriage confers on the husband the right to the companionship and services of the wife," and the wife could expect her husband "to protect and support her while in the substantial discharge of her duties."[27] Any agreement by the spouses to alter these rights and duties was unenforceable.[28] Indeed, these duties served to constitute marriage itself, as is illustrated by the Kansas Supreme Court's affirmance of a conviction for illegal cohabitation in 1887.[29] The defendants in this case had not obtained a marriage license, but had lived together professing to be husband and wife, which normally would have entitled them to the presumption of common law marriage.[30] However, they had proclaimed in their own wedding ceremony that marriage was a "strictly personal matter" immune from state regulation,[31] and the groom had acknowledged his bride's right to control her own property, to keep her own name, to have custody of any children upon divorce, and to call on him for equal child care responsibility.[32] The court declared of the parties that "they have lived together, but had no intention of creating that relation of *status* known and defined by law and by customs and usages of all civilized societies as marriage."[33]

As is well known, spouses could not enforce these duties against one another save in exceptional circumstances.[34] From one perspective, this seems to undermine identification with family roles by freeing family members to act as they wish without fear of legal sanction. From another perspective, however, the doctrine of "family privacy" that abjured "intervention" reflects an understanding of private life as irreducibly social. That doctrine lodged the right of privacy in the family, because it saw the family, not the individual, as the fundamental unit within the "private" sphere. For the Victorians, status merely embodied the dictates of nature, and family members were bound by "natural" inclination to perform the obligations embodied in status.[35] From this perspective, efforts to enforce duties risked the introduction of an individualistic ethic of rights at odds with the collective character of the family.[36] Unwillingness to command performance of status duties thus reflected a view that family members typically had a relational sense of identity that the law might undermine, rather than promote, if it intruded too far into the family.[37]

Third persons who induced a breach of spousal duty, however, often could be liable to the other spouse for alienation of affection, seduction, or enticement.[38] Such causes of action flowed from status expectations, the perpetrator being deemed to have interfered with a wife's entitlement to "the society and protecting care of her husband,"[39] or a husband's expectation of the "society and services of his wife[.]"[40] While not uniformly applauded, these causes of action served to reinforce an ethic of communal support and respect for spousal duty.

Given the social interest in marriage, separation or divorce could not be effectuated merely upon the wishes of the spouses. An agreement that could be construed as encouraging separation, for instance, such as a promise to provide support in case the parties were to live apart, was unenforceable.[41] Such agreements were regarded as attempts by the parties to disavow the spousal duty of cohabitation. As Bishop put it, "[m]arried parties cannot validly agree to do what the law forbids to be done on their agreement; namely, so to live in separation as to cut off the unforfeited right of either to demand a return to cohabitation."[42]

Similarly, divorce was "not a mere controversy between private parties[.]"[43] Rather, the view was that "marriage [is] a public institution of universal concern, and each individual marriage or its dissolution affect[s] the rights not only of the husband and wife, but of all other persons[.]"[44] As a result, spouses could not obtain a divorce simply by agreement between themselves.[45] Furthermore, any contract dealing with property distribution or alimony would be enforced only if construed as not stimulating divorce or discouraging the assertion of any defense to a divorce petition.[46]

The centrality of marriage as a status during this period is underscored by the fact that divorce was available only upon proof of some dereliction of marital duty, committed by a guilty spouse against an innocent one. As Joel Bishop put it, "a breach of marriage duties, such as authorizes divorce, is a civil tort, and the divorce is in essence an action of tort, though not technically known by this name[.]"[47] Thus, a spouse could obtain a divorce only by establishing that her partner had committed certain offenses against her,[48] the most common of which were adultery,[49] desertion,[50] and cruelty.[51] The parties could not cooperate to create a ground for divorce by, for instance, acquiescing in the other's misconduct,[52] suppressing evidence that might constitute a bar to divorce, or conspiring for one party to commit a marital offense.[53] Furthermore, any evidence that the wronged party had forgiven the guilty one would prevent divorce.[54] Finally, where both spouses had breached their duties, neither could obtain divorce from the other.[55] Such impediments reflected the premise that marriage was a public institution whose dissolution should occur only upon proof that one spouse had been wronged by the other's violation of status obligations.[56] The emphasis on duty over personal preference is underscored by Joel Bishop in words that have an odd ring to a late twentieth-century audience:

There are physical and mental unadaptations, or misfits—dissimilar aspirations and passions, non-assimilating loves and hopes, personal atmospheres mutually repellent, "incompatibilities of temper," and various other like things,—which plainly ought to have prevented marriage at the beginning, but which as grounds of divorce cannot be practically adopted without working more mischief than good.[57]

The gravity of a breach of marital duty was reflected in the fact that fault could serve to penalize a guilty spouse in decisions about property,[58] alimony,[59] or custody.[60] Furthermore, some states prohibited remarriage by the guilty party either completely or for a certain period of time, reflecting the notion of marriage as a status whose obligations one must be deemed capable of assuming.[61] "Thus," comments Herbert Jacob, "divorce was a very serious matter which impugned reputations and had the potential of depriving men and women of property and children."[62] To many in the Victorian era it was inconceivable that it could be any other way. As Joel Bishop stated in criticizing the notion that the law should simply seek to restore divorcing parties back to their premarital position, such a rule "puts innocence and guilt on one level, gives no damage for wrong inflicted, and affords no restraint against breaches of matrimonial duty."[63]

Victorian family law thus reflected the ideas that "marriage is an institution of society, and that the relation of husband and wife is a status of the parties, created and controlled by the law."[64] Even some laws that undermined traditional patriarchal prerogatives, such as married women's property law or presumptions in favor of mothers in some custody disputes, also can be seen as reinforcing status expectations.[65] In closing, perhaps the best expression of Victorian belief in the compatibility of legal duty and marital affection can be found in lines from Coventry Patmore's "The Wedding Sermon":

[T]he bond of law
Does oftener marriage-love evoke,
Than love, which does not wear the yoke
Of legal vows, submits to be
Self-rein'd from ruinous liberty.
Lovely is love; but age well knows
'Twas law which kept the lover's vows
Inviolate through the year or years
Of worship piec'd with frantic fears,
When she who lay within his breast
Seem'd of all women perhaps the best,
But not the whole, of womankind,
Or love, in his yet wayward mind,
Had ghastly doubts its precious life
Was pledged for aye to the wrong wife.[66]

The foundation of Victorian family law was based upon conceptions of identity and intimacy that can be viewed as responses to nascent modernization and its modernist sensibilities. Following Marshall Berman's definition of "modernization" as the processes fostering rapid material change in society, and "modernism" as the "visions and values" associated with them,[67] we can see status in Victorian family law as part of an effort to preserve a relational sense of identity in the face of rising individualism.

The Concept of the Modern

Several scholars suggest that it was the fate of the Victorians to be the first to confront the widespread press of modern forces.[68] As Daniel Walker Howe notes, cases can be made for identifying modernizing influences as far back as the sixteenth-century Tudor revolution, the seventeenth-century Puritans, and the late eighteenth- century industrial revolution.[69] The Victorians, however, were perhaps the first to experience the effects of this process in nearly all dimensions of everyday life. As Howe suggests, "The significance of the Victorian era, then, lies not in its encompassing the whole of modernization, but in being its exponential culmination."[70]

In discussing the idea of modernization, we must remain aware that much of the logic of modernization seems apparent only in our century, which creates the danger that we will project back into an earlier historical period a concern with the issues that we regard today as most pressing. The Victorian conceptual universe was not our own, and the pre-Freudian phase of the Victorian era may be particularly resistant to our efforts to map psychological concerns onto it. There is much work, however, that suggests that we contend today with many of the questions whose outlines the Victorians were dimly beginning to perceive. At times their perception was self-conscious, at times inchoate. Nonetheless, the concepts of modernization and modernism provide some basis for appreciating that Victorian structures of experience were different from ours, while still discerning within them a kinship with our own.

However, we must be careful not to reify concepts such as modernization. It is, after all, an intellectual construct, an abstraction from the ragged and contradictory texture of lived experience. As Peter Gay reminds us, for instance, "strictly speaking, there was no bourgeois experience in the nineteenth century; there were only bourgeois experiences."[71] Joyce Appleby has pointed out the dangers of utilizing social science concepts such as modernization in attempting to understand the evolution of culture.[72] She warns that, while generalization is inevitable in any historical account, the language of social science may be particularly insensitive to the richness and diversity of experience.[73] With respect to the concept of modernization in particular, she notes that an implicit attachment to continuity often tends to cast modernization as a disruptive force that preys upon traditional societies imbued with "a set of warm and wonderful features perpetually at risk."[74]

This word of caution is surely well founded. However, my use of the concept of modernization may in fact help to illuminate what Appleby describes as "the way that symbols and values interacted with routines and institutions."[75] In particular, framing the analysis this way, as opposed to using the myriad of other perspectives that are available, might shed light on the evolution of our conception of the relationship between the self and others. As Michael Zuckerman suggests, "Modernization may, indeed, afford a context in which it is possible to comprehend both the communal and the individualistic elements of American life."[76]

A working definition of what constitutes the "modern" experience is offered by Richard Brown, who suggests that traditional and modern society may be thought of as two ideal types, neither of which is likely fully to be represented in any period. With that caveat, he suggests that the expectation of constant and rapid change typifies modern society, such that time loses its character as endless repetition and becomes a scarce resource that recedes into the future.[77] Commitment to perpetual change is associated with the belief that there exists a "true" reality underneath the facade of appearances. This notion can of course be traced back at least to Plato's allegory of the cave,[78] but it enjoyed renewed vigor with the onset of the Enlightenment in the eighteenth century.[79] Modernism can be seen as an expression of the Enlightenment faith in reason as the means to pierce the facade and reveal to us the essence of things.[80] As such, "[c]entral to the modernist view was the assumption of *things in themselves.*"[81]

The role of reason as an engine of constant change is expressed in Anthony Giddens's description of modernity as characterized by "reflexivity."[82] This principle requires that social practices be justified not by tradition but by reason.[83] Reflexivity thus demands ceaseless rational reexamination and rejustification of everyday life. As Giddens puts it, "[t]he reflexivity of modern social life consists in the fact that social practices are constantly examined and reformed in the light of incoming information about those very practices, thus constitutively altering their character."[84] As a result, the past warrants no respect independently of the rational claims that can be offered in its behalf.[85]

A powerful tenet of modernism has been that this destruction of received wisdom is the means by which humanity can free itself from the yoke of superstition and oppression. Indeed, some Enlightenment thinkers had the expectation that the advance of reason would provide the key to understanding not only the physical world but also the principles that governed the social world and the happiness of those within it.[86] Modern life, therefore, ideally is perpetually open to improvement, as reflexivity promotes the concept of progress through development. Development represents the impulse toward constant transformation and open-ended growth, based on the application of new knowledge as it becomes available.[87]

The emphasis on reason over tradition underscores modernism's commitment to the individual as the primary unit of social life. With communal restriction more open to question, there emerged with modernism a heightened sense of the individual as possessing an integrity apart from her location within a particular community. In fact, as Steven Connor has suggested, modernism might be regarded as "the moment when self-consciousness invaded experience."[88] The modernist version of emancipation has proffered the vision of an individual whose essence is defined by her powers of reason and choice, apart from any context in which she may be situated. Under the prodding of modernism, individuals have gradually shed the raiments of context. Attributes such as religion, race, gender, place of birth, and ethnicity are increasingly seen as contingent, unconnected to the assessment of the individual *qua* individual.[89]

This notion of identity as fundamentally acontextual is captured in Roberto Unger's defense of the modernist personality.[90] For Unger, while we are always situated within a context, "we always break through the contexts of practical or conceptual activity."[91] This is because there is no ultimate context that does justice to the full range of human potential.[92] Nonetheless, our purpose in transcending context is to create new ones that might come closer to an ideal "natural" context. This latter context "makes available to those who inhabit it all the forms of practical collaboration or passionate attachment that people might have well-founded reasons to desire."[93] The natural context is thus the one in which the essence of humanity can realize itself. This state can never be attained, but it serves as the ideal against which other contexts can be evaluated.

Given both this ideal and the inability of any context to measure up to it, Unger regards the only appropriate mode of existence as the ceaseless revision of context. He thus holds up "the modernist ideal of a context so open to revision that the contrast between routine moves within a framework and revolutionary struggle about it loses its force."[94] As he declares, "[b]y making [contexts] increasingly open to revision we also qualify or transform the force of our commitment to any one of them."[95] Unger thus makes clear "how much in a view of our fundamental identity ultimately turns upon beliefs about the status of our contexts."[96]

Marshall Berman points up the connection between the modernist dynamic of physical development and the notion of relentless self-development that characterizes a theory such as Unger's. Berman suggests that Goethe's *Faust* is perhaps the quintessential tale of the experience of modernity. The self-development that Faust wants, Berman argues, is a "dynamic process that will include every mode of human experience, joy and misery alike, and that will assimilate them into his self's unending growth; even the self's destruction will be an integral part of its development."[97] Yet the cost of such a process is incessant transformation that undermines efforts to erect enduring structures of meaning within the world.[98]

These were the forces whose influence became so pervasive during the

Victorian era. In order to appreciate the Victorian response to them, it will be useful first to understand early modern social life before modernization became widespread. This background helps frame the Victorian family as a complex vehicle for both embracing and tempering the individualism that modernization was perceived as spawning.

Early Modern Social Life

Throughout the American colonial period, and even into the early part of the nineteenth century, the average individual participated in a social life that might be described as a matrix of overlapping experiences. The boundaries between groupings such as family, community, and church were relatively indistinct; those groupings were seen as defined not so much by their specific character as by their reciprocal interdependence within the broader structure of a hierarchical society.[99] As Mary Ryan has indicated in her study of the family in upstate New York, "[a]s of 1800 or even 1830, it was difficult to sort out private from public life."[100] Within this social structure, the family was the basic unit in an interconnected chain, rather than a distinct group with specified functions.

In this capacity, the family served, for instance, as the primary location of economic production, as all household members labored together in an interdependent economic unit.[101] The family also performed a number of social functions. John Demos, for example, has observed that the family in Plymouth Colony served as a school, a vocational institute, a site of religious worship, a house of correction, and a welfare institution.[102] Similarly, Mary Ryan points out that widows, orphans, the poor, and criminals were sent into respectable homes in Oneida County for care and rehabilitation.[103]

The integration of the family into community life made it susceptible to considerable community intervention, which militated against much family or individual privacy. Much of this surveillance was conducted by churches, which regarded families as possessed of no privacy that precluded scrutiny by church members.[104] Ryan suggests that "[t]he frequency, routineness, and casualness of these intrusions call into question whether these families were *private* at all in the current meaning of the term."[105] Even more prominent, she argues, were obstacles to the creation of individual privacy, as the community sought vigorously to discourage the development of a strongly individuated sense of self.[106] Generally speaking, then, the early modern family and individual were seen as relatively permeable rather than sharply defined, each subject to significant communal influence.[107]

The crucial economic and social functions performed by the family meant that the household typically was characterized by hierarchical relationships rather than close ties based upon individual feeling.[108] Such a foundation was generally deemed to provide a surer guarantee that the household would function effectively than the ostensibly more volatile bonds of emotion. At the same time, some measure of affection tempered hierarchical relations. The Puritan duty of conjugal love, for instance, reflected in part the recognition that emotional ties could serve to maintain a harmonious and cooperative household atmosphere.[109] This attention to the role of affection thus did not demarcate a distinct realm of personal sentiment; rather, "[a] woman's love for her husband, and his in return became, as a consequence, a 'duty,' a 'performance,' not a rarefied emotion."[110]

Furthermore, the family was not deemed the only or even the primary sphere for the experience of affection. Ryan points out, for instance, that on the New York frontier the sentiment of love was regarded as equally appropriate among church members as family members, suggesting relatively muted emotional distinctions among family, church, and the larger community.[111] Similarly, Stephanie Coontz concludes that "colonists had little sense that emotional interactions among people were qualitatively different within the family than outside it."[112] To the extent that emotional intimacy played a part in community life, it was thus diffused among various social experiences, rather than confined to a distinct sphere of "personal" life.

The multiplicity of tasks performed by the family also resulted in relatively indistinct gender roles. While men generally worked in the fields and women in the home, these areas were contiguous and part of a household unit that represented a relatively self- sufficient economic enterprise.[113] Furthermore, the variety of community functions performed within the household belied any notion of a "private" domestic sphere to which women were confined.[114] Within the agrarian household, therefore, "[w]omen's economic dependency was one strand in a web of interdependence of men's and women's typical work."[115]

In sum, social life until the early nineteenth century generally attached little practical significance or emotional valence to distinctions between public and private life. As Ryan concludes,

Social relations were too various, overlapping, and expansive to be corralled into the enclosed space connoted by the term ["private"]. Neighbors, church brethren, or the exuberant fraternity of the benefit association shared warmth and intimacy within a social, rather than a private, sphere. Conversely, the family was not the exclusive place of affectionate human contact. The family circle was not marked out as an especially secluded social space.[116]

This conceptual universe began to change, however, as the constellation of changes described as modernization began to spread more broadly in the early decades of the nineteenth century.

The Forces of Modernization

By the third decade of the nineteenth century, the convergence of a number of modernizing influences was beginning to create an acute sense of rapid change and dislocation. In the nineteenth century, observes Peter Gay, "the very nature of change underwent a change; it was more rapid and more irresistible than in the past."[117] Economic life saw the emergence of large industrial enterprises on a scale that dwarfed household enterprise, in which time was organized more rigidly than in the previous village economy. An ascendant system of wage labor provided individuals with direct access to income, giving them freedom to circumvent restrictive local economic arrangements, but also eroding interpersonal networks of reciprocity and interdependence. With expanding markets, local economies were suddenly more vulnerable to events that occurred far from their boundaries. Rapid technological development introduced a cycle of invention and obsolescence in which fortunes could be made or lost with novel rapidity. New forms of transportation and communication shattered familiar notions of time and space. The railroad and steamship opened up far-flung sources of supply and demand that created intense competition over new markets, and technological change created a pervasive sense of dynamism and instability. Finally, perhaps the most initially wrenching, and ultimately significant consequence of modernization was the separation of home and work into separate domains.[118] The world of work became more directly subject to impersonal market forces often far removed from the business site itself. As Walter Houghton observes: "To live in this dynamic, free-wheeling society was to feel the enormous pressure of work, far beyond anything known before."[119]

Equally significant was the emergence of modernist sensibility. Greater receptivity to change and development reflected a decline in deference to traditional sources of authority and the assertion of a more individualistic ethic that emphasized rational scrutiny.[120] Furthermore, developments in science began to inculcate an ethic of skepticism that called into question previous verities such as religious belief.[121] The burgeoning multitude of competing theories and philosophies eventually created an atmosphere in which an attitude of doubt became more prominent.[122]

Among many Victorians, modernization created an acute sense of instability and anxiety about the ability to find coherence in daily life. One character in a popular novel of the 1870s laments, "There is no reciprocal rule of life anywhere. Every one who does right at all only does what is right in his own eyes. All society, it seems, is going to pieces."[123] Similarly, Thomas Carlyle wrote, "The Old has passed away, but, alas, the New appears not in its stead; the Time is still in pangs of travail with the New."[124] The middle class in particular began to express concern about the fragmentation of the social order into an endless series of market struggles untempered by any moral restraints.[125]

These were the fears and hopes associated with the ascendance of a more explicit, self-conscious, widely accepted distinction between private and public life that middle-class reformers saw as a means of restoring both solidarity and order to social life. As Peter Gay puts it, "nineteenth-century middle-class culture was particularly emphatic about . . . making the gulf between private and public life as wide as it could manage."[126] The public sphere encompassed the market and much of politics, and came to be seen as remote and impersonal, governed by egoism and competition.[127] By contrast, private life, centered around the family, was the realm where ostensible feminine values of affection and moral refinement might be cultivated as an antidote to the profanity of the public sphere. The family thus assumed greatly heightened significance as a distinct institution in a newly prominent sphere known as "private" life.[128] This conception of the family as a private sanctuary was a hallmark of the Victorian age.[129]

As the following sections will show, recent scholarship suggests that the functions of the family within this new regime were complex, with attitudes toward family ties that were in some tension. On the one hand, the family was to serve as a haven of affection. While this might forge bonds of altruism, it also reflected greater emphasis on voluntary rather than patriarchal family cohesion. This emphasis, as well as the greater attention to emotional gratification, had the potential to reinforce an individualistic ethic. On the other hand, the family was to mold character in all its members by inculcating an ethic of duty and self-restraint that might hold egoism in check. I will argue that one way to view the creation of distinct roles within the Victorian family is as a device that attempted to accomplish this latter end. The Victorian construction of intimate personal life thus sought to draw on notions of both personal fulfillment and impersonal obligation. For the Victorians, the family became the vehicle for dealing with broader social tensions between nascent individualism and communal obligation.[130]

The Family as Haven of Affection

One powerful image of the family during the Victorian era was as a sanctuary of emotional comfort in the midst of a broader society increasingly governed by selfishness and materialism. John Ruskin's paean to the family is one of the best known and most representative expressions of this attitude:

This is the true nature of home—it is the place of Peace; the shelter, not only from all injury, but from all terror, doubt, and division. In so far as it is not this, it is not home: so far as the anxieties of the outer life penetrate into it, and the inconsistently-minded, unknown, unloved, or hostile society of the outer world is allowed by either husband or wife to cross the threshold, it ceases to be home; it is then only a part of that outer world which you have roofed over, and lighted fire in.[131]

Such an image reflected heightened emphasis on affection within the family unit. A trend toward greater emotional ties among family members had been gathering for some time,[132] but the ethic of familial affection gained widespread support during the Victorian age. It was in this era that intimate companionship became the broad cultural model for familial relations.[133]

The greater prominence of affection was evident in both the spousal and parent-child relationships. The idea of romantic attachment was of course not newly created in the nineteenth century, and in fact had been in evidence in various circles since at least the twelfth century.[134] Its association with marriage, however, was a more recent phenomenon,[135] and many scholars suggest that a "companionate" view of marriage first gained widespread acceptance during the Victorian era.[136] Popular periodicals of the middle and late nineteenth century, for instance, emphasized love and emotional attachment as the firmest basis for a lasting marriage. As one anonymous correspondent to Good Housekeeping magazine put it: "The first duty of a Man fit for a Husband should be the cultivation of a close companionship with his wife, and the combination with love of that communion of spirit and true sympathy, which is generally considered to be an attribute of friendship."[137]

Correspondence between nineteenth-century husbands and wives testifies to the significance of emotional ties between spouses. Steven Mintz and Susan Kellogg observe, for instance, that husbands' letters to their wives during this period reflected an increasing willingness to seek advice and openly express affection.[138] Mintz and Kellogg also note that spouses began to address each other less formally with the dawn of the nineteenth century, using first names or nicknames more often.[139] As Peter Gay suggests, the nineteenth-century middle class "gave affectionate love a consistent and persuasive ideology and an expressive vocabulary that would have struck their great-grandparents, and even their grandparents, as rather daring and very worldly."[140]

Several scholars suggest that Victorian emotional intimacy was accompanied by considerable sexual intimacy as well.[141] The stereotype of the Victorians portrays them as the essence of prudery, either suspicious of or hostile to sexual expression.[142] The kernel of truth in this characterization reflects the fact that, as I discuss in the following section, sexuality had symbolic significance for the Victorians with respect to issues of egoism and self-control, so that temperance and reserve were cultivated in sexual matters.[143] Extreme versions of this ethic downplayed or denied the experience of sexual passion, especially among women.[144] Yet, as Carl Degler has suggested, it may be more accurate to regard much of this writing as an effort in indoctrination by some elements of society, rather than as a description of actual behavior.[145] Degler maintains that we should doubt that actual practice faithfully reflected this ideology.[146]

One piece of evidence in support of this view is the Mosher Survey, a set of questionnaires given to forty-five women during the period 1892–1920 by Dr. Clara Mosher. While not necessarily fully representative or definitive, the survey is striking in its indication of a high degree of both sexual desire and satisfaction among the respondents. Thirty-five of the women stated that they felt desire for intercourse independent of their husband's interest, for instance, while a large percentage reported experiencing orgasm.[147] A good number of the women rejected reproduction as the sole justification for sex, regarding intercourse as a means of achieving emotional union that for some was almost spiritual in quality.[148] As Degler suggests, the survey indicates that for these women sexual expression was a natural and satisfying aspect of daily life.[149] It thus lends support to Peter Gay's argument that, despite Victorian reserve, "[i]t would be a gross misreading of this experience to think that nineteenth-century bourgeois did not know, or did not practice, or did not enjoy, what they did not discuss."[150]

Greater affection between parents and children also marked the Victorian family.[151] Emphasis was placed on the child as a being with unique needs and desires, whose individual character development was an important parental project.[152] In place of harsher child-rearing practices designed to break the will of the child,[153] parents began to rely more on the child's desire for affection as a means of promoting compliance with parental expectations.[154]

The Victorian image of the family as an emotional haven thus visualized a realm in which affection forged bonds of altruism in opposition to market egoism. Some aspects of this image, however, in fact had the potential to reinforce an individualistic ethos that exalted subjectivity as the ultimate arbiter of personal conduct.

First, the idea of the family as a haven fostered the notion of a retreat from and rejection of the larger world. As Gillian Brown has observed, nineteenth-century "domestic individualism" operated to "locate the individual in his or her interiority, in his or her removal from the marketplace."[155] Similarly, DeTocqueville identified in American life in the 1830s a tendency for citizens to withdraw into a circle of family and close friends, to the detriment of more expansive social relationships.[156] The creation of a private sphere dissociated from the larger world thus threatened to weaken a sense of communal obligation, contributing to the emergence of a self divorced from social context.

Second, emphasis on ties of affection drew in part on the increasing legitimacy of concepts of volition and consent in family life, as patriarchy declined to some degree as a basis for ordering family relationships.[157] These concepts prompted more solicitude for individual feelings and desires. As Carl Degler points out, for instance, "[l]ove as the basis for marrying was the purest form of individualism; it subordinated all familial, social, or group considerations to personal preference."[158] This heightened attention to individual sentiment meant that marriage was more likely to be valued as an arrangement designed to serve the happiness of the particular couple who entered into it.[159]

Mary Ryan illustrates the greater resonance of choice and preference in family relations in her description of the effects of industrialization in Utica. She suggests that, while urban middle- class family connections were not severed by industrialization, they were transformed. "The members of the household were no longer meshed together by common productive property and shared work experience,"[160] but rather by deliberate decisions, such as whether to finance education or training.[161] As a result, family life rested on a foundation of greater subjectivity, as family ties came to be "knit of more intangible materials of affection, self-sacrifice, guilt, and all the mysterious machinations of conscience."[162] A similar emphasis on choice is noted by Steven Mintz, who observes that the shift to reliance on affectionate influence in child-rearing emphasized at least the appearance of consent,[163] which meant greater reliance on the "voluntary cohesion" of family members.[164]

Perceptions of more widespread acceptance of an ethic of voluntary commitment generated concern among Victorians about the rise of an individualism that stressed private gratification as its paramount principle.[165] Many saw such an ethic as creating the "dilemma of the unfettered self,"[166] the individual who enjoyed apparently expansive freedom but who was unable to "create the moral self in a rapidly changing world[.]"[167]

Finally, the romantic love that was the basis of the companionate ideal had the potential to encourage self-absorption and resistance to social strictures. As Karen Lystra notes, "[r]omantic love was based upon the 'fiction' of the independent self, acting as a 'free agent' in terms of personal needs."[168] The emphasis on personal emotion fostered more intense concentration on the individual's internal life, and "added further impetus to the development of a personal identity separate from social obligations and public roles."[169] Indeed, the ethic of romantic love saw social convention as an obstacle to intimate relations, and posited "free-form subjectivity" as the only basis for a true union with another.[170]

Victorians were especially alarmed by the egoistic potential of the romantic ethic because romantic love was seen as a force that culture was virtually powerless to control.[171] This sense of anxiety was perhaps most acute with respect to sexuality.[172] As we have seen, much recent scholarship suggests that Victorians welcomed sensuality as an important element of emotional intimacy. At the same time, the volatility of sexuality raised what Louis Kern calls "the ethical question at the heart of nineteenth-century culture[:] the role of the self in society and culture."[173] The considerable public interest in sexuality during that century, maintains Kern, reflected the realization that this question was "intimately bound up with interpersonal relations and that certainly no other social act was more closely linked to the individual self."[174] Debate over birth control,[175] prostitution,[176] adultery,[177] sexual temperance in marriage,[178] and masturbation[179] all raised in the Victorian mind the issue of the proper scope to afford the pursuit of individual gratification.

The notion of the family as emotional haven therefore answered the need to preserve the "finer" human emotions, but a family ordered on this basis alone likely could not serve as a source of social cohesion. The inculcation of a sense of restraint was essential in maintaining an ethic of personal responsibility and self-control. This ethic was to serve dual, and to some extent contradictory social purposes: to instill those traits increasingly important in a more rational and competitive economy,[180] and to ensure that egoism was checked by an internal sense of duty.[181] Thus, while the idea of the family as haven visualized a retreat from society, the idea of the family as a vehicle for inculcating self-restraint imagined a reconnection with it.[182]

Victorian family roles can be seen in part as an effort to fulfill the "public" function of preserving a relational sense of self that would be attentive to communal obligation. By fostering individual identification with family roles, Victorian culture held up the family as "one important source of social cohesion in a society deeply anxious about questions of order and disorder."[183]

Role Identification and the Victorian Family

Role Identification. The work of Erving Goffman provides a useful point of departure in clarifying the concept of role identification. Goffman uses the term "role embracement" to refer to situations in which persons conform to their role expectations with little or no idiosyncratic variation in behavior. As he puts it, "[t]o embrace a role is to disappear completely into the virtual self available in the situation, to be fully seen in terms of the image, and to confirm expressively one's acceptance of it."[184] The extent to which this "virtual self" is seen as an integral part of one's "real self" depends on the extent to which the person sees the latter as anchored in the "institution" in question.[185] A person whose sense of self is strongly constituted by being a judge, for instance, will see herself as realized in the activity of pursuing judicial objectives, rather than as having her "real" self constrained by the demands of that position.[186]

I define "role identification" as identification with the virtual self that is associated with performance of an institutional role.[187] The orientation of a person characterized by role identification is captured by Ralph Turner's discussion of the person whose sense of self has an institutional anchor. For this person, the real self is the self that adheres to high social standards, particularly in the face of strong temptation to behave otherwise.[188] Furthermore, the real self is "revealed only when the individual is in full control of his faculties and behaviors"; when such control is impaired, "an alien self displaces the true self."[189] Hypocrisy for this person means failing to live up to one's standards rather than failing to behave in accordance with one's desires or impulses.[190] Those with an institutional anchor are oriented toward the future, and construct a meaningful environment through the use of commitments that necessarily limit their freedom of action.[191] Finally, for this person, individualism means resisting the pressures that can "divert a person from achievement, from adherence to ethical standards, and from other institutional goals."[192]

Role identification can endow individual conduct with shared meaning, and thus permit moral judgments about how well individuals perform their roles.[193] The role in question serves to "adjust the expression of impulses to the controlling paragon, or character ideal" associated with that role.[194] As a result, socialization that encourages role identification can inculcate a relational sense of identity, a sense of self defined in part by one's relationships with others and the expectations that they create.

In my view, the family emerged as a particularly well-defined "institution" during the Victorian era, and the creation of roles within this institution reflected an effort to foster role identification among family members. This effort may be understood as an attempt to use the family as a vehicle for preserving a relational sense of self and obligation in a period of ascendant individualism.

The Victorian Family as Institution. As we have seen, the family became a more sharply defined and prominent social arrangement during the Victorian years. As such, it began to take on features of an institution. By this I mean that it began to be regarded as a natural and essential part of the social landscape, associated with certain prescriptions about proper behavior. As Peter Berger and Thomas Luckmann have written, institutions serve to control human behavior by channeling it in a particular direction, as opposed to the numerous alternative directions that are theoretically available.[195] A crucial quality of institutions is their apparent "objectivity."[196] As Berger and Luckmann explain, this means that "the institutions are now experienced as possessing a reality of their own, a reality that confronts the individual as an external and coercive fact."[197] The emergence of a social arrangement as an institution is associated with the assumption of roles, which allows persons to develop relatively stable expectations about each other's behavior.[198]

One way of inculcating a sense of the family as an institution was to cloak it with the mantle of tradition. Victorians did so by casting the family as "the most important symbol of stability and continuity, the only embodiment of a tangible past in a period of rampant change and self-seeking individualism."[199] They also did so by creating new traditions centered around the family. Mintz and Kellogg point out, for instance, that the nineteenth century featured the appearance of such family oriented celebrations as the birthday party, Christmas, and Thanksgiving, along with the birthday cake, the Christmas tree, Christmas presents, Christmas caroling, and the Thanksgiving turkey.[200] Indeed, heaven itself was increasingly described as a home in which family members eventually would be reunited.[201] The status of the family as an institution was also established and strengthened by the inculcation of emotional attachment to domestic life. The most prominent example of this was of course the campaign to persuade women to seek their destiny in the domestic sphere.[202] Men also, however, were the targets of educational efforts, which exhorted them to seek their nonworking satisfaction within the home rather than in the taverns and meeting places that they had favored in the recent past.

An editorial in a California newspaper quoted by Robert Griswold is illustrative of efforts to convince men to look toward home for happiness: "The idea of looking beyond the sphere of home for enjoyment is at the root of many of our modern ills. Home should be the very centre and sanctuary of happiness; and when it is not there is some screw loose in the domestic machinery."[203] One indication of the relative success of this campaign is John Stuart Mill's suggestion that a measure of the advance of civilization in the nineteenth century was the extent to which men had been persuaded to turn away from their former amusements toward greater involvement in home and family life.[204] The family thus took on the emotional aura of an institution in the sense that "there were few aspects of their society the Victorians regarded with greater reverence than the home and family life within it."[205] As a result, this institution was at the center of the newly prominent private sphere of life.

The idea of the family as an institution and the process of role iden-tification were mutually reinforcing. On the one hand, the image of the family as a natural institution that commanded deep allegiance fostered willingness to identify with family roles. On the other hand, these roles were what constituted the family as an institution; to the extent that these roles were regarded as natural, family members would be committed to the family as an entity that could make legitimate demands on them. The Victorians thus propagated a "teleological view" of the family,[206] in which each family role was premised on a supposedly universal un-derstanding of the function of the family.

It will be useful to examine the roles that were associated with family life in the Victorian period in order to understand the kind of relational identity that family members were encouraged to develop. As we know well, roles within the Victorian family were assigned on the basis of ostensibly "natural" gender traits.[207] This subject has received extensive scholarly attention, which I don't plan to recount here.[208] Rather, I want to focus on the way in which these roles operated to restrain the play of individual drives by creating a sense of self defined in part by one's relations with and responsibilities to other family members. Appreciation of this point will give us insight into how the Victorian construction of intimacy could include the idea of impersonal obligation, a formulation that seems inconsistent with modern notions of intimate private life.

The basic principles of nineteenth-century married life were that "[m]en and women had specific duties and lived with concrete restraints on their behavior and demeanor."[209] For Victorian husbands and wives, "the limits and duties were clearly defined: husbands were to provide the necessities of life, treat their wives with courtesy and protection, and exercise sexual restraint.... A wife's duty was to maintain a comfortable home, take care of household chores, bear and tend to the children, and set the moral tone for domestic life."[210]

These role expectations were presented as the standard for all husbands and wives, and a flood of didactic nineteenth-century literature served to foster identification with them.[211] The degree of this identification is suggested in research by both Elaine May and Robert Griswold, which indicates that the failure to meet sex-role obligations was the most common ground asserted as a basis for Victorian divorce.[212] Entry into marriage involved automatic assumption of a specific role, a process that linked individual self-realization to adequate performance of the obligations associated with that role. For nineteenth-century culture, "[o]ne came to selfhood through obedience to law and ideals,"[213] and few ideals were more important than those associated with family life. As a result, powerful cultural sanctions encouraged reliance on family roles as fundamental elements in the development of identity. For women, "[n]ineteenth-century American society provided but one socially respectable, nondeviant role for women—that of loving wife and mother."[214] For men, "[w]ork by the husband was a responsibility owed to the wife, and nothing more detrimental could be said about a man than that he did not support his wife and family."[215] Role identification was not uncontested, especially by women, and its precepts were in fact used at times to transcend conventional role expectations.[216] Nonetheless, it exerted a powerful hold on the cultural imagination well into this century.[217]

These roles each required the exercise of restraint for the sake of purposes that transcended the self. For a man, the role of provider required that impulse be disciplined and personal desire subordinated to the exigencies of the commercial world, for the sake of both family members who depended on him for sustenance and a nation intent on modern economic development. "Restraint was important, for the sake of the men themselves and their ability to function in the economy. At the same time, it guaranteed their role as provider and producer, contributing to domestic harmony as well as national progress."[218] For a woman, the role of domestic angel required that personal needs be effaced in favor of the needs of others. This served both the practical function of ensuring performance of domestic tasks and the symbolic function of providing a model of self-denial for others.[219] Thus, the egoistic potential of the self-restraint ethic was arrested to some degree by linking cultivation of self-control to the achievement of social ends.

Reciprocity of role obligations enhanced the extent to which role identification encouraged the formation of a relational sense of identity. That is, husband and wife regarded the functions they performed as complementary and equally important to the success of the household. This sense of reciprocity could create a sense of interdependence and shared purpose, as each was aware that meeting role expectations was necessary for the success of a joint enterprise.[220] Indeed, an understanding that marriage was an undertaking for the achievement of joint and social purposes ideally checked any inclination to look to marriage as the vehicle to achieve narrower individual purposes. As Henry Seidel Canby said in memoirs of his Victorian upbringing, " 'God bless our home'...never meant make our home a happy one. The blessing was asked upon those virtues which were often more conducive to moral conduct and material success than happiness."[221]

The sense of gender roles as representing complementary and equally vital family functions is underscored by the conclusion of many scholars that the demarcation of a "separate sphere" for women was an advancement in the esteem and importance that women enjoyed. Certainly, by today's standards, Victorian gender roles seem stifling and oppressive in their denial to women of access to large areas of social life. Equally offensive is the suggestion that such restrictions are justified by the innate qualities of the sexes. Yet scholars such as Daniel Walker Howe maintain that "though it seems somewhat paradoxical to us, Victorian domesticity represented a phase in the modernizing liberation of women from their traditional subjugation."[222] The attribution of moral superiority to women reflected a considerable improvement over the negative images that had influenced previous generations.[223] Furthermore, it was the basis for assigning to women the crucial function of taming the egoism and individualism that seemed to be in ascendance in nineteenth-century society. Women referred to this function in justifying a host of reform efforts that took them out of the home and into society, focusing on issues such as temperance, sexual conduct, and poverty.[224] Furthermore, the idea of women's moral superiority provided an ethos that made women the actual, if not nominal, authorities within the home.[225] As such, they could make demands on family members in the name of moral improvement, thus transforming an ostensibly passive role into an instrument of influence.[226]

Identification of an explicit women's sphere also contributed to a heightened sense of gender consciousness on the part of women.[227] For most of the nineteenth century, reform efforts drew on the concept of the "special" role of women, rather than more universalistic tenets, and thus did not challenge the "separate spheres" ideology.[228] Nonetheless, growing awareness of womanhood as a shared experience laid the foundation for eventual challenges to gender limitations.[229]

In sum, current awareness of the limitations and deficiencies of Victorian gender roles should not obscure the fact that for many men and women these roles represented an arrangement of mutual support. While women were still relegated to secondary status, that status took a somewhat less oppressive and grating form. As Mary Ryan observes, "The balance of sexual power had not been turned upside down, but it had shifted on its axis a few degrees."[230]

Aside from assigning men and women to interdependent spheres, role identification also sought to cultivate a relational sense of identity by fostering an ethic of duty in the emotional relationship between husband and wife. As we've seen, one element in the notion of the family as a haven of affection was the greater romantic intensity of the bond between spouses. The perception that such intensity sprang from voluntary personal feelings that could not be commanded raised the specter of a "private" sphere beyond communal control, in which the individual operated unfettered by a sense of duty to others. Role obligations represented a response to this concern. Unlike romantic love, "[r]ole duty was conceived as willable, therefore the individual could be held accountable both in his own mind and in a social sense."[231] Internalization of a sense of obligation ensured that the "private" sphere was not governed solely by the dictates of individual emotion.

Role expectations relating to the emotional bond between spouses emphasized the importance of "sympathy, a compassionate understanding of another person's needs and weaknesses together with an ardent desire to alleviate these."[232] An attitude of sympathy regarded as paramount the qualities of mutuality and restraint. A husband, for instance, was admonished to temper his sexual drive to accommodate his wife's desires, to pay heed to his wife's more refined sensibilities, and to accept her instruction on matters of moral improvement.[233] A wife was directed to be solicitous of her husband's needs, to be a constant source of emotional succor to him, and to help him attain a state of "higher" moral development.[234]

The emphasis on sympathy rejected the notion that the vagaries of individual passion should serve as the foundation for married life. Rather, "[l]ove could be a secure basis for marriage only when it was transmuted into something purer and more selfless."[235] The concept of sympathy offered a way to conceptualize marriage as a relationship of mutual dependence, in which each spouse unselfishly provided the other with moral support and direction.[236] The role of spouse demanded restraint and self-denial, qualities that linked one's sense of self to the welfare of another. Role identification thus checked the individualistic potential in companionate marriage, for the spousal role was based on the tenet that "[t]rue marriage was to be found in mutual dependence and transcendence of self."[237]

In many quarters, the idea of spousal selflessness had a religious component. An example of this is the "sacramental" view of marriage that was prominent during the Victorian era. This view was particularly strong among Evangelical Christians, but also gained acceptance in broader circles through the efforts of ministers, moralists, educators, and writers.[238] It saw marriage as a vehicle for transcending egoism and achieving a "higher" moral state in which spousal conduct was guided by the duty spouses owed to each other rather than by baser selfish desires. On this view, the purpose of marriage went beyond the happiness of the couple and their children. Rather, it was to "strengthen and discipline the will and to master the desires."[239]

Steven Mintz suggests that sacramental imagery offered a way to reconcile notions of freedom and obligation within marriage, as Christian love emphasized the attainment of selfhood through union with another.[240] Mintz maintains that as the scientific advancements and tumultuous change of the nineteenth century began to sow the seeds of spiritual anxiety and doubt, many Victorians began to look to marriage as a vehicle for preserving and vindicating the religious tenets of selflessness and sacrifice. The idea of marriage as a sacrament reflected the identification of the spouse as the source outside oneself through whom one could achieve true selfhood.[241] Rather than a lapse of religious belief, says Mintz, we might think of this process as a displacement of religious aspirations onto secular objects.[242] Through such displacement, sacramental imagery harnessed the freedom of romantic love to the performance of duties that arose outside the self.

The significance of the sacramental view was practical as well as symbolic. As Mintz puts it, "[l]ike a legal fiction, to which it bears a resemblance, it furnished a vocabulary and a set of sanctions invoked in actual marriages."[243] He illustrates this point by examining the correspondence from Harriet Beecher Stowe to her husband. Stowe consistently used the language of moral improvement when she requested changes in her husband's behavior, such as that he exhibit less concern about minor physical ailments, be less hasty in censuring her for her mistakes, devote more time to family prayers and less to the daily newspapers, and even that he moderate his sexual demands.[244] Furthermore, she asked that she might be given responsibility for the family finances so that he might be able to spend more time on self-purification.[245] All such concerns were voiced as part of "an earnest attempt to correct & reform all in us that needs reforming[.]"[246] Mintz suggests that emphasis on the duties associated with the spousal role should be seen as "a peculiarly Victorian mode of discourse, through which one party to a marriage might legitimately make demands of another."[247]

By investing marriage with traditional religious symbols of selflessness, the sacramental view offered a vision of connection during a period of acute anxiety about tendencies toward atomism. Mintz suggests that the ability to portray marriage as a sacrament that could transform human emotions into an instrument of selflessness was a way to resist the atomizing pressures of modern life.[248]

We can see, therefore, that with respect to the emotional bond between spouses the concept of role, whether infused with religious significance or not, made it possible for William Gladstone to proclaim: "Marriage derives its essential and specific character from restraint."[249] Role identification served, both literally and figuratively, to "domesticate" romantic passion by tempering the instability and potential solipsism of personal feeling with appreciation of more impersonal duties toward one's spouse.[250] It was this conception of marriage as the reciprocal performance of roles, and the realization of self through such performance, that was the foundation for Victorian family law's reliance on status as an organizing principle.

Conclusion

Confronted with the onrushing forces of modernization, Victorians feared the loss of both the "finer" human sentiments and a sense of social cohesion. They responded with the vision of an ordered intimacy. They demarcated a distinct sphere of "private" life, centered around the family, for the pursuit of intimacy. At the same time, they sought through role identification to temper that pursuit with obligations rooted outside the vagaries of subjective preference. Victorian family law sought to reinforce this orientation by expressing those shared expectations about behavior through the vehicle of status. An individual's formal legal identity within the family reflected a relational identity that was intended to be a part of one's sense of self.

Victorian private life thus did not represent simply a retreat from the world and its demands, but was marked by "the integration of public and private roles[.]"[251] As Mary Ryan points out, we must be careful to distinguish privatization from individuation. While both move away from more expansive social relationships, in the middle to late nineteenth century "[t]he doctrine of privacy venerated not the isolated individual but rather a set of intense and intimate social relations, essentially those of the conjugal family."[252] These relations reflected a network of complementary obligations rather than the purely voluntary commitment of individuals to each other. As such, they were intended to provide a model of how a sense of community might be preserved in a more egalitarian society that found more room for "private" life. This perspective helps us see that the notion of the "private" is itself a social construction rather than a reference to a natural domain of existence.[253]

For a variety of reasons, the Victorian construction of intimacy has not held, but has given way to a different ideal in the late twentieth century. It's not my intent to explore in detail the reasons for this evolution; complex economic and social changes have contributed to it,[254] as well as factors such as the increasing influence of Romanticism,[255] the diminishing role of the family in the transmission of wealth,[256] the emergence of a mass consumer society,[257] and heightened gender consciousness.[258] My focus in the next chapter is more cross-sectional: I want to examine how the family law regime of contemporary society reflects a distinct construction of intimacy that differs from the Victorian model. The late twentieth century is more apt to conceptualize private life as the domain of the acontextual self, who views with suspicion the efforts of culture to shape the terms of intimate relationships.

2. The Modern Construction of Intimacy

Modern family law is quite different from Victorian family law. Indeed, many aspects of current law offer a striking contrast to the family law regime of even a generation ago. Greater commitment to personal choice in family matters reflects the belief that status is an obstacle to the cultivation of genuine intimate relationships. Recent legal trends thus emphasize the family as a domain of contract, rather than status. In general, then, late twentieth-century family law has rejected the basic tenets of Victorian family law. In part, of course, this reflects displeasure with the sexism that permeated those tenets. I will argue in this chapter, however, that this rejection also is based on a distinctive understanding of personal identity and intimacy.

Specifically, I want to explore the idea that, in contrast to the Victorian era, the late twentieth century is marked by a heightened sense of subjectivity as the source of guidance for personal conduct.[1] This phenomenon is complex, but one way to view it is as a more widespread acceptance of the modernist sensibility that the Victorians sought to restrain. That sensibility reflects the idea that no context in which the individual finds herself— no set of relationships of which she is a part— should enter into her self-definition so as to limit her freedom of action. Put another way, modernism holds the view that personal obligation must be voluntary in order to be legitimate. If the Victorian era was marked by role identification, then, the late twentieth century is marked sby "role distance"—a greater sense of an authentic self that stands apart from the roles that it may be asked to play.[2]

As a result, there has been a shift in the way that we tend to think about the "private" realm, from a vision of it as an arena defined in large part by family relations to a vision of it as a zone of individual autonomy. Modern private life is seen as a domain in which the individual can realize herself by forging intense relations of intimacy with others, the obligations of which are determined by the parties themselves rather than imposed by standard cultural expectations. The family is but one of many such relationships, sustained now more by generic interpersonal skills than by a distinctive sense of ineluctable duty.

It's worth emphasizing at this point that what follows is not an attempt to describe the "essence" of contemporary life, but an effort to explore one strand in its complex fabric. Furthermore, I'm interested less in the extent to which this strand may be dominant or uncontested than in what it suggests about the changing *relative* influence of certain notions from the Victorian era to our own. At the same time, of course, my focus reflects the belief that this orientation is influential—that it presents a set of metaphors and images increasingly accessible to the popular imagination in making sense of ourselves and our relations with others.

Family Law: From Status to Contract

Modern family law has steadily moved toward contract as its governing principle. I mean "contract" in both a literal and figurative sense: that the law is more willing to enforce agreements that tailor family life to individual preferences, and that the law is more solicitous in general of individual choice in family matters. In this section, I want to focus on changes in family law that reflect the increasing resonance of two inter-related propositions: (1) that private ordering, rather than public regulation, is the preferable means of governing intimate relationships; and (2) that formal status is less important than the substance of intimate relationships.

First, however, it is important to note that positing trends in family law is hazardous for at least two reasons. One is that there is no definite consensus on exactly what constitutes family law; taxation, government benefits, torts, criminal law, health care, and property law, to name only a few areas of the law, may have a significant impact on family life. The other is that despite the recent greater prominence of federal constitutional decisions concerning the family, family law is overwhelmingly state law. Fifty states and the District of Columbia are unlikely to approach anything in uniform fashion, and may in fact sharply disagree on occasion. Any purported trend thus will not be unqualified; exceptions and even countertrends can usually be identified.[3]

It's also important to recognize that the movement toward contract, broadly defined, is not equivalent to a withdrawal of the state from involvement in family matters. Greater freedom of spouses to contract, for instance, also means intensive court scrutiny of the terms of the contract, and often the spousal relationship itself, in the course of enforcing those contracts. In addition, relatively recent "equitable distribution" statutes in most states have vested courts with remarkably broad discretion in supervising the division of marital assets upon divorce.[4] Furthermore, courts typically are empowered to determine custody on the basis of the "best interests of the child,"[5] and have ongoing jurisdiction to modify custody and support awards depending on changed circumstances or parental behavior. The supervision of courts also may be invoked as a substitute for parents in matters such as minors' requests to obtain abortions.[6]

Greater solicitude for personal choice thus may place the individual in a more direct relationship with the state, thereby creating different forms of government involvement in the family.[7] As a result, greater emphasis on contract is not tantamount to delegalization of family life. At the same time, however, as Bruce Hafen observes, current legal intervention is "more a matter of defense than of offense, based less on the affirmative enforcement of social aspirations and more on the negative need to protect particular family members[.]" In other words, modern family law, in contrast to the Victorian era, regards its mission less as the effectuation of a substantive moral vision and more as the prevention of harm.[8] With this perspective as background, let's take a look at some recent trends in family law.

Private Ordering. Recent years have witnessed considerably greater receptivity to private ordering of family matters. As one observer puts it, the law "has evolved far toward recognizing the need for private choice and the untenableness of uniform public policy as a strategy for governing the conduct and obligations of intimacy."[9] This is evident with respect to entry into marriage, the terms of the marital relationship, and departure from marriage.

Entry into marriage is subject to a decreasing number of substantive and formal prerequisites. The Uniform Marriage and Divorce Act (UMDA), for instance, eliminates most traditional marriage prohibitions and all exclusions based on affinity.[10] Furthermore, marriages entered into in violation of the UMDA requirements are valid unless decreed null, and the Act significantly limits the circumstances under which an annulment may be obtained.[11] Consistent with state laws, the Act also contains minimal formalities for the marriage ceremony itself, acknowledging the more prevalent desire of couples to devise their own marriage ceremony.[12] As a result, some suggest that current regulation of marriage entry in the United States is simply a process of licensing and registration.[13]

In part, these changes reflect sensitivity to the Supreme Court's proclamation that the ability to marry is "one of the 'basic civil rights of man,' fundamental to our very existence and survival."[14] On the basis of this principle, the Court has struck down a prohibition on interracial marriage,[15] a requirement that a noncustodial parent obligated to pay child support obtain permission from the state to marry,[16] and a requirement that prison inmates obtain the warden's permission to marry.[17] While the Court has been careful to proclaim the validity of reasonable regulations that do not significantly interfere with the marriage decision,[18] the clear message is that individual choice regarding marriage is an exercise of personal autonomy to which the state should defer in most cases.

Once persons enter into marriage, the law is now more willing to let them define the terms of their relationship. In a series of cases, for instance, the Supreme Court has struck down statutes premised on the traditional sex roles that formerly provided the governing model of how family life should be organized.[19] As the Court has proclaimed, "No longer is the female destined solely for the home and the rearing of the family, and only the male for the marketplace and world of ideas."[20] Furthermore, the Court has indicated that certain decisions relating to procreation, such as contraception[21] and, to some degree, abortion,[22] are those that, absent some compelling reason, should be made without state interference.

Receptivity to private ordering of the terms of family life is underscored by greater willingness of courts to enforce marital contracts. Courts traditionally were reluctant to enforce most antenuptial agreements between spouses for fear that they might alter the "essential incidents" of marriage or that provision for property division or support upon divorce might encourage marital dissolution.[23] With the decline of consensus about the terms of marriage, and with the prevalence of divorce, most states have adopted the view that it is unreasonable to regard marital contracts as contrary to public policy.[24]

Consistent with this attitude, the Uniform Premarital Agreement Act (UPAA), adopted in several states, provides that the parties may contract with respect to various economic matters, the choice of law governing the contract, and any other matter, "including their personal rights and obligations, not in violation of public policy" or criminal law.[25] Similarly, the Uniform Marital Property Act (UMPA) provides that marital property agreements are enforceable.[26] Prospective spouses may contract regarding property division, spousal support, and any other matter relating to property not in violation of public policy.[27]

States are also more amenable to enforcement of separation agreements established at the end of the marriage. Section 306 of the UMDA is the model for many states. It provides that a court must accept as binding a separation agreement relating to all subjects except child support, custody, and visitation, as long as it finds that the agreement is not unconscionable.[28] The parties have the option to decide whether the agreement will be incorporated into the divorce decree,[29] and, except for terms concerning child support, custody, and visitation, may agree that even an agreement so incorporated will not be modifiable by the court.[30] The comment to this section emphasizes that the section explicitly rejects the traditional view that marital property settlement agreements are against public policy.[31]

To be sure, courts have not been willing to enforce marital contracts in exactly the same fashion as commercial contracts. Some states, for instance, will review the substantive fairness of certain antenuptial agreements at the time of enforcement to take account of changes in circumstances since execution.[32] Some states will subject to particularly close scrutiny contract terms dealing with support,[33] impose formalities beyond those required for ordinary contracts,[34] or toll during marriage statutes of limitation relating to claims arising out of antenuptial agreements.[35] Such practices create more uncertainty about the enforceability of marital contracts than other agreements.[36] Furthermore, notwithstanding authorization and support in some quarters for contract terms dealing with personal obligations,[37] some doubts have been raised about the enforceability of such terms.[38] Notwithstanding these qualifications, greater receptivity to marital contracts mirrors the increasing insistence that the family is a domain of private ordering. As Lenore Weitzman maintains, "opponents of intimate contracts regard marriage primarily as a public institution, while proponents view it as a private relationship."[39]

In addition to greater control over entry into and the terms of marriage, parties now also are able to determine for themselves when to leave the marital relationship. All states now provide for some form of no-fault divorce,[40] with all but two authorizing divorce on the motion of only one party.[41] In contrast to the Victorian notion of marriage as a relationship involving the performance of certain socially important duties, a no-fault regime reflects a conception of marriage as a private matter, controlled by the preferences of the parties. Indeed, the Supreme Court's decision in *Boddie v. Connecticut*,[42] striking down a filing fee for divorce, can be read to suggest, although it did not hold, that there may be some form of right to divorce.[43] The conceptualization of marriage as a private matter is underscored by the trend to disregard or define very narrowly marital fault in determinations concerning property division,[44] alimony,[45] and custody.[46] Such a posture reflects the view that there is little if any social consensus about standards that should govern marital behavior, and that states should refrain from passing judgment on the substance of marital interaction unless some direct harm can be demonstrated. The connection between this agnosticism about marital behavior and no-fault divorce is apparent: if the state feels less able to assess the propriety of behavior in an existing marriage, then it is in a poor position to proclaim what behavior justifies ending the marriage.

Determination of the economic consequences of divorce reflects to some degree the belief that, having changed their minds about the value of the marriage, divorcing spouses should be able to move on without being unduly encumbered by their past choice. Virtually every state now gives courts broad authority to divide property equitably, often with disregard for legal title.[47] The strong preference is that lump-sum property division, rather than alimony, serve as the vehicle for dealing with the financial consequences of divorce.[48] This regime reflects the view that in a scheme of private ordering a "clean break" between spouses best preserves the flexibility to act on the basis of revised preferences, without ongoing obligations flowing from prior choices.[49]

Greater acceptance of private ordering in entering and leaving marriage, as well as with respect to the terms of the marriage itself, reflects the notion that marriage has become "a personal rather than a social institution."[50] On this view, "[s]ince the new function of marriage is happiness and fulfillment of the individuals," we should defer to private ordering of the marital relationship.[51]

The Declining Importance of Status. A second development, related to the first, is that formal legal status has decreasing significance in determining rights and obligations in matters of intimate personal life. The law is now more likely to see "individuals" rather than husbands, wives, parents, or children, and to see "relationships" rather than "marriages" or "families."

Modern substantive due process "privacy" doctrine is a straightforward expression of this perspective. Access to contraception and to abortion, for instance, are available to persons regardless of marital status.[52] Indeed, the Supreme Court has emphasized, in words now well known, the primacy of the individual apart from whatever relationship of which she may be a part:

The marital couple is not an independent entity with a mind and heart of its own, but an association of two individuals each with a separate intellectual and emotional make-up. If the right of privacy means anything, it is the right of the *individual*, married or single, to be free from unwarranted governmental intrusion into matters so fundamentally affecting a person as the decision whether to bear or beget a child.[53]

The Court has underscored this point in holding that a woman may not be required to obtain the consent of her husband in order to procure an abortion,[54] nor may a minor be required to obtain parental consent before having such a procedure.[55] These decisions make clear that, with respect to procreation decisions, status as wife or minor child cannot be the source of distinctive obligations that are not imposed on persons who do not occupy that status. They have also been perceived in some quarters as providing the basis for a more general right of autonomy in sexual conduct, which would reflect displacement of marital status as the basis of distinctive sexual rights.[56] Of course, this displacement has already occurred to some extent by the repeal or nonenforcement of statutes prohibiting adultery, fornication, or cohabitation, all of which classified offenses on the basis of marital status.[57]

The declining importance of status is evident in the greater willingness of courts to impose on unmarried cohabitants who separate some of the same responsibilities imposed on divorcing spouses. These obligations may be based on an explicit contractual agreement,[58] may be deemed to arise as part of an implied understanding,[59] or may be imposed on a quasi-contractual *quantum meruit* theory.[60] In any event, the concept that underlies enforcement is that formal status should not determine rights or obligations in the context of a long-term emotional relationship that is substantively equivalent to marriage. Greater willingness to enforce contracts between unmarried cohabitants reflects the mutually reinforcing character of increased deference to private ordering and the declining significance of status.[61] As Frances Olsen has observed: "If marriage is seen as nothing more than what the parties agree to, and if the parties' agreement is all that is enforceable by the courts, a couple's agreement should not be less enforceable just because it does not include formal marriage."[62]

The lessened importance of status is also reflected in the Supreme Court's ruling that marital status may not be used to deny to unmarried fathers the rights afforded married fathers. Instead, the Court has decreed, the enjoyment of paternal rights depends on the substance of the relationship between the father and his children.[63] The Court has also established in a series of cases that discrimination against the children of unmarried parents is unconstitutional in many instances.[64] Several jurisdictions also now prohibit discrimination on the basis of marital status,[65] and these prohibitions have been held in some states to void antinepotism rules that proscribe employment of spouses in the same enterprise or organization.[66] Finally, status as a family member is now less likely to immunize a person from tort liability. A majority of states have abolished or limited interspousal tort immunity,[67] and, while the trend is more complex with respect to parental immunity, most states have enhanced the ability of children to sue their parents.[68]

In sum, as Mary Ann Glendon has put it, "the traditionally central position of legal marriage in family law has been extensively eroded everywhere."[69] It is certainly true that status distinctions are still made in several areas of family law, often with serious repercussions.[70] In fact, "despite a growing sense of ambiguity about the meaning of 'family,' state laws defining that term remain relatively stable."[71] Yet, by comparison with a generation ago, even those distinctions that remain are less likely to designate relationships that are exclusively associated with certain rights and obligations. Rather, as Glendon observes, the primary significance of formal marriage may be that it gives rise to certain presumptions that have legal significance.[72] Without these presumptions, for instance, the child of unmarried parents may have to prove paternity to receive certain benefits,[73] and a partner in an unmarried relationship may have to prove that the relationship was sufficiently like marriage to warrant sharing certain assets when the partners go their separate ways. This willingness on occasion to look beyond formal status reflects greater acceptance of the view that the authenticity of both individuals and relationships is a quality that can be assessed independently of certain socially prescribed forms. Such a perspective is consistent with the modern insistence on personal choice in intimate matters.

Each of the legal developments that I have discussed could itself be the subject of a book or article. Each has its own peculiar history and rich complexity. I don't mean to minimize this fact by treating them here together, nor do I suggest that the common threads that I have identified are the only ones that run through them. Furthermore, I don't mean to deny the continued existence of much in family law that reflects a status orientation.[74] Nonetheless, recent trends can be seen as evidence of a movement from status to contract, in the sense that the past couple of decades have featured the ascendance of individualistic tenets that traditionally have been suppressed in family law.[75] As a result, we are now more apt to think of family life as "part of the individual tradition, resting upon political power, contract, self-interest, and a concept of liberty that will impose a sense of normative duty only when the power of the State can enforce it."[76]

In the remainder of this chapter, I want to explore the sensibility that is the implicit foundation for much of modern family law. That sensibility tends to see the self in acontextual terms, in possession of a core identity separate from any relationship in which it's involved. Such an understanding leads to an attitude of "role distance," which regards social roles as "external" constraints on individual liberty. Yet, paradoxically, the acontextual self sees intimacy as a particularly important vehicle for self- realization. This combination of detachment and desire, I will argue, leads to a distinctively modern pursuit of intimacy. That pursuit is shaped by the understanding of the individual as a consumer in a personal relations market, in which the family is but one intimate option among many. As a result, much as the acontextual self may desire a haven of unqualified support within the family, its quest for authenticity may undermine the conception of obligation that has enabled the family to perform this function.

Role Distance and the Authentic Self

From Role to Self. "Since the 1950's, Americans have gained considerable freedom in their personal lives. . . . Family and gender roles are much more flexible and being free to develop oneself is becoming a goal for both men and women."[77] Individuals are now more apt to think of themselves as possessed of a unique identity that requires nurture and expression, and that can be threatened by conformity to the demands of role and status.[78] A survey of American values in 1957 and 1976 documented this increased attention to individuality. It noted that while people in 1957 tended to define themselves in terms of normative role expectations, by 1976 there was greater emphasis on individuated concepts of self.[79] This tendency to define oneself apart from social roles has continued in the intervening years. A woman in another study in the 1980s expresses this attitude in terms increasingly familiar in modern life:

I used to be naive enough to think my identity revolved around my relationship to other people. My identity used to be my role as wife and mother. My earlier views toward success and toward myself were what other people defined, not what was inside me. Now my identity is more as a person in my own right.[80]

The work of Louis Zurcher bolsters the idea that self-definition is less closely linked to social role than in the past.[81] He reports a shift in recent years in the way that respondents define themselves on the Manfred and Kuhn Twenty Statements Test (TST), an instrument designed to elicit statements describing the self. Traditionally, reports Zurcher, responses tended to reflect a category of self-concept that identified the self with institutionalized roles that were the sources of both rights and duties.[82] More recently, responses have tended to fall within a category indicating that "the self is much less closely identified with norms and roles."[83] For such a person, "self-concept is fairly fluid among external social roles, each of which is evaluated rather continually by the person, who 'stands apart' from the roles[.]"[84]

The late twentieth century is thus marked by what might be described as a movement "from role to self."[85] As a result, one observer suggests that our era is distinguished by the pervasiveness of the belief that one may justify actions on the ground that a more authentic inner self does not fit well within a given social role.[86] Such a view draws on the modernist belief in essences to posit the existence of a "true" self that lies underneath the contingent appearances of social role.[87]

This attitude may be described as a greater sense of "role distance," in contrast to the Victorian tendency toward "role identification."[88] Role distance reflects the belief in a core self that stands apart from the relationships in which it is enmeshed. While the individual may behave in accordance with the expectations associated with a given role, she is apt to see that conformity as a performance, rather than as conduct that serves in part to define who she is.[89] As Erving Goffman puts it, "the individual is actually denying not the role but the virtual self that is implied in the role for all accepting performers."[90] Role distance therefore provides a perspective from which the demands of role may be seen as artificial constraints on the development of one's "authentic" self.

One way to view role distance is as a reflection of the modernist doctrine that "all contexts can be broken."[91] On this view, the individual self is defined fundamentally by its capacity for choice and transformation, rather than by any particular choice that it might make. A given context—a personal relationship, a job, a religious affiliation—may help the individual understand herself better, may affect the values that she holds. She is never limited, however, by that understanding or those values, because she can always transcend them. On the modernist view, individual biography involves the possible realization of a number of identities.[92] We see this, for instance, in the changes that have become more characteristic of contemporary life. How many people work at the same job all their lives, live in the same city, practice the same religion in which they were raised, or even stay married to the same person?

The open-ended nature of the modern self is a basic premise of the humanistic psychology that has influenced popular ideas about personal identity. For Carl Rogers, for instance, a person is a "continually changing constellation of potentialities, not a fixed quality of traits."[93] In Abraham Maslow's formulation, the self is constituted by a hierarchy of needs, and is completely fulfilled only rarely during ephemeral moments of "peak experience."[94] The imperative of such a being can only be growth, the opportunity to realize the self's own unique dynamic. Discovery and development of one's authentic personality thus requires the "willingness to be a process."[95] This means that whatever forms of life in which we may be involved should always be subject to reevaluation in terms of "the only question which matters[:] 'Am I living in a way which is deeply satisfying to me, and which truly expresses me?' "[96]

I've suggested that the Victorians sought to use self-restraint through role identification to ground the individual in the broader culture.[97] By contrast, the modern search for identity is distinguished more by its subjectivity—the sense of an individual outside any ordered social scheme.[98] An attitude of role distance tends to regard with suspicion any voice other than the individual's own feelings and preferences. As Philip Rieff argues, the result is that the basis for evaluating conduct shifts from adherence to shared moral ideals to the more idiosyncratic criterion of furthering individual health; "[n]ot the good life but better living is the therapeutic standard."[99]

From this perspective, the Victorian emphasis on self-restraint in fact may be counterproductive. Humanistic psychology, for instance, tends to depict impulse as benign, something toward which we should be attentive rather than censorious.[100] On this view, feeling offers the best guide to discovering one's authentic self. This privileged character of affect and emotion can be seen in part as a reflection of what Charles Taylor has called the "expressivist turn,"[101] which builds on the Romantic ethic that arose during the Victorian era.[102] This ethic was a reaction against the emphasis on rationality in Enlightenment modernism, a reaction grounded in the belief that devotion to rationality threatened to distort and suppress natural human sentiment in the name of instrumental reason.[103]

While Romanticism takes issue with the rationalist dimension of modernism, it is nonetheless modernist in its belief in the existence of a natural self that lurks beneath surface appearances.[104] To oversimplify a bit, Romanticism substitutes passion for reason as the essence of this self.

Emotion and feeling are the voice of nature in the individual; as a result, we must privilege those attributes that are most spontaneous and free of social convention.[105] For Romanticism, "[i]t is through our feelings that we get to the deepest moral and, indeed, cosmic truths."[106] The result is what Robert Bellah and his colleagues have termed "expressive individualism," the belief that self-actualization occurs through the expression of each individual's unique emotional core.[107]

Romanticism reinforces the modernist movement toward subjectivity, since only the individual can discern the inner voice that speaks through feeling and emotion. Thus, while the expressivist turn may be in tension with the modernist emphasis on rationality, it furthers the modernist quest for the self because "it intensifies the sense of inwardness and leads to an even more radical subjectivism and internalization of moral sources."[108] From this perspective, sources of obligation "outside" the self come to seem more problematic. The obligations of role, for instance, are imposed without regard to the wishes of the particular individual who happens to occupy a given role. Yet, modern sensibility is more inclined to believe that the individual is the best judge of what course of conduct is most consistent with her unique personality and potential. Heightened regard for subjectivity thus gives rise to the notion that individuals should be free from constraints to which they have not consented.[109]

One final way of understanding contemporary role distance is as a shift from a sense of self anchored in institutions to one anchored in impulse.[110] Recall that the Victorian era can be seen as one in which an individual achieved selfhood by overcoming impulses to meet "higher" institutional standards of behavior.[111] By contrast, Ralph Turner suggests, contemporary life is marked by a growing sense that the true self is "a set of impulses that have been repressed or dissipated under institutional constraint[.]"[112] In this paradigm, the real self is revealed when she does something not out of a sense of duty, but because she spontaneously wishes to do it.[113] Similarly, while an institutional model might regard hypocrisy as the betrayal of certain standards of behavior, the impulse model sees hypocrisy as adherence to standards even if the behavior required is not what the individual really wants to do.[114] Turner's framework thus allows us to compare the Victorian and contemporary eras in terms of "the shared and socially produced intuitions through which people identify their true selves."[115]

I should emphasize here that the portrait I have sketched is a qualified one. First, acceptance of the ethos I have described likely varies by region and class, and is most closely identified with so-called social elites: urban middle- and upper-middle class professionals.[116] Furthermore, it is contested, even by certain social elites, who decry its purported atomistic character.[117] Particularly critical have been some feminist scholars, who see the commitment to unfettered self-development as associated with a traditionally male orientation toward social life and personal identity.[118]

At the same time, however, social elites are in fields such as law, media, social services, and education that have powerful influence in generating models for understanding everyday life. In addition, elite attitudes seem to be penetrating even traditional pockets of resistance.[119] Finally, those who point to competing traditions or perspectives often see themselves as engaged in an effort to retrieve visions that are losing resonance for most Americans.[120] We thus seem increasingly likely to see ourselves as residents of what Lawrence Friedman calls "the republic of choice": a society committed to "the right to develop oneself, to build up a life suited to oneself uniquely, to realize and aggrandize the self, through free, open selection among forms, models, and ways of living."[121] As the following section suggests, acceptance of these ideas has left its mark on modern family life.

Role Distance and the Family

As we have seen, one hallmark of the Victorian era was the significance of family role in self-definition, which was associated with a sense of private life as a realm centered around the family.[122] With a heightened sense of role distance, and greater resistance to the notion that any given relationship can constitute a part of the self, the individual comes to replace the family as the center of private life. As a result, the family now tends to be perceived more as one optional relationship among many, rather than as a set of relationships essential to achieving selfhood. Furthermore, even when the individual chooses that option, she now has far more latitude to structure its terms as she wishes.

Let's begin with what I call the rise of the *optional family*. As one scholar observes, "There has been a dramatic and pervasive weakening of the normative imperative to marry, to remain married, to have children, to restrict intimate relations to marriage, and to maintain separate roles for males and females."[123] We can appreciate how marriage and family have come to be seen as rooted more in the domain of individual choice by tracing the path of an individual across various stages of life.

First, children are leaving home at an earlier age than in the recent past.[124] Their departure is increasingly prompted not by marriage but by a desire to establish a household of their own. Living independently of one's parents has become a strong expectation of young adults, and is generally encouraged by the larger culture.[125] Remaining single is now more acceptable, and in some ways easier, than ever before. Furthermore, various services once provided by family members can now be obtained in the market, which makes it easier in a practical sense for individuals to live apart from families.[126]

Once a person becomes involved in an intimate relationship with another, there is less pressure to formalize that commitment through marriage. Cohabitation is rapidly increasing as an acceptable alternative to marriage; the number of unmarried-couple households increased by 80 percent from 1980 to 1990.[127] While both the absolute number and percentage of couples cohabitating without marriage is still relatively small, it appears that unmarried cohabitation is coming to be regarded as an acceptable mainstream arrangement.[128] The lessened premium on marriage is also reflected in the rising age of first marriage in the period since World War II, and in the increasing proportion of persons never married.[129] Individuals are now able with little cultural disapproval to choose to live outside of marriage either singly or with another.

While many cohabitants ultimately marry, there are some indications that cohabitation may not represent simply a period of preparation for marriage. Cohabitants, for instance, generally dissolve their relationships in a briefer period of time than those who are married separate or divorce.[130] Furthermore, some research concludes that persons who had lived together before marriage reported significantly lower marital communication and satisfaction after marriage than couples who had not.[131] One suggested explanation for this phenomenon is that cohabitants may adapt less readily to those role expectations that still attach to being married.[132] Cohabitation thus may represent an alternative track for an increasing number of persons who are averse to the loss of flexibility that they perceive marriage to represent.[133]

Once an individual does decide to marry, traditional assumptions about behavior associated with marital status are less applicable. For instance, marriage no longer automatically implies that a couple will have children. As fertility rates continue to decline over the long term, voluntary childlessness has become more prevalent as an acceptable way of life.[134] Those who do have children now tend to have them later in life and to have fewer of them.[135] At the same time, marital status is now treated as less of a prerequisite for those people who want to have children. More than one-quarter of all children born in the United States are now born out of wedlock.[136] As one senator has commented, "Illegitimacy levels that were viewed as an aberration of a particular subculture 25 years ago have become the norm for the entire culture."[137] Another observer suggests that this phenomenon may be the latest phase in the lessening salience of the formal family. The first phase was the movement away from marriage as the locus of sexual relations, and the second was the detachment of childbearing from wedlock. We now may be entering a phase, he speculates, in which marriage is no longer the locus of childrearing.[138]

The emphasis on individual choice is also underscored by the fact that marriage is seen as far more revocable than before. Divorce has lost its stigma for the most part, and is generally regarded as an acceptable personal choice.[139] Americans continue to divorce at high rates, with the annual rate having doubled between 1960 and 1980 and remained relatively stable since then.[140] About half of all marriages now end in divorce; one detailed analysis of demographic and divorce data estimates that two-thirds of all marriages will face disruption through separation or divorce.[141] The average duration of American marriages before divorce also continues to fall.[142]

Status as parent has also been more affected by the emphasis on personal choice. "When parenting competes with other adult interests and roles, we increasingly acknowledge the legitimacy of self-interest as the decision criterion."[143] Thus, the presence of children is now generally not regarded as a reason for a couple who desires a divorce not to obtain one.[144] Furthermore, it also appears that a large number of noncustodial parents choose to spend little time with their children, so that their status as parent plays a diminishing part in the ordering of their lives.[145] This is especially the case if the noncustodial parent remarries and if he or she acquires stepchildren as a result. Some researchers now suggest that the significance of biological parenthood may be waning, as divorce and remarriage represent "a mechanism for building an extended family by choice rather than by ascription."[146] Thus, even the ostensibly ineluctable tie of biology may be dissolving as a barrier to the exercise of choice over family matters.

While many divorced persons ultimately remarry, such marriages tend to dissolve at a higher rate than first marriages.[147] Research suggests that remarriers have even less of an expectation of permanence than do persons marrying for the first time.[148] One study concludes that individuals who have experienced divorce tend to hedge their commitment because they are more sensitive to the prospect of marital dissolution. The authors suggest that "persons who remarry are increasingly likely to view marriage as a conditional contract."[149]

As the culture places less emphasis on either getting or staying married, "marriage is occupying a less central place in the lives of men and women in the United States."[150] A survey of Americans in 1957, for instance, reported that most persons saw great difficulty for the unmarried in achieving happiness. By 1976, however, the majority of persons felt that one need not be married in order to lead a satisfying life.[151] Similarly, the 1980 Survey of American Families revealed that mothers and daughters disagreed with both the statement that it is desirable to be married and the statement that it is desirable to be single. Most people considered marrying or remaining single as equally acceptable alternatives, which researchers describe as an attitude quite different from the traditional orientation.[152]

With the declining cultural emphasis on marriage, it is not surprising that compared to earlier cohorts, contemporary adults spend a smaller proportion of their lives as members of family households.[153] This phenomenon is partly attributable to the tendency to delay, rather than reject, living in a family setting. Even so, this means that "more and more young people are spending an important part of early adulthood in a context in which family roles may be much less salient, and are developing tastes and skills that are likely to reduce their orientation to family roles."[154] Furthermore, as those persons move through life and experience cohabitation, marriage, children, separation, divorce, and possibly remarriage, they will encounter many more transitions from family to nonfamily settings than in the past.[155] They will be increasingly accustomed to defining their lives in terms of their own needs and development, rather than in terms of the particular family of which they might be a part at any given time.[156]

As fewer particular expectations accompany family life, and as marriage becomes less integral to the process of family formation,[157] differences between being married and being unmarried may tend to diminish. Some research suggests, for instance, that marriage has become less significant as a determinant of personal happiness, since it no longer provides the emotional and psychological security that it once did.[158] "The shift from singlehood to marriage no longer carries the profundity in obligations and commitment that it once did in the past,"[159] so life in a family setting may now be a less distinctive living arrangement than it once was. Role distance and greater emphasis on self-development have therefore given rise to the optional family, so that the question of entering and remaining within family life is more a matter of choice than it was a generation ago.

In addition, these cultural trends have also fostered the emergence of what I call the *negotiated family*, which means that those who elect to participate in family life wield far more choice about its terms than in the past. The negotiated family is a product of the fact that the greater prominence of role distance in current life means that family relationships are less likely to be organized around common expectations of behavior. Rather, they now depend more on "performance and achievement."[160] Status as husband or wife, parent or child now counts for less than individual personal qualities.[161] Expectations and obligations within the family, therefore, are now more likely to be products of personal interaction and negotiation.[162] With respect to marriage, for instance, "[e]ach couple must decide for itself between marriage and just living together; it must shape its own rituals, its attitudes toward stability and change, its own stand toward exclusiveness vis-à-vis other relationships."[163] The demands and rewards of marriage are seen as fashioned, rather than assumed; this places emphasis on understanding the particular options available so that persons can weigh the relative desirability of the expectations embodied in each. Such expectations are not fixed, but are subject to renegotiation if either spouse regards them as no longer satisfying.[164] As one set of scholars puts it, the basic tenet of the modern intimate relationship, including marriage, is that "[e]verything is negotiable except the principle that everything is negotiable."[165]

The parent-child relationship also seems decreasingly ordered by role expectations. Researchers in the *Inner American* study, for instance, found that one of the clearest trends in American culture is the desire of parents to develop a personal relationship with their child; parental authority increasingly rests on the quality of that relationship rather than the parent's status as parent.[166] As a consequence, discussion and negotiation have assumed greater importance in influencing the child's behavior.[167] As one study of the portrayal of families on television concluded: "Today's TV parents are less likely to give their children rules or to pass on family beliefs and values. Rather, TV parents and kids tend to discover life's important values and beliefs in a process of mutual learning."[168] Furthermore, once children leave home, the extent of contact and degree of involvement tend to depend on the quality of personal interaction rather than the expectations that flow from the parent-child relationship itself.[169]

Interpersonal skills are also crucial in shaping relations in the "blended" family, comprised of parents and children from different marriages. There are virtually no established expectations as to how the members of the blended family should relate to one another.[170] As a result, relations among family members are primarily a product of negotiation, as individuals have "a choice of whether or not to be related when they are no longer connected by an intact marriage."[171]

The language in which negotiations among family members is likely to occur is one that places greater emphasis on satisfying the needs of the authentic self. It is by now a commonplace assertion that marriage is valuable to the degree that it serves as a vehicle for individuals to realize their unique potential.[172] Furstenberg and Spanier, for instance, report that those who regard remarriage after divorce as successful typically attribute success to the fact that their current spouse recognizes the way they "really" are or helps them to become the person they "really" want to be.[173] Similarly, Philippe Aries has suggested that the decision to have children is increasingly influenced by the belief that parenthood will be a satisfying experience that will enhance individual growth and development.[174]

The extent to which family relationships are an enduring source of support therefore depends more today on individual performance, since "whatever its 'commitment,' the current interpersonal relationship must include a commitment to continuing negotiation."[175] This naturally flows from a heightened sense of role distance and commitment to self-development, and the consequent emphasis on consensual obligation.[176] As a result, the modern family has taken on many of the characteristics of a voluntary association. As one scholar observes, to argue that there is a heightened emphasis on individual satisfaction within the family "is not to say that there is an absence of generosity or love. . . . It is *relative* emphasis that is important here, and the point is that the individual will not only come first, he or she will have a social structure that will allow individual agendas to be accomplished."[177]

The attitudes underlying the optional and the negotiated family did not emerge *ex nihilo* in the past two or three decades. They were latent in the Victorian family, which gave heightened attention to individual feeling and personal choice. The Victorians, however, sought to restrain this subjectivity through the vehicle of role identification. As that solution has unraveled, however, the modernist self has slipped its fetters and has come to dominate our conception of private life. As I discuss in the next section, one important vision of that private life is as a realm in which one can nurture the self through intimacy with others. A result is heightened emphasis on the *intimate* family. As we shall see, however, role distance makes it more likely that the family will be seen as but one possible source of intimacy, rather than as a distinctive and enduring set of relationships.

Intimacy and Authenticity. Role distance promotes the view that an understanding of one's authentic self is difficult to achieve if persons relate to each other through artificial role expectations that suppress individuality. This suspicion of social roles leads to emphasis on the exchange of genuine feeling as the ideal mode of social interaction. Each person's willingness to reveal herself ideally elicits the discovery and expression of "real" selves freed of pretense and social convention. The modernist self thus finds appealing "an intimate vision of society,"[178] in which the dominant aspiration is "to develop individual personality through experiences of closeness and warmth with others."[179]

The increasing influence of this vision is indicated by a longitudinal study of American values, which found that the desire for more satisfying and warm relationships became a more pervasive cultural theme from 1957 to 1976.[180] Researchers note a greater tendency to describe all social relationships in interpersonal terms, and conclude that their survey reveals the "increasing importance of intimacy as a good in our society."[181] Similarly, Daniel Yankelovich's research indicates that by the early 1980s a large percentage of Americans regarded as a serious void in their lives the fact that they had many acquaintances but few close friends.[182] The desire to transcend barriers to closeness is reflected in a variety of cultural phenomena. Sexuality is now the object of more open and pronounced attention, and has taken on great significance as a vehicle for self-realization.[183] Television and radio talk shows commonly seek to create a sense of shared personal experience by eliciting revelations that ostensibly narrow the distance between famous and ordinary persons,[184] or between viewers or listeners themselves. Many television news programs now include informal chatter and bantering between newscasters, and advertising often tells us how much companies "care" about their customers. Personal qualities of warmth and authenticity also have assumed increasing importance in modern political campaigns.[185] Finally, Daniel Bell has suggested that contemporary art often attempts to achieve the "eclipse of distance,"[186] the disruption of detached contemplation in favor of "immediacy, simultaneity, envelopment of experience."[187]

Anthony Giddens suggests that personal intimacy has become not only a desirable but a necessary aspect of the modern quest for authentic identity. Trust, he argues, is essential for self-realization, because it makes possible confidence in the relative stability of the environment in which the self must operate.[188] "External" criteria for behavior such as roles can serve as a basis for trust, because they serve as normative codes that will likely be followed by others.[189] Declining reliance on such criteria makes other persons less predictable and more volatile, because their behavior depends more on "internal" idiosyncratic considerations. In this world, the achievement of trust depends on the ability of a person to convince the other that the sentiments that she reveals are expressions of her "true" self, in whom the other can trust. Trust, and the self-realization that it makes possible, therefore depends on keen awareness of the feelings of oneself and others. As a result, the intimate relationship, which offers maximum opportunity for cultivating such awareness, becomes the model of how social interaction should proceed in order to foster self-development.[190]

Today's pursuit of intimacy is thus an individual quest for authentic self-definition rather than, as with the Victorians, conduct that occurs within the context of a set of relationships whose terms are prescribed by a common code of behavior. Richard Sennett captures this difference when he contrasts the nineteenth- century "seduction" and the twentieth-century "affair":

A seduction was the arousal of such feelings by one person—not always a man—in another such that social codes were violated. This violation caused all the other social relations of the person to be temporarily called into question; one's spouse, one's children, one's own parents were involved both symbolically through guilt and practically if discovery of the violation occurred.[191]

By contrast, says Sennett:

It would seem illogical now for a person conducting an affair, whether inside or outside the bonds of marriage, to see it innately connected to parental relations, so that whenever one makes love to another person one's status as someone else's child is altered. This, we would say, is a matter of individual cases, of personality factors; it is not a social matter.[192]

The Intimate Family. While the attainment of intimacy has become a more widespread goal in personal relationships generally, the aspiration finds its most intense expression within the modern family. From its inception as a relatively self-conscious institution, the family has been seen as a source of intimacy for its members.[193] At the same time, the family also traditionally performed a variety of social functions.[194] These functions provided additional criteria for evaluating family life, and served to impose certain expectations of behavior that made family a source not only of intimacy but also of obligation.[195] Over time, the family has relinquished many of the social functions that it once performed.[196] As a result, the family today is seen as specializing to an even greater degree in the task of "gratifying people's psychological needs—for understanding, affection, and happiness."[197]

The past two to three decades have seen an intensification of the ideal of family intimacy, especially with respect to marriage. Companionate marriage is now the consensus model, depicting a "modern, intimate,

highly interactive ideal communicated in the self-development literature."[198] Researchers replicating the Middletown studies, for instance,
found that in contemporary Middletown husbands and wives provided
each other considerably greater emotional support than did couples in
the 1920s.[199] Similarly, reflecting more recent trends, Bellah and his coauthors found that many of their respondents feel that their marriages are
better than their parents' because of greater intimacy and sharing of
feelings.[200]

The emergence of intimacy as the dominant purpose of family life has
increased the potential for emotionally rewarding family relationships.
At the same time, the dominance of this ethic against a backdrop of role
distance may be at odds with our vision of the family as a refuge of
enduring and distinctive support.[201]

First, an ethic of intimacy bases assessment of satisfaction on subjective, inherently dynamic emotional states, as opposed to the performance of family roles whose dictates are perceived as more objective.
As a result, "[t]he love that must hold us together is rooted in the
vicissitudes of our subjectivity."[202] As Bernard Farber observes, the
modern emphasis on "commitment- reinforcing" activities implicitly
reflects an assumption that such activities are necessary in order to
counter natural tendencies to give priority to individual gratification,
and to evaluate relationships by that standard.[203] The instability that
flows from reliance on subjectivity as the source of validation for
family relationships reflects the dynamics of reflexivity associated with
the modern self.[204] Reflexivity demands that social and personal arrangements be justified on the basis of reason, rather than past
practice.[205] No arrangement is immune from the need for such ongoing
justification. In the modern world, "the revision of convention [is]
radicalized to apply (in principle) to all aspects of human life[.]"[206]
As a result, any intimate relationship is subject to continuing reevaluation of its performance. Thus, while heightened emphasis on intimacy
in the family holds out the promise of a more secure source of emotional support, the dynamism of both emotional states and the process
of reflexivity may in fact reduce the ability to realize that promise.

A second source of tension between the model of intimate disclosure
and our aspirations for family life is that this model is not distinctive to
the family, but is now regarded as an ideal for all personal relationships.
Even though we generally expect the family to provide a particularly
high level of emotional support, both the family and other personal
relationships are now more apt to be evaluated by the common standard
of intimacy. Since satisfaction in all relationships is seen as dependent

on the deployment of generic interpersonal skills, other relationships theoretically can substitute for the family by providing a sufficient level of intimacy.[207]

Data in fact suggest that persons nowadays rely less exclusively on the family and draw upon a more diverse set of sources for emotional support than even a generation ago. One longitudinal survey, for instance, reported an increase from 1957 to 1976 in the variety of people relied upon for emotional support, and a decrease in reliance on family members.[208] The increased acceptance of psychotherapy has been a particularly prominent manifestation of this phenomenon. Not only adults but children as well are exposed to the prospect of multiple options for emotional support. Many schools now attempt to deal with disarray in families by instituting counseling to help children deal with divorce, learn about sex, or confront their anxieties.[209] Once they become adolescents, children often become part of a relatively auton-omous "youth culture" that to some degree displaces the family as an agent of socialization. Surveying the trend toward extrafamilial sources of support, one observer goes so far as to speculate that there is "very likely to be an increasing proportion of the population who rely on friends for short-term help, on professionals for long-term help, and on kin for not much more than shared celebration of family holidays."[210]

A person therefore need not participate in family life to obtain the benefits of intimacy. While the family in some sense may be the implicit ideal by which other personal relationships are assessed, this is different from saying that the family meets distinct needs that other relationships cannot meet. The evaluation of family life according to the calculus of intimacy makes family and nonfamily relationships seem more commensurable.

This commensurability has led some family scholars to question the analytical utility of the concept of "family" itself.[211] John Scanzoni, for instance, maintains that most persons "seek certain *generic* ingredients in their close relationships regardless of structure."[212] From such a per-spective, thinking in "attribute" categories such as family and nonfamily relationships may be less useful than employing a more general approach that focuses on the "*close relationship situation.*"[213] Within such a par-adigm, the family is but one of several forms of connection arrayed on a single continuum of intimate relationships.[214] The focus of research then shifts more toward the individual and those factors that influence the choice of one relationship over another.[215] Such an approach reflects a view that the family is one possible choice among similar alternatives, rather than a way of life with a character qualitatively different from other personal relationships.

This lessened distinctiveness of family relationships reinforces the attitude of role distance. On the one hand, role distance reflects the resistance to defining oneself in terms of family life. At the same time, the ability of the family to serve as the basis for self-definition is undercut by the fact that it seems less distinguishable from other personal relationships. As Ralph Turner suggests, "the potential of any institutional role for self-anchorage depends on the degree to which it incorporates distinctive privileges, responsibilities, and skills. Such monopolies may have been progressively undermined in recent years."[216]

Indeed, there is some indication that the definition of the family itself has become more fluid, as persons rely more on subjective criteria and less on communal standards. A recent survey indicated, for instance, that most people define family ties in terms of personal feelings, rather than according to marriage or blood lines.[217] The survey also noted that only half the respondents included their stepchildren in their definition of their close family. As researchers concluded, "[t]his can be seen as the negative side of a definition of family based on the presence of loving emotions. Where the emotions are absent, so are the bonds of family, law or custom notwithstanding."[218] Thus, in a certain sense, even the understanding of the family of which one is a member is now more apt to be seen as governed by subjectivity.

Despite aspirations to the contrary, the ascendance of subjectivity can't insulate the individual from the culture in which she is located. In fact, the disengagement from those roles that constitute the "middle distance" between the individual and the society at large may make her even more susceptible to the messages of mass culture. In the next section, we'll explore a particularly powerful self-image propagated by that culture: the self as consumer. This self-image, I will argue, may lead to a tendency to regard all relationships, including those within the family, as potential sources of intimacy in a personal relations market. The result may be an even wider gulf between aspiration and experience, as family relationships become less able to provide the kind of stable commitment that many seek from them.

Self as Consumer

Modern Consumer Culture. In this section, I want to make the case that a current prominent way of thinking about identity and experience is that the individual is a consumer in a marketplace that offers various sources of satisfaction. I don't mean to suggest that persons consciously regard themselves in this way; indeed, they often resist such descriptions. Modern culture, however, is particularly insistent in offering the image of the consumer as a model for behavior, and, with a greater sense of role distance, there are fewer obstacles to the internalization of this message. The result is what Albert Borgmann has called "commodious individualism": the understanding that what privacy vindicates is the right to individual consumption free from "judgmental intrusion."[219] The implication of these developments is that the quest for self-development and intimacy is increasingly shaped in subtle ways by the images and metaphors of the modern consumer experience.[220]

People have always been consumers; the human condition is such that we have had to make use of objects in the world to fulfill basic needs such as food, clothing, and shelter. The exchange and consumption of goods may also serve more subtle purposes. Objects of consumption may serve as a means of denoting status, of sending signals about social inclusion or exclusion, or of providing occasions for predictable social interaction that reaffirms a sense of solidarity.[221]

What distinguishes contemporary culture, however, is the relative prominence of the sphere of consumption. In traditional societies, custom and tradition typically place limits on the amount and type of goods that are consumed, the manner in which they are consumed, and the desires that are considered legitimate.[222] While a household might have the means to acquire novel or luxurious goods, this does not automatically translate into a willingness to do so. More commonly, economic surplus is either hoarded or used to purchase more leisure.[223] The sphere of consumption thus is generally a tightly bounded realm subject to considerable cultural regulation.

By contrast, modern consumer culture regards individual desire, not cultural norms, as the ultimate judge of the worth of goods and services. Such a view is of course consistent with the modernist tenet that the individual is the source of all value judgments. Furthermore, modern consumer culture sees the sphere of consumption as open-ended: "For all practical purposes, human wants may be regarded as limitless. An occasional individual may have everything he wants, but man's capacity to generate new wants as fast as he satisfies old ones is well-known psychologically."[224] Such a notion is consistent with the conception of the individual as someone with unbounded needs whose only ultimate sense of fulfillment can come from continued growth. The heightened significance of consumption in modern culture sends an increasingly powerful signal that a coherent way to see oneself is as a consumer in a marketplace of various opportunities for satisfaction. With such an understanding, the exercise of individual choice so central to modern sensibility is regarded as the exercise of consumer sovereignty.

Perhaps the primary vehicle for reinforcing this vision is advertising. With mass production, urbanization, and greater geographical and social mobility, advertising media help erase provincial boundaries by offering a broader world of consumer choice.[225] The vision communicated by such media is the equation of self-fulfillment with consumption. Persons are encouraged "to interpret needs . . . as needs for commodities,"[226] and to "identify states of feeling systematically with appropriate types of commodities."[227] From such a perspective, the world takes on significance in large measure as something that offers a multitude of opportunities for fulfillment, if only one shops carefully, armed with both an understanding of one's preferences and an openness to novel forms of satisfaction.

The images and language of consumer advertising of course do not afford the only way of understanding fulfillment in the modern world; alternate and even antithetical conceptions exist. Nonetheless, as Michael Schudson observes, "no other cultural form is as accessible to children; no other form confronts visitors and immigrants to our society (and migrants from one part of society to another) so forcefully."[228] Schudson draws a provocative analogy between consumer advertising and the prevalence of religious imagery in the French countryside in the nineteenth century. While this imagery did not necessarily mean that the French peasant was a devout Christian, it did mean that "[w]hen one thought of salvation or, more modestly, searched for meanings for making sense of life, there were primarily the materials of the Church to work with."[229] Similarly, when one seeks clues to the nature of modern happiness, the logic, metaphors, and images of consumption come naturally to mind. Indeed, as Thomas Luckmann has suggested, religion itself has become an object of consumer choice, as religions compete with other sources of " 'ultimate' significance" for the allegiance of customers.[230]

Even a superficial examination of modern language reveals the resonance of the consumer model. One person attempting to persuade another is commonly regarded as trying to "sell" her ideas; if she is successful, the listener often concludes, "I'll buy that." The Washington *Post* declares: "Our role in election coverage is to tell you what the supermarket is offering for November."[231] The President of the United States reflects on the accomplishments of his administration in protecting freedom, applauding a child's notion that happiness in America means "choosing among 200 flavors of ice cream."[232] The director of a task force recommending changes in libel law states that the group's proposal has been announced "to put it out in the marketplace."[233] Ubiquitous tee shirts and bumper stickers proclaim "Born to Shop" and "When the Going Gets Tough the Tough Go Shopping." These examples suggest that the perspective of the consumer in the marketplace seems a natural way to describe a variety of otherwise diverse experiences.

The resonance of the consumer model is also reflected in the increasing application of economic theory to ever more diverse domains of life. Spearheaded by "Chicago school" theorists, the discipline of economics has come to assert explanatory jurisdiction over all forms of human behavior.[234] Gary Becker, for instance, has declared that "all human behavior can be viewed as involving participants who maximize their utility from a stable set of preferences and accumulate an optimal amount of information and other inputs in a variety of markets."[235] This approach explicitly posits that individuals are fundamentally consumers, and that the paradigmatic form of human interaction is the market transaction. As a result, economic analysis has been applied to areas as diverse as adoption,[236] employment discrimination,[237] criminal justice,[238] and sexual conduct.[239] Each application of the theory is intended to demonstrate that, despite superficial appearances, ultimately all behavior is a form of market conduct in which persons perform cost-benefit calculations with regard to alternatives that promise varying amounts of utility to the individual.[240] This view has not gone uncontested,[241] but its emergence as an intellectual force points up the apparent plausibility and resonance of the understanding of oneself as a consumer.

Thus, as consumption gains more importance in modern life, self-definition as a consumer gains currency. This is significant not merely because of whatever materialism it may generate. Rather, individuals seeking to understand themselves and the world around them through use of the consumer metaphor draw on an experience that is distinctive in subtle ways. The next section will analyze this distinctiveness by exploring the inner world of the modern consumer.

Modern Consumer Experience. The modern consumer can best be described as restless. Two features of her experience contribute to this condition. The first is the expectation of constant change and novelty, which leads consumers to view their choices as impermanent and qualified. Few people today expect the products that they purchase to remain a fixture in their lives for any extended period of time. Rather, consumer satisfaction comes to be linked to the stimulation of novelty.[242] Consumers are encouraged to jettison past purchases in response to such novelty, and to interpret their needs expansively so as to fuel the market for further novelty. The person who is resistant to such blandishment, who makes do with the old model or dresses in last year's fashion, may invite ridicule. With the rise of consumer advertising, the experience of new needs and their stimulation became mutually reinforcing.[243] As a result, modern patterns of consumption are inherently unstable. "The consumption pattern of the moment is seen not as part of a way of life, but a temporary adjustment to circumstances. We expect to take the first available chance to change the pattern."[244] This expectation of constant change leads to a sense that choices and commitments should be qualified rather than irrevocable. The modern consumer must be flexible; no prior choice should impinge on the ability to make future choices. Keeping one's options open becomes a paramount consideration.[245] The modern consumer thus strives less to choose certain things than to remain free to choose.[246]

The emphasis on the provisional nature of consumer commitments is congruent with the insistence of the self-development ethic that satisfaction is not a stable achievement but a constant process of revision and growth. The healthy individual is open to new experience; the healthy consumer is open to new products. Belief in the growth of the self parallels belief in the growth of the market. Furthermore, the proliferation of new specialized products for distinct needs reinforces the notion of oneself as a person with an ensemble of needs. The more specialized the product, the more consumer needs tend to be seen as fragmented and potentially limitless. Any product is always subject to improvement, and even the improved product can satisfy only a fraction of a consumer's needs.

A second distinctive feature of modern consumer experience that fosters restlessness is that it tends to be characterized not so much by having as by wanting. Consumption itself often appears to provide only momentary satisfaction, with disappointment soon on its heels, followed in turn by renewed longing for other goods or experiences. In part, of course, this is a function of the fact that a constant parade of new products makes older ones seem inadequate, so that consumers tend to reevaluate their needs in light of an expanding market.[247]

The pendulum of longing and disappointment is also the result, however, of a subtle change in the relationship between the consumer and the product. In modern life, it is not quite accurate to say that consumer choice simply reflects the process of matching specific needs with the particular attributes of a product. In contrast to the early part of this century, for instance, contemporary advertising does not see its role primarily as one of providing detailed product information to enable the consumer to make a rational choice. Rather, advertising seeks to create a diffuse aura of desirability around a product, through association with various symbols.[248] As a result, "images and symbolic meanings are as much a 'real' part of the product as its constituent ingredients."[249]

As a consequence, consumer advertising creates a realm of dreamlike images and juxtaposition of objects that seem not to profess to be taken literally, yet that appear simultaneously to "promis[e] intense 'real life' to their clientele, and [to] implicitly defin[e] 'real life' as something outside the individual's everyday experience."[250] Advertising creates a relationship between consumer and product in which floating, detached images tend to be more common than symbols with specific referents.[251] The ambiguity of advertising images encourages the projection of idiosyncratic desires and fantasies upon the product, permitting the consumer to "attach his favoured day dream to this real object of desire."[252] This results in the "dissolution of the commodity into an unstable network of characteristics and messages," so that "the nature of the object itself becomes largely a function of the psychological state of those who desire it."[253] Modern consumers thus increasingly inhabit a world defined by its subjectivity—a world made up not of objects with definite attributes, but one composed of their own dreams and desires.[254] Those dreams and desires both shape and are shaped by advertising, which represents as normative those fleeting moments of intense satisfaction.[255]

This projection of expectations onto products lays the groundwork for disappointment in two ways. First, the consumer often has little sense of the specific satisfaction desired from a product. "If an individual feels a sense of accomplishment in a particular consumption choice, can he determine what specific bits of [her] needs assortment, in association with what specific characteristics of the purchased item, helped to bring this about?"[256] Often the answer is no, which suggests greater ambiguity in the assessment of personal well-being.[257]

Second, the act of consumption may rarely measure up to the fantasies of the consumer. The condensed and highly charged emotions evoked by advertising create a standard of personal experience that more complex everyday life can only imperfectly approximate.[258] As a result, consumption often provokes disillusionment because of its failure to live up to the promise of imagination.[259] Life then seems a poor version of the diffuse dreamworld of advertising, which prompts dissatisfaction with one's circumstances.[260] The modern consumer thus is often enmeshed in "the basic pattern of first associating a dream with a product, followed by the disillusionment consequent upon its use, so that fulfillment seems just out of reach."[261]

Hard on the heels of disappointment, however, comes rekindled desire, as fantasies are projected upon some different product. The impetus for consumers' renewed longing is the hope that each new product will be the vehicle for realizing the intense experience already enjoyed in the imagination.[262] Somewhere, the modern consumer is convinced, it must be possible to attain the transcendent satisfaction that is the ideal. This aspiration resembles Maslow's model of self-actualization, a state of being devoutly pursued but only fleetingly experienced.[263]

The restlessness of the modern consumer therefore is attributable in part to her involvement in a cycle of desire and disappointment, in which the predominant mood is one of longing. "[T]he modern hedonist is constantly withdrawing from reality as fast as he encounters it, ever casting his day-dreams forward in time, attaching them to objects of desire, and then subsequently 'unhooking' them from these objects as and when they are attained and experienced."[264] The contemporary consumer often lives for expectations of consumption, rather than actual consumption itself.[265]

In a world in which autonomy is often equated with consumer sovereignty, it therefore becomes more natural to draw on the consumer metaphor and its distinct model of experience to understand and define personal life. In the next section, we'll explore the implications of this self-definition for the experience of intimate relationships and family life. While this account is not necessarily a literal description of late twentieth-century intimate life, the concept of consumerism nonetheless provides some suggestive insights into intimate experience.

The Personal Relations Market. Perhaps nothing better expresses the influence of consumerism on self-definition than the tendency to refer to one's life as a "lifestyle." The metaphor of style, drawn from the fashion world, connotes something that is subject to change as newer and ostensibly better alternatives become available. It suggests that a person's own life as lived is but a contingent feature of her self. This orientation reflects the premises of modernism, abstracting the individual from her context so that all that remains is her capacity to shift from one style to another. A lifestyle is not constitutive of identity. Rather, it is an object of choice—something one has, rather than something one is. On this view, experience can be regarded as a commodity, which can be compared to other experiences in the vast marketplace that constitutes personal life.

As we have seen, the experience of interpersonal intimacy is a particularly valued element of the modern lifestyle. As such, intimacy can be seen as a commodity as much as any other part of one's experience. From this perspective, the pursuit of intimacy is akin to shopping in a personal relations market. Consumers have come to enjoy greater sovereignty in this market in recent years. The family no longer holds a monopoly on the experience of intimacy; there is now more competition from other personal relationships. As a result, we are now more apt to regard the family as simply one consumer choice among many in the personal relations market.

The influence of the consumer model in thinking about personal relations is reflected in psychological exchange theory, which models human interaction as a series of exchanges in which each person tries to maximize the satisfaction available in the encounter. For this theory, "the analogy of the market place has proved a useful one. . . . Satisfaction can be looked at as *benefit* and dissatisfiers as *costs*. The difference between the two can be looked at as *profit* or *loss*, depending on which is the larger."[266] Kenneth Gergen observes that the extension of such consumer calculations to all domains of life is a natural result of modernist logic.[267]

Some family scholars have also adopted concepts that closely track the notion of consumer behavior. Bernard Farber has suggested, for instance, that individuals in modern relationships are likely to operate on the assumption of "permanent availability," the idea that any person, married or not, is potentially available as a partner in another relationship that might offer greater rewards.[268] Implicit in this concept, says Farber, is the notion that one always might be able to do better with another marriage partner.[269] Similarly, Furstenberg and Spanier employ the concept of "conjugal career" to describe the phenomenon of divorce and remarriage, since most persons who remarry see themselves as progressing from one stage of satisfaction to a higher one.[270] Another family scholar, William Goode, has examined recent changes in the willingness of persons to "invest" in family relationships.[271] Furthermore, scholars arguing the need for a new paradigm that focuses on the generic intimate relationship rather than the family likewise emphasize what can be regarded as consumer behavior.[272] They note their reliance on schools of thought that assert that persons enter into relationships "for their own purposes," and change either those relationships or their purposes when they are thwarted in achieving their objectives.[273] Finally, Gary Becker has argued that unmarried persons pursue companions in "marriage markets,"[274] that "[a]n efficient marriage market develops 'shadow prices' to guide participants to marriages that will maximize their well being,"[275] and that altruism, reproduction, childrearing, inheritance, divorce, and remarriage are among the forms of family behavior that can be explained by economic theory.[276]

This body of diverse work reflects an increasing ability to feel comfortable with the consumer model as a way of understanding personal life and the family. The underlying vision that unites these approaches is that "[e]ach person is continuously comparing his or her marital bargain with other marital bargains which he or she might be able to negotiate with other persons, and with his or her potential benefits from not being married at all."[277]

Awareness of the influence of consumer culture on the pursuit of intimacy may offer a novel perspective on certain features of modern family life. First, it suggests that the relative instability of modern family life may in part reflect the fact that for the modern consumer the family, just like all other personal relationships, is regarded more as an object of choice than an element of identity.[278] Commitment thus must be conditioned on ongoing calculations of individual utility, which theoretically are always open to recalculation. The ethic of personal growth counsels the individual to "weigh and balance" the "relative weight and intensity" of each stimulus, so as to select the alternative that maximizes her satisfaction.[279] The past has little independent moral force in such a calculation. Rather, relationships must always earn their allegiance though current market performance. As one family scholar maintains, "*permanence has no value for its own sake. It is not an inherent good[.]*"[280] Furstenberg and Spanier report in their study, for instance, that few who have divorced and remarried see marriage as a lifetime commitment. Rather, remarriers profess to adopt a realistic attitude that acknowledges that changes in sentiment can occur, and that often there is little that the other partner can do about it.[281] From this perspective, change in an intimate relationship is not an anomaly but is its essence.[282]

A second insight of the consumer metaphor is that it points up the homology between the increasingly refined and open-ended needs of the modern self and the increasingly specialized mass consumer market. Just as the product market features specialized products that both satisfy and create more esoteric needs, so the personal relations market offers relationships that serve a variety of purposes—professional, spiritual, financial, emotional, political, artistic, avocational, and countless others. Kenneth Gergen, for instance, suggests that the emergence of a variety of specialized organizations that address specific kinds of personal problems tends to reduce reliance on family members for support.[283] It is easier to think of the family as a product in a specific market niche, a source of a particular type of satisfaction, rather than a distinctive way of life qualitatively different from other personal relationships.

Finally, the consumer model may help explain how the modern experience of family life can be squared with the fact that most individuals profess devotion to the family as the source of their deepest commitments and aspirations. If we see the family as a consumer choice, we can see that individuals may encounter the same cycle of desire, disappointment, and rekindled desire that characterizes the modern consumer experience.

On the one hand, the family evokes powerful images of unqualified commitment and unconditional emotional support. Marriage continues to have emotional resonance as a relationship that can offer acceptance of the individual as a full person in the face of fragmented modern relationships that can create anxiety about both meaning and identity.[284] Ideally, many believe, the family serves as a sanctuary of emotional support in a competitive and egoistic world.[285] Our daily world is suffused with the images of close-knit families that serve as a condensed metaphor for intimacy. Research indicates, for instance, that the depiction of marital intimacy in advertising has increased significantly since the early decades of this century.[286] Similarly, respondents in a recent national survey indicated that "family was by far their greatest joy."[287]

How can we reconcile such sentiment with considerable evidence that individuals experience family life as less distinct from other relationships, and that their commitment is more qualified than in the past? One way to do so is to posit that, much as consumer products may serve as the locus of amorphous yearnings that consumption never quite satisfies, so the family may serve as a highly charged symbol of intimacy that actual family life rarely realizes. Modern culture often presents as ideal those intense, but relatively rare, moments of deep communion.[288] Life in the family, with its inevitable demands for compromise and sacrifice, may generate a vague sense of discontent, of intimacy less vivid than the dream of family seems to promise. This discontent may be intensified by the tendency to regard family obligations as located more within the realm of choice than they were in the past. One longitudinal study of American society concluded, for instance, that we may be entering an era in which individuals are more apt to experience families as a network of burdensome roles and responsibilities.[289] If we think of the family as a consumer product, then, the act of consumption may fall short of the expectations generated by cultural advertising.

Our high rate of both divorce and remarriage may thus reflect phases in the cycle of the modern consumer experience. As many observers suggest, high rates of divorce may indicate not so much a rejection of marriage as the fact that individuals' expectations of marriage are so high that they will not settle for anything less than the perceived ideal.[290] As Furstenberg and Spanier comment,

[A]s the cultural importance placed on the personal gratification of marriage grows, the commitment any given couple makes to a marriage becomes more conditional as either partner must be able to exit from the relationship in the event that it is not living up to his or her expectations.[291]

The consumer in the marketplace is often provoked by disappointment to search for another product that will offer greater satisfaction; those who divorce may search for another marriage that holds out the promise of deeper and more unqualified intimacy. The consumer engaged in a quest for greater utility confronts a constant array of new products that offer the possibility of fulfillment; in the personal relations market, "the required novelty is guaranteed by the very number and diversity of persons which an individual will normally encounter in a life-time of social interaction, consequently ensuring that there are plenty of 'strangers' upon whom one can project one's dreams."[292] In such a world, the family becomes more a lifestyle than a way of life with distinct rewards and obligations.

In the realm of family life, then, individuals are apt to long for both unconditional commitment and flexible obligations. Both aspirations fuel the pursuit of intimacy: the first provides a vision of the object of the search, the second ensures that no choice will preclude a renewed search. As Robert Bellah and his coauthors observe, many in modern life yearn for the unqualified commitment that their parents seemed to have, yet are repelled by the sense of fatalism that such commitment appears to reflect.[293] As a result, many modern individuals both envy their parents and vow never to be like them.[294]

Insistence on the sovereignty of the acontextual self therefore may make the individual particularly receptive to a consumer model of identity. As I've suggested, this metaphor may illuminate how it is that calculating rationality seems more prominent in the family, and why there seems to be such a divergence between our aspirations for and experience of family life. It's worth reiterating that I don't regard the consumer model as a literal account of modern behavior in family settings. In fact, there is considerable resistance to thinking of family life in such terms. At the same time, we need to attend to the effect of cultural messages on the strength of that resistance. My point is that while role distance generates a vision of freedom from roles, it ironically paves the way for the adoption of a new role: that of the consumer. This role may seem increasingly incompatible with the dutiful performance of family obligations.[295]

Conclusion

Modern family law reflects an increasing commitment to contract as the basic legal principle that orders much of family life. This commitment is based in part on a modernist conception of both identity and intimacy, which reflects progress in the quest for the acontextual self. The Victorians posited a private realm marked by role identification, in which the individual was situated within a set of family relationships that were the source of both personal affection and impersonal obligation. By contrast, the modern private realm is marked by role distance. At its core stands the individual, defined apart from any relationships in which she may be involved, for whom subjectivity is the arbiter of conduct in personal life.

Role distance places a premium on intimate relationships untainted by "external" social expectations. In these relationships, intimacy ideally promotes self-realization. Each person serves as the catalyst for the discovery and expression of genuine feelings in the other; those feelings in turn serve as elements in the construction of an authentic sense of self. This development is a double-edged sword for the family. On the one hand, it holds the promise of more emotionally satisfying family relationships. On the other hand, it grounds those relationships in inherently dynamic emotional states, which may undermine the ability of the family to serve as a source of stable support. Furthermore, to the extent that the understanding of oneself as a consumer gains resonance, the family may come to be seen as but one intimate option in a personal relations market. As such, it could begin to lose whatever distinctive character it may have in the cultural imagination.

In the next chapter, I will explore what may be the logical culmination of the quest for the acontextual self: a postmodern world in which both enduring identity and enduring intimacy appear to fade from view.

3. Postmodern Personal Life

In this chapter, I want to explore one aspect of what some observers have described as our postmodern condition: the loss of the self as a coherent category of analysis.[1] From different perspectives and with different metaphors, a number of scholars have expressed the idea that our sense of individuals as unified selves over time may be fading. The implication of this idea, which loosely might be called postmodern, is not that a new conception of the individual is emerging, but that the category of the individual itself is becoming less salient in our understanding of social life. As stable identity becomes a more precarious achievement, intimate commitment also becomes more problematic. The idea of commitment is premised on the assumption that a person will feel bound by earlier promises, because those promises were made by the same person who now is asked to fulfill them. If no overarching sense of self unites a person at different times, then there seems no basis for holding someone to a commitment that another "self" may have made at an earlier time. The culmination of a loss of belief in stable identity thus might be a world in which intimacy consists of discrete moments of connection, with no more extensive promise of attachment beyond each experience.

Exploring the postmodern perspective on identity will be valuable because it offers a glimpse into a world that reflects the culmination of modernist logic—a world in which the modernist quest ironically negates itself.[2] In a postmodern universe, the pursuit of an authentic self results in an effacement of the self, and the pursuit of intimacy results in an even more attenuated sense of connection. This prospect suggests that an acontextual model of the self ultimately may be misguided, because it fails to root the self in those relationships that make possible both coherent identity and intimate commitment.

The Postmodern Loss of Self

Observers draw on a variety of perspectives in suggesting that we may be entering an era marked by the fragmentation of self. One approach, exemplified by Kenneth Gergen, links this development to the tremendous increases in exposure to and stimulation by other persons that modern technology makes possible.[3] Various technologies begin to dissolve time and space as barriers to this exposure and stimulation, making possible "*self-multiplication*, or the capacity to be significantly present in more than one place at a time."[4] This phenomenon increases the range of relationships in which one may be involved at any given moment.

Air travel, for instance, makes easier face-to-face contact with persons in far-flung locations. Telephones, of course, can put one person in touch with another almost instantaneously in virtually any part of the world, while teleconferencing can link numerous persons in different locations with each other on the same call. Telephone lines such as 976 prefix numbers provide the opportunity for total strangers to talk about common interests and concerns, with electronic anonymity paradoxically fostering a sense of intimacy and self-revelation. Computers have electronic mail features that can permit the transmission of messages to persons within an organization or an even broader network of persons with similar interests. Computers can also provide electronic "bulletin boards" that transmit information and solicit responses from persons without face-to-face contact, as well as on-line information services that provide immediate exposure to financial reports, press releases, judicial opinions, and other pronouncements. Some programs are interactive, permitting, for instance, an individual to make a stock purchase on-line, place orders for other goods or services, or register an opinion. "Laptops" can ensure that space is no barrier to this access to interaction with others.

Impediments of time and space are also eroded with devices such as overnight delivery, available even on weekends, and FAX machines, which provide almost instantaneous transmission of documents back and forth. Being in transit is now less of an obstacle to interaction, with telephones available on airplanes and trains, and FAXes available on trains and in airports. Furthermore, "Walkman" units and automobile radio, cassette, and compact disc units ensure that transit on foot or in the automobile will not be bereft of stimulation. Video cassette recorders permit a person to experience another's presence even without physical proximity, as tapes of weddings, graduations, vacations, or other events can be experienced vicariously by the recipient, as well as reexperienced by the actual participants.

The electronic media also make possible interaction with distant figures—politicians, entertainers, athletes—whom one may well never see in the flesh. Talk shows on radio and television encourage personal revelation by such celebrities, and often provide an opportunity for listeners or viewers to ask questions of or speak with the guests. The significance of these figures is reflected in research that indicates that when young persons were asked about those people who influenced them, almost a quarter were individuals such as entertainers with whom the young people had never had any direct contact.[5]

A sense of immediate interaction is also created by eyewitness television and radio reports, which can often portray dramatic events even as they are occurring, such as the Cable News Network's coverage of the bombing of Baghdad during the Persian Gulf War. On such occasions, viewers and listeners "experience" first-hand the same events that persons on the other side of the world simultaneously experience. Indeed, television can cut rapidly from one location to the next, thus providing exposure in rapid succession to a variety of experiences: the anguish of a grieving mother, the euphoria of a bomber pilot, the solemnity of a Pentagon spokesman, the anxiety of inhabitants in a bomb shelter, the anger of antiwar protestors. If we've taped the show, time is no obstacle to our reexperiencing these events.

Through these various technologies, Gergen argues, "the number and variety of relationships in which we are engaged, potential frequency of contact, expressed intensity of relationship, and endurance through time are all steadily increasing."[6] The significance of this development for personal identity is that each experience locates the individual in a different network of relationships, values, expectations, and self-images.

One way to appreciate this phenomenon is by considering the multitude of settings in which someone might function in a given day. Someone we'll call Tom, for instance, is a divorced father and a law partner in a firm that does corporate litigation. When focused on legal matters, he is compulsive and demanding, quite willing to insist that junior colleagues stay well into the night with little notice. A phone call about a pro bono matter, however, transforms him into a patient and supportive audience for a low-income tenant who faces eviction. It also rekindles doubts that he wants to continue in corporate law, as he joins with the legal aid lawyer in denouncing the ability of developers to demolish affordable housing in favor of more profitable projects. Lunch with a friend who has helped him pursue his artistic avocation brings forth Tom the artist, who loosens his tie when he enters the punk rock/exhibition space cafe where they'll be eating. During lunch, he professes disdain for the compulsiveness of a work routine, and declares that he's devising a plan that will allow him to leave the firm within two years in order to pursue painting. A FAX from a client upon his return to the office may send him into a litigator's rage because it indicates that a paralegal has overlooked an important document in a case. A phone call from his mother makes Tom the son feel bad that he hasn't been to visit since his father died three months ago. He promises to fly out to see her next weekend, even though he'll have to miss a friend's opening at a gallery in town. A summons for a conference call with a client cuts his conversation short.

Driving home, Tom hears a financial adviser on a radio talk show emphasize the importance of having a strategy for weathering what look to be turbulent economic times in the next several years. This triggers fears based on his family's financial problems when Tom was growing up, and leads him to dismiss as immature fantasy his plan to leave the firm. Tom the financially responsible adult places a call on his car phone to the senior partner in his firm, and tells him that he'd like to accept the offer of a position on the firm's management committee. When Tom stops to work out at his health club, he's struck by how poorly he seems to compare to the sleek and fit bodies that surround him. Despite the fact that an important case will be going to trial within the next two months, he signs up for squash lessons and resolves to begin rising early to jog. When he arrives home, Tom says a brief hello to his daughter Jessica, of whom he has custody every other week, and retrieves a message from his answering machine from the minister of his congregation. Tom has taught Sunday school classes for the last two months, which has stirred spiritual feelings that he didn't know he had. He agrees to attend a retreat for instructors in two weeks, although he's not certain how he'll be able to rearrange his work schedule in order to do so.

Tom and his daughter eat a quick dinner, because Tom has to get the place ready for this month's meeting of his men's discussion group. During dinner, Tom impresses upon Jessica the importance of self-restraint in sexual behavior. In a phone conversation with a friend after dinner, however, he brags about the number of women he's met at singles bars since his divorce. During his men's group meeting, Tom speaks eloquently about the costs of professional achievement. After the meeting, he declines Jessica's request to continue their dinner conversation, because lunch with his friend has made him resolve to focus more seriously on his art. As he begins, however, the telephone rings. He doesn't answer it, but he hears a message from his office that triggers the need to draft a legal document. He puts down his brush, leaves his canvas, and sits down at his personal computer to begin the document.

Tom could be described in terms of a variety of "selves" in the course of the day, depending on the context in which he found himself. Each is part of a relationship with others, which contains its own perspective and values. This is because each relationship organizes the world around a distinct narrative. As a lawyer, Tom is part of a story about a profession that meets the legal needs of clients; as a public interest advocate, he is part of a story about our responsibilities to those in need; as an artist, he is part of a narrative about the need to express individual creative impulse; as a father, he is located within a story about providing guidance to those in the next generation; as part of certain friendships, he may see himself playing out the script of a single heterosexual male for whom sexual "conquests" reflect achievement.

As the number and intensity of our relationships with others increases, Gergen suggests, we become "populated" with their voices and perspectives.[7] As more voices become "present," either in person or in memory or through technology, the individual has that many more contexts that evoke a response. A person thus begins to acquire a variety of possible identities that can be evoked in different situations.[8] The result, says Gergen, is the development of a "multiphrenic" personality, which is the "splitting of the individual into a multiplicity of investments."[9] Each context or investment may seem to evoke intense feeling about who one "really" is and what one should be doing, as Tom's encounters suggest. Yet the accelerated pace of contemporary life often shifts us from one context to another, so that a person confronts voices from a number of contexts in rapid succession.

As Tom's day also highlights, these voices often offer conflicting guidance. Which self to choose becomes more difficult; "as new and disparate voices are added to one's being, committed identity becomes an increasingly arduous achievement."[10] As we confront a variety of incommensurable accounts of the self, "[f]or everything we 'know to be true' about ourselves, other voices within respond with doubt and even derision."[11]

The result, suggests Gergen, is that the notion of a stable self over time begins to dissolve. "As one moves from one perspective to another, the objectivity of self recedes from view. And in the end one is left with perspectivity—itself a product not of the individual but of the surrounding communities in which one is embedded."[12] Identity becomes a fluid concept, not so much a "core" narrative that organizes experience as much as an aggregation of narratives, each of which speaks to a distinct dimension of one's relations with others. The concept of authenticity loses meaning in such a world, for that notion assumes some underlying sense of self that is the basis for identifying superficial from more permanent versions of the self.[13] Furthermore, the idea of playing a role becomes incoherent, because "[t]he sense of playing a role depends for its palpability on the contrasting sense of a 'real self.' If there is no consciousness of what it is to be 'true to self,' there is no meaning to 'playing a role.' "[14] With each incremental increase in the assemblage of "possible selves,"[15] unitary identity becomes more problematic.[16]

Frederic Jameson is another scholar who has explored the idea of the loss of the self, from a perspective that focuses on our changing experience of time.[17] Jameson uses the metaphor of schizophrenia to describe the type of personality that may be emerging in the postmodern era. He hastens to clarify that he uses the term not in a clinical sense, but as symbolic of the type of experience that results from postmodernism's "peculiar way with time."[18] Jameson suggests that contemporary society has begun to lose the capacity to retain its past by virtue of relentless changes that undermine historical traditions.[19] As a result, contemporary experience is more likely to be characterized by "the fragmentation of time into a series of perpetual presents."[20]

For Jameson, such experience begins to resemble the world of the schizophrenic, who is "given over to an undifferentiated vision of the world in the present,"[21] in which "the various moments of his or her past have little connection and [in] which there is no conceivable future on the horizon."[22] Because her sense of temporal continuity has been disrupted, the schizophrenic has a far more vivid and intense experience of each moment than most other people. She also, however, has a less stable sense of identity over time, since identity is the product of a certain unification of past, present, and future.[23]

Jameson's metaphor of schizophrenia thus parallels Gergen's concept of multiphrenia, in which the unified subject dissolves amid exposure to a succession of vivid contexts, each of which seems to have its own integrity and force. Our friend Tom, for instance, surely is not a candidate for a mental institution. Yet had he been required to make a decision about his life at any given moment in the day, it might have differed depending on the context that he was in. At one moment, he might strive for professional success at any cost, at another to spend more time with his daughter or his mother, at another to devote himself to painting, and at yet another to revel in a hedonistic way of life.

One might suggest that Tom is capable of "stepping back" and making a decision based on an overview of his life. The postmodernist would reply, however, that wherever he does this—in his office, at home, talking on the phone to a friend—is itself simply another context, which cannot help but shape his decision. Furthermore, whatever the context, Tom's deliberation will necessarily draw on the multitude of voices that he has encountered, each of which offers a particular way to characterize his situation. Thus, the postmodernist would say, it would seem more insightful to focus on these contexts and these voices than to abstract from them some individual who stands apart from them.

Jean Baudrillard echoes both Gergen and Jameson in his account of the postmodern loss of self. First, he draws on the metaphors of modern communication networks to depict a self immersed within the "connections, contact, contiguity, feedback, and generalized interface that goes with the universe of communication."[24] Like Gergen, Baudrillard sketches a portrait in which the individual is bombarded with information and messages to which she must respond. We are all, Baudrillard suggests, part of pervasive communication networks in which stimuli and responses are increasingly linked in time, thus provoking an ever more rapid chain of counterresponses.

Those who have worked in Wall Street law firms or multinational corporations, for instance, know how technology spanning time and space successively reduces "down time." In this world, the idea of a private space insulated from such stimuli, a space where one can "be oneself," begins to seem problematic. Rather, it is sometimes difficult to avoid the sensation of being a center for the receipt, transformation, and transmission of information. Baudrillard suggests that such experience erodes the sense of a private sphere in which an individual can contemplate her unique identity free from "external" influences.[25] With ever greater exposure to multiple communication networks, "I no longer succeed in knowing what I want, the space is so saturated, the pressure so great from all who want to make themselves heard."[26]

Baudrillard also echoes Jameson's theme of schizophrenia. What characterizes the "new form of schizophrenia,"[27] Baudrillard suggests, is "the absolute proximity, the total instantaneity of things, the feeling of no defense, no retreat."[28] This sense of a perpetual present marks for the individual the end of a distinction between interior and exterior life.[29] In Baudrillard's dramatic metaphor, the postmodern individual "is now only a pure screen, a switching center for all the networks of influence."[30]

Jean-François Lyotard similarly focuses on communication as the point of departure for his assessment of the postmodern dissolution of the self.[31] He locates the individual within a network of "language games,"[32] which he takes as the prerequisite for any society to exist.[33] Lyotard suggests that the increasing intensity and pervasiveness of contemporary communications have heightened our awareness of the multitude of language games in which we are situated. This focus suggests that individual conduct can be seen as "moves" within these games, and that the notion of individual intention may be a less fruitful way to examine these moves than an emphasis on the shared character of the "rules" that constitute the games themselves.[34] Lyotard declares, "A *self* does not amount to much, but no self is an island; each exists in a fabric of relations that is now more complex and mobile than ever before."[35]

Other contemporary observers have similarly suggested that a postmodern era is emerging that is characterized by an accelerated pace of stimulation, a fragmented sense of time, and difficulty in sustaining a stable sense of self. David Harvey, for instance, suggests that increases in the rapidity of production, exchange, and consumption cycles under capitalism have produced "time-space compression"—a world in which "[v]olatility and ephemerality . . . make it hard to maintain any firm sense of continuity. Past experience gets compressed into some overwhelming present."[36] David Miller celebrates what he terms a new "polytheism," characterized by a self comprised of "equally real, but mutually exclusive" aspects, uncoordinated by any single ego.[37] Similarly, Steven Connor describes postmodernism as a sense of "the loss of history, the dissolution of the centred self, the fading of individual style,"[38] and Gianni Vattimo notes a feeling of nostalgia for "an imaginary self that refuses to yield to the peculiar mobility, uncertainty, and permutability of the symbolic[.]"[39]

Finally, some observers suggest that the loss of belief in the existence of an authentic self is reflected in the arts. Jameson, for instance, argues that "pastiche"—that evocation of the past through the use of stylized nostalgic devices—reflects a sense that no more authentic experience is available for communication than the surface form that it takes.[40] Christine Brooke- Rose has commented on the "dissolution of character" in the contemporary novel, as flatter and less emotive characters bespeak the diminishing significance of the individual amid collective networks of influence.[41] Italo Calvino has linked this condition to a situation in which "time has been shattered[;] we cannot live or think except in fragments of time each of which goes off along its own trajectory and immediately disappears."[42]

By contrast, music television (MTV) seems to some the paradigm of a postmodernist art form. MTV presents a rapid barrage of intense visual and auditory stimuli, in which, says Lawrence Grossberg, "the construction and dissemination of moods is increasingly separated from the communication of any particular meanings or values."[43] Grossberg suggests that MTV is powerful not because of its particular videos, but because of its relentless refusal to take anything seriously, including itself.[44] This terminally ironic stance creates a sense of "authentic inauthenticity": "[i]f every identity is equally fake, a pose that one takes on, then authentic inauthenticity celebrates the possibilities of poses without denying that is all they are."[45] Virtually by definition, the concept of an authentic self is alien in such a universe.

Postmodernism thus paints a portrait of a world in which the inescapability of context seems so vivid that the sense of an authentic and unified self over time begins to dissolve. In such a world, subjectivity seems to become a chimera, an antiquated way of accounting for daily life. In the next section, I'll explore how this state of affairs can be seen as the culmination of the modernist quest for the acontextual self.

Postmodernism and Subjectivity

Identity and Context. Postmodernists depict the individual as immersed in one context after another without respite, to the point that she seems akin to a chameleon without any core identity. From one perspective, we might say that postmodernism asserts that context is constitutive of identity. In fact, each context so envelops the individual within it that each creates a different "self." On this view, the postmodern emergence of multiple selves—that is, the lack of a unified self—reflects the dissolution of distance between context and self. Thus, one might argue, postmodernism reflects the demise of the modernist view that the self can be defined apart from the context in which it is situated.

If we look more closely, however, we can see that in one sense modernism and postmodernism are equivalent: a self for whom every context is constitutive is one for whom no context is constitutive in any meaningful way. Neither radical engagement nor radical disengagement can support any notion of a coherent sense of identity. If a context were in fact constitutive, it would limit the extent to which other contexts could enter into one's self-definition. This is because the identity forged in the first context would shape one's reaction to subsequent contexts, thus limiting the radical openness to experience that permits each context to be constitutive. If membership in the Communist party were essential to a person's identity, for instance, then that person might well decline a lucrative opportunity to become an entrepreneur. An orientation in which identity limited openness to context would be contrary to modernism because it would accept the idea that some contexts can be constitutive. It would be contrary to postmodernism because it would reject the notion that all contexts are constitutive.

Let's look at this phenomenon more closely. Modernism envisions the authentic self as a person defined by her capacity for growth and her receptivity to new experience. Put another way, she derives her essence not by any choice that she has made, but by her capacity to rethink her choices. She is a process of perpetual transformation, and each experience is the raw material for her continual metamorphosis.[46]

Such a being ideally must be fully open to the stimuli of each context that she encounters. Each context offers the potential for her to reshape or realize some aspect of her personality, so each has equal weight and legitimacy. To return to our earlier example, modernism advises Tom that he should attend equally to his multiple voices—aspiring painter, spiritual seeker, achieving attorney—because each of them represents a dimension of his personality whose expression should not be stifled. Tom should be guided by the idea of "omniattention, the sense of [the] contemporary [person] as having the possibility of 'receiving' and 'taking in' everything."[47] He should ultimately be guided only by his subjectivity—his sense of his own feelings and desires— to arbitrate among these stimuli. Indeed, his authenticity is realized in his sovereignty to move among these contexts without outside interference.

Yet feelings and desires can be remarkably volatile. Each context elicits a different combination of them, which can seem vivid in its insistence that this set of preferences should serve as the basis for action. If no context is constitutive, then at the extreme there is no concept of identity capable of providing a transcontextual perspective from which to weigh the claims of each moment of experience. In this case, as Michael Sandel observes, there is the risk that there will be "no non-arbitrary way, either for the self, or for some outside observer, to identify [any particular] desires, interests, and ends, as the desires of any particular subject. Rather than be *of* the subject, they would *be* the subject."[48] The subject they would be, however, "would be indistinguishable from the sea of undifferentiated attributes of an unarticulated situation, which is to say it would be no subject at all, at least no subject we could recognize or pick out as resembling a human person."[49]

This situation sounds precisely like the postmodernist loss of the self. It is one characterized by the "radically situated subject,"[50] a subject inundated by, and ultimately merged within, her surroundings. Yet this dissolution ironically flows from an image of the individual whose essence is her capacity to stand apart from her surroundings, whose authenticity lies in the power to choose which voice will guide her conduct. The postmodernist loss of the self thus turns out to be premised on the "brute objectivity of random subjectivity."[51]

A unified identity therefore serves as a perceptual filter that gives priority to some contexts over others. This function is underscored by Frederic Jameson. In his discussion of schizophrenia as a metaphor for the postmodern personality, Jameson maintains that it is the absence of such a filter that distinguishes the schizophrenic from the more conventional personality. "Our own present," he says, "is always part of some larger set of projects which force us selectively to focus our perceptions."[52] Jameson observes: "We do not, in other words, simply globally receive the outside world as an undifferentiated vision: we are always engaged in using it, in threading certain paths through it, in attending to this or that object or person within it."[53] By contrast, the schizophrenic "is not only 'no one' in the sense of having no personal identity; he or she also does nothing, since to have a project means to be able to commit oneself to a certain continuity over time."[54]

I do not mean to suggest that we are completely at liberty to select which experience we will incorporate into ourselves and which we will not. Such a formulation begins to reintroduce the specter of the modernist self, completely free to fashion an identity from among competing contexts. All contexts are to some degree constitutive, in the sense that we are different in some way because we have had *this* experience instead of *that* one. Yet we do give more weight to some contexts than others, based on our interpretations of their significance. Those interpretations in part reflect the cultural messages that we receive about the relative importance of various contexts.[55] My point is that a culture helps shape a unified sense of identity to the extent that it signals that some contexts should be privileged over others. Conversely, a culture puts at peril the achievement of unified identity to the extent that it signals that all contexts warrant equal attention.

We can gain a fuller sense of this connection between the modernist self and its postmodern effacement by examining modernist analyses of identity. Those who might be called the modernist forerunners of postmodernism posit the existence of a distinct self independent of context, but the self they depict is so fluid and variable that we lose a sense of its integrity. Upon close examination, then, the supposedly sovereign acontextual self dissolves into its surroundings.

I should make clear that the account that follows is one in which the quest for the modernist self ultimately *leads to* the postmodern loss of self. This assumption of a certain historical evolution might be criticized by postmodernists as a "metanarrative"—an effort to impose an overall order on phenomena that are fundamentally incommensurable.[56] A postmodernist might say, for instance, that it makes no sense in postmodern terms to say that the loss of self depends on a self that is radically disengaged from context, because that assertion reflects the modernist view that self and context are distinguishable. On this view, if modernism and postmodernism organize the world differently, then there exists no common discourse by which to construct a story that links them together in a coherent manner.[57]

We can grant validity to postmodernism's suspicion of metanarratives, however, without abandoning historical explanations. I needn't claim that my account of the evolution of modernism into postmodernism is the only story that can be told. My claim is simply that it is a narrative that has persuasive power. In part, this is because it implicitly operates within the modernist framework that still dominates the culture, a framework premised on the notion of temporal progression. My argument in what follows, therefore, is that modernism and postmodernism can be fitted into a coherent narrative in which postmodernism represents the logical culmination of the quest for the modernist self. As such, it provides a glimpse of where we might be headed if the vision of the acontextual self continues to gain influence.

Modernism as Postmodernism. As we saw in chapter 2, Louis Zurcher can be seen as a scholar who suggested the emergence of a fully modernist individual, whom he described as the "mutable self."[58] This person is more fully aware than previous individuals of the different dimensions of her existence, represented by four types of self-concepts classified as A, B, C, and D. The A mode of understanding oneself focuses on one's physical attributes, the B mode on one's roles within various social institutions, the C mode on the ability to reflect on one's feelings apart from any social role, and the D mode is characterized by an "oceanic" or transcendent sense of merger with the larger universe.[59] Previous surveys indicated the predominance of type B self-concept, observed Zurcher, while more recent surveys suggest that the type C orientation— the mutable self—is becoming more prevalent.[60] On the one hand, the mutable self seems the paradigm of autonomy and authenticity. She has the "maximum opportunity for role selection and portrayal, rather than merely role accommodation. The person can become distanced from role models previously emulated[.]"[61] Operating in the C mode "seems to arm the individual with the greatest degree of control in the environment."[62] The mutable self is sensitive to the fact that the four types of self-concept represent distinct aspects of her being, all of which must be reconciled and accommodated for her to realize her potential. She alone can determine which of them will be given precedence in any given situation, for she is aware that her four selves are capable of change, and should be "maintained in specific forms only as long as they contribute to a sense of fullness, a sense of *living*."[63]

When we try to gain a clearer picture of this mutable self, however, she is elusive and seems to dissolve. Indeed, she is defined by an acceptance of change and inconsistency: "[t]he focal point of self-concept [is] process or change itself—stability [is] based on change[.]"[64] Her sense of self may reflect either of the four orientations, depending on the particular situation at hand. We begin to suspect, then, that it is the context that drives the self-concept rather than the self-concept controlling the context.

This suspicion is reinforced by Zurcher's suggestion that it is the D mode that may reflect full self-realization. He observes that "the oceanic D mode usually is the penultimate experience."[65] Yet the D mode is one in which the self is perceived as merged into, rather than distinct from, the universe at large. Indeed, statements reflecting a D orientation " 'do not lead to socially meaningful differentiation of the person who makes the statement.' "[66] Typical type D statements are those such as " 'I am one with existence; I am a pebble on the beach of time[.]' "[67] The radically separate mutable self thus turns out to be not much of a self at all. Put another way, the modernist quest to liberate the self from context seems to lead to a postmodernist condition in which the self is nothing but context.

A similar paradox characterizes Robert Jay Lifton's "Protean Man."[68] Lifton suggests that a new type of personality might be emerging, and describes it by reference to the Greek myth of Proteus, who "was able to change his shape with relative ease from wild boar to lion to dragon to fire to flood."[69] Protean Man seems the master of his identity: "elements of the self can be experimented with and readily altered," and "idea systems and ideologies [can] be embraced, modified, let go of and reembraced, all with a new ease that stands in sharp contrast to the inner struggle we have in the past associated with these shifts."[70] The impetus for initiating and reevaluating these shifts is Protean Man's "expanding sensitivity to the inauthentic."[71] Protean Man thus asserts his priority over any context that he may occupy, in the name of a more authentic identity that is always defined apart from the situation in which he is involved. He is the quintessential modern self, relying on his subjectivity to navigate through the stream of modern experience.[72]

Yet, as with the mutable self, it ultimately seems difficult to distinguish Protean Man from his immediate environment. His openness to each moment and his refusal to foreclose any options "permit each individual everywhere to be touched by everything, but at the same time cause him to be overwhelmed by superficial messages and undigested cultural elements, by headlines and by endless partial alternatives in every sphere of life."[73] The result, according to Lifton, is that "as an individual one can maintain no clear boundaries";[74] there emerges the "blurring of perceptions of where self begins and ends."[75] The supposedly authentic Protean Man thus comes to be characterized by his "formlessness."[76] His insistence on being guided only by his distinct personal voice results in a cacophony of voices, none of which he can identify as his own.

The comparison with Proteus is an apt one. Defined essentially by his capacity to assume different forms, Proteus nevertheless cannot escape being defined at any given moment by the form that he has assumed. When he has assumed the form of a lion, for instance, he is not playing the role of a lion—he *is* a lion. His "essential" identity thus has a purely abstract quality, one that is of no help in locating him within the flow of time that is the hallmark of human existence.

Lifton sees both promise and peril in the arrival of Protean Man, but acknowledges that his emergence raises fundamental questions about the nature of personal identity. "The whole stability-change issue badly needs general psychological reevaluation," he says, "especially in regard to the kinds of significant change that can take place within a person while much else remains constant."[77] Once again, allegiance to subjectivity seems to create the prospect that the subject herself may become a meaningless category for understanding daily life, as a person and her experience become merged into a succession of different moments.

Finally, Erving Goffman is a scholar whose work seems to posit the existence of a modernist subject who stands apart from and chooses which of various roles to play. In the end, however, this subject seems to be nothing more than a collection of those very same roles. On the one hand, the imagery of the individual as "performer" pervades Goffman's work, suggesting a person who occupies a public stage for a certain period and then retreats backstage to nurture a more authentic self.[78] Goffman maintains, following Ralph Linton,[79] that the basic unit of role analysis is "the individual enacting his bundle of obligatory activity."[80]

In this metaphor, roles as "bundles" are the *possession* of the individual. They are objects that are distinguishable from her, which can be deployed by her as she wishes.

The metaphor of possession is even more explicit in Goffman's description of the individual as a "holding company" for her roles:

It is a basic assumption of role analysis that each individual will be involved in more than one system or pattern and, therefore, perform more than one role. Each individual will, therefore, have several selves, providing us with the interesting problem of how these selves are related. The model of man according to the initial role perspective is that of *a kind of holding company for a set of not relevantly connected roles*; it is the concern of the second perspective to find out *how the individual runs* this holding company.[81]

Thus, in the midst of all this variegated role activity, there is still someone in charge, someone who evaluates each situation and produces the behavior that is appropriate to it.[82]

At the same time, Goffman's analysis points up the difficulty of identifying an individual apart from her roles. In discussing his concept of role distance, for instance, which I've utilized in chapter 2,[83] Goffman suggests that the "self" that a person "holds apart from" a given role in such an instance is simply a self constituted by other role identities. His analysis of a surgical team, for instance, identifies periodic "role distancing" behavior on the part of the chief surgeon, which takes the form of wisecracks, mock sternness, and feigned casualness.[84] At first glance, such behavior may seem an effort to express the fact that the surgeon has a "real" personality behind the surgeon's mask that she wears.

Yet, as Goffman points out, this behavior can be seen as an effort by the surgeon to preserve morale and reduce tension among the surgical team. As such, it represents the surgeon's temporary subordination of her role as physician to her "role function of anxiety management[.]"[85] Thus, even role distance may simply reflect the fact that "one of the claims upon himself that the individual must balance against all others is the claim created by the over-all 'needs' of the situated activity system itself, apart from his particular role within it."[86] Role distance, in other words, may ultimately reflect role-oriented behavior.

Goffman is in fact explicit about the implications of this insight. Noting the varied impulses that an individual may experience while involved in a role activity, he declares that "these various identificatory demands are not created by the individual but are drawn from what society allots him. He frees himself from one group, not to be free, but because there is another hold on him."[87] In such a universe, the individual who is distinct from all contexts once again seems up close to be an illusion. As a result,

[W]hen the individual withdraws from a situated self he does not draw into some psychological world that he creates himself but rather acts in the name of some other socially created identity. The liberty he takes in regard to a situated self is taken because of other, equally social, constraints.[88]

The modernist belief in a self defined apart from any situation, a person radically open to every experience, thus ironically appears to be the predicate for the postmodern loss of the self. In the next section, I'll explore the form that intimacy might take in this postmodern world.

Postmodern Intimacy. Postmodern fragmentation of identity carries the potential for changing the way in which we pursue intimacy, or close personal relationships with others. Specifically, a postmodern orientation may lead to a world in which commitment over time becomes subordinated to the experience of a variety of intense moments of connection, no one of which significantly influences behavior in other contexts. We can gain an appreciation of this possibility by first examining our conventional idea of commitment.

Commitment typically rests on the notion of a self experienced as unified over time, a self that is transcontextual, if you will. For many people, for instance, marriage as a commitment means that spouses declare that their identities as spouses will serve a guide to their behavior in a variety of contexts. Thus, for instance, a husband may refuse the opportunity to develop a romantic relationship with a female colleague with whom he shares a passionate interest in art, even though such a refusal prevents the full realization of the "self" that is located in, or potentially "defined by," that particular context. Similarly, a wife on a business trip may refuse the overtures of an old college friend, even though the "self" in that situation otherwise might find such a prospect quite appealing.

Our sense of what it means to make a commitment thus depends on the belief in a coherent self who spans several contexts, whose relatively stable preferences serve as the basis for foreclosing certain courses of action that may seem temporarily attractive, but that threaten to undermine those preferences over the long run.[89] Commitment thus involves the deliberate withdrawal from the full range of experience that each situation offers, a restraint on the free play of subjectivity.

For the full-fledged postmodernist, however, such an orientation is problematic. First, she is more apt to regard the multiplicity of relation-ships in which she is involved each day as involving different "selves" who require nurture, rather than as myriad experiences of the same person. At a minimum, she is likely to regard each of those relationships as calling forth different yet equally valid dimensions of her personality. In our earlier example, for instance, Tom may have experienced in a single day moments of intense connection with his law partners, his artist friend, his mother, his daughter, his minister, and members of his dis-cussion group.

Each of these encounters was intimate in the general sense of the term, yet none seemed significantly to diminish his receptivity to new experi-ences of intimacy as they became available. Indeed, each may have height-ened his sensitivity to the intimate potential in each succeeding encounter. Not to pursue this potential may have seemed to Tom the denial of either an authentic "self" or an authentic dimension that deserved expression. For the postmodernist who is sensitive to the diversity of her potential, then, "[i]n each commitment may lurk a multitude of small deaths,"[90] as each moment forecloses certain previously available options.[91]

Commitment may become problematic for the postmodernist for a second reason. Even if a person were inclined to make a commitment, how is she to decide which "self" and which "context" is to serve as the touchstone for that commitment?[92] One may share a love of literature with one romantic companion, outdoor activity with another, and profes-sional interests with yet a third. If each "self" is regarded as equally "real," then any choice will seem arbitrary. Heightened awareness of the contextual nature of choice may well lead to suspicion of any choice that is made. As Kenneth Gergen points out, "when lived reality is continu-ously punctuated by consciousness of its limitations and artifice, com-mitment becomes arduous."[93]

Third, commitment may become difficult because awareness of the myriad selves or dimensions of one's being may create an extremely high standard for the foreclosure of experience that commitment entails. A cartoon by David Sipress reflects this tendency, as a man says to a woman over coffee,

"The way I see it, all we need to do to make our marriage work is to learn to communicate so we can resolve our conflicts, develop an intense sexual intimacy, find a whole new set of really interesting friends, have a lot more fun together, create a spiritual life for ourselves, and grow enormously as individual people."[94]

Commitment may be difficult because there may always seem to be some need that remains unsatisfied, some aspect of self not fully realized.

Finally, even for persons surmounting these hurdles, the increasing volume of interaction with others, in person or through media, may constantly threaten those commitments that are made. We can appreciate this prospect by analogizing commitment to what Joshua Meyerowitz calls a sense of "place."[95] "Place," says Meyerowitz, "define[s] a distinct situation because its boundaries limit[] perception and interaction."[96] This demarcation of a distinct context makes possible the creation and enactment of roles, because it limits the intrusion of stimuli that depict other relationships and their expectations.[97] Thus, for instance, a school-room is a "place" in which the flow of "external" stimulation and information is controlled so that the roles of teacher and student can be performed without interference. Commitment can be compared to the creation of a distinct "place," in which certain stable expectations can be fostered because stimuli that offer alternative possibilities have been minimized.

The susceptibility of contemporary individuals to myriad forms of media, however, reflects the penetration of formerly insulated "places." To use a simple example, a man may be watching television at home, a milieu in which his commitments as husband and father may be particularly salient. At the same time, and in the same location, he may be exposed to a series of programs that offer alternative "places" to inhabit, in which his self-image as free spirit, intellectual, entrepreneur, or cynic may be evoked. Each instance of stimulation thus has the potential to diminish the extent to which his identity as husband and father is dominant while he's at home. This dissociation of physical location and the roles characteristic of that location fosters a sense of role distance. Meyerowitz suggests that with the declining sense of place in contemporary life, "[m]any people feel that they have stopped 'playing roles,' that they are now behaving 'naturally' and just 'being themselves.' "[98]

Similarly, commitment may be vulnerable to disruption by virtue of exposure to a variety of others who evoke alternative dimensions of the self. An attitude of role distance counsels that no one place is really home, so one should attend to all experiences— all stimuli—as possible vehicles for self-realization. As a result, it may be difficult for any one relationship to stabilize for any significant length of time, since a parade of potentially competing self-images may call into question the "self" in that particular relationship.

These conundra may make commitment less tenable in a postmodern world, and may lead to a distinctly postmodern pursuit of intimacy. That pursuit would be organized around the acceptance of the self as fragmented, and would not seek to reconcile the sometimes contradictory demands of each fragment into some more coherent whole. As Kenneth Gergen speculates, "the disappearance of 'true self' encourages one to search for the kinds of persons or situations that will enable the various actors in one's ensemble to play their parts."[99] The idea of intimacy as involving commitment over time would thus fade in favor of the "*fractional relationship*, a relationship built around a limited aspect of one's being."[100] Gergen suggests that fractional relationships have a tendency to lead to a "microwave" effect, in which the parties seek to make up for the limited duration of the interaction with intense expressions of intimacy. As he puts it, "[o]ne must somehow demonstrate the significance of one's feelings and the high esteem in which the relationship is held. And because there is little time, the demonstrations must be loud and clear."[101] Parents concerned about not being able to spend much time with their children, for instance, may stress "quality time," periods of intense interaction in which highly condensed feelings are displayed and exchanged. Similarly, lunch with an old friend whom one sees once a year may evoke powerful feelings of connection and empathy. In each instance, the emotions aroused by the context in question may not linger into the next context. After "quality time" is over, for instance, a father may immerse himself in his hobby and brook no interruption. At the end of lunch with an old friend, the desire to take advantage of a book sale may make a person reluctant to drive her friend to the airport. The world of the fractional relationship thus has both an intense and an ephemeral quality to it.

The tendency to regard each fractional relationship as serving certain distinct needs begins to bring into focus a familiar figure: the consumer. The basis for evaluating a relationship can be narrowed to the question of whether it satisfies the particular need in question. This makes it more amenable to analysis in instrumental terms, because there are fewer variables to complicate the assessment. If a friendship centers around playing tennis, for instance, and an opportunity to join a group closer to home arises, the friendship may no longer thrive. If a relationship rests on a shared interest in film, and a partner meets someone even more knowledgeable, the relationship may wither.

The fragmentation of postmodern life therefore can make experience seem like a personal relations market, an array of possible connections whose relative utilities can be assessed and reassessed from moment to moment. The "temporary contract," rather than the stable commitment, becomes the best mode of operation in such a market,[102] for it provides the greatest flexibility for the consumer in constant pursuit of optimum utility. It should not be surprising, then, that some have suggested that postmodern culture and consumerism are closely linked, each reinforcing a way of life in which "ceaseless exchanges and mutations...recognize no formal frontiers which are not constantly transgressed."[103]

Postmodern experience thus can be seen as the logical conclusion to the modernist quest for intimacy. Once intimate personal life comes to be seen as the domain of the authentic self, the way is open for "pure" subjectivity to seem the only legitimate basis for intimate connection. The increasingly fragmented nature of that subjectivity, however, makes any connection fragile, and tends to limit the influence of any relationship over time and space. Once again, the ethereal subject seems to float from context to context, visiting all but at home in none. From our current perspective, at least, she seems destined to know neither herself nor what it means to know another. In short, she seems bereft of both identity and intimacy.

The result may be a world in which there is no stable repository of meaning beyond the self, nothing that seems worthy of the foreclosure of possibility that intimate commitment necessarily entails. The postmodern condition, then, may be the perception that "it is ever more difficult to make sense of our affective experiences ('life's a bitch and then you die') and to put any faith in the taken for granted interpretations of our lives and actions."[104]

Conclusion

The suggestion that we are entering a postmodern era in which maintenance of stable individual identity is more problematic offers a glimpse of what may be the culmination of the quest for the acontextual self. The precondition of the fragmentation of self paradoxically is the assertion of its radical freedom from context. Only then are there no barriers to the ability to move from context to context, open to the full, albeit temporary, immersion within the stimuli of each. Under such circumstances, the notion of an authentic identity begins to crumble, because no setting provides the relatively privileged vantage point necessary for judgments of authenticity. As identity becomes more fragile, so may the capacity for intimate commitment, since commitment assumes a unified self whose promises in the past bind the same person in the future.

Few people may actually live the life of the postmodern consumer in the personal relations market. Each of us lives within competing narratives that offer different messages about identity and intimacy. We may be in danger of losing the resonance of some of these narratives, however, as contemporary culture more insistently and vividly promotes the drama of personal choice and autonomy. This prospect should lead to skepticism about the wisdom of adopting contract as the governing principle of family law. In the next chapter, I'll argue that status can serve as a vehicle for preserving an alternative account of identity and intimacy, one that provides a corrective to the increasing influence of the acontextual model of the self. Ironically, then, formal legal identity may enhance the prospect that the pursuit of intimacy will be successful.

4. Status and Intimacy

Status is commonly regarded as the antithesis of intimacy because it vindicates impersonal standards rather than personal sentiment. On this view, status has little to offer in any quest to bolster intimate commitment. In this chapter, I want to contest this assumption. I will argue that status can foster commitment because it's sensitive to the connection between intimacy and identity in ways that an emphasis on private ordering is not.

First, status can promote intimacy because it's attentive to the ways in which intimate relationships can be constitutive of one's sense of self. Status protects the reliance that arises in this process from the disruption that changes in sentiment can bring. Status therefore can be justified on classic liberal grounds as a means of preventing harm to those in intimate relationships, once we understand the distinct potential for harm that arises within those relationships.

The postmodern vision suggests, however, that protection of reliance may be insufficient alone to promote intimacy, because the fragmentation of the self may result in less emotional investment in any particular personal relationship. I therefore will spend more time responding directly to this prospect of a diminished capacity for intimate commitment, arguing that status can promote intimacy because it contributes to the sense of a unified self over time that is the prerequisite for such commitment. Status has this potential because it offers a model of identity defined in terms of communal norms, which can root the self in context. My first contention, therefore, is that status is sensitive to the fact that intimacy can shape identity; my second is that status is responsive to the fact that committed intimacy depends on coherent identity.

Status and Reliance

The Market. My exploration of the use of status to protect reliance begins not with the family but with the market. Even as family law has tended to move from status to contract in recent years, the law governing commercial affairs has steadily moved from contract to status over the last century. Family law may have something to learn from commercial law about the perils of an uncritical embrace of freedom of contract as its governing principle.

Even as it exalted status within the family, society for much of the nineteenth century adopted a rhetoric that proclaimed a commitment to freedom of contract in the commercial sphere.[1] The vision was neither uncontested nor unqualified at the time, but it powerfully shaped legal understanding into the early decades of this century. The domain of private ordering through contract was associated closely with the market.[2] That realm was comprised of individuals who enjoyed equal freedom from restraint on their ability to contract, and who themselves determined the obligations to which they were subject. Contracts therefore were expressions of individual will, and contract enforcement was seen as a vindication of human self-determination.[3]

On this view, judicial inquiries into the fairness of contract terms, such as efforts to evaluate the adequacy of consideration, largely were considered inappropriate. Only the parties themselves were in a position to judge the value of the goods and services involved, and the existence of the contract itself generally was deemed to reflect each party's un-coerced acceptance of the terms of exchange.[4] Similarly, legislative efforts to regulate the terms of contracts were regarded as "external" interference with individuals' ability to assume only those obligations that were freely chosen. The best-known expression of this position is of course *Lochner v. New York*,[5] a Supreme Court case from early in this century that struck down a law limiting the working hours of bakers to ten hours a day. Such regulation, held the Court, was "an illegal interference with the rights of individuals, both employers and employees, to make contracts regarding labor upon such terms as they may think best, or which they may agree upon with the other parties to the contract."[6] On this view, the "private" realm represented the exercise of free will, which required protection from distortion by "public" influence.

The model of the self that underlies such a vision is fundamentally acontextual. As Lawrence Friedman puts it, "pure" contract theory "is blind to details of subject matter and person."[7] The essence of the individual is her capacity to make a choice free of any "external" restraints. This formal freedom is the common thread that justifies treating quite diverse experiences—accepting a job, buying a car, or paying one's last dollar for bread—as identical contractual exchanges.[8] Rather than being shaped by any context, the contractual actor creates her own contexts.[9] Inequalities of bargaining power, for instance, are merely the result of prior individual choices, rather than restraints on choice. As such, they can't serve as the justification for altering contracts negotiated in the absence of manifest coercion.

Gary Peller has suggested that classical contract doctrine's emphasis on an abstract chooser reflects a view of the subject as a consumer of social relationships.[10] As long as formal capacity to contract exists, any relationship in which the individual may be involved, regardless of its balance of power, is merely a contingent choice that she has made, rather than part of who she is. As such, that relationship can't be regarded as impinging on the will of the individual, and therefore is irrelevant in determining contractual obligation. This perspective underscores the connection between the nineteenth-century embrace of freedom of contract and a commitment to what Roscoe Pound called "abstract individual self-determination."[11]

Categorical devotion to contract as a governing principle of social life has come under increasing criticism since the last decades of the nineteenth century. The Legal Realists in particular argued that an emphasis on the abstract individual obscured relationships of dependence that systematically shaped contractual outcomes.[12] Individuals bargain, they pointed out, against a background of entitlements that represent the delegation of authority to engage in various forms of coercion. A property owner may lawfully withhold her property from others, regardless of their need for it, unless they agree to use it on terms satisfactory to the owner.[13] Given the importance of property to production of the means of subsistence, those without property therefore have little choice but to agree to terms demanded by those who own it. As a result, for instance, workers often must choose between accepting work on conditions set by the employer or having no source of income. Consequently, suggested Morris Cohen, "[t]here is in fact no real bargaining between the modern large employer . . . and its individual employees."[14]

Such criticism called into question the assumption that some "natural" state of affairs exists apart from social context, which the law should merely ratify.[15] Instead, a concern for vindicating actual, rather than formal, freedom demands attention to the reliance and dependence that exist in specific situations. This perspective focuses on the texture of particular relationships, rather than on individuals abstracted from context.

The result has been an increasing willingness to regulate the terms of commercial life on the basis of what we might call status, in an effort to protect those deemed to be the vulnerable party in a given relationship. The Uniform Commercial Code, for instance, distinguishes between merchants and nonmerchants, and holds each to different standards of behavior.[16] Negotiations between employers and unionized employees must be conducted in accordance with requirements under the National Labor Relations Act,[17] and the erosion of the employment-at-will doctrine creates certain rights based on a person's status as an employee.[18] Legislation such as the Employee Retirement Income Security Act (ERISA),[19] the Occupational Safety and Health Act (OSHA),[20] and the Fair Labor Standards Act (FLSA)[21] completely remove large areas of the employment relationship from contractual determination. Similarly, the landlord-tenant relationship has become increasingly governed by regulation that prescribes the terms on which rental housing contracts may be executed,[22] and special principles govern the arrangement between insurer and insured.[23] These are but a few of the instances in which one's status—as merchant or nonmerchant, employer or employee, landlord or tenant, insurer or insured—dictates to a large degree the terms on which one deals with others.[24]

In each instance, the use of status reflects a relational notion of obligation. That is, certain relationships by their nature are seen as characterized by vulnerability and dependence, which makes inappropriate a regime of unqualified private ordering. In each case, the law reflects the view that the stronger party owes certain responsibilities to the weaker, responsibilities that flow from the fact of the relationship itself rather than solely from individual choice.

This relational orientation is embodied as well in those areas of contract law still relatively free of systematic regulation. Contemporary scholarship has demonstrated that few commercial transactions between business firms can be characterized as a single interaction by atomistic parties who henceforth go their separate ways—the vision of a contract theory that emphasizes individual will and the "meeting of the minds." Rather, commercial dealings typically occur in the context of an ongoing relationship, which the parties seek to preserve through norms of accommodation and reciprocity.[25]

Modern contract law has evolved to take account of this reliance, through doctrines such as promissory estoppel[26] and the covenant of dealing in good faith.[27] Indeed, some contract scholars have suggested that reliance, rather than consent, is in fact the underlying basis for contract law as a whole.[28] From this perspective, the basis of obligation can be seen as status—not so much in terms of a formal legal category, but in the sense that participation in a certain relationship that induces reliance gives rise to particular duties. Classical contract law's vision of a free market of unfettered bargainers therefore has been considerably tempered in many instances by appreciation of the texture of actual economic relationships.[29]

Family law thus seems to be moving toward contract precisely at a moment when that paradigm's influence over commercial life is waning, and when the analytical foundation of contract law itself seems to be shifting. The fact that these changes in commercial law are occurring because of the need to acknowledge dependence is of direct relevance to family law, because family relationships also feature considerable vulnerability and reliance. Just as protecting the vulnerable through the use of status can enhance freedom in commercial life, so acknowledging reliance through the use of status can promote intimacy in family life.

The Family. Current claims for the primacy of freedom of contract in family life resemble earlier arguments in favor of freedom of contract in commercial life. Proponents of a regime of private ordering in family matters implicitly posit a self that is prior to and independent of personal relationships. That self requires a domain in which it can express its will to self-determination free from "outside" influence.[30] The "private" sphere of intimate relations is such a realm, a space in which individual subjectivity governs the interaction of the parties. Just as contracting parties once were regarded as the only persons capable of evaluating the terms of their commercial agreement, so intimate partners now tend to be regarded as the only legitimate arbiters of the terms of their relationship. In each instance, the "public" sphere is deemed incapable of passing judgment on the fairness or desirability of "private" arrangements. While freedom of contract once governed the market for goods and services, it now rules the personal relations market. In each instance, the rallying cry is consumer sovereignty.

One might claim that the forces that undermined reliance on private ordering in commercial life aren't sufficiently pressing to warrant caution about the use of contract as the governing principle in family life. The commercial world, the argument might go, features systematic imbalances in power between parties such as producers and consumers, landlords and tenants, and, in general, those with capital and those without. Intimate dependence, however, exhibits no such regularity. Emotional or psychological vulnerability depends on idiosyncratic factors that differ from person to person and relationship to relationship. In addition, the brute demands of physical subsistence can serve to vitiate the idea of meaningful consent in commercial life, but don't exert a comparable influence in intimate matters. An individual is much freer to decide whether to enter relationships based on her own judgment about whether the other person would meet her needs. Furthermore, the availability of no-fault divorce makes exit from undesirable partnerships relatively easy. Thus, one might argue, concerns about dependence and reliance that justify the use of status in commercial matters are less pressing within the family, and shouldn't outweigh commitment to self-determination in intimate relationships.

This argument, however, fails to take into account the way in which a relationship such as marriage comes to shape the identities of both spouses, and therefore is the source of mutual dependence. The assumption of an acontextual self envisions marriage as an encounter between two separate people, who lend each other support in their efforts to fashion authentic identities. Each spouse is a valuable assistant in the construction of the other's identity, but is not a constituent of that identity itself. The marriage thus is akin to a valuable possession—something that can be enormously useful in meeting personal objectives, but that ultimately is separate from the person that one is. This perspective is reflected in what two scholars describe as a common perception: that upon entering marriage "one's world, one's other-relationships, and, above all, oneself, have remained what they were before—only, of course, that world, others, and self will now be shared with the marriage- partner."[31] Put differently, the consumer is separate from the personal relationship that she chooses.

An alternative view, however, is more sensitive to the way in which marriage serves as a "nomos-building" relationship: a partnership that creates a structure of meaning within which the individual can make sense of her experience.[32] This perspective acknowledges that a meaningful world is essentially a human creation, in which we need validation by others in order to gain assurance that existence is relatively stable and coherent. Marriage represents a process in which subjective experiences gain such validation and become the common property of the spouses.[33] Through this process, a person obtains grounding for her beliefs that the world works in a certain way—that some actions deserve praise and other blame, or that intimacy involves certain demands but not others. The ability to locate oneself within this structure of meaning then becomes an important element of self-definition.

Spouses therefore typically don't simply help each other construct separate individual identities. Rather, together they participate in the creation of a shared reality in which each partner's identity is dependent in part on interaction with the other. Each spouse's understanding of reality is continuously shaped and reshaped with reference to the other, which in turn means that "the identity of one spouse is constantly in interaction with the identity of the partner."[34] The existence of the relationship itself makes each person different than before, a performer in accordance with a jointly written script.

Carol Gilligan offers a simple yet instructive example of this phenomenon in illustrating a different point. She tells the story of a girl and boy at play. The girl wants to pretend that they are next-door neighbors, while the boy wants to play pirates. One solution is for the children to take turns playing each game. This vindicates the separate preference of each child and the separate identity of each game. The relationship between the children in this instance is the occasion for accommodation of separateness: the children can satisfy their independent desires if they will only wait their turns. By contrast, Gilligan recounts a different approach, in which the girl says to the boy, " 'Okay...then you can be the pirate that lives next door.' "[35] Gilligan suggests that in this solution each child enters the other's imaginative world and transforms that world by his or her interaction with the other. In this instance, the relationship between the children is not an occasion that preserves the separate identity of the game that each child independently desired. Rather, the relationship is the impetus for a new game, which incorporates but is different from the games that the children separately had imagined.[36] Similarly, spouses create a shared reality that draws on, but is not reducible to, the spouses' individual experiences.

The notion of oneself as a spouse thus tends to be an important element of the self-definition of most married people.[37] The power of this relational view of identity is underscored by studies of divorce, which emphasize the transformations in one's basic sense of self that accompany the end of a marriage.[38] Furthermore, even with a greater sense of role distance, individuals are apt to find that it is difficult to disengage from the role of spouse without some lingering effects on identity. Helen Rose Ebaugh's studies of "role exit," for instance, have found that past identification with a social role tends to persist to some degree, as those who exit a role attempt to incorporate past identity into current self- understanding.[39] As a result, role exiters tend to maintain some amount of "hangover identity" from past roles even as they move beyond them.[40]

This effect of marriage on identity means that marriage and family life involve a considerable amount of emotional and psychological vulnerability. One's very sense of both a meaningful universe and a coherent self are dependent in crucial ways upon relationships with other family members. From this perspective, marriage, for instance, is not simply a valuable vehicle for achieving personal satisfaction. Rather, it is a web of interdependence, "a shared history in which two people are bound together in part by what they have been through together."[41] As Robert Goodin has observed, the notion that we have special responsibilities to persons such as family members rests on the recognition that others are dependent on us, and are especially vulnerable to the courses of action that we choose.[42] Marriage as an entity thus has a moral force not reducible to voluntary exchanges of benefits and obligations.[43]

If a relationship such as marriage has moral significance as an entity in itself, then status as a spouse also in itself gives rise to obligation. The creation of a structure of meaning through marriage involves mutual reliance and creates mutual vulnerability. Being a spouse means assuming an obligation to honor that reliance and to refrain from exploiting that vulnerability. This is a responsibility that we impose on all spouses because of the interdependence that typically characterizes marriage. Status is the embodiment of that responsibility, a proclamation that certain intimate relationships in themselves give rise to obligation because they shape each partner's sense of self.

We know, of course, that a marriage may be more fragile these days, given a greater tendency to perceive it as but one option among many in a personal relations market. Spouses in the modern world may be particularly vulnerable because of the volatility in sentiment that characterizes the modern consumer experience. Feelings may change, devotion may wane, and other alternatives may come to seem more attractive. Status provides a buffer against the full force of the relentless tides of these market forces. It proclaims that some things can be taken for granted as long as a marriage lasts, and that some obligations may remain even when a partner has decided to leave. Status asserts that a person's "public" identity as a spouse sometimes may take precedence over one's "private" identity as a chooser. The individual therefore may not always be able to act immediately in accordance with revised preferences when others may be injured as a result.

The first way in which status can promote intimacy, therefore, is by protecting those who are willing to make intimate commitments. The vision of a free market of perfectly mobile bargainers doesn't do justice to the ways in which family relationships can implicate identity, and thus neglects the special kind of reliance that arises from emotional interdependence in these settings. Status is a way of acknowledging that individuals do not pass in and out of intimate relationships untransformed, but rather create a shared life that provides an important source of meaning for each. Just as we have come to appreciate the limitations of unfettered freedom of contract in commercial life, then, we should be sensitive to the danger of this vision in family life as well. In each realm, status can serve to protect those who are particularly vulnerable to the actions of others.

Status and the Self

The "I" and the "Me." A second way in which status can promote intimate commitment is by fostering a stable sense of self over time. Commitment involves binding oneself in the name of a self that is relatively constant as it encounters a variety of contexts. We've seen how the postmodern loss of self can be traced to insistence on the radically autonomous self, for whom no context is constitutive. Exaltation of subjectivity as the only appropriate guide to individual conduct risks fragmentation of the self, and its eventual dissolution within the stimuli to which it is exposed at any given moment. This suggests that stable identity may depend upon a vision of the self as social in character, for whom certain relationships are constitutive. In the remainder of this chapter, I want to examine how the concept of status might provide a relational understanding of self that is crucial to this process.

The work of George Herbert Mead provides one useful way to begin to grapple with these issues. In particular, in his *Mind, Self, and Society*, Mead examined what it means to have a sense of self, and what preconditions must exist in order for this experience to occur.[44] His thinking is relevant here because Mead conceptualized the self not as separate and autonomous, but as fundamentally social in origin. At the same time, Mead provides a way of thinking about how the self unifies its experience so as to give meaning to those relationships in which it is engaged. This analysis sheds light on how a culture may foster a sense of continuous identity over time. Mead's work is useful for my purposes not so much as a literal account of the emergence of self-consciousness. Rather, I want to use it as a general framework for thinking about how we might preserve a sense of self that is both relational and relatively stable, and how legal status might help us do so.[45]

For Mead, the "essential psychological problem of selfhood" is, "How can an individual get outside himself (experientially) in such a way as to become an object to himself?"[46] The necessity for the self to be perceived as an object flows from the fact that, without this character, the individual organism doesn't distinguish between itself and its environment. Consciousness per se is the awareness of various types of stimuli, but until the emergence of *self*-consciousness "the individual experiences his body—its feelings and sensations—merely as an immediate part of his environment, not as his own[.]"[47] As an object, then, the self becomes differentiated from other stimuli. This differentiation in turn makes it possible to say that the self has certain experiences that are peculiarly its own.[48]

Mead maintains that a person can become an object to himself only through interaction with other persons. Only through the eyes of others can he grasp himself as something different from the flow of his own consciousness. Their perspectives provide the distance necessary in order for him to see himself as an object in a field of experience. A person becomes such an object to himself only by taking the attitudes of other individuals toward himself in various social situations.[49] Self-consciousness, then, depends upon the experience of relationships with other individuals.[50]

For Mead, language is the minimum condition for this process, because it makes possible the creation and communication of meaning from one person to another. When I utter a certain word, I can roughly anticipate the kind of reaction that another person will have to that word, and thus can provoke in myself the kind of response that she is likely to have. As Mead argues, "What is essential to communication is that the symbol should arouse in one's self what it arouses in the other individual."[51] If it does not, language is unable to function as a symbolic system.[52] This internal incorporation of the attitude of others through communication permits the development of a sense of self. By using various symbols and anticipating the responses that they will provoke, a person can see herself as others see her: as an object of experience distinguishable from her flow of subjective sensation. As Mead maintains, when a person "not only hears himself but responds to himself, talks and replies to himself as truly as the other person replies to him, [then] we have behavior in which the individuals become objects to themselves."[53] For Mead, then, even the possibility of identifying separate selves depends on the existence of a "universe of discourse," which consists of a group of individuals participating in shared experience.[54]

The awareness of oneself as an object is what Mead calls the "me." The "me" is the "organized set of attitudes of others which one himself assumes."[55] Put another way, the "me" represents the imprint of the community upon the individual, that form of awareness that locates oneself within a matrix of social relationships.[56] As such, the "me" orients itself in terms of the performance of social roles, and is attentive to the reciprocal expectations that define the roles that characterize each situation. As Louis Zurcher has written of this concept, "The Me is the social component of self, manifesting conformity to the values, norms, statuses, and roles of a social structure."[57] If we think of the "me" as an individual, we might say that she is characterized by "role identification."[58]

Mead posited, however, that the individual is comprised not only of the "objective" dimension of "self" or "me." She is also made up of the "subjective" dimension of the "I." The "I" is that margin of existential freedom to act differently from conventional expectation. As Mead expresses it, "The 'I' gives the sense of freedom, of initiative."[59] The "me" presents the individual with the situation that she must confront, by locating her as a "self" within a particular social setting. By doing so, the "me" generates awareness of the expected conduct within that setting.[60] The "I" is the response of the individual to those expectations.[61] This response is never completely predictable, and always differs, if ever so slightly, from precisely what the situation calls for. The demand of the "I" is for "freedom from convention, from given laws."[62] Were we to characterize the "I" as an individual, we might say that she is marked by an attitude of "role distance."[63]

For Mead, the interplay between the "I" and the "me" constitutes individual and social experience. As he notes,

We are individuals born into a certain nationality, located at a certain spot geographically, with such and such family relations, and such and such political relations. All of these represent a certain situation which constitutes the "me"; but this necessarily involves a continued action of the organism toward the "me" in the process within which that lies.[64]

This ongoing process is one in which "the individual is continually adjusting himself in advance to the situation to which he belongs, and reacting back on it."[65] The "me" presents a set of communal expectations, and the "I" responds to those expectations. This response in turn changes the community; it creates a new situation and a new "me" that is located within that situation.[66]

The "me" and the "I" are thus dependent upon one another.[67] Without the "I," for instance, the "me" would seem virtually an automaton; it is the "I" that represents the "possibilities of the self that lie beyond our own immediate presentation."[68] Even more important for my purposes here, the "I" needs the "me." An individual needs the "me" in order to be able to regard experience as *her* experience, as belonging to a self that spans the series of existential moments that the "I" confronts. The "me" makes possible the "establishment of a coherent and continuous identity."[69] It thus "give[s] the form of the 'I.' "[70] That is, it provides a self upon which the "I" can reflect, an object rooted in experience, so that the actions of the "I" can be seen as the actions of a particular agent. The "I" may not be wholly confined by that "me" and the situation in which it is located. Without it as a point of departure, however, it cannot exist as an "I."

One implication of Mead's analysis, then, is that the postmodern loss of self can be seen as the result of the pursuit of a pure "I" without a "me"—that is, the quest for an individual defined apart from any social context. For Mead, attainment of human identity necessarily demands recognition of its relational character. "We cannot realize ourselves except in so far as we can recognize the other in his relationship to us. It is as he takes the attitude of the other that the individual is able to realize himself as a self."[71] Without a "me," the "I" is the familiar disembodied self that floats from one context to another without being rooted in any of them. Mead thus sheds light on the first precondition of stable identity: that there be some sense of self. As he illustrates, that sense is dependent on acknowledgment of the social nature of the self. Only a self that is part of a community can be a self at all.[72]

In his analysis of the "full development of the self,"[73] Mead also provides some insight into what it might mean for a self to unify its experience so as to develop a relatively stable sense of identity. Central to this process is the concept of the "game."

"Play" and the "Game." While Mead regards language as the minimum condition for the emergence of a self, he posits two general stages of self-development that language makes possible.[74] In the first, "the individual's self is constituted simply by an organization of the particular attitudes of other individuals toward himself and toward one another in the specific social acts in which he participates with them."[75] Mead likens this orientation to "play." In play, he says, the child can assume a role in the sense that she can invoke the particular response or responses that are appropriate to that role.[76] Indeed, the child can assume a succession of roles, responding intelligently each time to the demands of each. In play, however, the person's behavior is "just a set of responses that follow on each other indefinitely," without any larger sense of organization.[77] Says Mead, "[t]he child is one thing at one time and another at another, and what he is at one moment does not determine what he is at another. . . . You cannot count on the child; you cannot assume that all the things he does are going to determine what he will do at any moment."[78] There

is thus a succession of "me's," but no stable "me" that unifies them in some larger pattern of experience.

This situation calls to mind the multiplicity of selves that some characterize as the postmodern condition. In this condition, the self fulfills the demands of one role after another, without any sense of a coherent self beyond the particular role in question.[79] In "play," no context is constitutive, in the sense that no context elicits behavior that has implications beyond the situation at hand.[80] Each role is a discrete stimulus, which calls for a distinct response. Mead regards the self in such an instance as not yet fully developed, because it does not relate to experience as an organized whole.[81] The person "has no definite character, no definite personality."[82]

By contrast, the individual reaches full self-realization in the "game." The game features a logic that serves to organize various roles into a specific relationship to each other.[83] In order to participate in the game, the individual "taking one role must be ready to take the role of everyone else."[84] Mead uses the example of a player on a baseball team to make his point. The player "must have the responses of each position involved in his own position. He must know what everyone else is going to do in order to carry out his own play."[85] The "other" whose attitude is internalized in such an instance is the "generalized other," which represents the organized set of attitudes of the relevant community—in this case the team.[86] This "generalized other" is the "organized community or social group which gives to the individual his unity of self[.]"[87]

The significance of the game is that it makes possible this unity of the self over time, so that each moment has significance not simply in itself, as in "play," but as part of a larger purpose to which it is related. In one instance, one may play the role of fielder, in another the role of batter, in yet another the role of baserunner. From one perspective, these situations all involve different contexts, but the behavior in each is shaped by the overarching sense of oneself as the member of a baseball team. The game is thus constitutive, in that it provides to a player a relatively stable identity that guides conduct in different situations.

Of course, the game itself can also be seen as a single context, whose influence does not extend to other contexts. In other words, we can think of individuals as participants in a number of games with different purposes or objectives. From this perspective, the self is not necessarily any more stable than in "play," since it simply moves from game to game. If, however, the individual saw herself as a participant in an ongoing "game," a game regarded as more important than others, her identity as a player in that game would affect how she behaved in the other games in which she was involved. That is, the self defined by its specific location within that particular set of relationships—i.e., one's position within *that* game—would alter the significance that flowed from occupying a different position in another game.

A person's position as mother, for instance, might limit her willingness to act as dissatisfied employee and quit her job, if she saw the "game" of family breadwinner as one in which she participated even while at work. By contrast, a person's position as sports fan might not extend into the workplace so as to dictate her job decisions. Mead's metaphor of the "game" as the occasion of full self-development thus suggests that one way to think of the establishment of a relatively stable sense of self across different contexts is as a participant in an ongoing game. A game that is ongoing may be regarded as a context that is constitutive.

One way to locate the individual within a game, to invoke in her a sense of the attitude of others, is through the use of legal status. Status creates a "public" identity that is social in nature—a self defined in terms of its relationship to others. Status thus establishes a "me," a self that has an "objective" character that lies "outside" the subjectivity of the "I." The rights and obligations expressed in this status represent the voice of the "generalized other." This voice speaks the language of impersonal obligation, those communal expectations that arise by virtue of the self's location in a particular web of relationships. Mead captures the stabilizing effect of this phenomenon when he observes, "One of the greatest advances in the development of the community arises when [the] reaction of the community on the individual takes on what we call an institutional form. What we mean by that is that the whole community acts toward the individual under certain circumstances in a certain way."[88]

As a participant in a game that gives meaning to her actions, a person with a particular status therefore has a source of guidance beyond her own subjective preferences. The creation of legal identities such as spouse and parent, for instance, "objectifies" individuals, thereby establishing a self distinguishable from the undifferentiated flow of subjectivity. This objectification occurs through the declaration that to occupy these statuses means to be subject to communal expectations that arise "outside" the individual.[89] Status thus uses the voice of the "generalized other" to posit a "me," a relational self that makes it possible for the "I" to regard itself as agent with a certain continuous identity over time.[90] The rules of the "game" in which this "me" as, say, a spouse participates are comprised by the sets of reciprocal expectations of family members toward one another.

This sense of a relatively stable self offers greater potential for the achievement of intimacy than does a perception of the self as fragmented over a variety of contexts. First, from the perspective of the actor, it does so by enhancing the ability to make commitments. The promise made in one context can have force in a different one if it is seen as made by a self that is relatively constant in both. Commitment makes possible those islands of intimate emotional support within the flux of daily life, because it helps organize the flow of time into a meaningful pattern. To act on the basis of a prior commitment is to link both past and present, and to make a commitment is to link both present and future.

We can draw on Joshua Meyerowitz's concept of "place"[91] in conceptualizing how status can contribute to a unified self and a capacity for intimate commitment. Recall that Meyerowitz regards a distinct place as defined by the particular information and stimulation that it admits and denies.[92] Recall also that he argues that we are losing our sense of place—are coming to have "no sense of place"—because of the penetration of ubiquitous electronic media into more and more corners of social life.[93]

We can think of status as preserving a distinct sense of psychic "place." It does so by declaring that the individual is not to approach each context fully open and receptive to all the stimuli that it may offer. Rather, the experience of that context should be filtered through the perception of a unified self, who will find some stimuli rewarding and some not in light of the identity that has been shaped by her commitments. As I suggested earlier, for instance,[94] a person whose identity as husband shapes his behavior at work may not be fully receptive to the romantic opportunities that this context offers. His identity provides a "place" that denies or deflects certain stimuli to which he might attend under other circumstances.[95] The spatial metaphor reflects the fact that what otherwise might be experienced as a flow of unconnected contexts, each offering a set of distinctive possibilities, has been ordered and interpreted according to an overarching meaning. As a result, the experience of each context is different than if this interpretive framework had not been employed. A relatively stable sense of self thus increases the prospects for achieving intimacy by enhancing the ability to make commitments.

Second, from the perspective of others, a sense of the actor's unified identity promotes intimacy by inspiring trust. Trust increases the willingness to share one's emotional vulnerability with another. As Niklas Luhmann has suggested, "trust is extended first and foremost to another human being, in that he is assumed to possess a personality, to constitute an ordered, not arbitrary, centre of a system of action, with which one can come to terms."[96] This assumption that the other is a relatively coherent self over time then creates the expectation that she will act in a relatively consistent fashion.[97]

Luhmann underscores that the creation of trust does not consist, as modernism would have it, of the interaction of two persons who reveal "true" selves defined apart from social context. As Luhmann points out, the specter of the radically free acontextual self is in fact what gives rise to efforts to establish trust in the first place. "Freedom," he notes, "in the—as it were—pre-social sense of other people's uncontrollable power to act, is the source of the need for trust[.]"[98] By contrast, "freedom bound up with and moderated through the social order ... is the source of the ability to learn trust. In order for trust to emerge and fulfill its function, freedom must be transferred from the 'pre- social' context to the other."[99]

Modern sensibility tends to regard status as antithetical to intimacy because of its impersonal character. Mead, however, provides a basis for suggesting that status can enhance the potential for intimacy precisely because it is impersonal. Status contributes to the creation of a unified self capable of making commitments and inspiring trust. It does so by using communal obligations to root the self in context, thus locating the self within forms of life in which it can act meaningfully as an agent. Status expresses the social aspects of the self that are the precondition for its exercise of autonomy and its participation in intimate relationships.

"Family" can be seen as a form of discourse about the relational self—a self that acknowledges the constitutive character of certain contexts in which we participate. These contexts reflect what Berger and Luckmann call the "typification" of certain "forms of action."[100] That is, they are constitutive by virtue of certain shared expectations that people have of one another. Status provides the vocabulary of family discourse, a way of publicly expressing these shared expectations. This expressive function of status reflects the fact that, as Berger and Luckmann put it, "[t]he typification of forms of action requires that these have an objective sense, which in turn requires a linguistic objectification."[101] From among the sea of relationships in which we are involved, family status designates those that are to serve as exemplars of the constitutive relationship. It gives concrete substance to abstract concepts such as the relational self and committed intimacy, by demarcating a set of relationships that we expect to embody those concepts. We can think of family law, then, as providing "a vocabulary referring to ... forms of action"[102] that we take as indicative of how the relational self should interact with others. While other relationships may be constitutive as well, the family has served as the most prominent model of this process.

This differentiation among relationships meets what seems to be a need for some way in which people can express those commitments that they regard as more serious than others. Even those who advocate greater private ordering in family matters assume the existence of this need. Marjorie Schultz, for instance, maintains that, while the particular form of the family may be mutable,

[w]hat is not mutable is the individual's need to form bonds of a deep and continuing nature, involving commitment, intimacy, and a degree of public acknowledgment and affirmation. Marriage is our predominant historical, legal, and cultural symbol of that need. Whether or not that is inevitable is less important than that it is true.[103]

Similarly, Jennifer Jaff, who is critical of what she perceives as legal preferences that favor married persons, acknowledges that "[e]liminating distinctions" can have the "negative consequence" of "eliminating choices by merging options[.]"[104] When law imposes certain obligations on a spouse because he is a spouse, then, it affirms the view that marriage involves a level of commitment distinctive from other personal relationships.

A couple of qualifications are in order at this point. First, I don't mean to reify status. It is, after all, a human product that is shaped continually by human interaction. As Mead makes clear, the "me" may present a set of expectations to the "I," but the "I" is not compelled to fulfill them. Indeed, "the 'I' is something that is never entirely calculable. The 'me' does call for a certain sort of an 'I' in so far as we meet the obligations that are given in conduct itself, but the 'I' is always something different from what the situation itself calls for."[105] In turn, this reaction of the "I" reshapes the "me," reflecting a revised set of communal expectations.[106]

One impetus for this revision, for instance, is that the demands of status may be perceived as unjust and repressive. The expectations associated with the status of "wife," for example, have changed considerably since the Victorian era. Furthermore, as Martha Minow has demonstrated, even wives in the nineteenth century utilized opportunities afforded by their status to reshape and redefine what it meant to be a wife.[107] In other words, while status may provide a sense of relative stability, it's important to keep in mind just how relative that stability is, as social expectations are fashioned and refashioned in the course of everyday life.

Second, I want to reiterate that I'm not positing some radical freedom to choose which context will affect us and which won't; all contexts leave their mark in some way. At the same time, the socially created meaning of those contexts can differ, and we are capable of acting differently on the basis of those meanings. When a culture signals that a context is constitutive in some strong sense, it is indicating that the "me" of that context is a self whose voice should be heeded in other contexts as well. One way to think of "family," then, is as a discourse that uses status to designate a "me" whom the "I" should regard as particularly influential across contexts.

Why is it important, however, to preserve this discourse over the many others that might express a relational identity? Why can't relationships at work, or in the neighborhood, or elsewhere serve as discourses about the constitutive relationship if the family is losing its distinctive character? The answer, I contend, lies in the historically powerful resonance of "family" in American culture as a discourse of opposition to market logic. If we look closely at the way this discourse has operated in the public imagination, we'll see that its power indeed has rested upon its function as the model of a relational sense of identity.

Dueling Discourses. "The dichotomization of market and family pervades our thinking, our language, and our culture."[108] We tend to think that the market represents an arena in which self-interested behavior is appropriate, while the family is characterized by selfless conduct.[109] The discourse of the market and the discourse of the family can be seen as expressing alternative, albeit simplified, visions of human conduct.

Indeed, one way to look at the family is as a discourse explicitly opposed to its market counterpart. It acquired much of that oppositional tenor, of course, during the Victorian era. It was in that period that the family acquired a particularly significant social identity and emotional valence, which can be seen in part as a reaction against the perceived ascendance of market logic.[110] The family was to be a "redemptive counterpart" to the market,[111] an antidote to its egoistic, calculating, and competitive ethic. As such, family discourse served both a defensive and an affirmative function. In the former role, it articulated the vision of the family as a haven that was insulated from the reach of market principles. In the latter, it provided a foundation for challenging, or at least tempering, the operation of those principles within the market itself.

The defensive strain of family discourse is reflected in the prominent Victorian image of the family as a haven of affection: a realm in which qualities such as sharing, altruism, and sympathy might be preserved.[112] The imagery bears some resemblance to the United States cold war rhetoric of Communist containment. The market was seen as a force whose influence threatened to penetrate further and further into the world; the family was to serve as the line of defense that prevented civilized life as we know it from being overrun. As Walter Houghton puts it, the home was to be "a shelter for those moral and spiritual values which the commercial spirit and the critical spirit were threatening to destroy."[113]

The effect of this vision of containment is that we generally have viewed families as entities that ought to be insulated from market forces to a considerable degree.[114] This function of family discourse is reflected, for instance, in the New Jersey Supreme Court's opinion in *In the Matter of Baby M*, which involved the enforcement of a surrogate motherhood contract.[115] In refusing to enforce the contract, the court declared, *inter alia*, that "[t]here are, in a civilized society, some things that money cannot buy."[116] The court regarded the existence of a financial incentive for the biological mother to surrender the child problematic in at least two respects.

First, from the perspective of the child, the court regarded such an incentive as an inappropriate consideration in determining who should obtain custody.[117] For this reason, the law could not adopt its typical deferential stance toward the judgment of the natural parents about the care of their children. That deference is premised on the belief that decisions in the family domain will be altruistic—that is, that parents will be guided by the best interests of the child. The prospect of financial gain, however, adulterates the decision process, according to the court, because it introduces the market logic of parental self-interest into the equation.[118] From this perspective, the court saw its decision as a way of protecting the family domain from being invaded by its opponent.

The second way in which the court regarded a financial incentive as inappropriate is from the perspective of the biological mother. The court said that the fact that the mother had entered into a contract to surrender the child for money might cause her decision to be less "voluntary" than it otherwise would be.[119] The implicit premise of this view is the same as above: that the mother "normally" would be guided by family discourse, but her contractual commitment might distort this natural predilection. From either perspective, it's clear that the court regarded economic motivation as suspect in this context.[120] The basis for this assumption is the defensive strain of family discourse, which asserts that the family should be insulated from the calculating egoism of the market.[121]

In performing its affirmative function, family discourse has served as the foundation for a critique of the market itself. As we have seen, one of the tenets of the Victorian "cult of domesticity" was that family values, and the women who safeguarded them, were often characterized as morally superior to market values and the men who lived by them.[122] There emerged during the nineteenth century "a growing consensus that only women, through their uplifting influence over the home and children, could be a source of moral values and a counterforce to commercialism and self-interest."[123]

The far-reaching potential of this discourse is reflected in the fact that it provided the justification for extensive involvement of women in matters *outside* the home. In the name of perpetuating family values, women were active in numerous social welfare movements; religious revivals,[124] temperance, antislavery, education, social work, settlement houses, and protective labor laws describe only a few of these efforts.[125] Some of these campaigns directly challenged market logic as a governing principle, arguing that state regulation was necessary to prevent the market from undermining important human values.[126] Others attempted to temper the operation of the market, softening its harsher outcomes by providing the kind of support that reflected a familial orientation. In either case, women sought to extend the influence of family values with the justification that "[t]he world is only a larger home."[127]

Martha Minow sheds light on this function of family discourse in her analysis of the women working in the textile mills of the Lowell Corporation in the first half of the nineteenth century.[128] Many of these women experienced unprecedented economic independence as a result of their participation in the marketplace, which created expanded possibilities for personal growth and development. In many respects, then, these women might seem particularly receptive to the ethic of individual achievement and autonomy exalted by market logic.

Yet, as Minow points out, these women used their economic success as an opportunity to affirm familial values in at least two ways. First, they provided financial and emotional support for family members less able to exploit market opportunities.[129] Second, they created networks of mutual assistance within the workplace itself. When one worker became ill, for instance, others filled in for her so that she would not lose any wages. Similarly, women readily shared tasks within the mills, as well as their knowledge and experience with new employees.[130] Thus, as Minow puts it, "the mill girls brought the mores of the family to the work place."[131]

Minow's analysis helps us appreciate the dialectic between behavior guided by role and behavior guided by notions of individual autonomy. The Lowell mill women not only used role-oriented family discourse to give meaning to their relative independence; that independence in turn reshaped their role identities.[132] For my purposes here, the important point is that family discourse made this interplay possible by providing an alternative to market logic. As Minow observes, "Even when reaching some form of autonomy in economic and daily life, women routinely recreated patterns of connection and care-taking; their family roles persisted unsupplanted by an individualism that could have been available to them."[133]

Family discourse has continued to perform its affirmative function in our day. Perhaps the most prominent example of this in recent years has been Mario Cuomo's speech at the Democratic National Convention in 1984, which virtually overnight transformed him into a national figure. The centerpiece of Cuomo's speech was an emphasis on the "family of America," in contrast to what he assailed as the social Darwinism of the Reagan administration.[134] The idea of family, declared Cuomo, involves "[t]he sharing of benefits and burdens for the benefit of all."[135] Regarding ourselves as the family of America, said Cuomo, therefore, means that

at the heart of the matter we are bound one to another, that the problems of a retired school teacher in Duluth are our problems. That the future of the child in Buffalo is our future. That the struggle of a disabled man in Boston to survive and live decently is our struggle. That the hunger of a woman in Little Rock, is our hunger. That the failure anywhere to provide what reasonably we might, to avoid pain, is our failure.[136]

Cuomo's speech thus indicates that family discourse continues to provide "a vantage point for criticizing autonomous individualism."[137]

It's important at this point to offer a qualification that acknowledges the complexity of the relationship between family and market discourse. Family discourse has not been purely oppositional. In fact, in some respects the family can be seen as a complement to the market, an institution whose heightened ideological significance in the nineteenth century was necessary in order for market principles to gain acceptance. As such, the family lent support to the market in both a practical and symbolic fashion.

On a practical level, the Victorian designation of the family as the primary vehicle of socialization provided an institution that could produce the new type of personality that the market needed. "Traditional personal behavior, with its unplanned, natural rhythms, did not fit comfortably within modern society."[138] As Steven Mintz and Mary Ryan have independently suggested, a middle class anxious about the ability to transmit its status to the next generation seized upon the development of "modern" character traits of self-control and restraint as the key to success in the emerging market economy.[139] From one perspective, these traits can be seen as a way of instilling a sense of responsibility that would temper the drives of unfettered egoism. They also, however, served to foster the myth of the "self-made man," the very embodiment of market autonomy.[140] Seen in this light, the family in fact contributed to the development of a distinct market discourse.

The emergence of family discourse also can be seen as lending support to the market on a symbolic level. Extravagant Victorian proclamations about the superiority of family values freed persons to act on the basis of market logic in the "public" sphere, by suggesting that the "finer" virtues were being preserved at home.[141] Ann Douglas has termed this phenomenon "sentimentalism," a process that operates through "the manipulation of nostalgia."[142] On this view, one can argue that the very vehemence with which Victorians asserted the moral superiority of women and the family was merely a symbolic expression of regret, which was "calculated not to interfere with their actions."[143] Nancy Cott has suggested, for instance, that the cult of domesticity undercut opposition to workplace exploitation, because it held out the home as a source of compensatory comfort for indignities at work.[144] Thus, family discourse can be seen as a rhetoric that served to legitimate both the dominance of market values and the repression of women.

Realizing that family discourse can be supportive of market logic makes clear that the effect of this discourse is not determinate. Rather, the nature of its contribution will depend on the give and take of social and political life. For this reason, the way in which we interpret the opposition between family and market is crucial. One way of thinking about this opposition undermines the subversive power of family discourse, because it ironically reinforces the atomism of the market vision. A second interpretation offers the prospect of preserving family as an oppositional discourse, because it sees that discourse as signaling that certain personal relationships should be constitutive. Analysis of the dichotomy between the family and the market in the cultural imagination will thus confirm that one important way to view the family is as a discourse that encourages the formation of a relational sense of identity.[145]

Family Discourse and the Relational Self. One way to think about the family/market dichotomy is that the market is the realm of rational self-interest, while family is the realm of spontaneous altruism. On this view, the paradigm market actor uses the concept of "exchange value" to relate to the world. This concept allows an individual to assess persons and things in the world in terms of a common coin: the relative satisfaction that they can provide.[146] Life then consists of a series of choices that reflects the attempt rationally to maximize the satisfaction that one enjoys.

By contrast, the argument goes, persons within the family ideally operate according to the principle of "use value." They don't see persons or things in terms of the possible utility that they can provide. Rather, they value them "in themselves," for their intrinsic worth.[147] Instead of a quest to maximize satisfaction through rational choice, life in this realm is the occasion for the spontaneous expression of one's deeper and fuller sentiments. Frances Olsen describes this perspective as the belief that

each succeeding political [reform of the family] seems to leave the family a more *natural* entity, a freer expression of human impulses. . . . Insofar as people consider that the family exists only to serve human emotional wants, that it lacks practical purpose, they believe that it is becoming more pure and family- like.[148]

While this version of the family/market dichotomy seems to resonate on one level, it in fact has serious shortcomings. First, in one respect it seems counterintuitive. Why else would people get married or have a family if they didn't rationally anticipate that it would bring them some satisfaction? Why wouldn't a spouse choose to stay in a difficult marriage unless she believed that she would be worse off in some way by leaving? The belief that relative satisfaction doesn't enter into family-oriented behavior seems to contradict what seems on one level an irrefutable (and potentially vacuous) axiom of economics: that people will try to live their lives so as to be happy. Why do people do what they do in families if they don't perceive that they will gain some reward from doing it? This first account of the family/market dichotomy thus seems to generate a portrait of the individual that doesn't square with our understanding of how most of us actually go about leading our daily lives.

On a deeper level, this account of the dichotomy reintroduces the modernist quest for essences. It posits the market as a realm of appearances, where our perception of persons and things is filtered through the framework of our purposes. As a result of this filtering process, everything is treated as a means to an end, as one possible source of satisfaction. By contrast, the family is the realm in which we can perceive the real character of persons and things, because we're not simply viewing them with an eye to what they can do for us. Since our vision is undistorted by any purposive orientation, we can regard everything as an end in itself. This permits us to be more sympathetic and less calculating.

This interpretation draws on the modernist belief in some ideal sphere in which we can apprehend the world in its "true" nature, a realm in which our perception is untainted by the fallibility and contingency of our own interests. It reflects the desire to "isolate and defend an ideal zone of use value" that can be insulated from the variability and mutability of human purposes.[149] Yet, as pragmatism reminds us, the world cannot be understood apart from our purposes within it.[150] Belief in the possibility of unmediated perception reflects an attempt to distance ourselves from our particular situation so as to judge ourselves by some absolute standard. Our sense of the world, however, is unavoidably intertwined with our purposes. As Richard Rorty argues, "The question of what propositions to assert, which pictures to look at, what narratives to listen to and comment on and retell, are all questions about what will help us get what we want (or about what we *should* want.")[151] What would it mean, for instance, for the family to have some essence apart from the human purposes that it served? We should therefore recognize that "[t]he family is just what we make it—it exists only to please us."[152]

This first version of the family/market dichotomy thus supports the search for "authenticity" that we discussed earlier. It leads to the view that efforts to mold family life to some communal purpose through, for instance, the imposition of status obligations, are illegitimate. Rather, we should simply leave people alone, because they inhabit a realm of "natural" feeling that should be left undistorted by efforts to treat it as a means to something else. As I've argued, the metaphor of authenticity runs the risk of providing individuals with nothing but their subjectivity as a guide, leaving them vulnerable to pervasive cultural messages that promote the understanding of oneself as a consumer.[153] The notion of the family as a realm of "natural" sentiment opposed to the market sphere of rationality therefore ironically creates the prospect that family life itself will begin to reflect a market orientation.

An interpretation of the family/market dichotomy in terms of the difference between rational choice and spontaneous expression thus threatens to rob family discourse of its oppositional character. Yet we often do experience family and market in this way. A better interpretation, I believe, acknowledges the experiential resonance of the first interpretation, but focuses on the different conceptions of identity promoted by market discourse and family discourse. It is the family's relational notion of the self, I contend, that gives rise to our perception of acting altruistically in the family setting, and that provides family discourse with its oppositional power.

This focus on a distinct conception of identity begins with the difference between conscious and unconscious choice. When we consciously choose and weigh alternatives, persons and things seem to have the character of objects that are distinct from us, which we can take or leave. We sense that we are "free to choose" because we can hold ourselves apart from these objects; no alternative is so compelling that we feel that our selection is foreordained. The greater the abstraction of the self from its surroundings, then, the more existence seems best captured by the metaphor of choice. Our experience seems to be an ongoing series of choices among various potential sources of satisfaction. The rational actor then appears to be the best model for our lives as persons in the world. The experience of conscious choice thus draws on a sense of the self that is relatively atomistic.

By contrast, the less conscious our sense of choice, the more relational our sense of self. The relational self is not the detached self who is free to take or leave alternatives as she wishes, but someone who is defined in part by her relationships with others. This identity places constraints on her, because certain courses of action now seem foreclosed in light of their consequences for those with whom she is enmeshed. The more that alternatives are foreclosed, the less salient seems the metaphor of choice. Conduct now seems spontaneous and unplanned, because the sense of rational deliberation is diminished.

A stranger at a deserted lake who sees a child flailing in the water far from shore, for instance, may well decide to try to rescue the child. She is more likely to experience the decision to do so as a deliberate choice, however, than is that child's mother. The mother's sense of who she is is in part constituted by her relationship with the child. This means that there are many fewer options for her than for the stranger in that situation. Indeed, she may well feel that she has *no* choice; her rescue effort is likely to be interpreted as the natural, spontaneous, uncalculating response that typifies the conduct of family members toward each other.

Yet on some level the parent did have a choice; she could have stayed on the shore rather than gone into the water. What distinguishes her from the stranger who stays on shore is not necessarily that she did not make a rational choice to maximize self-interest. Rather, it is that the self whose interest was maximized is one that includes the child. From this perspective, only one option would contribute to this self's welfare. The action is not experienced as a rational choice in any significant way, however, because the concept of deliberation doesn't seem to capture what went on. From this perspective, the person animated by family discourse pursues a set of human purposes as much as the person animated by market discourse. The difference is that family discourse casts those purposes as shared purposes, which forecloses more options than does a market discourse focused on the purposes of the individual. Family discourse thus takes its oppositional character from its challenge to the individualistic ontology of market logic.[154]

An illustration of this phenomenon under conditions that permit more time for deliberation is provided in a study of rescuers of Jews in Nazi Europe.[155] Researchers interviewed a sample of rescuers drawn from various backgrounds, as well as a sample of nonrescuers who lived in Nazi Europe and a sample of entrepreneurs. They found that the latter two groups tended to conform to rational actor theories of altruism. That is, they appeared to "make some conscious calculation about what they could afford to give and what they needed or wanted to keep or pass on to heirs."[156] None of the rescuers, however, saw their decision to rescue Jews in terms of weighing the costs and benefits of doing so. Instead, all of them insisted that there simply was no choice to make.[157]

Researchers conclude that the reason for this perception is that rescuers have a more expansive view of their identity than do members of the other two groups. As one rescuer put it, "[g]radually, by opening your eyes, you see that . . . everyone is you."[158] This "perception of self as part of a common humanity" foreclosed certain courses of action for these rescuers:

Because the rescuers' identities were so strong, there was no conscious choice for them to make in the traditional sense of assessing options and choosing the best one. Instead, their perception of themselves in relation to others limited the options available to *them*. Certainly, they knew most people did not risk their lives to save Jews and so they knew that theoretically this choice was available. But they did not believe that this choice was an option for them.[159]

One of the rescuers succinctly summarized the way in which this sense of self seemed to foreclose alternatives: " 'I don't make a choice. It comes, and it's there.' "[160]

These rescuers thus tend to lack that sense of sharp distinction between the self and its surroundings that permits persons and things in the world to be regarded as objects of choice. For them, the self could not remain untransformed by its choices. For them, rescue activity reflected action on the basis of an identity that necessarily embraced certain kinds of behavior and not others. As a result, "[f]or rescuers, the concept of a cost/benefit analysis became meaningless, since to deviate from the pre-scribed behavior would necessitate a fundamental shift in the actor's basic identity construction."[161] From this perspective, choices served less as options than as opportunities for self-affirmation.[162]

Rescuers' perception of their conduct as spontaneous rather than de-liberate thus reflects rejection of the ontological individualism of market discourse. The sense of a relational self is underscored by the subtle contrast between that orientation and what the researchers describe as a feeling of empathy. The latter sentiment encourages ethical behavior toward another because it generates the realization that the person in need "could be me."[163] Yet the authors suggest that rescuers' responses indicated that "[t]hey were not rescuers because they knew they could be in a similarly needy position."[164] Rather, they were motivated by the sense of an indistinct boundary between the self and others. "Indeed, rescuers made no distinction between their own needs and those of their Jewish guests."[165]

In sum, these rescuers illustrate the way in which the experience of conduct as spontaneous altruism can rest not so much on the absence of an orientation toward self-interest as on an expansive view of the self whose interests will be promoted. As the researchers in this study conclude,

Our impression of rescuers is that they do not consider the individual the basic actor in society. All of our interviews suggest that rescuers view themselves as part of a shared humanity rather than as individual beings, separate and distinct from others.[166]

If we examine family as a discourse of opposition to the market, then, we see that it holds out a model of altruistic conduct that is premised on a relational sense of self. I suggested earlier that this self-conception can provide a relatively stable sense of identity because it creates a psychic "place" that limits the amount of stimuli with which one must contend in any given context.[167] Our examination of the roots of altruism confirms this idea because it indicates that altruism can be seen as premised on the existence of a relational identity that limits the choices that seem to be available in a given situation.[168] Family discourse offers a vision of the self as rooted in connections with others, connections that impose limitations, but that also make possible the continuity of identity essential to understanding oneself as a unified human agent over time. As Michael Sandel observes, "While the notion of constitutive attachments may at first seem an obstacle to agency—the self, now encumbered, is no longer strictly prior—some relative fixity of character appears essential to prevent the lapse into arbitrariness which the deontological self is unable to avoid."[169]

Family discourse therefore makes available a "middle distance" that creates the possibility of a relational sense of self that is nonetheless relatively stable. This spatial metaphor points up the fact that a self either radically disengaged from or radically engaged in context is one that risks losing its distinctive identity.[170] A stable sense of self seems to depend on the establishment of some distance from context, even while acknowledging that one is inescapably situated within it. The constitutive relationships that comprise the middle distance meet this need, by providing a vantage point from which the "I" as subject can reflect on the "me" as object. As Sandel puts it, "[a]s a self-interpreting being, I am able to reflect on my history and in this sense to distance myself from it, but the distance is always precarious and provisional, the point of reflection never finally secured outside the history itself."[171]

Status contributes to the preservation of family discourse by demarcating an "objective" middle distance to which this discourse refers. It provides a distinctive form within the social world that we take as embodying abstract concepts such as altruism and commitment. By establishing such a referent, status prevents the family from becoming a diffuse image that may stir certain aspirations and desires, but that has little connection to actual daily experience.

The family may take a variety of forms. The statuses of husband and wife, for instance, have different implications than they did a century ago. We are now committed to the idea that status should not assign family roles on the basis of gender. Our notion of family form thus changes over time; indeed, family law reflects an ongoing process of deciding exactly what it means to be a member of a family. The idea of family as a discourse means that what Bruce Hafen calls "familial attitudes" are more important than any particular social arrangement as such.[172]

What *is* important, however, is that there be *some* distinctive social form that is seen as embodying those attitudes. A world in which this is absent, a world characterized by the individually crafted "close relationship," is one in which the culture provides negligible support for those who wish to live out a commitment to an intimate relationship with another. This is not to say that individuals cannot fashion such relationships. The heightened sense of their contingency, however, combined with the ethos of modern consumer culture, may make commitment difficult to sustain. The constitution of family through status may be a way of acknowledging "our collective demand that the social order restrict the overwhelming universe of interpersonal possibility, and that it present this restriction to us disguised as 'nature.'"[173]

Status, therefore, can promote intimate commitment by fostering the cultivation of a coherent self that is capable of making and keeping promises. The prerequisite for such relative stability is recognition of a self that is constituted in part by its relationships with others. Discourse about the family provides a powerful cultural narrative about this process of self-definition. Family status is integral to this narrative because it offers examples of the relational self through its creation of legal identities with distinct rights and obligations.

Conclusion

At first glance, impersonal legal status and personal intimacy seem natural enemies. I have argued, however, that this inherent antagonism is only apparent. Status in fact can be used in family law to foster intimate commitment because it's sensitive to the ways in which intimacy and identity are connected. First, status can be used to limit the vulnerability that results from the character of intimate relationships as shared structures of meaning that help shape personal identity. Second, status can be used to constitute a social self, whose mooring in communal norms enhances a sense of stable identity that is the prerequisite for intimate commitment.

In the next chapter, I want to move from the rarefied air of personality theory to the practical ground of family law. Specifically, I will explore just how we might begin to give status adequate weight when we deliberate about how the law should respond to the complexities of family life.

5. Status, Contract, and Family Law

In this chapter, I want to explore how a new model of status might inform our consideration of several family law issues. I have several purposes in doing so. First, I hope to illuminate the limitations of an emphasis on private ordering in thinking about family law. Second, I intend to suggest concrete ways in which a new model of status might promote a relational sense of identity and responsibility in family matters. Finally, I hope that working through the analysis of several topics will clarify how a new model of status would differ from the traditional family law model. Specifically, I want to illustrate how we might use status in a way that is sensitive to both the egalitarian ideal and the pluralistic character of contemporary family life.

My treatment of these issues is therefore suggestive rather than comprehensive. Each topic warrants far more detailed analysis than I will be able to present here. Furthermore, while I offer suggestions on how we should deal with many of these matters, I don't argue that a new model of status would necessarily dictate these or any other specific outcomes. We typically want many things of families and of family law, and each situation presents a different configuration of interests to consider. I don't intend to offer definitive resolution but rather to indicate how we might begin to give adequate weight to a perspective that emphasizes shared norms of responsibility.

The basic elements of this perspective are twofold. First is acknowledgment of the importance of promoting a relational sense of identity among family members. Second is appreciation of the role of legal status in creating and maintaining institutions that support this aim. My analysis explores the possibility of affirming these notions in a realm that we've come to regard as uniquely private and intimate. My hope is to offer a point of departure for a richer and fuller consideration of what is at stake when we deliberate on family law issues. What follows, then, is an opening conversation in a much longer dialogue about how law might better mediate between the demands of freedom and responsibility in family life.

Family Formation

Same-Sex Marriage. Marriage traditionally has been restricted to heterosexuals. Some states explicitly limit marriage to men and women,[1] while courts in other states have interpreted statutes that are silent on the issue as implicit rejections of same-sex marriage.[2] In the latter instances, courts have based their conclusion on long-standing Western disapproval of homosexual liaisons, historical restriction of marriage to heterosexuals, the importance of procreation as a function of the marital unit, and concern that same-sex marriage would undermine the central role of the family as a unit of socialization. Indeed, some judges have taken heterosexuality as so integral to marital status that they have denied that law differentiates among those eligible to marry on the basis of sexual orientation. Rather, they have said, two members of the same sex are simply incapable of entering into marriage. As one court put it, "Appellants were not denied a marriage license because of their sex; rather, they were denied a marriage license because of the nature of marriage itself."[3]

G. Stanley Buchanan has offered a thoughtful defense of restricting marriage to heterosexuals.[4] The very notion of a society, argues Buchanan, depends upon the ability of a majority to define norms of behavior in areas of social life that are deemed fundamentally important.[5] He argues that Western culture traditionally has held up opposite-sex marriage as "the standard of moral excellence in the core areas of sexual conduct and childrearing."[6] As such, marriage has served as the expression of beliefs about matters of morality regarded as crucial to human development and the constitution of the community. Crucial to this function has been the exclusivity of opposite-sex marriage, which has intensified marriage's appeal as the model for intimate conduct. The loss of this exclusivity, maintains Buchanan, would deprive the majority of the ability to promote the standards of morality to which it aspires. As a result, legislatures should be free to restrict marriage to heterosexuals, and should be under no obligation "to prove empirically that legal recognition of same-sex marriage would impair the ability of opposite- sex marriage to advance the values it has traditionally promoted."[7]

I agree with Buchanan's contention that marriage is the central institution through which we express our aspirations about intimate behavior, and that marriage best serves this function if it represents a distinct status. I would maintain, however, that the moral aspiration that marriage has expressed is not heterosexual intimacy per se, but the more general vision of responsibility based on the cultivation of a relational sense of identity. If we regard the concept of family as a discourse about how a self might be constituted in part by relationships with others, there is no reason to exclude same-sex relationships from that discourse. My conception of status, then, invites an imaginative reconstruction of the traditional values promoted by marriage that supports legal recognition of same-sex relationships.[8] Furthermore, this focus on the substantive ends promoted by marriage may be preferable to an argument for legalization that rests on the claim that the state should defer to private ordering of intimate relationships.

Considerable research on same-sex couples suggests that their values and experiences are similar to those of heterosexuals involved in intimate relationships.[9] As one scholar who has studied same-sex couples concludes, "Whatever their sexual preferences, most people strongly desire a close and loving relationship with one special person."[10] A nationwide survey of homosexuals indicated, for instance, that 63 percent of the men and 70 percent of the women defined themselves as being in a relationship characterized by permanent commitment.[11] Partners in same-sex relationships score high on scales designed to measure attachment, caring, and intimacy, with scores indistinguishable from heterosexual couples.[12] In-depth interviews with gay men and lesbians round out this portrait, containing statements such as, "[I]f Michael were to become seriously ill and bedridden, I would take care of him until he died. I love him in every way that is possible to love another human being. No matter what happened to him, I would be his and he would be mine. I love him."[13]

Despite the aspiration to commitment among many same-sex couples, there is some reason to believe that these relationships are more fragile than those that receive legal recognition. Studies of male couples in particular tend to indicate that partners are considerably less likely to be sexually exclusive than either lesbian or heterosexual couples.[14] While this may reflect in part the acceptance of nonexclusivity by the partners, there is evidence that it may also reflect the absence of social reinforcement of desires for self-restraint. One study, for instance, found that almost a quarter of the men in nonexclusive relationships were unhappy with this arrangement.[15]

Another study, by Joseph Harry, indicated that, among male same-sex relationships that partners regarded as equivalent to marriage, a majority were unfaithful even when both agreed on the desirability of fidelity.[16] According to Harry, this suggests that "individuals were incapable of adapting their own behavior to either their own desires or those of their marital partner."[17] Harry maintains that the absence of any institutional support for fidelity means that the "market mentality" that characterizes activities such as the gay bar and the steam bath tends to extend as well into those relationships in which the partners desire commitment.[18] The result, he fears, is greater "inability to sustain an enduring relationship of intimacy."[19] His conclusion is that "the gay relationship will become a more rewarding affair for its participants only when the fidelity version of that relationship acquires substantially greater structural, cultural, and socialization supports."[20]

The primary form of such support for intimate relationships is of course marriage. One lesbian writer in a permanent relationship describes the significance of not having this institution available to reinforce her commitment to her partner:

We had not had a wedding. Aunts and uncles did not come to visit and admire our home. We never received anniversary cards. As trivial as these things may seem, they represent something vitally important: heterosexual couples are encouraged to stay together. Their union is celebrated and shared with loving and supportive families and friends.[21]

This desire for public support and recognition is what leads some same-sex couples to engage in a "commitment ceremony."[22] As one psychologist who counsels homosexuals puts it, "a public commitment is especially important to some gay people. They feel a symbolic statement strengthens their relationship, just like a heterosexual couple."[23] If we appreciate the role of marriage in promoting a relational sense of identity, then we should make that institution available to same-sex couples who aspire to live according to such an ethic.

It's true that marriage traditionally has served as the principal relationship within which procreation and childrearing have occurred. This fact, however, needn't justify preventing homosexuals from marrying. First, as chapter 2 discussed, childlessness is now more acceptable among heterosexual couples, and emotional support has come to be perhaps the central expectation that defines marriage.[24] Same-sex partners are as capable of providing this support as heterosexual partners. Second, the availability of various fertilization technologies have made it possible for same-sex couples to procreate outside of sexual relations.[25] Many homosexuals are quite willing to assume parental responsibilities, and to offer the kind of stability for children that spouses have traditionally provided.[26]

An argument for same-sex marriage based on the ethic of relational obligation offers some advantages over an argument based on a right to autonomy or choice in intimate settings.[27] The latter approach simply argues that we should tolerate homosexual behavior despite what may be our disapproval of it.[28] The result at best may be a grudging willingness to permit certain "private" activity, conceptualized as occurring on the margins of society. This willingness can be distinguished, however, from the "public" approval that marriage would bestow. Furthermore, even if privacy were deemed to compel recognition of same-sex marriage, that principle would not necessarily challenge stereotypes that denigrate homosexuals.

By contrast, an argument based on the substantive ends for which we value intimate relationships emphasizes the commonality between heterosexual and same-sex partners.[29] It acknowledges that intimate behavior is of moral interest to the community, but asks that the community engage in an act of empathetic imagination that provides the basis for respecting homosexuals and accepting them as full members.[30] A focus on the importance of the family as an arena of relational responsibility therefore may provide a more secure grounding for same-sex marriage than an emphasis on individual privacy.

Unmarried Cohabitation. Recent years have seen a considerable increase in unmarried cohabitation.[31] Couples in these relationships vary in the extent to which their relationship involves emotional attachment, economic integration, or expectations of permanence. The situation that has generated the most legal controversy, however, is one in which someone claims that an informal relationship was equivalent in substance to marriage, and that she therefore is entitled to certain assets acquired while the couple lived together. I will refer to persons in this kind of relationship as cohabitants. The claims of cohabitants raise the issue of whether the law should recognize different obligations and benefits for persons based on marital status.

Traditionally, the law sharply distinguished between the married and unmarried. A strong preference for marriage led courts categorically to deny relief to parties in dissolving informal relationships, even when the parties had entered into an express agreement.[32] Cohabitants were treated essentially as outside the law, in contrast to the elaborate regulation of the consequences of divorce.

Recent courts have been far more willing to grant relief to unmarried partners when their relationship dissolves. Contract theory has been the most prominent ground on which this relief is based. Some states will impose obligations only on the basis of an express agreement,[33] while others will enforce implied contracts deemed to arise from the behavior of the parties.[34] A smaller number of courts have also used broad, equitable powers to impose financial obligations in the absence of either express or implied contracts.[35] This trend toward greater legal supervision of the dissolution of unmarried relationships has reduced the extent to which married and unmarried cohabitants are subject to different obligations when partners go their separate ways.[36]

To a lesser extent, there also has been a greater willingness to afford unmarried cohabitants the benefits that spouses enjoy with respect to third parties. Some courts, for instance, have permitted a cohabitant to recover for loss of consortium when a partner has been injured by a tortfeasor,[37] while others have provided to cohabitants benefits traditionally confined to spouses under worker compensation statutes.[38] In addition, some jurisdictions have adopted "domestic partnership" legislation that makes it possible for cohabitants to obtain benefits ordinarily available only to formal family members, such as health insurance, family leave, pensions, and survivor's benefits.[39] While there remains resistance to the extension of formerly exclusive marital benefits to the unmarried,[40] the difference in treatment is not as stark as it was even a couple of decades ago. Indeed, several scholars have issued recent calls for the extension to unmarried cohabitants of the legal benefits currently available only to spouses.[41]

The notion that the obligations and benefits of married status should be available to cohabitants thus has some momentum. How might the concerns that underlie a new model of status inform our deliberation about whether this is a good idea?

First, that model proceeds from the assumption that marriage is preferable to unmarried cohabitation for intimate relationships that involve emotional and financial interdependence. Marriage provides a set of norms about commitment that are more strongly established than those for cohabitation; those norms provide social reinforcement for the cultivation of a relational identity.[42] Causal relationships in this area are complex and uncertain. Nonetheless, it may be reasonable to assert, for instance, that one reflection of the force of marriage is the fact that unmarried unions tend to be less stable than married ones.[43] A new model of status would be sympathetic to the claim that the social interest in promoting marriage justifies preserving a firm distinction between the legal treatment of married and unmarried couples.

On occasion, however, the concern for promoting relational identity that underlies the preference for marriage militates against sharp distinctions based on status. The issue of obligations between unmarried cohabitants is one such instance. Unlike the traditional model of status, a new model would reject the claim that the law should refuse to enforce any obligations at all when cohabitants dissolve their relationship. The widespread increase in cohabitation, its greater social acceptance, and the fact that the overwhelming majority of states are willing to adjudicate claims between unmarried partners, indicates that cohabitation has become an important form of emotional and financial interdependence. For many, cohabitation is comparable to the relationship once primarily, if not exclusively, associated with marriage. Forty percent of cohabitant households, for instance, have children in them,[44] which means that many unmarried unions are fulfilling functions comparable to those of marriage.

If the law ignored the reliance and vulnerability that arises in these relationships, it would be party to considerable hardship. Nonenforcement would undermine the cultivation of relational identity by reinforcing the idea that by refusing to marry one can escape the responsibilities that flow from an intimate relationship. The message would be that these relationships of interdependence are purely "private" matters of no social concern. Furthermore, the failure to compensate partners likely would have a disparate gender impact. Women in such relationships tend to be less wealthy than men, tend to make more sacrifices for the man's career than vice versa, and often would like to marry but are unable to convince the man to do so.[45] Failure to entertain claims of unmarried partners thus would leave men with control of resources that women helped to create, thereby creating a disincentive for the unselfish behavior associated with a relational sense of identity.

As my analysis of other issues in this chapter will suggest, the existence of a certain pattern of behavior is not necessarily in itself a warrant for legal ratification of that behavior. Unmarried cohabitation, however, is widely accepted and raises important issues of responsibility in intimate relationships. Failure to respond to the claims of cohabitants thus could undermine the relational ethic that family law should reinforce.

A new model of status, therefore, first would counsel that we take account of the prevalence of cohabitation and its dynamics by adjudicating claims between unmarried partners. Second, this model might lead us to eschew contract theory as the basis for recovery, in favor of an approach that applied to cohabitants the same obligations imposed on divorcing spouses. Thus, an unmarried partner would not need an express contract to gain relief, nor would a court be required to infer the existence of an implied contract based on the parties' behavior.

A willingness to enforce only express contracts neglects the fact that most people in intimate relationships simply don't enter into contracts about their financial affairs. Indeed, persons involved in perhaps the closest emotional relationships may well find the very idea of a contract distasteful. The requirement of an express agreement, therefore, would leave outside the law a large number of relationships that feature a considerable amount of interdependence and reliance.

Furthermore, the requirement of a written agreement sends the message that responsibilities in intimate relationships arise only through explicit consent. The image is of individuals who otherwise have no responsibilities to each other, who surrender their sovereignty only grudgingly on terms that they themselves have accepted. If we're concerned about reinforcing a relational sense of identity in these relationships, however, we will want to encourage the idea that obligation in certain instances can arise from the fact of relationship itself. A willingness to review a partner's claims even in the absence of a written agreement expresses this principle.

A second option is to utilize a theory of implied contract to expand the proportion of unmarried partners eligible for relief. Several courts have followed this approach, attempting to determine whether the conduct of the parties reveals an intention that they share assets if the relationship ends.[46] This theory is more realistic than the requirement of an express contract. It recognizes that intimate relationships often proceed on the basis of tacit shared assumptions, and that conduct reflecting interdependence is often the best evidence of the partners' expectations. Furthermore, a court's inquiry into those expectations necessarily will draw upon communal notions of equity and responsibility. A judge must determine, for instance, whether a person under the circumstances would have felt indebted to a partner for her sacrifice, and whether the partner who made the sacrifice expected that the benefits from the relationship would provide some form of compensation. The "intent" of the parties in such instances largely is a legal construction, shaped considerably by assessment of what a typical person would expect given prevailing social norms. In this sense, a theory of implied contract incorporates a social understanding of obligation.

Yet problems remain. First, partners often have different expectations about the relationship, which makes it perilous to assert the existence of some unitary intention.[47] Furthermore, the more selfish partner may be the one to express her intent more aggressively. A court might well take that sentiment as the clearest expression of expectations about the relationship, and assume that the parties had no intention of sharing their assets.[48]

Most important, the formal justification of the outcome in these cases is still couched in contract rhetoric, rather than in the language of relational obligation. As fictional as the "intent of the parties" may be, a court is still constrained to describe the responsibilities it imposes as based on the consent of the parties. This emphasis perpetuates the notion that unmarried cohabitation is a "private" matter of concern only to the participants. It promotes the vision of a domain in which freely choosing selves assume their obligations free of communal "interference."

By contrast, courts in Washington state have adopted an approach that would better vindicate a public ideal of responsibility. Once the court establishes that an unmarried relationship is "tantamount to a marital family except for a legal marriage,"[49] it applies to that relationship the same rules that govern divorcing couples.[50] This makes clear that certain shared norms should shape the way in which persons deal with each other in intimate settings, and that society will enforce those norms when the relationship ends.

A new model of status, therefore, might treat cohabitants as having assumed a certain status upon a finding that their relationship substantively resembles formal marriage. Division of property, responsibility for support, child custody, and the enforceability of contracts relating to these matters would then be adjudicated as they are for divorcing spouses. Outcomes under this approach may not differ dramatically from those under an implied contract theory, since many cohabitants' expectations are shaped by an implicit understanding of how the law deals with divorcing partners.[51] Nonetheless, as Margaret Radin reminds us, "we cannot be sanguine about radically different normative discourses reaching the 'same' result."[52] Contract is primarily the language of private ordering, signaling that certain behavior is essentially the business of those who directly engage in it.[53] Status in this context communicates the message that intimate relationships typically implicate personal identity in a way that creates special obligations for those involved in them. The theory under which a cohabitant can gain relief matters because, as Katharine Bartlett observes, law "defines norms that parties reproduce when they articulate their claims in certain ways."[54] In sum, while it's important to preserve marriage as a distinct status, this concern is based upon the desire to promote a relational sense of obligation between intimate partners. On balance, enforcing comparable obligations toward each other for married and certain unmarried partners would seem to further this aspiration more effectively than a sharp distinction based on legal status.

Distinctions based on marital status seem more justified, however, with respect to claims of benefits from the government or third parties. In those instances, the issue is not how the parties should act toward each other, but what kind of recognition the relationship should receive from those outside it. If society has an interest in promoting marriage as the model of the constitutive relationship, it seems justifiable to deny to the unmarried certain benefits afforded to spouses.

Thus, for instance, if same-sex marriage is legalized as I suggest, we might regard as inadvisable "domestic partnership" ordinances that provide to cohabitants many of the same benefits that spouses enjoy. Furthermore, the exclusion of unmarried partners from Social Security awards,[55] worker compensation benefits,[56] and wrongful death claims[57] can all be justified as expressions of a legitimate social preference for marriage. Treating cohabitants as eligible for all these benefits would permit unmarried couples to enjoy the same treatment as spouses, without being subject to public supervision of the beginning or end of those relationships. Furthermore, to the extent that cohabitants come to resemble spouses both with respect to their obligations to each other and their treatment by outsiders, marriage loses much of its distinctive character.

It may seem unfair to deny benefits in these cases to persons who are "married" in all but form, particularly given my willingness to ignore the absence of legal status with respect to economic matters upon dissolution. Yet there's an important distinction between the two situations. The substantive fact of interdependence in certain relationships gives rise to expectations based on the experience and vision of a shared life, even when partners are not married. We want persons in these relationships to attend to the vulnerability of the other, and we therefore should apply social norms of sharing in order to protect reliance and promote responsibility.

By contrast, unmarried partners haven't been willing to declare their commitment to the larger public through the social institution that's designed to do so. They themselves have indicated that outsiders should deal with them as unmarried persons, which carries the connotation of a lesser commitment than if they were spouses. They have indicated this despite the fact that marital status is often used as the basis for the distribution of various types of benefits, from the use of library cards to eligibility for insurance coverage. Denial of a benefit with respect to third parties thus is less likely to defeat a strongly held reliance interest than is the denial of a claim by one partner against the other. An unmarried partner will have available the assets created and acquired during the relationship even if, for instance, she doesn't receive statutory widow's benefits.[58] Furthermore, with respect to government benefits, it is reasonable for society to conclude that honoring claims by cohabitants on public resources might send a signal that the decision whether to marry is a matter of social indifference. A new model of status, therefore, can ensure that parties receive the fruit of their common life together, even as it expresses a preference for the relationship of marriage.

The Ongoing Family

The Marital Rape Exemption. Most states treat the rape of a married woman by her husband differently than they do the rape of an unmarried woman. Some states exempt a husband from prosecution for rape, substituting a lesser offense of spousal sexual assault.[59] Others exempt husbands from all but first-degree rape charges.[60] Still others withhold prosecution unless actual or threatened physical force is used.[61] Many states impose periods within which an alleged marital rape must be reported that are considerably briefer than the statute of limitations for nonmarital rape.[62] Some states have responded to charges that the exemption constitutes gender discrimination by extending the exemption to both men and women.[63] Others have responded to claims that the exemption discriminates on the basis of marital status by making the exemption available to unmarried cohabitants.[64] Such measures indicate the continuing apparent persuasiveness of various arguments that have been offered in favor of the exemption. These include concern that marital rape will be difficult to prove in the context of an ongoing sexual relationship, fear that a rape charge will be used by a vindictive wife, the belief that prosecution will inhibit reconciliation that the parties might be able to achieve without the threat of legal sanction, and the assertion that a wife has alternate remedies such as actions for assault and for divorce. All these arguments have been subject to cogent critique, which I don't intend to reproduce here.[65] Despite widespread criticism of the exemption, however, it remains a fixture in American law. In large measure, this is probably based on the prevalent belief that "it may well be that spousal rape is an act, the very nature and quality of which differs from, and is less serious than, ordinary rape."[66]

The marital rape exemption understandably has been attacked as an improper vestige of status, which must yield to appreciation of the individual rights of married women.[67] This critique is a powerful and important one. I want to argue here, however, that an argument based on a new model of status can complement this perspective by offering a critique that focuses on marital obligation. Indeed, the argument from status avoids some of the dangers of an exclusive focus on individual rights, and is responsive to sentiment that marriage is a distinctive relationship.

A status-based critique of the exemption begins with the assertion that people assume special responsibilities to each other when they marry. Marriage is meant to embody a relationship in which one's sense of self is constituted in part through connection with another. This interdependence gives rise both to mutual trust and to mutual vulnerability. Marital rape is a violent betrayal of that trust and a blatant exploitation of that vulnerability. Rather than being responsive and attentive to his wife's needs and fears, a husband who rapes his wife ignores her wishes and subordinates her to the satisfaction of his own desires. This is not only the violation of bodily integrity but also the abrogation of a mutual pact that a wife has relied upon to order her life and give it moral meaning. It is, in short, the destruction of a "nomos."[68]

Research underscores this distinctive dimension of the trauma of marital rape. One extensive study indicates that 52 percent of women raped by their husband reported serious long-term effects from the rape, compared to 39 percent of women raped by a stranger.[69] Another study states that the destruction of trust is the single most common long-term effect of marital rape.[70] More than a third of the interviewees in this study reported that their ability to trust and develop intimate relationships with men had been impaired, because marital rape constitutes "not only a sexual assault, but a betrayal of trust and intimacy."[71] Another researcher found that more women raped by husbands became sexually dysfunctional than women raped by either dates or strangers.[72]

The dynamics of marital rape thus produce a "powerful sense of betrayal, deep disillusionment, and total isolation."[73] A woman raped by her husband can seek no solace at home from the person who has pledged to guard her welfare. As a result, she feels particularly bereft of support. Furthermore, psychological or financial dependence often leads a wife to minimize or even deny the rape, and to attempt to stay and placate her husband. The result usually is that she is raped again, often repeatedly.[74] This sequence in turn reduces her self-esteem and leads to a tendency to blame herself for her abuse, which triggers more rape and makes it even more difficult for her to leave.[75] This reflects a cycle in which the husband exploits his wife's trust and dependence in a way especially destructive to her sense of self. A victim of marital rape describes the particular anguish of her experience:

I feel if I'd been raped by a stranger, I could have dealt with it a whole lot better. ... When a stranger does it, he doesn't know me, I don't know him. He's not doing it to me as a person, personally. With your husband, it becomes personal. You say, This man knows me. He knows my feelings. He knows me intimately, and then to do this to me—it's such a personal abuse.[76]

It's probably unwise to differentiate in rape law among different types of relationships between the victim and rapist, for fear that we may undermine appreciation of the gravity of the crime under any circumstances. If we did, however, there is good reason for marital status to give rise to *greater*, rather than lesser, punishment.

The argument that the exemption is antithetical to the promotion of relational identity in marriage is buttressed by the history of marital rape law. The origin of the exemption in Anglo-American law is commonly attributed to Lord Hale's statement that a husband cannot be guilty of rape because a woman who marries provides her irrevocable consent to sex with her husband.[77] This rationale suggests that marriage places the wife's sexual services at the husband's disposal; he is free to disregard her wishes and to treat her as perpetually available to satisfy his sexual desires. In short, the exemption conveys the notion that a wife is the property of the husband. This message is consistent with the common observation that rape law originally was intended "to protect the chastity of women and thus their property value to their fathers or husbands."[78] Such a perspective reflects precisely the kind of objectified image of the "other" that marriage is intended to combat.

The connection of marital rape with objectification is underscored by studies indicating that husbands who rape their wives appear to "devalue women and to feel that their wives were obligated to service them sexually in whatever ways they desired."[79] A consistent theme throughout the research literature is the purposive attempt by the husband to humiliate his wife, subjecting her to intercourse in ways that he knows will be especially offensive, painful, and even dangerous.[80] Marital rape typically occurs as part of a pattern of physical abuse, rather than simply unwanted sexual relations, which underscores the husband's treatment of his wife as an object.[81] Nothing could be further from our aspiration that spouses will cultivate a relational sense of identity.

A status-based argument against the marital rape exemption thus emphasizes the location of the woman within the context of marriage, drawing attention to marital rape as a breach of the husband's obligation. Its emphasis is subtly different from the individual rights approach, which argues that women generally, regardless of marital status, have a right to be free of sexual violence.

The individual rights approach has been important in affirming the integrity of wives as individuals who deserve concern and respect in their own right. Yet it has attracted criticism because it "abstracts away from the reality of power relations," visualizing the rights- bearer as "the solitary woman, safe in her bedroom."[82] This emphasis on acontextual autonomy is vulnerable to the argument that if the wife doesn't report the rape immediately, or stays with her husband, or has sex with him again, then the alleged rape likely was in fact consensual sex.[83] As a generic individual, a wife is always free to choose. If we place her in context as a wife, however, conduct that seems inconsistent with her assertion of rape may become more intelligible. She is part of a relationship that typically involves emotional and financial vulnerability, and her extrication from that interdependence may be ambivalent and painful.[84] Indeed, faced with the abrupt disruption of a major strand in the fabric of her life, she may avoid coming to grips with the incident in order to avoid facing the bleak prospect of isolation.

A status-based argument against the marital rape exemption therefore emphasizes the husband's obligation to his wife and her expectation that he will honor it. By seeing victims of marital rape as wives rather than simply generic women, we may gain insight into the distinctive trauma that these women suffer and the complexity of their responses to it.

Conclusive Paternity Presumption. Several states have adopted a conclusive presumption that a child conceived and born to a woman living with her husband is the child of that husband, unless the husband or wife challenge paternity within a certain period of time.[85] Even if another man is likely the biological father in such instances, he is barred from introducing evidence that establishes this fact. Historically, the presumption served the purpose of limiting the number of instances in which children would be classified as illegitimate.[86] With states now less able to discriminate on the basis of legitimacy in providing legal benefits,[87] and with less social stigma attached to the fact of illegitimacy, an important modern rationale for the presumption is to protect the marital unit from disruption.

The Supreme Court upheld the constitutionality of such a presumption in the recent Supreme Court case of *Michael H. v. Gerald D.*[88] The decision has been widely criticized as an unfair subordination of the biological father's interest to the interest of the married couple.[89] I will argue, however, that the presumption is a defensible way that a state might attempt to reinforce spousal commitment under circumstances that are likely to be especially stressful. Appreciation of the distinctive character of this commitment justifies favoring marital over nonmarital relationships in situations such as those in which the presumption comes into play.

The statute at issue in *Michael H.* was a typical version of the presumption.[90] It provided that a child of a woman living with her husband is conclusively presumed to be a child of the marriage, as long as the husband is neither impotent or sterile. The husband may challenge paternity within two years after the child's birth, as may the mother if the putative father has filed an affidavit acknowledging paternity.[91] A declaration of paternity would grant the father visitation rights unless visitation would be detrimental to the interests of the child. It also would provide the right to consideration as the parent who should have custody. If designated the custodian, a parent has authority to make a variety of decisions about the child's upbringing.[92]

The *Michael H.* case involved Carole D., the child's mother, who had married Gerald D. in 1976. In 1978, Carole had an affair with Michael H., a neighbor. In September 1980, Carole conceived a child, Victoria D., who was born in May 1981. Gerald was listed as the father on the birth certificate, although Carole informed Michael that she believed that he might be the father. In October 1981, Gerald moved from the couple's California home to New York for business reasons, while Carole decided to remain in California. After Gerald's relocation, Carole, Michael, and Victoria had blood tests that indicated that there was a 98.07 percent probability that Michael was Victoria's father.[93]

Over the next two and a half years, Carole and Victoria lived twice with Michael, twice with Gerald, and twice with a third man, Scott. The involvement with Michael included an eight-month period when Michael lived with Carole and Victoria in Los Angeles when he was not in St. Thomas on business. In June 1984, Carole reconciled with Gerald and rejoined him in New York, where the couple, Victoria, and two other children born into the marriage lived at the time of the litigation.[94]

Michael's lawsuit asserted his paternity of Victoria and his right to visitation; Gerald defended on the ground that California's presumption precluded Michael's challenge. Michael claimed that he had a substantive due process liberty interest in his relationship with Victoria that was not outweighed by the state's interest in protecting Gerald and Carole's marriage. He also claimed that he had a procedural due process right that prevented the state from terminating that interest without a hearing.[95]

Justice Scalia's plurality opinion concluded that, while the California statute was framed in terms of a procedural presumption, it was designed to implement a substantive rule of law that the husband is the father of his wife's child unless either spouse claims otherwise.[96] Thus, Scalia concluded, Michael was asserting a substantive, rather than procedural, due process claim. In order to prevail, he therefore had to demonstrate that his interest was one traditionally protected under American law. Scalia acknowledged that the Court has protected the paternal interest of an unwed biological father who has established a relationship with his child. But none of those cases, he observed, involved a situation in which the claimant was the father of "a child conceived within, and born into, an extant marital union that wishe[d] to embrace the child."[97] In these circumstances, the opinion concluded, there is no traditional legal protection for the unwed father.

Furthermore, the plurality opinion noted that *Michael H.* was a case in which the assertion of a liberty interest by the putative father necessarily conflicted with the husband's assertion of a liberty interest in the integrity of his marital unit. "Here, to *provide* protection to an adulterous natural father," Scalia observed, "is to *deny* protection to a marital father, and vice versa."[98] In such circumstances, he concluded, it is permissible for the state to favor the marital father.

Justice Brennan's dissent criticized the plurality for focusing on the specific circumstances of Michael's claim, rather than on his general claim to the rights of an unwed natural father who had maintained a relationship with his child.[99] The plurality's approach, the dissent argued, allowed the state's interest in the relationship that might be disrupted to determine whether a liberty interest existed. The state's interest, however, should be weighed only *after* the existence of a liberty interest has been independently identified.[100] Michael, Carole, and Victoria are a family, said Brennan, just as are Gerald, Carole, and Victoria. The only difference is that the latter is a marital family, but the unwed father cases establish that "marriage is not decisive" in determining which parental relationships will be given constitutional protection.[101] Finally, Brennan maintained that Michael's claim should be treated as the assertion of a procedural due process right, and that no state interest in administrative efficiency could justify the exclusion of evidence directly relevant to the issue of paternity.[102]

How might a new model of status inform our consideration of the issues presented by this case? First, the *Michael H.* case represents an instance in which two men are willing to make a commitment to care for a child. Family law generally should promote this assertion of a desire to cultivate the relational identity of parenthood.[103] In this case, however, there is reason to fear that the pursuit of one person's family interest will undermine the ability of the other person to maintain a family unit.

Specifically, a marriage such as Gerald's and Carole's has suffered considerable turmoil. It's reasonable to believe that when at least one person has had an affair, and when a wife has begotten a child by another man, a couple's desire to reconcile may be particularly fragile and vulnerable to disruption. These circumstances require patience, compassion, and devotion in the face of emotional vulnerability. When the man with whom the wife has had an affair wants to assert paternity, it's likely that the challenge itself will place additional strain on the relationship. Even if the challenge is only for the purpose of a declaration of paternity, with substantive rights determined separately, it involves a public recitation of events that the spouses are doing their best to put behind them. The further prospect of a separate hearing to determine what rights to afford the biological father will surely be even more stressful. Finally, the demands of actually sharing childrearing with a biological father who has been given that right would be an constant reminder of past infidelity and a likely source of continuing suspicion and emotional strain. A paternity challenge by a putative father thus might well set in motion forces that would make reconciliation even more difficult than it already is in these cases.

The state has a legitimate interest in being concerned about this prospect. Marriage represents a public commitment to another, the assumption of a responsibility widely regarded as more binding than that involved in nonmarital relationships. The state has reason to promote this commitment and to prefer that children be raised within marriages by willing parents. When spouses are willing to forgive past transgressions and make a renewed effort to stay together, the law should reinforce this willingness to make the marriage work. When a husband is aware of his wife's infidelity and is still willing to raise as his own a child conceived through her adultery, he has expressed a commitment both to the child and to the marriage.[104] A paternity presumption honors this commitment by insulating the spouses from having to deal with a third party who has powerful emotional significance for the married couple. The presumption thus tries to provide a more stable environment in which the spouses can pursue what may be the slow and difficult task of strengthening their marital bond.

The presumption also operates less directly to promote the idea of spousal commitment, by expressing a preference for marital relations over adulterous liaisons. It's true, of course, that the mother as well as the putative father has engaged in adultery, and that only the father is left in the cold. The law can reasonably reflect the view, however, that this is a reasonable risk that a person takes who becomes involved in an affair with a married person. A person who contemplates such a prospect knows that a third party—the other spouse—is likely to be affected in some way, if only through diversion of the spouse's time and attention away from the marriage. The knowledge that one may not be able to participate in rearing a child conceived through an affair sends a signal, however indirect, that a person should be cautious in cultivating a romance with someone who is married. Adultery generally is no longer a crime, and most states have eliminated a spouse's cause of action against a lover for alienation of affection. It's still reasonable, however, for the law to express general social disapproval of adultery by disfavoring it in certain situations in which parties assert otherwise comparable claims.

Two aspects of Justice Brennan's dissent illustrate the difference between the relational approach that I've outlined and a more individualistic analysis. First, the dissent insisted that the Court must examine Michael's interest without regard to the other persons who will be affected by the exercise of his right.[105] Michael is thus the acontextual rights-bearer, seeking to vindicate his own interest notwithstanding his location within a web of relationships that will be affected by his actions. The dissent's approach offers no vantage point from which to see, as does the plurality, that acknowledging Michael's interest necessarily diminishes Gerald's.

This points up that an individual rights approach to family law sometimes may be insensitive to the complex layers of interdependence that characterize intimate relationships. Rights discourse traditionally has focused on the relationship between the individual and the state, but many family law issues involve conflicting individual rights claims. An emphasis on rights alone offers no basis for resolving such controversies.[106] The case of *Michael H.*, for instance, demanded not the mechanical assertion that biology plus relationship equals constitutional right, but a delicate adjustment among various relationships that each had a claim on our sympathy. The presumption attempts such an adjustment by, for instance, deferring not to the mere formal status of the spouses, but demanding that they themselves exhibit a willingness to raise the child. A father who finds such a commitment too difficult can be relieved of his obligations. A father who desires to raise the child can still be overridden by the child's mother—but only if the putative father has acknowledged his paternity. Furthermore, the presumption may be inapplicable if the mother and her husband divorce—depending on the situation.[107] In short, a focus on the context of relationships rather than on isolated rights suggests that the presumption may be the best way to take account of all the interests implicated in a complex set of circumstances.[108]

Second, to the extent that the dissent acknowledged that there are competing family claims, it assumed that the state must be agnostic between them. Both Michael and Gerald are involved in a family relationship with Carole and Victoria, the dissent maintained, and "the only difference between these two sets of relationships . . . is the fact of marriage."[109] That fact alone, however, can't justify favoring one relationship over the other; to do so denies the "freedom not to conform" to conventional family forms.[110] Indeed, the dissent chides the plurality for its repeated references to Michael as the "*adulterous* natural father,"[111] implying that such language bespeaks an anachronistic moralism.

As Robert Nagel has pointed out, the dissent assumes that "[t]he imminence and inevitability of social change make judgments about its desirability futile."[112] By contrast, appreciation of the cultural significance of marriage leads to the conclusion that we need not assess Michael's behavior as a morally neutral choice of "lifestyle," but may disfavor that conduct in the face of a competing claim by the married couple. This approach reflects a belief that law's purpose is not simply the passive accommodation of private behavior. Rather, law may shape behavior in complex ways through its affirmation or condemnation of various types of conduct.[113] The dissent's claim that the situation in *Michael H.* "repeat[s] itself every day in every corner of the country"[114] therefore provides no warrant in itself for legal acquiescence in that conduct. Law may still express a preference for commitment and loyalty, despite the tenacity of contrary behavior.

A final point deserves attention. One may argue that divorce and remarriage are resulting in more and more children who have both marital and nonmarital parents. Insistence upon the priority of one father to the exclusion of others neglects this fact, one might claim, and inhibits the development of what may be a more useful nonunitary concept of parenthood.[115] This argument has considerable force in the context of divorce, where strong parental relationships exist and emerge both inside and outside the marital household. That context, however, doesn't pose the same potential for disruption of marriage as does a situation such as the one in *Michael H.* In the case of divorce, the other parent with whom the father may share the child is a former husband. While this may be the source of some awkwardness, this person doesn't have the same emotional significance to the current husband as does a person with whom his wife has had an affair during their marriage. In the latter situation, there is reason to believe that shared parenthood would be a greater ongoing source of difficulty for the marital unit.[116]

The conclusive paternity presumption thus may be the best we can do under difficult and painful circumstances. Appreciation of the significance of marital status directs our attention in such cases to the interrelated character of the parties' claims. Furthermore, it suggests that the state has a legitimate interest in responding to these claims in a way that reinforces spouses' commitment to each other.

Divorce

Fault. As chapter 2 indicated, the trend in family law is to minimize or eliminate considerations of marital fault in the divorce process.[117] All states now have available a no-fault ground for divorce, and fifteen states have eliminated fault grounds altogether. In addition, fault plays a declining role in determinations regarding property, alimony, and custody. Some states explicitly exclude fault as a consideration in property and alimony decisions,[118] while others, by statute or judicial interpretation, have limited the type of fault regarded as relevant in both economic and custody determinations.

With respect to property and alimony, the most common limitation on the consideration of fault is that misconduct is regarded as relevant only to the extent that it dissipates marital assets. Some courts accordingly have regarded as irrelevant for property division purposes one spouse's attempted murder[119] or abandonment[120] of the other, because this conduct constituted no such dissipation. In the custody context, a narrow interpretation of fault focuses attention on whether the misconduct had a direct impact on the child.[121] As a result, one scholar suggests, in most cases "domestic violence is either deemed irrelevant to custody decisions or is not taken seriously."[122] In many states, then, divorce law is solely a means of adjusting the future financial and parental affairs of the spouses, a function that avoids moral judgments about the parties' past behavior unless that behavior has harmed assets or children. This reflects the tendency of modern family law to see its function as providing a framework for private resolution of family matters, with exceptions limited to the prevention of harm.

The justification for eliminating or circumscribing consideration of fault is that it reduces acrimony in divorce proceedings, and that it avoids the necessity for assessments of marital behavior that a court is ill-equipped to make. If fault is a consideration, the argument goes, spouses will have an incentive to gain advantage by making accusations of misconduct. In addition, they will regard the divorce action as a vehicle to vent the disappointment, frustration, and anger that often accompany dissolution of an intimate relationship. The result too often will be an emotionally wrenching process that makes more difficult a rational assessment about how to order the parties' postdivorce affairs.

Furthermore, some argue, even if we were willing to tolerate this unpleasantness, we lack any consensus about what constitutes acceptable marital behavior. Marriage now encompasses a variety of arrangements and expectations, and we are in no position to say that one pattern of behavior should serve as the norm.[123] For these reasons, we are better off letting the parties work out between themselves feelings of betrayal, guilt, or blame. The law should simply make it possible for them to go their separate ways, by allocating their assets and protecting their children without passing judgment on their actions.[124]

These arguments have some force. Yet we must weigh them against the problems spawned by such agnosticism. First, persons typically regard marriage as a moral venture, which implicates in fundamental ways concepts such as trust, fairness, sacrifice, loyalty, and care. Daily married life derives much of its meaning from shared assumptions about what it means to live a good life together. Our earliest moral lessons are learned within the family; it remains a powerful symbol of what we can legitimately expect from others and they from us. The creation of a new family through marriage is an effort consciously to construct a way of life that resembles, even if it does not replicate, our earliest experience of a shared moral order.

Divorce represents the loss of this structure of meaning. In many cases, that loss occurs despite the desire of one party that it not. At a minimum, there is often asymmetry in the rate at which each party comes to accept the dissolution.[125] As a result, studies indicate that spouses tend to care very much about moral responsibility when they go through a divorce.[126] Spouses struggle to fashion an interpretation of events that can serve as the basis for constructing a new order of meaning that still draws upon certain basic precepts of the old.[127] Legal insistence on a sharp distinction between past and future may be misguided in the divorce context, since "examination of the past and planning for the future may well be part of the same exercise."[128] In sum, there is good reason to believe that divorcing spouses do not regard divorce as simply a technical exercise designed to allocate assets and children.

The excision of fault from the divorce process thus may eliminate any outlet for divorcing spouses to express themselves on things that matter deeply to them. A wife who has provided nurture for her husband through difficult times, only to be abandoned for another woman as soon as his prospects improve, receives no legal recognition that her conduct has been honorable and that her feeling of betrayal is legitimate. It's not surprising, then, that research suggests that a good deal of bitterness still characterizes divorce actions.[129] Despite the reduction in the opportunity for formal assertions of fault, disputes over property and custody are often battlegrounds on which spouses indirectly work through their feelings about the end of the marriage. We must ask whether the provision of an explicit mechanism for dealing with marital misconduct in certain instances might better channel and control these impulses. In sum, one danger with the banishment of fault from the divorce process is that "the people the law seeks to affect themselves think in moral terms. A law which tries to eliminate those terms from its language will both misunderstand the people it is regulating and be misunderstood by them."[130]

A second possible reason for concern is that the failure to provide any sanction other than divorce for misconduct may encourage opportunism in marriage. A wealth of literature, for instance, recounts the necessity for preserving incentives for good-faith behavior in long-term commercial relationships.[131] Parties in these instances often make considerable investments in reliance on the continuation of the relationship, and must remain flexible in their dealings with one another as unexpected circumstances arise. Despite the open-ended character of these arrangements, a body of law has developed that encourages parties to make commitments to these relationships, by assuring them that their investments will be protected if the other party breaches the understanding that has arisen. Standards of fair dealing thus inhibit any inclination to take advantage of a partner's reliance.[132]

Marriage is obviously different from commercial relationships in many important respects. Nonetheless, it's reasonable to assume that all but the most saintly altruist will have some expectation of eventual reciprocity when she acts unselfishly. Some scholars have argued that the consideration of fault in a divorce proceeding is akin to the award of damages for breach of a long-term contract. As such, fault discourages opportunism.[133] If fault is not taken into account, they argue, marriage is essentially an illusory contract, unenforceable because no party will ever be deemed to have breached it. We might then expect a higher incidence of opportunistic behavior, because that behavior will not be penalized in a divorce proceeding.[134] One study, for instance, suggests that spousal abuse occurs more frequently in states that have abolished consideration of fault in the adjudication of divorce and its incidents.[135] Thus, to the extent that law creates a set of behavioral incentives, elimination of fault from divorce discourse may remove a barrier to undesirable conduct.

A final danger is that the declaration that fault is irrelevant may send a message that society is indifferent about marital misconduct. Even if a law technically decrees only that fault is legally, rather than morally, irrelevant, this distinction may carry little weight in a culture in which people often equate legal and moral responsibility.[136] To the extent that this occurs, it would weaken an understanding of the family as the embodiment of relational responsibility. That's not to say that spouses will stop acting altruistically or that egoistic behavior will reign supreme within the family. It is to say, however, that we may lose one form of cultural reinforcement for the notion that marital behavior is amenable to moral evaluation.

The elimination of fault considerations is therefore not responsive to how many parties actually experience divorce, may make opportunism more frequent, and may convey a message about marriage at odds with our deepest aspirations. How might we respond to these concerns in a way that takes note of the problems that we encountered under a fault-based divorce regime?

First, we can conceptualize a fault determination primarily as the identification of behavior that violates certain basic norms of marriage, rather than as the assignment of responsibility for the breakdown of a marriage. The reasons that marriages fail are often complex, fraught with nuances and subtleties that tax our ability confidently to blame one partner for the union's demise. There is reason to believe that the identification of one blameworthy and one innocent spouse didn't do justice to how the parties themselves perceived their relations under a fault regime, given the reports of widespread collusion in manufacturing grounds for divorce.[137]

We should be more confident, however, that there are certain minimal standards of marital conduct on which most persons would agree. Spousal abuse, for instance, is something that the vast majority of people finds reprehensible. Promiscuous sexual infidelity may be another. It's difficult to establish bright-line rules in this area, because circumstances so often determine the moral significance that we attach to given behavior. The range of ways in which spouses can inflict serious injury on one another is limited only by the imagination. Nonetheless, it's reasonable to assume that the average person is capable of identifying conduct that constitutes an egregious breach of marital trust. The law therefore can use fault determinations judiciously to promote the idea of marriage as a relationship of mutual care and responsibility.

More specifically, states can preserve the option of using either fault or no-fault grounds for divorce. We can be reasonably certain that most divorces will proceed on a no-fault basis, given the large number of uncontested divorces even under the fault-based system.[138] We should leave available, however, a divorce action based on fault when a spouse desires legal recognition that a genuine abuse of trust has occurred. This option provides a way of affirming that there are shared social norms that should guide spouses in their dealings with one another. It gives those who have been victimized by the breach of those norms the opportunity to obtain a declaration of that fact and a vindication of their feelings of pain and betrayal. Permitting battered wives, for instance, an opportunity to recount their experience may lessen the prospect that women will blame themselves for the violent behavior of their husbands.[139] The language of fault in such instances is a far more sensitive expression of experience than dry no-fault language that depicts the reason for divorce as mere incompatibility.

In addition, fault should play some role in financial and custody determinations even in states that provide only no-fault grounds for divorce. Treating serious misconduct as irrelevant in these matters sends the message that those who abuse the marital relationship ought to share its fruits equally with those whom they have abused. The notion that only misconduct that produces specific circumscribed forms of "harm" should be taken into account ignores the fact that marital behavior necessarily occurs within a context of interdependence in which cause and effect can't be easily isolated. Serious misconduct disrupts this web of relationships and those who are reliant on it. It constitutes harm to the family unit, not simply to discrete assets or children.

It seems fair to penalize this disruption through property and support awards because the end of the marriage often exposes a spouse to economic hardship that she wouldn't have endured had the marriage continued. Most states, for instance, permit a divorcing spouse to bring a separate tort action for physical or emotional abuse.[140] If there is general agreement that a spouse who seriously misbehaves should suffer a financial penalty through a tort action, there is no reason to refuse to levy that penalty in the form of property and support determinations instead. The law will not want to leave an offending spouse penniless because of misconduct, but the financial effect of the award on that spouse would necessarily be one of the factors that a court would take into account.

It seems fair to take fault into account in a custody determination because the spouse's misconduct has made the child more vulnerable than if the marriage had continued. Furthermore, while the spouse's relationship with the child may be relevant in awarding custody, that relationship can't be segregated from the larger pattern of irresponsibility that the spouse has exhibited toward the family as a unit. A parent ideally provides an example of moral integrity, a concept that necessarily draws on a unitary, rather than fragmentary, understanding of personality. One spouse's serious misconduct toward another must at least be taken into account in determining which parent can better provide this example.

Consideration of certain kinds of fault in financial and custody determinations therefore would affirm the view that marital conduct can be evaluated according to basic shared norms of behavior. It would reject the view that relations between spouses are "private" matters as to which society is incapable or unwilling ever to pass judgment. Instead, law would posit that marital status necessarily involves the assumption of certain basic responsibilities toward one's spouse.

One argument against this approach is that it grants excessively broad discretion to courts to evaluate marital conduct. It's true that a court scrutinizing an allegation of misconduct necessarily would be required to engage in a fact-specific determination with few bright-line rules as guidance. Limiting a finding of fault to serious abuses of trust, however, would narrow the range of behavior potentially subject to sanction. Furthermore, courts already wield considerable discretion when carrying out directives to distribute property "equitably," to decide custody based on the "best interests of the child," or to make various determinations based on a "reasonable person" standard. Achieving justice in the individual case inevitably requires open-ended adjudication, but that is a price that we are willing to pay in many instances in our legal system.[141] Few occasions would seem worthier of the exercise of discretion than responding to serious breaches of the norms that should govern married life.[142]

A second criticism is that fault is unnecessary as a deterrent to misconduct because of the widespread abrogation of spousal tort immunity. An aggrieved spouse can achieve relief through a tort action for, say, infliction of emotional distress without reintroducing fault into the divorce proceeding. A separate tort action, however, is expensive, and there are procedural complexities that may render its use problematic.[143] In addition, some states already require that tort actions be brought as part of a divorce proceeding,[144] which means that a fault determination would introduce no greater animosity than already exists in divorces where a spouse alleges serious misconduct. Furthermore, tort actions may not reach certain conduct that we otherwise would find unacceptable. A requirement that infliction of emotional distress be intentional, for instance, may be difficult to satisfy when a spouse has secretly engaged in a long-term affair that has resulted in systematic neglect of spouse and children. Finally, relegating a spouse to a private cause of action sends the message that her injury is a "private" matter. A tort suit doesn't focus attention as well as a divorce proceeding on the distinctiveness of the marital relationship or the social interest in upholding standards of marital behavior.

A final criticism is that the reintroduction of fault would increase hostility in divorce actions, and would encourage baseless accusations by vindictive spouses or those seeking advantage in property or custody determinations. First, firm application of standards of pleading under Rule 11 of the Federal Rules of Civil Procedure should deter unsubstantiated claims. Courts could make clear that only colorable claims of serious misconduct will pass this test. Second, the abrogation of spousal tort immunity contemplates that acrimonious contests may occur, with the same potential for abuse as allegations of fault. It's better to adjudicate these claims in the divorce forum, where the marriage as a whole is already under review. Third, even under a fault regime, with a lower standard of fault, most actions were uncontested and straightforward. There is reason to think that the availability of no-fault divorce, combined with a more stringent standard of fault, will lead the overwhelming number of couples to file for no-fault divorce without claims of misconduct.

Finally, in those cases in which allegations are brought and emotions run high, the law should acknowledge that it has a responsibility to provide a forum for the expression of these feelings. Providing a peaceful vehicle for airing these grievances may lessen their deleterious effect outside the courtroom. Divorce for many will be their major experience with the legal system. We owe it to them to vindicate their expectation that the law will do justice according to shared norms about how spouses should act toward one another.

Property and Alimony. There has been considerable change in recent years in the way that the law addresses the postdivorce financial needs of spouses. There also has been controversy about the extent to which these changes have contributed to the serious economic hardship of women and children after divorce.[145] The result has been a particularly self-conscious attempt to formulate a theory of postdivorce spousal obligation. In this section, I want to describe how the belief that divorce should effect a "clean break" between spouses has influenced both the initial round of reforms and, more subtly, prominent recent responses to it. I will argue that this belief rests on individualistic premises that need to be supplemented by a relational theory of obligation.

The primary thrust of the reforms that began in the 1970s was to emphasize property division over alimony as the means of ordering divorcing spouses' economic affairs. Traditionally, most states had divided property according to title or other presumptions that favored husbands.[146] Alimony, while never widely available,[147] was intended to provide a source of ongoing financial support for the dependent spouse, either for an indefinite period or until remarriage. While the law has never articulated a specific theoretical justification for alimony,[148] spousal support was generally associated with the responsibility of a spouse at fault to compensate the other spouse for an ostensible breach of marital obligation.[149] In the past two decades, however, all states have made no-fault divorce available, and most states have authorized courts to divide between the spouses all property belonging to either or both of them regardless of legal title.[150] Furthermore, courts are given broad discretion to distribute this property "equitably."[151] Many states explicitly direct that the financial needs of the spouses be taken into account in making this allocation.[152]

Under this scheme, property division comes to take on the function traditionally served by periodic alimony payments. This reflects a preference for a "clean break" under no-fault divorce, which minimizes the need for spouses to deal with each other after divorce.[153] The theory is that all assets are put into a pot, each party is awarded a share, and each then uses this stock of capital to start a new life unburdened by the claims of the past. The image is of members of a voluntary association who withdraw their contributions in order to move on to other ventures; the law's purpose is to help them do so efficiently. This orientation is underscored by explicit declarations that equitable distribution is based on a view of marriage as an "economic partnership."[154]

Alimony's imposition of an ongoing support obligation comes to look suspect in such a universe. The Uniform Marriage and Divorce Act reflects this suspicion in establishing a presumption against alimony, rebuttable only by a showing of exceptional circumstances.[155] Other states provide that property division should precede consideration of the need for alimony, and should supplant alimony awards whenever possible.[156] Still other states limit the receipt of alimony to a relatively brief period.[157] Courts in some states have declared that alimony should be considered for "rehabilitative" purposes only, that is, "payable for a short, but specific and terminable period of time, which will cease when the recipient is, in the exercise of reasonable efforts, in a position of self-support."[158] In the early stages of reform, some courts' perception of a mandate to disfavor alimony led to a limitation on awards even in cases in which the dependent spouse thereby was left in considerable need.[159] Subsequent cases have rejected such harsh results,[160] but alimony awards nonetheless have declined sharply in the last two decades.[161] The first round of reforms thus emphasized the transformation of divorcing spouses into separate individuals, with minimal postdivorce obligations toward each other once assets had been divided between them.

More recent work, however, has criticized this approach as insensitive to the fact that spouses typically have little tangible property available for distribution.[162] Future earning capacity is the most important asset of most married couples, but is one that each spouse takes with him after divorce. Access to postdivorce income thus appears to be crucial to the postdivorce welfare of women and children.[163] Such access is difficult to justify, however, since traditional theories of postdivorce obligation appear to have been undermined by no-fault divorce.

The result has been a renewed effort to find a principled basis for imposing financial responsibility after divorce. One approach has been to broaden the definition of marital property to include items such as professional degrees, advanced training, medical residencies, licenses, and professional practices and goodwill. The theory is that any enhancement of earning power that occurs during the marriage represents "human capital" that is the product of joint spousal efforts.[164] Each spouse therefore is entitled to a share of this capital. Since few couples have enough assets for this entitlement to be paid in full at divorce, the person in whom the investment has been made is liable for periodic payments to the other spouse of her share. This approach justifies postdivorce obligation as the payment of a return on the other spouse's investment.

This theory has met with mixed results. While some states have accepted the approach,[165] most balk at classifying income enhancements as property,[166] while others are selective in doing so.[167] Resistance is based on the speculative calculations necessary to value future earnings; the fact that enhancements do not possess many of the attributes conventionally associated with property, such as open market value or alienability; and the belief that it is inequitable "to pay a spouse a share of intangible assets that could not be realized by sale or another method of liquidating value."[168]

Courts have been more comfortable with a second approach. This is to recognize a right to reimbursement for contributions made during the marriage by one spouse to enable the other spouse to acquire human capital.[169] On this theory, one partner typically sacrifices enhancement of her own earning power by assuming greater household and childrearing responsibility in order to help her spouse increase his. For the latter spouse to retain all the benefits of this sacrifice would be unjust enrichment. Efforts have been made to refine this approach by specifying what kinds of sacrifices should be compensable under what circumstances.[170] Whether the payments are classified as a cash award in lieu of property[171] or as alimony,[172] they are based on a theory of postdivorce obligation as restitution.

Human capital theory is more sensitive than were initial reforms to the effect of marriage on the welfare of spouses after divorce. Its approach, however, still reflects a "clean break" philosophy that emphasizes voluntary rather than relational obligation. Entitlement to postdivorce assets is earned through the specific exchanges and sacrifices that a spouse makes during the marriage. Postdivorce obligation is based on voluntary acceptance by the other spouse of the benefits of such efforts. The objective is to make sure that no spouse gets something for which he hasn't paid full price. Human capital theory thus reconstructs the marriage according to an exchange model of the relationship, which focuses on the implicit costs and benefits of each spousal interaction.[173] Beyond providing compensation for the benefits bestowed by one's partner, a spouse has no obligations that extend beyond the marriage.[174] The emphasis is on paying one's bills and getting on with a new life.

Basic economic justice between the parties is important, and the law should vindicate the principle that spousal sacrifice should be recognized. Human capital theory also is useful in drawing attention to the value of women's nonmarket contributions to marriage. Its limitation of obligation to a strict accounting model, however, has some serious drawbacks. For instance, a husband whose earning capacity has been enhanced by his wife's economic sacrifice would seem to have a plausible argument that she has been compensated for her efforts if the couple has been able to enjoy a higher standard of living as a result.[175] Such an outcome would seem to undermine the theory's utility as a basis for taking career sacrifice into account, but is also consistent with the underlying logic of this approach.

Second, the theory isn't fully responsive to the character of marriage as a shared life. For instance, what of a spouse who became ill or disabled during the marriage, and thus represented a net economic drain on the household? Does she owe compensation at divorce to her husband for his sacrifices that preserved her earning potential? What of a single mother who works two jobs for many years, then marries a man sufficiently wealthy that she can finally afford to go to college? If the couple divorces, does she owe her husband at least tuition and expenses for her college years, if not a portion of her future salary?

In each instance, the logic of human capital theory would demand that the wife compensate her husband. Yet I suspect that a good number of people would be unwilling to impose this burden on her. Indeed, many would argue that she is entitled to some postdivorce support from him. The reason for this difference is a consideration that human capital theory regards as irrelevant: need. The belief that need can be a source of obligation is based on the idea of marriage as a commitment of two people to care for one another. Marriage is a proclamation that one need not battle alone the vicissitudes that life can bring, but can rely on a partner to share the burdens of living in what sometimes seems a capricious and indifferent universe. Spouses agree in essence to pool their risks in face of an uncertain future.

Seen in this way, marriage ideally involves the cultivation of a relational identity that infuses costs and benefits with an intersubjective character. Individual acts take on meaning only against a background of shared commitment; to analyze them apart from this context fails to capture their full significance. Spouses generally have access to marital resources without regard to a strict accounting based on individual merit.[176] The longer they are married, "the more their human capital should be seen as intertwined rather than affixed to the individual spouse in whose body it resides."[177] Over time, then, occurs a process in which daily actions are made with reference to a collective welfare that powerfully informs the calculation of individual utility. Put differently, the boundaries of both identity and self-interest are not sharply demarcated by the individual body.

Human capital theory is reasonable in assuming that, despite this communal experience, spouses still expect some rough equivalence of individual costs and benefits. They expect this equivalence to occur, however, within the context of an ongoing marriage. Specifically, a spouse anticipates that she and her partner will enjoy a roughly comparable standard of living. If we want to vindicate the development of a relational sense of self in marriage and still do justice between the parties, then, it seems appropriate not to try to reconstruct spouses' past behavior, but to compare their postdivorce financial condition. In this formulation, we might think of need as the gap between the higher- and lower-income spouse's standard of living. The difference in earning potential between the spouses arose within a community that deemphasized such individual comparisons. The lower-income spouse relied on the continuation of this community in ordering her life, and the higher-income spouse achieved greater earning potential because of this reliance. This interdependence gives rise to a responsibility that the higher-income spouse can't abruptly disavow at divorce.

How strong was this interdependence? We can't measure it precisely, but time is a good indication of its likely intensity. The longer the marriage, the more the spouses have arranged their lives around its existence, even if their relative satisfaction with the relationship has varied. This suggests that the duration of the marriage should be a crucial, if not the primary, consideration in financial arrangements made at divorce. Specifically, we might aim at equalizing the postdivorce standard of living between the spouses for a certain period, based in some way on the length of time that the parties were married.[178] This approach might replace calculations based on human capital theory, or might be used in conjunction with them to justify allocations that exceed what that theory would provide. The important point is to affirm a theory of postdivorce obligation that is based on the responsibilities that inherently arise within marriage—responsibilities that may continue for some time after it ends.

We should be wary about letting the "clean break" philosophy dominate discourse about property and alimony. Not only does that philosophy have limitations in the context of relations between spouses, but its influence may also attenuate a sense of postdivorce obligation toward children. As Elizabeth Scott notes, in every matter except child support, "modern divorce law encourages parties to put the marriage behind them. Many fathers apparently adopt the general norm and fail to preserve their parental role and responsibility."[179] An approach sensitive to the cultivation of relational identity can help strengthen the sense of both marriage and parenthood as a communal experience that does not leave the individuals within it untransformed.

Marital Contracts. Marital contracts include both antenuptial contracts, executed by parties planning to marry, and separation agreements, negotiated by parties who have decided to divorce. A court typically is asked to enforce these contracts at the time of divorce. Courts in recent years have become increasingly receptive to distributing assets according to the parties' agreement. Some suggest that courts also generally are deferential to provisions relating to child custody and support, even though judicial review of such matters theoretically is supposed to be more searching.[180] One scholar maintains that greater willingness to defer to the terms set forth in marital contracts "dramatizes the preference for private ordering over the intrusion of outside norms as the basis for choices about life- styles."[181]

To be sure, most courts are unwilling explicitly to treat marital contracts identically to any other form of contract. Some states review separation agreements more closely than antenuptial agreements,[182] and contracts relating to alimony more closely than those relating to property division.[183] Some states will review agreements according to their fairness at the time of divorce.[184] In addition, a disproportionate division of assets may create a presumption that the contract was not entered into voluntarily or was the product of fraud.[185]

Despite these qualifications, deference to private ordering seems to be gaining strength as the governing principle in judicial review of marital contracts.[186] Even those states that conduct a fairness or conscionability review at the time of enforcement, for instance, will refuse to enforce a contract only if it leaves a spouse destitute or a public charge.[187] Furthermore, a considerable number of courts focus only on procedural fairness, attempting to determine merely if the contract was entered into voluntarily with adequate financial disclosure by both parties.[188] The Uniform Premarital Agreement Act (UPAA), adopted in eighteen states since its promulgation in 1983, provides that a contract is unenforceable only if a party didn't enter it voluntarily or if the agreement was unconscionable at the time of execution and there was inadequate disclosure.[189] A Texas court describes the UPAA as reflecting the principle that "[p]arties should be free to execute agreements as they see fit and whether they are 'fair' is not material to their validity."[190] Similarly, the Uniform Marriage and Divorce Act makes separation agreements relating to matters other than children enforceable unless unconscionable, and authorizes the parties to agree that the contract may not be modified by a court.[191] Finally, the growing use of mediation in determining the incidents of divorce is consistent with the idea that the parties themselves are best situated to determine postdivorce obligations.[192]

Appreciation of the social significance of marriage as a constitutive relationship, however, leads to some skepticism about claims that contract should be privileged over status as the source of obligations at divorce. First, the interdependence and vulnerability that characterize intimate relationships systematically create unique opportunities for overreaching. The cultivation of a relational sense of identity by definition indicates a disposition inclined to regard the parties' interests as largely coterminous. Such an attitude may undermine the willingness to engage in self-interested bargaining that normally makes us confident that a contract accurately reflects each party's preferences.[193] The party who has a more individuated sense of self is likely to be the one to propose a contract in the first place, to distinguish more sharply the resources belonging to each party, and to seek to limit the other partner's access to assets. Yet this is not the sense of self that the law should necessarily privilege in family matters.

There is also reason to believe that on average men's interests may be better represented in contracts than women's, especially where an agreement is the result of divorce mediation. Men typically have greater economic leverage in negotiating contracts, and some suggest that they are more willing to bargain aggressively than women in contexts in which neither party is represented by counsel.[194] Others maintain that women are more concerned than men about retaining custody of children, and are willing to make financial concessions to achieve this result.[195] The contract paradigm of separate individual bargainers thus may reflect a distinctly male orientation toward personal relationships that systematically disadvantages women. Yet a focus on formal bargaining equality as the criterion for enforceability neglects this more subtle asymmetry.[196]

In addition, there are concerns specific to both antenuptial and separation agreements that militate against deference to private ordering. With the former, the blush of romance may introduce cognitive biases that undermine our confidence that contract terms are the product of clear-headed deliberation.[197] Furthermore, an agreement may be several years old by the time of divorce, and significant changes may have occurred that have undermined the premises on which the original contract was based.[198] While partners may make a concerted effort to speculate on all possible contingencies, there is simply no way to predict the myriad twists and turns that life together may take. Even if the parties or the law provide that the contract is unenforceable in the event of changed circumstances, what changes are sufficient to meet this test will be a source of uncertainty and contention.

Indeed, contract law might disfavor a spouse who responded to changed conditions by being flexible rather than insisting on behavior in accordance with the contract. While this partner might be accommodating because of an expectation that her spouse would eventually reciprocate, she might be estopped from demanding any relief for her sacrifice at the time of divorce, on the ground that she waived her rights under the contract. The only sure way to avoid this is for a spouse to insist on contract performance or periodic amendment of the contract. Yet it's unlikely that parties would avail themselves of the opportunity to do so, and it's not clear that we would want them to. This behavior would regularly inject an orientation that emphasized the distinct interests of the individual parties, and their need to rely on text rather than trust to ensure personal welfare.

Separation agreements have similar defects. They are negotiated during one of the most stressful events in a person's life, when the parties may be in radically different emotional states. The financial and psychological interdependence that typically characterizes marriage creates significant opportunities for overreaching. Yet, as Sally Sharp has shown, contract law generally is inadequate to deal with such dynamics.[199] Doctrines designed to protect reliance, such as fraud, misrepresentation, concealment, undue influence, and duress require the existence of a confidential relationship between the parties. While spouses in an ongoing marriage may be deemed to be in such a relationship, courts often hold that it dissolves when the parties become antagonists. This may occur when one spouse files for divorce,[200] hires an attorney,[201] or simply separates or announces an intention to do so.[202] Furthermore, promises of reconciliation or threats to contest custody often are not treated as instances of duress warranting invalidation of the agreement.[203] Deference to separation agreements treats as classic arms-length bargainers parties whose lingering relational sense of identity should undermine our confidence in the outcome of private ordering.

Problems thus systematically arise in family law from the application of a body of law that takes as its subject a highly individuated self who sharply demarcates his interest from that of his contracting partner. We might be willing to deal with these problems through expanded contract defenses if we nonetheless were committed to private ordering of the incidents of divorce. Yet there are reasons that we should not be.

Deference to marital contracts sends the message that divorce is a "private" matter solely of interest to the immediate parties. Society as a whole, however, has an interest in the welfare of family members after divorce, and in promoting a relational sense of identity within marriage. These interests are vindicated by the position that parties who marry assume certain obligations toward each other based on shared norms. Those norms are reflected in statutes that govern property distribution, alimony, custody, and child support at divorce. Courts already are authorized to conduct an independent inquiry into a child's best interest notwithstanding marital contract provisions relating to custody and child support. The interest in marriage as a public institution also should permit a court to review an agreement regarding property and alimony for substantive fairness at the time of divorce.

This task is no more open-ended than the current directive that a court do equity in dividing property and in arriving at a level of alimony payments in the absence of an agreement. A review for substantive fairness would compare contract terms with what the parties would receive under the statute, demanding justification for material departure from this allocation. It would thus impose a more stringent standard than current fairness review, which typically asks only if a spouse would be rendered destitute or eligible for public welfare. Furthermore, the exercise would be the same as that conducted by courts who examine the substantive fairness of an agreement as the basis for drawing an inference about the voluntariness of the contract. The difference, of course, is that the focus would be not on the procedural adequacy of private ordering, but on the substantive outcome for each party.

The greater judicial responsibility that would result from application of this standard shouldn't be regarded as a nuisance that diverts the courts from more important tasks. Society has a powerful interest both in promoting an ethic of responsibility in family life and in ensuring that those who cultivate this ethic are not penalized for it. It's true that freedom of contract in family law has been of particular symbolic importance as a challenge to the sexism of the traditional model of status.[204] The defects of that model shouldn't lead us, however, to deny the social interest in the terms on which parties divorce. Judicial review of marital contracts based on a new model of status can accommodate our egalitarian commitments while still vindicating shared norms about marriage. It rejects the model of the self that sees these norms as an "intrusion" upon private choice,[205] asserting instead the role of communal values in the constitution of individual identity. Closer scrutiny of marital contracts, therefore, would reinforce the notion that spouses take on distinctive responsibilities that have both public and private significance.

Conclusion

My examination of several family law issues has suggested ways in which we might begin to reclaim a language of responsibility in family life by using a new model of status. Recognizing same-sex marriage would extend institutional support to those who desire to proclaim their commitment to each other. Providing legal protection to certain unmarried cohabitants would protect reliance in intimate relationships by enforcing norms about the responsibility to one's partner that arises from interdependence. Even as we do this, we can still express a preference for marriage by limiting to spouses certain benefits available from the government and from those outside the relationship. A status-based critique of the marital rape exemption emphasizes the distinct obligation that a husband assumes toward his wife, and illuminates how the exemption undermines this sense of obligation. A conclusive paternity presumption can be seen as an effort to reinforce the willingness of spouses to make a renewed commitment to each other despite a history of marital difficulty.

With respect to divorce, retaining a role for fault determinations affirms that there are certain basic norms of marital conduct. We may vindicate these norms by preserving fault along with no-fault grounds for divorce, and by taking serious misconduct into account in financial and custody decisions. In the context of property and alimony, using the duration of the marriage as a basis for equalizing postdivorce standard of living acknowledges the relational identity that emerges in the course of a marriage. This approach recognizes expectations that arise that are not fully captured by cost-benefit accounting. Finally, review of the substantive fairness of marital contracts affirms the social interest in the welfare of those affected by divorce. It proclaims that private ordering is constrained by norms of spousal behavior that can't be readily disavowed.

Analysis of these issues suggests how a new model of status might influence our thinking about family law. In the next chapter, I want to describe and respond to three potential objections to my proposal to reinvigorate status. These objections raise important concerns about both status and family law, and addressing them should help deepen an understanding of how we might begin to construct a new model of status.

6. Objections

In this chapter, I want to address three particularly prominent objections that are likely to emerge in response to my call for a new model of status in family law. The first objection is that status traditionally has been used in family law to reinforce gender stereotypes. A relational identity has been closely associated with women, the argument goes, and women's cultivation of it has been largely responsible for their economic and social disadvantage. A reinvigoration of status in family law therefore would risk perpetuating gender inequity.

A second objection is that status is an artifical intrusion into a realm that should be governed by spontaneous personal emotion. The only meaningful commitment within the family is that which comes from authentic feeling, not legal obligation. By imposing standard rights and obligations regardless of individual wishes, status represents a form of forced loyalty. On this view, the impersonality of status is antithetical to the authenticity we desire in intimate relationships. A reemphasis on status in family law, therefore, would risk distorting intimate family ties.

A final objection is that, even if we surmount the first two objections, it's simply unrealistic to expect family law to affect behavior. It's unlikely that persons in intimate settings take law into account in deciding what to do. A focus on the message that family law may be sending thus neglects the possibility that there may be no audience listening in the first place. On this view, reinvigoration of status in family law would be simply a futile exercise.

These concerns about gender, personal feeling, and the law's effectiveness raise important issues about the role of both status and family law in contemporary society. I address each of these objections in turn in the remainder of this chapter.

Status and Gender

The Objection. A first objection to the reinvigoration of status in family law is that status traditionally has promoted a relational ethic more vigorously for women than for men. The result has been that women are more likely than men to make career sacrifices in order to meet family responsibilities, and therefore often are economically dependent on men.[1] In addition, women take on a disproportionate share of work within the household even when they pursue a career.[2] Only recently have women begun to challenge this inequity by insisting that they be regarded as individuals rather than as "wives" or "mothers." A reemphasis on status in family law, the argument goes, would risk undoing this progress. Even if status is formally gender-neutral, the very concept is so laden with gendered connotations that, however unintentionally, it's likely to reinforce traditional images of men and women. Pepper Schwartz expresses this view in her reaction to calls for more selfless behavior by spouses: "Once again, women are being told that they should revise their lives because the family needs them."[3]

Recent work in what has been called "relational" feminism,[4] however, argues that women have suffered not because the adoption of a relational ethic is misguided, but because in important ways the culture has devalued that ethic. Thus, it is that devaluation, rather than the cultivation of a relational ethic, that should be challenged. The new model of status that I have proposed owes much to the insights of this branch of feminism. Indeed, the objection to status that I outlined above parallels a prominent critique of relational feminism: that it risks reinforcing traditional gender roles. Because of the similarity between relational feminism and my proposed new model of status, exploring the strengths and limitations of relational feminism is a useful way to evaluate the objection that reviving status in family law would perpetuate women's disadvantage.[5]

The Mixed Promise of Relational Feminism. While scholarship in relational feminism is diverse, it is distinguished by the assertion that women in our culture tend more than men to see their identity as constituted through connection with others.[6] The work of Carol Gilligan is the best-known example of this scholarship.[7] Gilligan reports that women in her studies consistently tend to describe themselves in terms of the relationships in which they are or have been involved.[8] This form of self-definition reflects the view that the individual is someone who emerges through interaction with others. Sociality, therefore, is a prerequisite for the development of a distinct sense of self. The result is an orientation that represents the "fusion of identity and intimacy."[9] By contrast, Gilligan suggests, men tend to define themselves in terms that emphasize the ways in which they are distinct or separate from others. This reflects the notion that the individual is prior to its interaction with others. For men, therefore, distance from others is essential in order to attain a coherent sense of self. On this view, intimate involvement with others presents the constant risk that one's identity will be compromised. In simplified terms, then, women tend to see others as a basis for self-realization, while men tend to see others as a threat to it.

Gilligan maintains that these distinctive orientations lead women and men to approach moral decision-making in different ways. Women, she posits, tend to be guided by an "ethic of care,"[10] which focuses on the potential of various alternative courses of action to sustain or fracture actual ongoing relationships. This perspective directs attention to specific people involved in particular relationships, and asks how each of their interests might be accommodated in order to preserve the connections between or among them. Men, on the other hand, tend to focus on generating impersonal rules of justice that are applicable across a variety of contexts.[11] What Gilligan describes as the feminine approach flows from belief that the self is constituted by the relationships of which it is a part, so that maintaining interaction with others is crucial. By contrast, the masculine view regards formal rules as the best way to prevent interference from others that might jeopardize the self. An ethic of care thus emphasizes sustaining connection; an ethic of justice emphasizes preserving independence.[12]

These different perspectives are illustrated in Gilligan's well-known account of the ways in which an eleven-year-old boy and girl approach a moral dilemma with which they have been presented. Each child is confronted with a scenario in which a man named Heinz must decide whether or not to steal a prohibitively expensive drug in order to save the life of his gravely ill wife. "Jake," the boy, formulates the problem as one that presents a conflict between the values of property and life.[13] His tendency to think in abstract terms is underscored by his suggestion that the dilemma is "sort of like a math problem with humans."[14] Jake identifies the logical priority of life over property, and is confident that the universality of this principle would lead a judge to conclude that Heinz had done the right thing.[15] "Amy," however, takes as her point of departure the effect that different courses of action might have on the interrelationships among Heinz, his wife, and the druggist. She is concerned that if Heinz steals the drug he might have to go to jail, which would leave his wife without him.[16] She also believes, however, that the druggist has a responsibility to respond to the wife's condition because he has something that she needs. She thus maintains that if Heinz were to make his dilemma known to the druggist, the latter ultimately would agree to provide it free or on reasonable terms.[17]

For Jake, then, Heinz inhabits a world that maximizes individual independence. The claims that individuals may have on one another arise from a system of rules. When those rules provide the basis for a claim, an individual may take unilateral action to vindicate his right to resources owned by another. The key to the dilemma, therefore, is determining whether the rules justify Heinz's seizure of the drug. For Amy, Heinz inhabits "a world comprised of relationships rather than of people standing alone."[18] The claims that individuals may have on one another arise from the web of interdependence in which each person is located. The key to the dilemma therefore is to make the druggist understand his location in this network of connections.

Relational feminists make the point that society largely has emphasized an ethic of self-sufficiency and independence, thereby devaluing a feminine orientation. Rewards in the form of money, power, and recognition, for instance, have been provided primarily for economic and professional achievements, rather than for less egoistic pursuits such as child care and family nurturance. Furthermore, even those who work outside the home in the care and training of children, such as teachers and child-care workers, tend to be paid relatively low wages. While a relational ethic has the potential to challenge this emphasis, by and large it has been subordinated to it. Society has devoted comparatively greater resources to the promotion of individual achievement than to encouraging attention to the needs of others.

Our implicit model of the person has reflected this set of values. For instance, the dominant theory of moral development to which Gilligan's work is a response asserts that developmental progress consists in moving from an understanding of fairness based on individual need, to a conception rooted in social convention, to a perspective that rests upon general principles of equality and reciprocity.[19] On this view, the ideal moral self is acontextual, distinguished by his ability to resist the pull of claims that arise from specific relationships. Thus, what Gilligan has characterized as a typically male orientation has been enshrined as the standard for all persons. Judged by this norm, feminine emphasis on the specific demands of particular relationships is an example of moral immaturity. Such a hierarchy necessarily marginalizes a relational sense of identity and its ethic of care.

Similarly, the workplace generally is structured around the idea that the typical worker has no family responsibilities.[20] Less than 15 percent of employees, for instance, have jobs that offer any flexibility in working hours.[21] A recent survey of firms with ten or more employees indicated that only 11 percent offered any childcare-related benefits or services to their employees.[22] The most common benefit is unpaid pregnancy leave, which is available to only one-third of employees in medium- and large-size companies.[23] Furthermore, pregnancy often is treated as an unusual condition that requires "special" arrangements, because women have needs that are "different" from those of the typical worker. By contrast, as Lucinda Finley observes, laws requiring employers to make accommodations for employees to participate in military service have not been seen as "special" provisions to benefit workers who are "different" from their colleagues.[24] By reference to the implicit male norm, such needs are not regarded as unusual, despite the fact that only a small minority of employees requires accommodation.

Those benefits that take the form of sick leave and other time off generally must be justified by the needs of the individual worker, and can't be used to take care of others who are ill or who need attention.[25] The exception is personal leave, which is available to only one-fourth of employees, at an average of less than four days a year.[26] Only two states have legislation requiring that family leave be made available to care for newborn or adopted children or for ill family members,[27] and federal legislation that would have provided employees with leave to care for newborn, adopted, or seriously ill children was vetoed by the president in 1990.[28]

Law and social practice thus operate to preserve a rigid dichotomy between the "public" world of work, organized around an implicitly male worker, and the "private" world of the family, tended by an implicitly female caregiver. As a result, women, but not men, "typically view their options as a choice *between* work and family."[29] On the one hand, women can pursue rewards within the workplace in accordance with a traditionally masculine set of values that radically limits their opportunities to establish and sustain family relationships.[30] On the other hand, they can reduce their work schedule or leave the work force for awhile, and face economic and professional marginalization as less than fully committed workers.

Financial arrangements at divorce traditionally also have emphasized individual autonomy rather than continuing responsibility, and thus have accentuated women's precarious financial position. Even before the divorce reforms of the last two decades, alimony was awarded in only a small percentage of cases,[31] and the amount and duration of awards has fallen even lower in recent years.[32] Equitable distribution statutes typically require that homemaking services be treated as a contribution to the acquisition of marital assets, but considerable evidence indicates nonetheless that women continue to suffer far worse economically from divorce than men.[33] A particularly harsh expression of devaluation is the notion that alimony should be "rehabilitative."[34] This suggests that a person who has devoted herself to nurturing others rather than developing market skills needs assistance in order to be remade into a normal individual. Similarly, the emphasis on a "clean break" between divorcing spouses is consistent with a traditionally masculine emphasis on preserving maximum freedom of action.

In a variety of ways, then, women have been disadvantaged by the relegation of a relational ethic to the margins of social life. Relational feminists argue that focusing attention only on achieving equality with men within the "public" sphere risks continuing this devaluation. Too often, the argument goes, equality is based on the argument that men and women are essentially the same. Yet the standard by which similarity is judged tends to be a masculine one, which posits the ideal individual as self-sufficient and unfettered by demands from others. The implicit message then is that true equality requires that women shed their ethic of care in order to become "unencumbered, equally-powered market actors."[35] Relational feminists argue that it would be a Pyrrhic victory if women's progress is defined in such traditionally masculine terms.

Relational feminism thus provides a basis for contesting the assertion that a regime of contract and private ordering in family law offers the best prospect for achieving gender equity. First, it highlights the fact that men typically are in an economically superior position to women within the household. This is because work tends to be organized around male values, and because society rewards those who emphasize career advancement over family responsibilities. This economic advantage in turn translates into greater influence over family decisions.[36] "Private" ordering of family life therefore typically reflects outcomes shaped by asymmetries in power. Contract doctrine, however, treats contracting actors as formally equal, an assumption that mirrors the masculine conception of the individual as separate and distinct from others. This formulation obscures the social context within which individuals interact, and leads to a tendency to regard inequitable outcomes as freely chosen.

Equally important, relational feminism focuses attention on the implicitly masculine model of obligation that underlies an uncritical embrace of private ordering. Conceptualizing responsibility primarily in contractual terms envisions society's basic task as the preservation of a zone of individual independence. In such a world, relationships with others are threatening, and their potential for "interference" must be contained. Treating consent as the basis for obligation in intimate relationships vindicates this image of the fundamentally separate individual. It treats as illegitimate a more typically feminine emphasis on the responsibilities that arise from the experience of a fundamentally social self. Relational feminism thus reveals the ways in which a regime of private ordering may injure women by denying imbalances in power, and by perpetuating those imbalances by continuing to devalue a relational ethic.

This school of feminism has provoked criticism for its attribution of a distinctive orientation to women.[37] Research revealing differences between men and women, critics argue, reflects not the existence of a distinctive feminine perspective but the effects of a system of gender privilege.[38] As Catherine MacKinnon expresses this critique, women's different voice is "the voice of the victim without consciousness."[39] Celebration of women's difference encourages women to eschew individualistic achievement in the name of an ostensibly more virtuous set of values. Emphasis on a relational ethic thus reflects the internalization of attitudes that serve to perpetuate the marginal status of women in supposedly egoistic realms such as the market and politics.

Critics of relational feminism point to the case of *Equal Employment Opportunities Commission (EEOC) v. Sears, Roebuck & Co., Inc.*[40] as an example of the way in which emphasis on a distinctive feminine orientation can be used to justify discrimination against women. In that case, the EEOC brought suit against Sears for sex discrimination with respect to hiring and promotion policies for potentially lucrative commission sales positions. Sears defended the significant underrepresentation of women in these positions as a reflection of women's own preferences. A prominent witness for Sears was Rosalind Rosenberg, a professor of American women's history, who testified that women "often view noncommission sales as more attractive than commission sales, because they can enter and leave the job more easily, and because there is more social contact and friendship, and less stress in noncompetitive selling."[41] The court ultimately ruled that Sears had demonstrated that men and women tend to have "different aspirations regarding work," and that this difference, rather than discrimination, explained the underrepresentation of women in commission sales positions.[42] For some observers, Sears's defense reflected the logical implications of relational feminism. Joan Williams, for instance, argues that the case demonstrates that "relational feminists delude themselves if they think they can rehabilitate domesticity's compliments without its insults."[43]

Fear of reinforcing traditional gender stereotypes also leads critics of relational feminism to oppose measures that arguably provide distinct benefits for women. An illustration of this is *California Federal Savings & Loan v. Guerra*, a case in which the Supreme Court upheld a state law requiring pregnancy leave for women even when disability leave was unavailable for other employees.[44] Some feminists argued that the law was a way of taking into account the fact that women's exercise of procreative capacity interferes with their ability to work in a way that men's exercise of procreative choice does not.[45] Other women's organizations, however, maintained that the provision of unique benefits to pregnant workers constituted sex discrimination, because it expressly used pregnancy as the basis for classifying employees.[46] They argued that an employer should be required only to treat pregnancy no differently from any other physical condition affecting ability to work. Singling out pregnant women for special treatment, they maintained, would encourage ostensibly protective measures that actually limited women's employment opportunities.[47] Critics of relational feminism therefore are wary of emphasizing a distinct women's orientation, arguing that a focus on the similarity between men and women is likely to be more successful in eradicating gender inequity.

Reconstructing the Individual. The critique of relational feminism points up the need for caution in the celebration of a relational ethic among women. First, it underscores that this celebration risks "essentialism"— perpetuation of the notion that women possess distinct qualities that overshadow the influence of race, class, or individual experiences.[48] Second, it points up that this ethic has arisen within a context of power, which has relied upon women's self-effacement for its continuation. As Gilligan herself has remarked, the equation of women's virtue with sacrifice means that too often women assume that "the conventions of feminine care in this society involve the silencing of women. 'Whatever you want, I will do it for you. I have no needs.' "[49] Emphasizing a distinctive feminine orientation thus ironically may be used to justify restricting women to the margins of society.

This suggests that relational feminism ultimately may be most valuable if we regard its affirmation of women's experience not as an end in itself, but as the catalyst for challenging the dominant model of identity.[50] Focusing on gender is important because it reveals the contingency of what I have called the modernist understanding of the self. Documenting the existence of an alternative understanding among roughly half the population suggests that our prevailing image of the person is incomplete, because it neglects important dimensions of actual experience. Demonstrating that the most influential conception of the individual reflects the self-image of a powerful social group challenges the universality of that conception.[51] Relational feminism's emphasis on women therefore can provide the foundation for thinking critically about what otherwise might be taken as natural.

The focus on women's experience is useful for a second reason. Even if we understand intellectually that the modernist view of identity is only a partial one, its dominance makes it hard to envision in practical terms how the self might be constituted through relationship with others. Put simply, what might it mean to live a life in which a relational ethic had more influence? Relational feminism's claim that women have been more attentive to this ethic suggests that we have a fund of concrete experience on which to draw in answering this question. Recent feminist legal scholarship, for instance, has explored the distinctiveness of women's perspective with respect to matters such as the concept of harm,[52] the concept of consent,[53] contract law,[54] the legal standard of the "reasonable person,"[55] tort and criminal law,[56] constitutional law,[57] legal practice,[58] and the process of judging.[59] Feminist historians have provided details about how an ethic of care has shaped the contributions of numerous women not only within the domestic sphere but in the larger community as well.[60] Gilligan's descriptions of the ways in which women in her studies approach moral dilemmas provide specific illustrations of how a relational perspective might shape the process of moral choice.[61] Works such as these offer a glimpse of what an emphasis on connection rather than separation might mean in everyday life.

Relational feminism thus has the potential to challenge the devaluation of a relational ethic, and to provide practical guidance on how all of us might incorporate that ethic more fully into our lives. That doesn't mean that the objective is to make men adopt the orientation of women. Rather, the point is to redress the current imbalance in our model of the human subject, as part of an effort to envision a self that is more attentive to the experience of connection. Ideally, the result will be a conception of identity for both men and women that sees the demands of freedom and relationship as complementary rather than antagonistic, as "distinct but not separate or opposed."[62]

Jennifer Nedelsky's analysis of the concept of autonomy offers a thoughtful example of how such a reconstructive project might proceed.[63] Nedelsky first observes that the conventional conception of autonomy is one that emphasizes the ability to make decisions without being constrained by anyone else's influence.[64] On this view, "[t]he most perfectly autonomous individual is the most perfectly isolated."[65] The central metaphor for this orientation, she suggests, is property.[66] Both literally and figuratively, property demarcates the boundaries between self and others so as to create a zone of individual sovereignty.[67]

If we focus on what actually enables us to be autonomous, however, "the answer is not isolation, but relationships—with parents, teachers, friends, loved ones—that provide the support and guidance necessary for the development and experience of autonomy."[68] As a result, Nedelsky suggests, our model of autonomy should not be property but childrearing. Through childrearing, we see that connection is not antithetical to autonomy, but is its prerequisite.[69] Indeed, the metaphor of childrearing vividly underscores the fact that emergence as a human being itself is crucially dependent on relationships with others. A focus on "autonomy within relationship"[70] would direct attention to the kinds of relationships that best nurture the exercise of individual capacities, rather than to the ways in which we can insulate the individual from having to deal with others. Nedelsky's analysis provides an example of how relational feminism might emphasize an ethic of care in order to prompt a reconceptualization of individual identity. As Lucinda Finley observes, an emphasis on responsibility within relationships posits that autonomy means not simply "determining one's actions through separation from others," but "determining actions by considering others."[71]

The value of this kind of reconstruction is that it enhances the prospect that men and women will recognize their common concerns. In other words, relational feminism's emphasis on difference can lay the foundation for appreciation of similarity. Martha Minow suggests that this is illustrated by the Supreme Court's acceptance in *California Federal* of a law requiring pregnancy leave for all female employees.[72] From one perspective, such a law emphasizes the distinctiveness of female employees, accentuating the way in which they differ from their male colleagues. The Court, however, upheld the provision, observing that it "allows women, as well as men, to have families without losing their jobs."[73] As Minow observes, "the 'difference' requiring 'special treatment' dissolves in the face of a larger similarity between male and female workers, each of whom has the task of juggling work and family obligations."[74] The Court thus replaced the implicit model of the employee as a person without family responsibilities, which labels women as "different," with a model that takes family duties into account. Acknowledging women's typically greater adoption of a relational ethic thus need not lead to women's continued marginalization. Rather, it can serve as the impetus for refashioning our model of identity with that ethic in mind.

This may be the most important step toward the achievement of gender equity, because it challenges the dichotomy between work and family that is the primary source of women's economic and social disadvantage. Furthermore, emphasis on a relational ethic focuses attention on the ways in which jobs often are structured with the implicit image of a male worker in mind. An example of this is the *Sears* case, which critics argue is an example of the dangers of relational feminism. Vicki Schultz points out that Sears's description of the commission sales position emphasized aggressiveness and drive, and that the test given to applicants included questions such as " 'Do you swear often?' " and " 'Have you played on a football team?' "[75] This construction of the job in masculine terms, however, was not inevitable. Earlier in this century, when stores were eager to attract women to retail sales jobs, firms described sales persons in terms of stereotypically feminine traits.[76] Sensitivity to a relational ethic thus can direct attention to the ways in which employers rely on gendered assumptions in creating and describing employment opportunities, and thereby can challenge the standard by which women in the workplace often are labeled as "different."

To speak of a new conception of the individual is not necessarily to assume that men and women will ultimately develop similar preferences. They might, which would suggest that orientations that we currently regard as distinctive to men and women are the product of socialization. Even if it doesn't provoke a synthesis that dissolves current gender differences, promotion of a relational ethic still may create more common ground between men's and women's perspectives. It's also possible, nonetheless, that there is some more intractable biological basis that accounts for some current differences. A reconstruction of our model of identity would account for this by insisting that we recognize the full range of human experience, and that we give at least as much weight to a relational ethic as we traditionally have given to an ethic of independence. Thus, even if some differences seem more durable than others, they could not be devalued as inferior because they deviate from an implicit male standard.

This insistence would dictate that no one, man or woman, be penalized economically or socially by a choice to give priority to family responsibilities. The emphasis would be on what Christine Littleton has called "equality of acceptance."[77] This concept is premised on the notion that equality between men and women should not rest on the premise that they are essentially the same, but on the principle that the choices and preferences of each are equally valid and warrant "equal resources, status, and access to social decisionmaking."[78] Mary Becker, for instance, offers examples of how those who engage in childrearing might receive benefits comparable to those who opt for more traditionally male occupations. Childrearers could be given preferences in employment such as those given veterans in many states; large employers could give parents extended leave while their children are young, just as male inductees were given extended leaves for military service during the operation of the draft; and childrearers could be given Social Security credits in their own accounts rather than being entitled only to claims as their spouses' dependents.[79] Thus, regardless of whether current gender differences persist, moving the relational ethic from the margin to the center of social life would foster a view of the human subject as both worker *and* parent. Achievement of this understanding may be the most important vehicle for realizing gender equity.

A new model of status in family law therefore would heed the demand of relational feminism that we take an ethic of care seriously. It has the potential in particular to impress upon men the importance of responsibility in intimate relationships. My discussion of several family law issues suggests, for instance, that men would not be able to escape obligations to partners by refusing to marry, by drafting contracts, or by filing for divorce. They would not escape accountability for sexual assault on their wives, nor would they avoid penalties at divorce for serious marital misconduct. In various ways, a new model of status would demand that those who typically enjoy more power within intimate relationships must be accountable to those who are more dependent. Even if this doesn't produce significant changes in male attitudes, at a minimum it provides more protection for women than the law currently provides. It demands that those who adopt a relational perspective not be penalized by those who have chosen to focus on professional and economic accomplishments. Ultimately, then, a new model of status can be consistent with our commitment to gender equity both within the family and in society at large.

Status and Emotion

The Objection. A second objection to the reinvigoration of status in family law is that status is antithetical to the cultivation of intimate relationships. Reliance on status as an important ordering principle may be appropriate in the economic realm, where persons enter relationships for the limited purpose of exchanging goods and services. The personal feelings and desires of individuals are largely irrelevant to such interactions, which means that it's reasonable to treat persons as occupants of abstract roles such as buyer and seller. In intimate private life, however, personal emotion is central. People involved in intimate relationships seek affirmation of themselves in all their particularity, and genuine intimacy necessarily flows from the mutual expression of and response to deeply felt emotion. The success of a personal relationship therefore depends on the ability of the partners to shape the terms of that relationship according to their own idiosyncratic desires. Status, however, deemphasizes particularity, attempting to create commitment by imposing standard obligations on occupants of a given role. It thus represents a misguided effort to shape sentiment in a realm that should be governed by natural and spontaneous feeling. Status, in other words, injects the inauthentic into what should be the domain of the authentic.

This criticism assumes that, but for the intrusion of status, intimate personal preferences and actions would spring from some natural wellspring of feeling unconstrained by any social context. As I've suggested, this "expressive individualism" has roots in the Romanticist tenet that the emotions provide a window onto the "true" self in its "natural" state unadulterated by human convention.[80] Recent scholarship into the nature of the emotions, however, places into doubt the account of emotions as internal states located "within" the individual. This work emphasizes that social influences are an integral element in the experience of emotion. Such a "constructivist"[81] perspective calls into question the dichotomy between natural and socially constructed sentiment. Review of this research will be useful in formulating a rejoinder to the claim that status and genuine emotion are antithetical.

Emotions as Internal States. Let's look first at the psychological premises of the notion that the emotions are expressions of an authentic inner self. The theory perhaps most closely associated with this idea posits that emotions consist of different forms of arousal that arise within the individual. From this perspective, each emotion corresponds to a distinct pattern of responses that distinguish it from other emotions. As one scholar observes,

The emotions are generally portrayed in psychology texts as noncognitive responses, mediated by phylogenetically older portions of the brain, and manifested peripherally by arousal of the autonomic (involuntary) nervous system and reflexive expressive reactions. Stated in more picturesque terms, the emotions are brutish, bestial, animalistic, gut reactions.[82]

Thus, for instance, grief can be distinguished from joy because each consists of a distinct constellation of features such as nervous system activity, heart rate, blood pressure, facial gestures, utterances, reports of mental images, and the like. We feel "grief" when we experience one combination of these elements, and "joy" when we experience another.

This perspective draws attention to the interior of the individual and her "internal happenings"[83] or "feeling-states."[84] It is there that the emotions "occur," because it is there that these different forms of arousal take place. As such, emotions are "private and psychological,"[85] and "beyond the scope of social convention and constraint[.]"[86] This suggests that emotions can be isolated and examined as relatively distinctive phenomena in their own right that are located within the individual. The implication of this understanding is that in order to analyze an emotion we should examine it apart from the particular context in which it occurs.[87] This methodology reflects the modernist belief in essences: it takes the view that it is possible to determine the essence of an emotion if we can abstract it from the contingent and superficial forms that it assumes in daily interaction. For instance, while one may feel sadness at the loss of a loved one and at failure on an examination, there is some fundamental quality of sadness that is common to each instance of the emotion.

Another tenet of this viewpoint is that one of the defining features of any emotion is that it is largely involuntary. While cognition may be used in an effort to control an emotion once it arises, it is not implicated in the initial experience of arousal itself. That is something that occurs apart from, indeed often in spite of, any conscious effort to manipulate it. Thus, "a person is 'gripped' by fear, 'falls' in love, is 'torn' by jealousy, 'bursts' with pride, is 'dragged down' by grief, and so forth."[88]

This account of emotion conceptualizes the individual as an essentially passive recipient of emotions. This is understandable in light of Theodore Sarbin's suggestion that "emotion was introduced into our technical language as a metaphor for the passions."[89] As passions, emotions are a class of events that happen to passive victims.[90] This point is underscored by the fact that the words "passion," "patient," "pathology," and "passivity" all stem from the same root, which connotes that a passion "is something that a person suffers."[91] The notion of passivity therefore has been a crucial element in our concept of emotion.[92] An emotion is something that happens to someone, not something she does.[93]

It is in fact this understanding of emotion as a "natural" and irresistible force untainted by human rationality that gives emotion its privileged status in expressive individualism. Romanticism sees the individual as overlain with various layers of social artifice and convention, which tend to repress individuality for the sake of the larger social order. Emotions, however, are those moments of epiphany when a person's true character bursts the bonds of propriety to assert itself in raw, unmediated fashion. The fact that the socialized self seems unable to repress these impulses, that they seem to be uninvited guests that are simply "there," is an indication that they are basic and fundamental to our unique personality.

This orientation sets up at least a distinction, and at times an antagonism, between emotion and culture. Emotions typically are viewed as authentic expressions of the "true" self, as distinguished from those artificial forms of behavior prescribed by social roles.[94] From this perspective, "enacted roles and genuine feelings [are] necessarily in opposition. Since sincerity [is] a matter of feeling, of conscious contents, of impulses and tugs, any mode that deals[s] with rules, standards, manipulated impressions—social constructions—could not approach sincerity."[95] From this perspective, it is not surprising that culture often is regarded as an impediment to the authentic experience of emotion.[96]

These are the premises that underlie the argument that the imposition of status in intimate matters is an intrusion on genuine emotional expression. Our era conceptualizes a realm called "private" life in which emotion is intended to serve as the vehicle for self-discovery and self-realization. Emotion fulfills this purpose because it seems to exist apart from context, and thus appears to provide a privileged window onto the modernist self. To the extent that law fails to defer to feeling, and instead attempts to impose its own standard of conduct in matters of intimate emotion, it interferes with the "natural" order of things. It may be necessary on some occasions for law to intervene to restrain individual behavior so that it doesn't inhibit others' opportunities for self-discovery. Those instances are rare, however; the imposition of status must meet a heavy burden of proof.

Emotions as Social Roles. A large body of recent research challenges the notion that emotions are internal episodes whose features can be examined apart from social context. This work suggests that a more useful way of conceptualizing emotions is as "socially shared patterns of feeling, gesture, and meaning."[97] As such, emotions illuminate not some "real" authentic self, but a more complex interplay between the individual and the the larger social relationships of which she is a part.

Research indicates, for example, that states of arousal generally don't seem to indicate the existence of distinct emotions. The existence of a certain visceral state may indicate generally whether someone is having a pleasant or unpleasant experience, but is not very useful in determining precisely what type of emotion is occurring.[98] At most, some crude form of innate patterning may occur prior to significant socialization, but this doesn't seem to account for the multitude of distinct emotions that people experience.[99] Thus, for instance, we can't identify grief simply by looking "within" the individual to ascertain a unique pattern of visceral reactions that constitute grief. Something more seems necessary to account for the emergence of grief, as opposed to some vague sense of general discomfort.

This point is illustrated by various psychological experiments. In one case, for instance, a patient suffering from a neurological disorder had electrodes implanted in her brain for diagnostic purposes. In the course of the diagnosis, an electrical current was activated that stimulated sensations that typically correspond to feelings of aggression and anger. An interview with the woman at the time of the stimulation indicates that she was well aware of her change in feeling, and that she expressed certain belligerent impulses. She did not, however, describe herself as experiencing anger. Indeed, she did not describe herself as experiencing any emotion at all. When asked to describe her feeling, she said, "I can't describe it, just can act it."[100]

Studies such as this suggest that mere activation of biological responses doesn't ensure that those responses will be experienced as emotions.[101] What was necessary for the woman to experience an emotion such as anger in this situation was a set of contextual cues that provided her the means to interpret the context as one in which anger was appropriate. This, however, was precisely what was lacking. As James Averill observes, "The context (e.g., the hospital setting, the supportive behavior of the interviewer, and the knowledge that her brain was being stimulated artificially) provided no basis for this patient to interpret her experience as, say, anger."[102]

Similarly, in another study volunteers were injected with epinephrine, a substance producing certain physical changes. One group was told of the nature of the changes that the members would experience, while the other was told that the drug would produce no change. Each volunteer was then placed into a room with a person who pretended to be either angry or euphoric. Those who had been told that they would experience no reaction tended to take on the emotion of the actor, while those who had been told of the effect of the drug became neither angry nor euphoric. Once again, context seemed to account for the experience of emotion. Those who were unaware of the physical basis for their sensations sought to account for them by taking their cues from the actor in the room with them.[103]

Such experiments point up the importance of "cognitive labeling" in producing emotional states.[104] The role of such labeling has been explored with respect to emotions such as pain,[105] hunger,[106] illness,[107] sexual arousal,[108] insomnia,[109] and intoxication.[110] In these studies, "the social definition of the situation was a crucial determinant of the meaning people assigned to their bodily sensations."[111]

Thus, for instance, I may experience a general state of anxious arousal in response to being caught in a traffic jam. If I perceive that the reason for the delay is a car going too slowly, I may experience the emotion of anger. If I see instead a sign that says that road repairs are being conducted for the next mile, I may be more likely to experience that same state of arousal as annoyance. Each emotion depends on an understanding of social cues. In the first instance, that understanding is informed by conventional driving practice and assumptions about proper road behavior. If I learn that the slowly moving car is being driven by a frail older person, for instance, my anger may be transmuted into something more akin to resignation or even sympathy. In the case of road repairs, the emotion is informed by an understanding of the practice of making road repairs and the typical consequences that flow from them. If, for instance, I learn that such repairs are being made only during rush hour, my sense of resignation may shift to anger, because this seems to contravene established social expectations.

This focus on the individual's assessment of the situation underscores the role of cognition in the experience of emotion. That is, "we cannot even begin to *identify* the emotion we are dealing with unless we take into account how a person is appraising an object or situation."[112] A person must conceptually organize her sensory experience into a meaningful pattern before she can properly be said to experience an emotion. On this view, a person is not a passive conduit through which emotions express her "true" self in some unmediated fashion. Rather, she is someone actively engaged in an interpretive process that gives rise to those emotions.[113]

This perspective on emotion places social context, rather than atomistic individuals, at the center of inquiry. It asserts that a person can express an emotion not because she has private access to internal states that correspond to a given emotion, but because she understands those circumstances that entitle her to feel certain things.[114] As Rom Harre puts it, we can't understand an emotion in isolation because

what there is are angry people, upsetting scenes, sentimental episodes, grieving families and funerals, anxious parents pacing at midnight, and so on. There is a concrete world of contexts and activities. We reify and abstract from that concreteness at our peril.[115]

Research suggests that individuals are able to ascribe emotions to particular contexts because culture provides certain paradigms that bestow meaning on what otherwise would be random sensory experience.[116] Cross-cultural studies provide illustrations of this phenomenon. Eskimo culture, for instance, emphasizes temperance in expressing both hostility and affection. Eskimos thus recognize several emotions that reflect subtle distinctions among these types of affective states.[117] Javanese culture places a premium on status differences, and the Javanese language gives rise to a range of emotions that reflect distinctions among forms of respectful behavior.[118] In Tahiti, feelings that we recognize as loneliness are not culturally significant. They give rise to no distinctive emotion, but are experienced as "nonspecific, troubled, or subdued bodily states, such as heaviness or weariness."[119]

The Czech author Milan Kundera also provides an illustration of the cultural differentiation of emotion in writing of *litost*.[120] *Litost*, says Kundera, "designates a feeling as infinite as an open accordion, a feeling that is the synthesis of many others: grief, sympathy, remorse, and an indefinable longing."[121] Kundera suggests that

it is no accident that the concept of *litost* first saw the light of day in Bohemia. The history of the Czechs—a history of never-ending revolts against stronger enemies, a history of glorious defeats setting the course of world history in motion but causing the downfall of its own people—is the history of *litost*.[122]

The experience of emotion is thus heavily dependent upon the availability of cultural paradigms.[123] These paradigms provide "sentiment vocabularies,"[124] which furnish categories for organizing and talking about the sensations that we encounter. Once an emotion is named through use of these vocabularies, it becomes "reified"—that is, it takes on the character of an "objective" social fact.[125] The name serves as a symbol around which physical and cultural elements of the emotion can be organized.[126]

James Averill's work on anger provides an example of how cultural paradigms operate. His studies have relied on detailed reports relating to the experience of anger, which contain information on almost one hundred dimensions of the experience;[127] to the reactions of others to the expression of anger, which contain information on more than seventy variables;[128] to the experience of annoyance as opposed to anger;[129] to the temporal dimensions of anger;[130] and to differences between and women in the experience of anger.[131]

Based on this research, Averill has identified at least twenty-eight rules and norms that govern the experience of anger.[132] Some of these rules may be said to be *regulative*. These rules govern when it's appropriate to express anger, such as the rule that anger is more properly directed at a peer or subordinate than at a superior.[133] Other rules, however, are *constitutive*. For instance, the rule that one has the right to become angry at intentional wrongdoing "helps constitute a response as anger (as opposed, say, to envy); it is part of what we mean by anger."[134]

The rules constituting anger indicate that the vast majority of people report feeling anger in response to incidents that are considered voluntary and unjustified, or in reaction to episodes that are regarded as potentially avoidable accidents or events.[135] The first category explicitly implicates concepts of moral fault or blame, while the second draws on the notion that certain conduct is correctable. Both categories thus have meaning only within the context of a culture's social practices. As Averill observes, "it should go without saying that what is considered justifiable (or unavoidable) is dependent in large measure on social norms and customs, and hence may vary from one group to another, from one context to another, and from one time to another."[136]

Averill suggests that the fact that anger typically is experienced in response to either unjustified or avoidable incidents indicates that anger serves the social function of correcting inappropriate behavior. "Drawing an analogy with the law," he says, "it might be said that angry appraisals are like judgments rendered in civil as well as criminal cases."[137] This function of anger makes clear why an understanding of this emotion must be sought in context rather than in the abstract. Almost any potential harm may provoke anger if the harm is regarded as unjustified or avoidable. By the same token, virtually any circumstance that serves to justify an event or make it appear unavoidable will diminish the prospect that an injured party will interpret her reaction as anger.[138] Interpretation of events according to the paradigm of anger requires attention to the nuances and textures of situated behavior. Did someone call to say that she might be late? Did she at least try to reach you even if she didn't call? Was it reasonable for her to leave a message with your seven-year-old son? Might that depend on whether she ever met your son? The experience of anger typically occurs against a backdrop of social practices that make it possible for this emotion, as opposed to another, to emerge.

This observation points up the fact that emotions serve to reproduce a cultural way of life. How we fall in love, when we get angry, when we feel jealous—all this behavior is inseparable from and perpetuates the shared understanding of a meaningful social world. Averill underscores this process when he refers to an emotion as "the enactment of a transitory social role."[139] As such, the experience of emotion is but one part in a larger social drama.[140] Theodore Sarbin also draws on dramaturgical metaphors in suggesting that emotions are rhetorical acts within a script that reflects cultural myth and narrative.[141] Far from representing some privileged realm of existence apart from social roles, then, emotions are inseparable from one's location within a particular context in a particular culture at a particular time.

How can we square this notion of emotion as social role with the perception of emotion as involuntary rather than deliberate? Averill argues that the perception of emotions as nonvolitional reflects not their essential character, but the social definition of those instances in which persons will not be held responsible for their conduct. Thus, he maintains, we might describe our cultural directive for anger as follows:

You should avoid becoming angry. However, under certain circumstances, for example, A, B, or C, a reasonable person cannot help but be angry. If under such conditions you respond in manner X, Y, or Z, then your behavior will be interpreted as a passion, and you will not be held responsible.[142]

The determination of which circumstances warrant such a reprieve depends on what social purposes are thereby achieved. A culture that values strict obedience in children, for instance, might legitimate the experience of anger toward the failure of children to observe strict forms of address toward their parents. By contrast, a culture that places a greater premium on close personal relations between parent and child might not. That culture might instead legitimate anger as a reaction to a child's unwillingness to be communicative about her school day. In each instance, what is crucial in constituting an emotion as nonvolitional is not the parent's internal state of arousal, but the social definition of when it is appropriate for the parent to relinquish close control over her behavior.

Objection to status on the ground that it constitutes artificial interference with authentic private emotions thus appears misguided. Rather than "natural" occurrences whose integrity must be protected from social distortion, emotions may be better conceptualized as enmeshed in a "feedback loop."[143] Culture provides paradigms through which individuals interpret states of arousal in specific contexts. Cognition stimulates arousal, which in turn generates further interpretation, which produces additional arousal, in an ongoing iteration between cognitive and biological processes.[144] The "private" realm provides no insulation from this process because the individual can't escape the fact that she is situated in a particular culture that continues to generate interpretive models of behavior.

More specifically for my purposes here, the experience of intimacy is not the *ex nihilo* product of two acontextual selves. Steven Gordon makes clear the imprint of context on that relationship in describing a lengthy catalogue of cultural influences:

> Lovelorn advice columns, religious tracts, guides to living, and other media are directed to shape our definition and expression of sentiments. Popular psychology books instruct us how to open up to grief, overcome shyness, read others' body language for erotic attraction, and how to say no without feeling guilty. Most popular songs are about love. Their lyrics provide love's vocabulary and the symbols through which it can be recognized. Music arouses appropriate moods as one hears how falling in love feels and what course love follows. Motion pictures depict vividly how sentiments begin, develop, and end in a relationship that is compressed into two hours on the screen.[145]

Similarly, Averill has suggested that the experience of love in American culture is shaped by a romantic ideal, which involves concepts such as suddenness of emotion, idealization of the partner, preoccupation with thoughts about the other person, and a willingness to sacrifice for that person. The ideal provides a perceptual filter through which people interpret and come to understand their experience with another as love.[146]

The analysis of emotions as social roles makes clear that "no desire is unaffected by social forces."[147] This recognition, however, doesn't necessarily justify direct regulation of all aspects of family life. Rather, it leads to the realization that we can't resist regulation of the family in the name of protecting a "natural" realm from the intrusion of artificial influences. The Victorians believed no less than we that their construction of intimate private life was no construction at all, but was merely the ratification of the natural order of things. Feminists in particular have revealed the fallacy of regarding the family as a "natural" zone of privacy,[148] but we need to be careful that we don't replace this image with one that has the individual at its center. There is no natural baseline of individual preferences apart from social context;[149] the question that confronts us is what context to choose.[150] Commitment to freedom of contract does not permit us to avoid this choice, for, as the *Baby M* case makes clear, we still must choose which contracts to enforce.[151] Indeed, one of the reasons that *Baby M* has so galvanized the public imagination is that it brings to the surface the realization that family life is not so much a natural as a socially created realm.[152]

This perspective forces us to see our task not simply as the implementation of existing preferences but also as the inquiry into what kinds of preferences we want people to have. Elizabeth Scott underscores this point in her discussion of the extent to which certain "precommitment" strategies might promote greater marital stability by imposing greater costs on divorce.[153] Scott suggests that spouses in some instances may be inclined to pursue divorce based on short-term desires that actually conflict with a longer-term preference for enduring commitment. Law may make effectuation of such short-term desires more costly by enforcing marital contracts that, for instance, impose a mandatory delay before moving for divorce, or that disfavor the moving party in the divorce settlement.[154] Furthermore, suggests Scott, we may want to make divorce for couples with minor children more costly by, for example, requiring counseling and evaluation of children before granting divorce, enforcing a delay of perhaps two years, and providing more substantial support obligations on divorcing parents.[155]

Scott regards such measures explicitly as vehicles for shaping attitudes about marriage. She argues that current divorce law vindicates a vision of marriage as an arrangement for individual gratification to which each partner makes a limited commitment.[156] By contrast, she maintains, modifications in divorce law may promote the idea of marriage as an enduring and stable relationship.[157] By becoming a part of the context of marital experience, then, precommitment mechanisms may help reshape the self and its sentiments so as to reinforce intimate commitment.[158]

In sum, the objection to status in family law as an artificial intrusion on authentic private sentiment is based upon an untenable dichotomy between social and individual experience. Indeed, belief that we can preserve a natural domain for the acontextual self can be perilous because it obscures the effect of numerous social messages, such as consumerism, that help shape the individual. As Ralph Turner has observed, "if impulses are generated in unrecognized ways by the social order and follow unsensed but consistent patterns, the impulsive self is as much a vehicle for social control as the institutional self."[159] A categorical embrace of private ordering thus can undermine the very quest for self-determination that is its professed rationale.

Appreciation that we are inescapably situated within context suggests that neither independence nor interdependence represents a stable "fact" of social life. Rather, these concepts are conclusions about whether our individual or social dimension should be regarded as more significant in a given situation. If we're to do justice to our complex duality, we need to preserve a place for status as a reminder of the web of connections that we spin and the responsibilities that arise from it.

Status and Family Behavior

The Objection. A final objection to a revival of status in family life is that, even if we concede that conceptions of intimacy are shaped by cultural influences, it's erroneous to assume that law plays an important role in this process. Most individuals probably know little about the laws that purport to govern their family matters. Furthermore, it's unlikely that those who do know the law take account of it in deciding how to behave in intimate settings. Other cultural influences, such as socioeconomic status, race, gender, the media, religious traditions, and personal family history vastly overshadow whatever contribution the law might make. A reinvigoration of status, therefore, would impose greater restraints on personal behavior without any corresponding benefits. Family law should attempt only to accommodate individual behavior, and leave the task of modifying that behavior to other social institutions.

This critique reflects what we might call a "regulative" view of law: law sets forth what people must do in order to accomplish their purposes, and people take these directives into account in ordering their behavior. On this view, law is driven by and reflects social attitudes. I want to contrast this understanding with what I will call a "constitutive" model of law. This posits that law serves in part to help constitute a culture, which means that it not only reflects but can shape the purposes that people pursue.[160] The constitutive view, I will argue, suggests that family law may play an indirect, but no less crucial, role in influencing behavior within the family. This perspective lends support to the argument that a new model of status may help reinforce an ethic of responsibility in family life.

Law as Regulative. Let's look first at the regulative theory. A representative example is Justice Holmes's well-known "bad man" theory of the law:

If you want to know the law and nothing else, you must look at it as a bad man, who cares only for the material consequences which such knowledge enables him to predict, not as a good one, who finds his reasons for conduct whether inside the law or outside of it, in the vaguer sanctions of conscience.[161]

On this view, law matters because people act differently than they would in its absence. Companies who want to undertake an initial public offering, for instance, are guided by statutes, agency regulations, and case law in determining what they must do in order to accomplish their objective. Similarly, police officers who desire to question a suspect in custody know that they must inform her of her constitutional rights in certain instances before they can commence interrogation.

The regulative perspective sees law primarily as a reflection of existing social attitudes and values that are formed apart from it. The image is of a group of people who want to do something and who utilize law as an instrument for accomplishing it. People who want to build a house, for instance, draw up blueprints. These blueprints govern what the people do on any given day, in the sense that they'll refer to them in ordering their behavior. The blueprint is followed, however, only as long as it seems to be an effective way to achieve the purpose for which it was created.

Furthermore, if people's purposes change, the blueprint will be changed as well, or even abandoned. The blueprint takes as given the purpose of building a house and is a vehicle for attaining that end. It doesn't, however, create the desire to build the house in the first place, nor does it prevent people from changing their minds and deciding to turn the land into a park. Preferences are thus exogenous to the blueprint; it is a passive means for their effectuation, not a catalyst for their reconsideration.

Holmes reflects this notion of preferences as exogenous in his description of the prototypical subject of the law as someone who finds his "reasons for conduct" in the "vaguer sanctions of conscience."[162] Similarly, Grant Gilmore articulates the idea that law is the passive repository of social attitudes: "Law reflects, but in no sense determines the moral wisdom of a society. The values of a reasonably just society will reflect themselves in a reasonably just law.... The values of an unjust society will reflect themselves in an unjust law."[163] The regulative theory thus regards law primarily as a conversation about means, not ends.

On the regulative view of things, family law doesn't seem to matter very much. It seems highly unlikely that people take account of the law in deciding how they'll interact with spouses, parents, or children.[164] At best (or worst), they take legal considerations into account after they have already decided that they don't want to live together as a family anymore. In that instance, of course, family law matters because it has consequences for things like property distribution and child custody. Family law thus seems to be irrelevant to the everyday functioning of ongoing families. It's as if the law were relevant to companies only when they decided to go bankrupt.

One prominent piece of evidence for this thesis is the fact that family law is marked by the virtual absence of any precise rules. There's nothing comparable, for instance, to the detailed requirements of what must be included in the prospectus for a stock offering, or the explication of conditions under which competitors may merge without running afoul of the antitrust laws. Instead, it seems, as one friend exclaimed to me after teaching family law for the first time: "There's no law; it's all equity!" Family law typically is framed in terms of broad standards: custody determinations are made according to the "best interests of the child," support awards are modified in the event of "changed circumstances," and marriages are dissolved if they are "irretrievably broken." Small wonder that family law seems to make no contribution to life in ongoing families, but appears merely to ratify what people already think and do. Instead of detailed blueprints for guidance, family law just seems to offer a picture of a completed house. A model of law as regulative would therefore be skeptical about the claim that a reinvigoration of status in family law would have much effect on behavior.

Law as Constitutive. A constitutive theory of law offers a bit more hope for family law. On that theory, "[i]deas in legal texts migrate into other contexts, connect there with other ideas, and are sometimes internalized."[165] Preferences are not exogenous to law, but in fact can be shaped by it. Law thus matters not only as a regulative phenomenon but also as a means of shaping the values of persons within a given culture. James Boyd White provides a statement of this view when he argues that law is

a language in which our perceptions of the natural universe are constructed and related, in which our values and motives are defined, in which our methods of reasoning are elaborated and enacted; and it gives us our terms for constructing a social universe by defining roles and actors and by establishing expectations as to the propriety of speech and conduct.[166]

How might family law do this? How might it "matter" in this way? One clue may be its overwhelming preference for standards over rules.[167] In its starkest form, a rule, in the words of Duncan Kennedy, directs someone to "respond to the presence together of each of a list of easily distinguishable factual aspects of a situation by intervening in a determinate way."[168] The minimum age for marriage, for instance, is one of the rare examples of this paradigm in family law. By contrast, a standard "refers directly to one of the substantive objectives of the legal order."[169] It requires a person to assess the facts in a given situation in light of the purposes embodied in the standard.[170] A statute that directs a judge to divide marital property "equitably" upon divorce, for instance, is exemplary of a standard. The court's mandate in that instance is to weigh various facts about the relationship of the parties and simply to do justice between them.

Standards therefore direct our attention immediately to purposes. This isn't to say, of course, that we don't talk about purposes with respect to rules as well. We do, but this typically isn't our point of departure. An argument over antitrust law, for instance, may have as its primary focus the issue of whether a firm does or doesn't have a certain market share, which in turn generates questions about the definition of the relevant market. At some point, one or both of the parties (more likely the one who would be disfavored under literal application of the rule) will invoke in her behalf the broader purpose of promoting competition. This is the end; preventing the accumulation of a certain market share is the means. An argument based on the "end" of a law, however, is often at the end of the brief as well. The reference to "policy" tends to be icing on the cake rather than the heart of the argument. Rules discourse thus tends to spend more time discussing means than ends.

By contrast, standards discourse from the outset explicitly requires consideration of ends. In this sense, it is indeed apt to say that family law offers a picture of a completed house for guidance rather than a set of blueprints. It forces us to talk about what we ultimately want to accomplish, and how a particular set of facts should be resolved so that we do so. This makes discussion highly contextual, dependent on a myriad of factors that are difficult to generalize from case to case.[171] A mother may be awarded custody because of a combination of, say, fifteen different factors. If any one of them had been different—the father rather than she helps with homework—the decision might have gone the other way. A standard puts a premium on what Clifford Geertz in another context calls "thick description"[172]: a focus on "what, in this time, or that place, specific people say, what they do, what is done to them, from the whole vast business of the world."[173]

The highly contextual and ends-oriented approach of family law makes it a particularly self-conscious form of practical reasoning.[174] That is, family law typically focuses on the question of what kind of conduct comprises "the means of living well,"[175] and poses this question in a way that requires full attention to the minute details of daily experience, rather than to rules that abstract from that experience. As practical reasoning, then, it deemphasizes "knowledge of a set of generalizations or maxims which may provide our practical inferences with major premises[.]"[176] Rather, it cultivates "the kind of capacity for judgment which the agent possesses in knowing how to select among the relevant stock of maxims and how to apply them in particular situations."[177] Is it better for a hostile child to be able to discontinue visitation with his father, or should contact be maintained for the sake of a possible future relationship? Should a spouse share in the benefits of a medical degree even though she didn't help pay for it? Should unmarried persons who separate share property in the same way as married persons who divorce? The persistent focus is on ends: What kind of life should we lead, and how can we lead it?

The examination of ends requires reflection on identity; I can only know what I want if I have a sense of who I am. The very notion of a person who wants to achieve certain purposes requires locating that person within a framework in which choices have meaning. Each direction that I can take moves me toward or away from the vindication of a certain identity. If I am an executive who sees myself as the steward of a family business that my children will inherit, I may not want to engage in a public offering for fear that the family will lose control over the company. If I see myself instead as a corporate manager whose career prospects depend on the profitability of the company, I may see a public offering as a desirable way of obtaining more capital. I may, of course, see myself partly as each. The point, however, is that each identity situates me within a different frame of meaning, in which I can evaluate certain courses of action as desirable or not.

While I can't know what's important to me without knowing who I am, I also can't know who I am without a sense of what's important to me. As Charles Taylor puts it, a sense of identity is dependent on locating the "self in moral space."[178] This is because

[to] know who I am is a species of knowing where I stand. My identity is defined by the commitments and identifications which provide the frame or horizon within which I can try to determine from case to case what is good, or valuable, or what ought to be done, or what I endorse or oppose. In other words, it is the horizon within which I am capable of taking a stand.[179]

Gaining a sense of this horizon can be seen as the process of thinking of oneself in terms of a narrative. A narrative defines me as an actor in a larger story, connecting the present meaningfully both to the past from which it emerged and the future that it might become.[180] Seeing oneself as the first-generation daughter of Vietnamese immigrants, or as African-American, or as a Democrat, or as a public official all invoke distinct frames of reference in which some things have more significance than others. "The narrative phenomenon of embedding is crucial," Alasdair MacIntyre observes, since "the history of each of our lives is generally and characteristically embedded in and made intelligible in terms of the larger and longer histories of a number of traditions."[181]

Practical reasoning thus involves situating oneself within narrative traditions that hold out visions of the good life. As we've seen, this requires a simultaneous understanding of both the self and its ends, neither of which has meaning apart from the other. From this perspective, the potential contribution of family law is that it can provide this understanding. It provides a narrative in which the actors are persons such as spouses, parents, and children. These actors are defined in terms of their roles within this script: a husband is "someone who" does X, Y, and Z. The script provides meaning, a lens through which the ragged texture of daily life takes on significance. Put differently, it provides a language in which to tell "stories about events cast in imagery about principles[.]"[182]

Family law thus provides an ongoing model of self-conscious practical reasoning about intimate human relationships. As such, it can offer powerful stories about the meaning of concepts such as love, betrayal, sacrifice, and selfishness. The treatment of divorce as a "no-fault" matter, for instance, may send a message that marital dissolution should be regarded more as a technical problem of incompatibility than as an issue of moral culpability. A presumption against alimony may send a message that the cost of divorce is a one-time exit fee rather than a continuing financial obligation. Treating spousal conduct as segregable into what will and will not harm a child may send the message that self and parent are different beings who can march to different drummers. Each message gives concrete content to what it means to live a good life in intimate settings with others.

These messages are communicated in diffuse ways throughout the culture, through magazines, television, popular novels, conversations with friends, and the like. This process is not a model of precision; we're not entirely sure exactly what message we're sending or how it's being interpreted.[183] "No one can chart with confidence the ways in which laws, customs, new lines of behavior, ideas about law, and ideas about morality reciprocally influence each other."[184] Nonetheless, there is reason to believe that law is a particularly significant source of imagery in American culture.[185]

Family law, therefore, may matter not because people pursue their purposes differently in light of the law. Rather, it may matter because it helps shape selves who find some purposes more worthwhile than others. At its best, as I have argued, it has fostered an understanding of identity as relational, constituted in part by others with whom one is connected in a web of interdependence.

Nothing makes it inevitable that family law will send this kind of message rather than some other. Indeed, if family law is what MacIntyre calls a "living tradition," it will be "an historically extended, socially embodied argument, and an argument precisely in part about the goods which constitute that tradition."[186] The deep resonance of family as a discourse about the relational self, however,[187] provides a rich fund of images and metaphors on which family law can draw. On the one hand, we've seen how this can create idealized expectations about family life that ironically produce a sense of constant disappointment about the gap between ideals and experience. Such disappointment underlies the perpetual longing that often seems to characterize the modern consumer.[188]

Yet these ideals can also serve as an incentive for narrowing the gap. Colin Campbell underscores this point in his discussion of the connection between consumerism and self-image. Ideals, observes Campbell, are inherent in the imaginative hedonism that characterizes consumerism, because "perfected or 'idealized' images naturally offer the greatest pleasure."[189] Thus, for instance, images of oneself as enmeshed in warm and caring family relationships may provide a great deal of emotional satisfaction. In turn, the satisfaction that this idealized self-image brings encourages belief that one resembles the image in some way.[190] This belief can only be sustained, however, "if the individual obtains some external proof, and this must necessarily take the form of conduct in the world."[191] As a result, the individual may be moved to try to realize in actuality the ideal that she has experienced in imagination: "In order to bolster and protect the idealized self-image the individual must now engage in some character-confirming conduct; it becomes necessary to 'do good' in order to retain the conviction that one is good."[192] Thus, the husband who draws from family discourse an emotionally resonant model of commitment may try to live up to that model in daily life.

Family law, therefore, is important because it provides ways in which people can act upon images of themselves as relational beings in the context of a family. If culture doesn't offer these models, it creates the risk that "family" will become a mere sentimental rhetoric providing diffuse images of connection that have no influence over how people actually lead their lives.[193] A poignant illustration of this possibility is provided by the recent survey on American families that I described in the introduction.[194] On the one hand, respondents overwhelmingly described the family in terms of emotional support, a sense of closeness, and shared intimate feelings. On the other hand, they tended not to describe their own families in this way. It's worth setting forth once again the conclusion of researchers: "It would seem that in many families members have positive feelings but lack the skills to express them to each other. They feel love and concern though they do not communicate it well. The caring and loving emotions are present in most families though many do not report the actions that are associated with those emotions."[195]

This portrait suggests a world in which aspiration seems not to affect action, a world where culture fails to provide a language in which people can express their deepest yearnings and realize their most generous impulses. It seems a world in which "family" is a diffuse mood, not a grounding for conduct. In such a universe, we project our intense longing for connection upon others, but lack the means to realize our desires through actual interaction with them. It appears plausible to project at least two scenarios that might result from this state of affairs. One is that the frustration of these desires will only increase their intensity, leading to even greater disillusionment with the everyday experience of family life. The other is that the absence of a vocabulary for expressing these impulses will cause them to atrophy, so that we lose the aspiration altogether.

I have suggested that family status is a way to bridge the gap between ideal and practice. Status creates an identity whose freedom of action is circumscribed by one's relationship to others. This imposition of obligation regardless of personal preference is a way of giving effect to the family ideal in daily life, preventing its degeneration into a sentimental icon that has no implications for actual conduct. Family law thus may matter in a way that is less direct, but no less important, than those laws that people directly take into account in deciding how to act. A new model of status in family law has the potential to contribute to the creation of cultural meaning by constituting and affirming a narrative about family members and their responsibilities to each other.

This is not to suggest that family law alone will bring about changes in attitudes. Indeed, it's probably most accurate to think of family law as interstitial, as providing subtle reinforcement of or resistance to sensibilities whose roots are complex and multifaceted. This suggests that we should be modest in making proclamations about the impact of law in a realm of life characterized by especially powerful sentiments. Yet we also shouldn't underestimate the particular significance of law in American culture.[196] Specifically, while a reinvigoration of status may not reverse modern attitudes that we find troubling, the categorical embrace of contract might well accelerate them by bestowing on them the imprimatur of law. At the very least, then, preserving a place for status may be a way of expressing our ambivalence about the direction of modern family life. As such, it can offer a reminder of the perils of any univocal account of intimate experience.

Conclusion

We need to be sensitive to concerns about gender, personal emotion, and the effect of law on behavior in fashioning a new model of status. None of these concerns, however, represents a compelling reason to eschew reliance on status in family law. First, a new model of status would call into question the devaluation of a relational ethic, which has been a significant source of women's disadvantage. Taking this ethic seriously has the potential to contribute to a new model of identity that is not dominated by a traditionally male emphasis on separation and independence. Second, understanding the social context within which emotions arise makes clear that the choice that confronts us in family law is not between social control and natural feeling. Rather, the question is, how can we promote shared values that reconcile the demands of both responsibility and freedom in specific contexts?

Finally, we can acknowledge that family law may work in both an indirect and diffuse way without dismissing it as insignificant. The law governing the family offers models of identity and behavior that contribute to the creation of cultural meaning. It can provide narratives of connection and responsibility within which individuals can locate the trajectory of their lives. Furthermore, even if family law has but a small effect on individual behavior, we still must choose what kind of incremental contribution we want it to make. The reinvigoration of status affirms that this choice is one that has significance for society as a whole.

7. Conclusion

A picture held us captive. And we could not get outside of it, for it lay in our language and language seemed to repeat it to us inexorably.
—Ludwig Wittgenstein, *Philosophical Investigations*

Raymond and Joan have been married for twelve years, and have a nine-year-old daughter, Melissa. Melissa is quite musically gifted, but has some emotional problems that have required both a great deal of patience from Raymond and Joan and some help from a child psychologist. Raymond is a doctor who is involved in genetic research, and Joan has been an elementary school teacher since she graduated from college twenty years ago. Joan helped put Raymond through medical school, from which he graduated four years ago. She's felt for some time that she'd like to leave teaching, but has struggled to decide what kind of career change she'd like to make.

Joan was diverted from this concern about a year ago, when she began having some problems with her sight. After consultation with various doctors, she was diagnosed as having optic nerve damage. Medication has improved her condition, but the doctors say that there's nothing more that can be done for her given the current state of medical knowledge. They've said that there's a chance that she may gradually begin to lose more of her sight after the next decade or so.

Raymond has advanced quickly in genetic research, and is highly regarded for both his dedication and his creativity. He has become more and more fascinated with the possible genetic component of diseases that are currently incurable, and hopes to contribute to breakthroughs that offer the hope of controlling these illnesses. He'd like to share his interests and sense of mission with Joan, but she's been subject to bouts of depression lately, and he finds it easier to spend more time with his colleagues at the laboratory. Aside from this disappointment, he's also a bit resentful that he's had to take time off from work recently to take Melissa across town to her therapy sessions, because Joan just hasn't felt up to it.

Raymond has begun to feel trapped. He wonders if he has begun to outgrow Joan. They seem to have less and less to talk about, and when they do talk it seems to be mostly about household chores, Melissa's problems, or Joan's efforts to find herself. Raymond has a friend at the laboratory, Brian, who was divorced last year after fifteen years of marriage. Since the divorce, Brian has been able to spend more time in the laboratory and has made a couple of significant discoveries that have advanced the team's research. Brian also seems to be gone every weekend on some outing: white-water rafting, sailing, or flying to New York for a Broadway show. A month ago, he and his girlfriend spent three weeks in the wine country of Italy. Brian is five years older than Raymond, but Raymond feels that Brian looks ten years younger.

Raymond thus has begun to give more serious thought to a divorce. His parents would probably be upset, but his brother has already been divorced. Besides, Raymond's parents live two thousand miles away in California, and he only sees them once every year or two. He figures that he'd miss Joan in some ways, but he could still call and try to be supportive; maybe they could be friends. Melissa would probably be better off living with Joan. He feels that he really hasn't been able to get close to her, and that Joan has been able to help her with her problems better than he has. He could still come and take Melissa to movies or come see her recitals; in fact, maybe they'd be able to relate a little better without having to deal with each other on a daily basis. Divorce sems like a big step, but Raymond doesn't want to see himself slowly stifled as the years pass by.

Right now family law defines Raymond as a husband, and therefore locates him within a particular narrative. His understanding of what this identity means comes from various sources—the media, his dealings with the law, his exposure to people over the years who have been legal persons known as husbands, wives, fathers, and mothers. This understanding makes some courses of action seem more attractive than others because they are more consistent with his part in this narrative.

If family law has worked well, Raymond's sense of what it means to be a husband will at least cause him to think very carefully about the ramifications of what he does for Joan and Melissa. To revert for a moment to Meadian terms, Raymond as "I" is always free to go; Raymond as "me" may feel it best to stay. Family law thus may matter not because it directly regulates Raymond's decision, but because it creates a "me" that can do so. As such, it has the "capacity to encourage the kind of human caring and sense of mutual responsibility for which the contemporary world cries out—even though such sensitivities cannot always be legally required or enforced."[1]

Whether he's fully conscious of it or not, however, Raymond also feels the pull of the acontextual self. The ways in which this ideal is transmitted are both subtle and pervasive. As Raymond deliberates about his situation, he knows little about "modernism," even less about "post-modernism," and would have no idea what an "acontextual self" looks like even if he saw one. If he looks at a recent copy of the *Bethesda–Chevy Chase Almanac*, however, he'll find a photograph of that self smiling back at him, seated behind the wheel of a convertible. The photograph is part of an advertisement entitled "Rent a Father's Day Convertible!"[2] Father's Day is of course a celebration of role. It's intended to honor all those men across the country who have in common the fact that they have helped give life to others who must rely on them to help find their way in the world.

What Dad would like best on this day, suggests the advertisement, is to have a rented convertible for the day or even the weekend. A rental car executive explains how this gift would be Dad's dream come true: "With unlimited mileage he can drive anywhere he wants. . . . Put the top down, fill up the back with clubs, rackets, rods, and coolers—and he's off on the first *all time fun* Father's Day."[3] In other words, the perfect way for Dad to celebrate his status as father—the embodiment of his relationship with others— is for him to hit the road by himself, with "unlimited mileage." The expectation that Dad is guided by a sense of role distance is reflected in the suggestion that he'll be so happy with the car that "he might even invite you for a ride in it."[4] Use of the term "might," of course, emphasizes that ultimately Dad's involvement with his family is a matter of personal choice.

The most important function of family law is to provide an alternative to the picture of the man seated behind the wheel of the convertible. I have suggested that status can make an important contribution to this task by promoting a narrative of the relational self. This process is less direct than the way the law may operate in other areas of life, and doesn't fit readily within the regulatory model of law. It's one that may be more important in the long run, however, because as a form of socialization it may promote "obedience to the unenforceable."[5]

A striking example of the need for such obedience is the continuing failure of millions of fathers to fulfill their child support obligations, despite intensified collection efforts in recent years.[6] Frank Furstenberg and Andrew Cherlin suggest that the lack of success in enforcing child support responsibilities may be attributable in large part to the fact that the law is attempting to "engineer a direct role for fathers in divorced families that doesn't often exist in nuclear families."[7] If this is so, they argue, significant change is not likely to occur as a result of enforcement efforts directed at absent fathers. Rather, what may be necessary is a "deeper and quite radical change in the way all fathers relate to their children. What may be needed is a greater sense of shared responsibility and partnership in childrearing."[8] In other words, the role of father needs to be regarded as constitutive, as part of who a man is, not as something that he might perform when he feels like it. Legal obligation without this picture of the self is likely to be ineffective. Thus, we might use family law to promote the welfare of children not simply by direct intervention in cases of harm but also by fostering a substantive vision of family life that makes a father less likely to inflict harm.

This point brings us back to the Victorians. For all their misguided efforts and flawed visions, they seemed to sense that we need to be rooted in communal responsibility in order to avoid a radical subjectivity that can undermine our efforts at connection. While they bequeathed to us specific family roles that we now reject, they also left to us a discourse in which the concept of family role is a way of expressing our desire for that connection. Despite our distance from the Victorians, the issues that they confronted are perhaps even more crucial in our own age. As Richard Sennett observes, concrete disruptions constantly challenge the notion of a "portable self" who can engage in "mobile role-playing" without scars from the loss of particular connections.[9] Yet, unlike in the nineteenth century, we tend to conclude that "there is no true place to which to return, no home now; if there ever was."[10]

As a result, "[l]acking their self-confidence and hopefulness, we are nevertheless still Victorians in our moral searching and our cosmic homesickness."[11] The closer our search leads us toward the acontextual self, the farther we find ourselves from home: fated to seek a self that continues to elude us, destined to pursue an intimacy that always seems just out of reach.

Notes

Introduction

1. MELLMAN & LAZARUS, MASS MUTUAL AMERICAN FAMILY VALUES STUDY 14 (1989).

2. *Id.*

3. *Id.*

4. *Id.*

5. *Id.*

6. This version of liberalism is commonly associated with J.S. MILL, ON LIBERTY 73–91 (E. Rapaport, 1978).

7. On the family as an institution, see R. BELLAH, R. MADSEN, W. SULLIVAN, A. SWIDLER & S. TIPTON, THE GOOD SOCIETY 11 (1991). On the character and significance of social institutions generally, see *id.* at 3–18.

8. A. MACINTYRE, AFTER VIRTUE 220 (1984 2d ed.). Similarly, Charles Taylor suggests that the characteristic understanding of the modern self is as "an identity that I can define for myself without reference to what surrounds me and the world in which I am set." C. TAYLOR, HEGEL 6 (1975).

9. Berado, *Family Research in the 1980s: Recent Trends and Future Directions*, in CONTEMPORARY FAMILIES: LOOKING FORWARD, LOOKING BACK 1 (A. Booth ed. 1991).

10. Martin & Bumpass, *Recent Trends in Marital Disruption*, 26 DEMOG. 37, 49 (1989).

11. Watkins, Menker & Bongaarts, *Demographic Foundations of Family Change*, 52 AM. SOC. REV. 346 (1987).

12. MELLMAN & LAZARUS, at 29.

13. *Id.*

14. *See* M. GROSSBERG, GOVERNING THE HEARTH 10 (1985).

15. *See* R. BELLAH, *et al.*, THE GOOD SOCIETY, at 3–18.

16. One might maintain that, in light of the historical association of status with ascription and social rigidity, I would be better advised to employ a new concept to express this social commitment. I have two reasons, however, for framing my proposal in terms of a reinvigoration of status. First, the concept is a recognized element of legal discourse,

providing a vehicle for confronting general issues of individualistic and communal dimensions of social life. *See* chapter 4, at 90–97. In particular, legal scholarship in the past few decades has questioned the automatic association of status with restrictions on individual freedom, and suggests that status can in fact serve to create the conditions necessary for meaningful autonomy. *See* M. PHILLIPS, THE DILEMMAS OF INDIVIDUALISM (1983); Friedmann, *Some Reflections on Status and Freedom*, in ESSAYS IN JURISPRUDENCE IN HONOR OF ROSCOE POUND 222 (R. Newman ed. 1962). Second, the concept of status provides a useful linkage to social science scholarship on roles, which seeks to explore the social dimension of individual experience, a subject that is central to my argument. *See* chapter 1, at 8–9.

17. The term is drawn from E. GOFFMAN, *Role Distance*, in E. GOFFMAN, ENCOUNTERS: TWO STUDIES IN THE SOCIOLOGY OF INTERACTION 85 (1961).

18. R. BELLAH, R. MADSEN, W. SULLIVAN, A. SWIDLER & S. TIPTON, HABITS OF THE HEART 111 (1985).

1. The Victorian Construction of Intimacy

1. Queen Victoria occupied the throne from 1837 to 1901.

2. L. STRACHEY, EMINENT VICTORIANS 1 (1918).

3. *See, e.g.*, P. SHELLEY, *Notes on Queen Mab*, in COMPLETE POETICAL WORKS 800, 806 (T. Hutchinson ed. 1933).

4. A. TENNYSON, IDYLLS OF THE KING (J.M. Gray ed. 1983).

5. As M. Jeanne Peterson has observed, "Much of our 'knowledge' of the Victorians has come from their children—Samuel Butler, Lytton Strachey, Virginia Woolf, and other, lesser writers—in what must be the most successful attack of children on their parents in the modern world." M. J. PETERSON, FAMILY, LOVE, AND WORK IN THE LIVES OF VICTORIAN GENTLEWOMEN ix (1989).

6. P. GAY, EDUCATION OF THE SENSES 5 (1984); Howe, *Victorian Culture in America*, in VICTORIAN AMERICA 3 (D.W. Howe ed. 1976).

7. *See* P. GAY, EDUCATION OF THE SENSES, at 17.

8. P. GAY, EDUCATION OF THE SENSES, at 24. *See also* E. MAY, GREAT EXPECTATIONS: MARRIAGE AND DIVORCE IN POST-VICTORIAN AMERICA 21 (1980).

9. *See* M. RYAN, WOMANHOOD IN AMERICA 142–43 (1975).

10. E. MAY, GREAT EXPECTATIONS, at 21. A further qualification is that the Victorian era in England and the United States were not identical. Daniel Howe suggests, for instance, that Victorianism in England had to contend with an often hostile aristocracy, and thus had more peripheral influence than the middle class in the United States. Howe, at 4. Nonetheless, while my focus in this chapter is on the United States, I do draw occasionally on English sources as illustrative of some Victorian attitudes. This is based on Steven Mintz's notion that what he describes as a "transatlantic literary culture" helped shape the Victorian family in both England and the United States through its emphasis on character formation and self-improvement. *See* S. MINTZ, A PRISON OF EXPECTATIONS: THE FAMILY IN VICTORIAN CULTURE 21–39 (1983).

11. Cornell, *Institutionalization of Meaning, Recollective Imagination, and the Potential for Transformative Legal Interpretation*, 136 U. PA. L. REV. 1135, 1144 (1988).

12. *Id.* at 1164.

13. *Id.*

14. In this sense, I see my project as similar to efforts to retrieve a latent civic republican ethic in constitutional discourse, an ethic that can serve as the basis for rejecting the exclusionary, gendered, and militaristic tenets that historically were part of the republican tradition. *See* Sunstein, *Beyond the Republican Revival*, 97 YALE L. J. 1539, 1539–40 (1988). *See generally* Michelman, *Foreword: Traces of Self-Government*, 100 HARV. L. REV. 4 (1986); Symposium, *The Republican Civic Tradition*, 97 YALE L. J. 1493 (1988). Both the civic republican enterprise and my own run some risks. One is the prospect of offering more charitable interpretations than are warranted, which is dangerous because "[t]o pretend that history offers us more than it does undermines the critique of the past[.]" Cornell, at 1205 n. 225. Furthermore, there are hazards in attempting to extract selectively from historical context an orientation rooted in a particular time and place. *See* Kerber, *Making Republicanism Useful*, 97 YALE L. J. 1663 (1988). While these concerns must be kept in mind, I believe that there is sufficient historical scholarship to support the interpretation that I offer.

15. H. MAINE, ANCIENT LAW 168–70 (1864 2d ed.).

16. B. BIDDLE, ROLE THEORY: EXPECTATIONS, IDENTITIES, AND BEHAVIORS 56 (1979).

17. *Id.* at 87, 92.

18. E. GOFFMAN, *Role Distance*, in E. GOFFMAN, ENCOUNTERS: TWO STUDIES IN THE SOCIOLOGY OF INTERACTION 85 (1961). Status and position often are used interchangeably in the sociological literature. Goffman, for instance, says that "[a] status is a position," *id.*, while Biddle prefers to use "position" instead of "status" because of the connotation of prestige that the latter term has acquired. B. BIDDLE, at 92. I prefer to avoid the use of "status" at this point because I will be using it to refer to the formal legal identity that is associated with a role.

19. E. GOFFMAN, at 85. Some scholars refer to those expectations themselves as a role. *See, e.g.*, Heiss, *Social Roles*, in SOCIAL PSYCHOLOGY: SOCIOLOGICAL PERSPECTIVES 94 (M. Rosenberg & R.H. Turner eds. 1981). For an overview of the various strands of role theory, see Lapata, *Role Theory*, in SOCIAL ROLES AND SOCIAL INSTITUTIONS 1 (J. Blava & N. Goodman eds. 1992).

20. This is not to suggest that persons performing roles are mere automatons who have no influence over the content of either those expectations or the extent to which they conform to them. The process is a more complex one, in which "[w]e are active rather than passive role enactors. We not only conform to role expectations, we interpret, organize, modify, and create them." L. ZURCHER, SOCIAL ROLES 13 (1983). Nonetheless, "[s]ome roles, because they are embedded in social institutions and organizations, are not very flexible." *Id.* Furthermore, some roles may be seen as more integral to a sense of self, and thus less consciously contested.

21. I thus follow Wolfgang Friedmann in regarding status as "a useful collective description of legal conditions imposed upon the individual by *public law.*" Friedmann, *Some Reflections on Status and Freedom*, in ESSAYS IN JURISPRUDENCE IN HONOR OF ROSCOE POUND 222, 226 (R. Newman ed. 1962). This definition is broader than one that treats status as arising through ascription, such as the duties and rights involved in the hierarchy of feudal society. *See, e.g.*, Rehbinder, *Status, Contract, and the Welfare State*, 23 STAN. L. REV. 941, 947–48 (1971). My definition encompasses what Rehbinder would regard as "role." *See id.* at 951.

22. Michael Grossberg, for instance, argues that the early part of the century was marked by the embrace of republican and egalitarian ideas that cast the family in relatively contractarian terms, that a reaction against this ideology occurred around midcentury,

which produced a "growing demand for coercive legislation," M. GROSSBERG, GOV-
ERNING THE HEARTH 11 (1985), and that by the end of the century a judicial patriarchy
emerged to reassert state control over family affairs. *See generally id.* (analyzing changes
in law of courtship, nuptial license, marriage qualifications, contraception and abortion,
illegitimacy, and custody). The nineteenth century also witnessed the passage of married
women's property acts in many states, which provided enhanced property rights for married
women. *See* N. BASCH, IN THE EYES OF THE LAW: WOMEN, MARRIAGE, AND
PROPERTY IN NINETEENTH-CENTURY NEW YORK (1982); Chused, *Married Wom-
en's Property Law: 1800–1850,* 71 GEO. L.J. 1359 (1983). Furthermore, the law of custody
underwent significant change within the century, undermining the traditional paternal
presumption in favor of an analysis of the best interests of the child that often relied on a
presumption that mothers were the best custodians of children of "tender years." *See* M.
GROSSBERG, at 234–85; Zainaldin, *The Emergence of a Modern American Family Law:
Child Custody, Adoption, and the Courts, 1796–1851,* 73 Nw. U.L. REV. 1038 (1979).

  23. *See* N. BLAKE, THE ROAD TO RENO (1962); L. FRIEDMAN, A HISTORY OF
AMERICAN LAW 435–38 (1973); W. O'NEILL, DIVORCE IN THE PROGRESSIVE
ERA (1967).

  24. *See* Minow, *"Forming underneath Everything that Grows": Toward a History of
Family Law,* 1985 WIS. L. REV. 819.

  25. 125 U.S. 190, 211 (1888).

  26. J. BISHOP, 1 NEW COMMENTARIES ON MARRIAGE, DIVORCE, AND SEP-
ARATION 7 (1891). *See also* J. SCHOULER, A TREATISE ON THE LAW OF DO-
MESTIC RELATIONS 22 (1870); J. STORY, COMMENTARIES ON THE CONFLICTS
OF LAW 100 (1834 ed.); Wade v. Kalbfleisch, 58 N.Y. 282, 284 (1874).

  27. J. BISHOP, Vol. 1, at 510. *See, e.g.,* Dallas & C. Ry. v. Spicker, 61 Tex. 427, 431
(1884).

  28. *See* J. SCHOULER, at 262. This doctrine had influence well into this century. *See,
e.g.,* Graham v. Graham, 33 F. Supp. 936 (E.D. Mich. 1940).

  29. State v. Walker, 36 Kan. 297 (1887).

  30. *Id.* at 303–4.

  31. *Id.* at 299.

  32. *Id.* at 300.

  33. *Id.* at 313.

  34. *See* W. BULLOCK, A TREATISE ON THE LAW OF HUSBAND AND WIFE IN
THE STATE OF NEW YORK 263 (1897); J. SCHOULER, at 56; Atwater v. Atwater, 53
Barb. 621, 625 (N.Y. 1868).

  35. "Positive law but enforces the mandates of the law of nature, and develops rather
than creates a system." J. SCHOULER, at 5.

  36. *See* S. MINTZ, at 136.

  37. We must also keep in mind, of course, the fact that the refusal legally to enforce
marital duties ratified existing power relationships within marriage, which were themselves
the product of the law. *See generally* Olsen, *The Myth of State Intervention within the
Family,* 18 MICH. J. LAW. REF. 835 (1985). For instance, the refusal to enforce a husband's
duty of support unless a wife was destitute left her dependent on her husband's judgment
as to what was an appropriate standard of living, since legally he controlled most economic
assets.

  38. *See* J. BISHOP, Vol. 1, at 567–73; Westlake v. Westlake, 34 Ohio St. 621 (1878)
(seduction); Higham v. Vandasol, 101 Ind. 160 (1884) (enticement); Rinehart v. Bills, 82
Mo. 534 (1884) (alienation of affection).

39. J. BISHOP, Vol. 1, at 567.

40. *Id.* at 568.

41. *See* J. BISHOP, Vol. 1, at 546; W. BULLOCK, at 140–41; J. SCHOULER, at 291; Durant v. Titley, 7 Price 577 (Pa. 1819).

42. J. BISHOP, Vol. 1, at 543. Provisions for support made after separation had occurred or while it was in process would be enforceable. *See* J. BISHOP, vol. 2, at 546–47; Rethmaier v. Beckwith, 35 Mich. 110 (1876). In fact, nineteenth-century law often treated as divisible that portion of the contract agreeing that the spouses would separate from the portion providing for support for a wife, and then enforced the latter in equity. *See* J. BISHOP, at 544–54, 554; J. SCHOULER, at 292; Hutton v. Hutton, 3 Pa. St. 100 (1846). The rationale for such a practice rested on status: "namely, that a husband cannot by his own wrong free himself from the duty to maintain his wife," and that a husband had the right to "contribute so much to [his wife's] support as he chooses." J. BISHOP, at 544.

43. J. BISHOP, Vol. 2, at 219.

44. *Id.* at 217. *See also* J. SCHOULER, at 291.

45. *See* J. BISHOP, Vol. 2, at 284; Haverty v. Haverty, 35 Kan. 438 (1886); Powell v. Powell, 80 Ala. 595 (1886). Any agreement not to defend a divorce action was void. *See, e.g.,* Kilborn v. Field, 78 Pa. 194 (1875), and a default in a divorce proceeding did not obviate the need to present proof in support of the divorce petition. *See, e.g.,* Scott v. Scott, 17 Ind. 309 (1861).

46. *See, e.g.,* Hamilton v. Hamilton, 89 Ill. 349 (1878); Snow v. Gould, 74 Me. 540 (1883). Bishop described bargaining over alimony as "rather treacherous ground, to be trodden only with care." J. BISHOP, Vol. 2, at 358.

47. J. BISHOP, Vol. 2, at 220 (footnote omitted). *See, e.g.,* Mangels v. Mangels, 6 Mo. App. 481 (1879).

48. J. BISHOP, Vol. 2, at 193.

49. *See, e.g.,* Mehle v. Lapeyrollerie, 16 La. Ann. 4 (1861); Holyoke v. Holyoke, 78 Me. 404 (1886).

50. *See, e.g.,* Fulton v. Fulton, 36 Miss. 517 (1858); Douglass v. Douglass, 31 Iowa 421 (1871). As Bishop stated, desertion was "an absolute and total refusal to discharge the duties of the marriage[.]" J. BISHOP, Vol. 1, at 27.

51. *See, e.g.,* Harratt v. Harratt, 7 N.H. 196 (1834); Smedley v. Smedley, 30 Ala. 714 (1857). As Bishop declared, alleged acts of cruelty "are accurately comprehensible only when contemplated in the light of the relative rights and duties of the parties[.]" J. BISHOP, Vol. 1, at 671.

52. *See, e.g.,* Cochran v. Cochran, 35 Iowa 477 (1872); Morrison v. Morrison, 136 Mass. 310 (1884). *See also* J. BISHOP, Vol. 2, at 110.

53. *See, e.g.,* Stokes v. Anderson, 118 Ind. 533 (1888); Smith v. Brown, 3 Tex. 360 (1848). *See also* J. BISHOP, Vol. 2, at 128.

54. *See, e.g.,* Pitts v. Pitts, 52 N.Y. 593 (1873); Hall v. Hall, 4 N.H. 462 (1828). *See also* J. BISHOP, Vol. 2, at 234.

55. *See, e.g.,* Peck v. Peck, 44 Hun. 290 (N.Y. 1887); Johns v. Johns, 29 Ga. 718 (1860). *See also* J. BISHOP, Vol. 2, at 165; W. BULLOCK, at 272.

56. "The dearest interests of the whole community require that the family should be made as far as possible inviolable, and the policy of the law is against judicial separation of husband and wife for trivial cause." W. BULLOCK, at 252. *See also* J. BISHOP, Vol. 2, at 130.

57. J. BISHOP, Vol. 1, at 23–24. This should not obscure the fact that the ease with

which divorce could be obtained was a controversial political issue in the nineteenth century. *See generally* W. O'NEILL; L. FRIEDMAN, HISTORY OF AMERICAN LAW, at 436–40. Liberalization of divorce laws through the addition of grounds for divorce occurred in many states until the 1870s or so, after which alarm over rising divorce rates and the condition of the family prompted retrenchment. *See* L. FRIEDMAN, at 436–40; E. MAY, at 4; W. O'NEILL, at 231–53. Despite these fluctuations in attitude, even movements toward leniency took the form of providing additional fault grounds for divorce, which reaffirmed the notion of divorce as available for breach of marital duty rather than mere spousal preference.

58. *See, e.g.,* Tumbleson v. Tumbleson, 79 Ind. 558 (1881); Varney v. Varney, 58 Wis. 19 (1883).

59. *See, e.g.,* Palmer v. Palmer, 1 Paige 276 (N.Y. 1820); Everett v. Everett, 52 Cal. 383 (1877). Nonetheless, some states authorized courts to make some provision for guilty wives when equity seemed to require it. *See, e.g.,* Sheafe v. Laighton, 36 N.H. 240 (1858); Miles v. Miles, 76 Pa. 357 (1874); Hedrick v. Hedrick, 28 Ind. 291 (1867). Exercises of such authority, however, were "not the rule, but the exception, which only seldom prevails." J. BISHOP, Vol. 2, at 351 (footnote omitted). *See* Fivecoat v. Fivecoat, 32 Iowa 198 (1871); Deenis v. Deenis, 79 Ill. 74 (1875). More generally, the demeanor and conduct of a wife toward her husband during marriage was to be taken into account, and could work either for or against her. *See, e.g.,* Burr v. Burr, 7 Hill 207 (N.Y. 1844); Stewartson v. Stewartson, 15 Ill. 145 (1853); Jeter v. Jeter, 36 Ala. 391 (1860).

60. An adulterous parent, said Bishop, "should only in the rarest circumstances be intrusted with the custody of a child." J. BISHOP, Vol. 2, at 466. *See, e.g.,* Helden v. Helden, 7 Wis. 296 (1858); Kremelberg v. Kremelberg, 52 Md. 552 (1879). While still disfavored, a parent who had deserted typically did not face quite as categorical a bar to custody. *See, e.g.,* Hewitt v. Long, 76 Ill. 399 (1875); Welch v. Welch, 33 Wis. 534 (1873).

61. *See, e.g.,* Cox v. Combs, 8 B. Monr. 231 (1848); Thompson v. Thompson, 114 Mass. 566 (1874); Peugnet v. Phelps, 48 Barb. 566 (1867); Reed v. Hudson, 13 Ala. 570 (1848). *See also* J. BISHOP, Vol. 1, at 303–8; W. BULLOCK, at 300.

62. H. JACOB, SILENT REVOLUTION: THE TRANSFORMATION OF DIVORCE LAW IN THE UNITED STATES 5 (1988).

63. J. BISHOP, Vol. 2, at 441.

64. J. BISHOP, Vol. 1, at 618.

65. As Richard Chused has pointed out, the enactment of married women's property laws may have represented not so much a challenge to coverture as a means of ensuring the availability of property that would enable women to perform their expanded family duties under the "separate spheres" ideology. *See* Chused. Similarly, the emergence of a maternal presumption for children of "tender years" reinforced the notion of women as primarily responsible for and specially suited to the task of child care. *See* Zainaldin.

66. C. PATMORE, *The Wedding Sermon,* in THE POEMS OF COVENTRY PATMORE 327–28 (F. Page ed. 1949). Patmore was English, but his lines reflect the Anglo-American Victorian premise that "marriage is both a sacred *and* a legal bond; and marriage laws are good and necessary, imposing obligations more to be trusted, as conducing to man's happiness, than the often false impulses of youthful desire." W. S. JOHNSON, SEX AND MARRIAGE IN VICTORIAN POETRY 76 (1975).

67. M. BERMAN, ALL THAT IS SOLID MELTS INTO AIR: THE EXPERIENCE OF MODERNITY 16 (1982).

68. *See, e.g.,* R. BROWN, MODERNIZATION: THE TRANSFORMATION OF AMERICAN LIFE, 1600–1865 (1976); Howe.

69. Howe, at 8.

70. *Id.*

71. P. GAY, EDUCATION OF THE SENSES, at 19. *See also* Howe, at 13.

72. Appleby, *Value and Society*, in COLONIAL BRITISH AMERICA: ESSAYS IN THE NEW HISTORY OF THE EARLY MODERN ERA 290 (J. Greene & J.R. Pole eds. 1984).

73. *Id.* at 307.

74. *Id.* at 308.

75. *Id.* at 293.

76. Zuckerman, *The Fabrication of Identity in Early America*, 34 WM. & MARY Q. 183, 185 (1977).

77. R. BROWN, at 12–13. *See also* A. INKELES & D. SMITH, BECOMING MODERN: INDIVIDUAL CHANGE IN SIX DEVELOPING COUNTRIES (1974).

78. PLATO, THE REPUBLIC 253–60 (B. Jowett tr. 1986).

79. *See* E. CASSIRER, THE PHILOSOPHY OF THE ENLIGHTENMENT (1951); P. GAY, THE SCIENCE OF FREEDOM (1969).

80. *See* Habermas, *Modernity—An Incomplete Project*, in THE ANTI-AESTHETIC: ESSAYS ON POSTMODERN CULTURE 3,8 (H. Foster ed. 1983).

81. K. GERGEN, THE SATURATED SELF: DILEMMAS OF IDENTITY IN CONTEMPORARY LIFE 112 (1991).

82. A. GIDDENS, THE CONSEQUENCES OF MODERNITY 36 (1990). The central role of reflexivity in the modern understanding of identity is explored in A. GIDDENS, MODERNITY AND SELF-IDENTITY (1991).

83. *Id.* at 38.

84. *Id.*

85. *See* D. HARVEY, THE CONDITION OF POSTMODERNITY 11 (1989).

86. *See* Habermas, at 9.

87. M. BERMAN, at 37–86.

88. S. CONNOR, POSTMODERNIST CULTURE 4 (1989).

89. *See* F. WEINSTEIN & G. PLATT, THE WISH TO BE FREE: SOCIETY, PSYCHE, AND VALUE CHANGE (1969).

90. R. UNGER, PASSION (1984).

91. *Id.* at 8.

92. *Id.* at 7.

93. *Id.* at 6.

94. *Id.* at 13.

95. *Id.* at 12.

96. *Id.* For a discussion of the complexity and tensions in Unger's treatment of this theme, see Weinrib, *Enduring Passion* (Book Review), 94 YALE L.J. 1825 (1985).

97. M. BERMAN, at 40.

98. *Id.*

99. *See* S. COONTZ, THE SOCIAL ORIGINS OF PRIVATE LIFE 73–115 (1988); J. DEMOS, A LITTLE COMMONWEALTH: FAMILY LIFE IN PLYMOUTH COLONY (1970); S. MINTZ & S. KELLOGG, DOMESTIC REVOLUTIONS: A SOCIAL HISTORY OF AMERICAN FAMILY LIFE xiv–xv (1988); M. RYAN, CRADLE OF THE MIDDLE CLASS: THE FAMILY IN ONEIDA COUNTY, NEW YORK 1790–1865 22 (1981); M. RYAN, WOMANHOOD IN AMERICA.

Ryan suggests that the frontier family was an inherently evanescent phenomenon, given the brevity and uniqueness of the frontier experience. M. RYAN, CRADLE OF THE

MIDDLE CLASS, at 20. She points out, however, that the frontier family and community drew extensively on New England social traditions. *See generally id.* at 18–59. Thus, the social life in this milieu provides some insight into late eighteenth- and early nineteenth-century social organization.

100. M. RYAN, CRADLE OF THE MIDDLE CLASS, at 233. I must emphasize that I am speaking in very general terms about the broad contours of early modern social life, and that some incipient notions of a distinctive realm of personal family life had already begun to emerge in some quarters before the onset of what we think of as full-scale modernization. Philippe Aries, for instance, maintains that a more self-conscious family organized principally around the task of child nurture began to take form in Europe in the seventeenth century. P. ARIES, CENTURIES OF CHILDHOOD (1962). Lawrence Stone argues that a more distinctive conception of the family informed by an ethic of "affective individualism" had arisen by the eighteenth century in the upper classes in England. *See* L. STONE, THE FAMILY, SEX AND MARRIAGE IN ENGLAND, 1500–1800 221–480 (1977). In addition, Alan Macfarlane has argued that individualistic and family-centered attitudes were well in place in England before the nineteenth century. A. MACFARLANE, THE ORIGINS OF ENGLISH INDIVIDUALISM: THE FAMILY, PROPERTY, AND SOCIAL TRANSFORMATION (1978).

With respect to the United States, Steven Mintz and Susan Kellogg assert that colonial life in Maryland and Virginia was generally characterized by more self-conscious family ties than was the case in New England, although they do emphasize the importance of "[n]etworks of kinship, friendship, and neighborhood" in the Chesapeake area. S. MINTZ & S. KELLOGG, at 36–41, 39. *See also* J. LEWIS, THE PURSUIT OF HAPPINESS (1983); Smith, *The Study of the Family Colonial America: Trends, Problems, and Prospects*, WM. & MARY Q., 3rd ser., 39 (1982). My point thus is not that the family was not recognized at all as an entity in its own right in early modern society, but that such an idea had not yet gained widespread acceptance as a basic principle of social organization.

101. *See* M. RYAN, CRADLE OF THE MIDDLE CLASS, at 25; N. COTT, THE BONDS OF WOMANHOOD: "WOMAN'S SPHERE" IN NEW ENGLAND, 1780–1835 22 (1977); A. DOUGLAS, THE FEMINIZATION OF AMERICAN CULTURE 50 (1977).

102. J. DEMOS, at 183–85. *See also* M. RYAN, CRADLE OF THE MIDDLE CLASS, at 24.

103. M. RYAN, WOMANHOOD IN AMERICA, at 39.

104. *See* M. RYAN, CRADLE OF THE MIDDLE CLASS, at 40. *See also* S. MINTZ & S. KELLOGG, at 7; D. LEVINE, FAMILY FORMATION IN AN AGE OF NASCENT CAPITALISM (1977); E. SHORTER, THE MAKING OF THE MODERN FAMILY (1975); Demos, *Images of the Family Then and Now*, in CHANGING IMAGES OF THE FAMILY 43 (B. Meyerhoff & V. Tuft eds. 1979).

105. M. RYAN, CRADLE OF THE MIDDLE CLASS, at 39.

106. *Id.* at 42.

107. *See* S. COONTZ, at 74.

108. M. RYAN, CRADLE OF THE MIDDLE CLASS, at 50–51. Again, it's worth noting that affective ties among family members, as well as romantic love, nonetheless had begun to gain influence in some quarters. *See* L. KERN, AN ORDERED LOVE 9 (1981); J. LEWIS; L. STONE, 221–480.

109. *See* M. RYAN, WOMANHOOD IN AMERICA, at 53–55; E. MORGAN, THE PURITAN FAMILY 29–64 (1966).

110. M. RYAN, WOMANHOOD IN AMERICA, at 55.

111. M. RYAN, CRADLE OF THE MIDDLE CLASS, at 41.

112. S. COONTZ, at 87.

113. M. RYAN, WOMANHOOD IN AMERICA, at 30–31.

114. *Id.* at 52.

115. N. COTT, BONDS OF WOMANHOOD, at 22. *See also* S. COONTZ, at 92–98.

116. M. RYAN, CRADLE OF THE MIDDLE CLASS, at 233. I must reiterate that there were exceptions to this orientation; my point is that this distinction was not widely accepted as a basic principle of social organization.

117. P. GAY, EDUCATION OF THE SENSES, at 47. *See also* D. CROW, THE VICTORIAN WOMAN 12 (1971); W. HOUGHTON, THE VICTORIAN FRAME OF MIND 7 (1957); Howe, at 3.

118. *See* N. COTT, BONDS OF WOMANHOOD, at 43; M. RYAN, CRADLE OF THE MIDDLE CLASS, at 231.

119. W. HOUGHTON, at 6. For other discussions of the changes associated with modernization and industrial development, see R. BROWN, at 122–58; S. BRUCHEY, THE ROOTS OF AMERICAN ECONOMIC GROWTH, 1607–1861 (1968); S. COONTZ, at 161–209; N. COTT, at 19–62; D. NORTH, THE ECONOMIC GROWTH OF THE UNITED STATES, 1780–1860 (1966); C. SMITH-ROSENBERG, DISORDERLY CONDUCT: VISIONS OF GENDER IN VICTORIAN AMERICA 79–89 (1985).

120. *See* N. COTT, BONDS OF WOMANHOOD, at 66.

121. *See* Meyer, *American Intellectuals and the Victorian Crisis of Faith,* in VICTORIAN AMERICA 59 (D.W. Howe ed. 1976).

122. W. HOUGHTON, at 12. John Stuart Mill's diary entry for January 13, 1854, contains the statement: "Scarcely any one, in the more educated classes, seems to have any opinions, or to place any real faith in those which he professes to have." J.S. MILL, 2 LETTERS 359 (H.S.R. Elliot ed. 1910). Houghton suggests that, while the Victorians wrestled with doubt, "doubt never reached the point of positive or terminal skepticism. It never involved a denial of the mind as a valid instrument of truth." W. HOUGHTON, at 13.

123. W.H. MALLOCK, THE NEW REPUBLIC; OR, CULTURE, FAITH, AND PHILOSOPHY IN AN ENGLISH COUNTRY HOUSE 54 (1877).

124. T. CARLYLE, *Characteristics,* in 3 CRITICAL AND MISCELLANEOUS ESSAYS 32 (Centenary ed. of CARLYLE'S WORKS H.D. Traill ed. 1896–1901). *See also* G.K. CHESTERTON, THE AUTOBIOGRAPHY OF G.K. CHESTERTON 20 (1936); J.S. MILL, THE SPIRIT OF THE AGE 6 (F.A. von Hayek ed. 1942).

125. *See* N. COTT, BONDS OF WOMANHOOD, at 98; C. SMITH-ROSENBERG, at 87.

126. P. GAY, EDUCATION OF THE SENSES, at 446.

127. M. RYAN, CRADLE OF THE MIDDLE CLASS, at 234.

128. *See* P. GAY, EDUCATION OF THE SENSES, at 445; M. GROSSBERG, at 6; W. HOUGHTON, at 393; S. MINTZ, at 194; E. ZARETSKY, CAPITALISM, THE FAMILY, AND PERSONAL LIFE xi (1986 rev. ed.). As I hope to make clear, by "private" I do not mean that the family was thereby insulated from legal intervention by the state. As Lee Teitlebaum has shown, that interpretation is problematic. *See* Teitlebaum, *Family History and Family Law,* 1985 WIS. L. REV. 1135. I mean rather that the notion of a discrete domain regarded as "private" became pervasive in public discourse and helped shape the understanding of social life.

129. *See* S. MINTZ & S. KELLOGG, at 49.

130. *See* M. GROSSBERG, at x.

131. J. RUSKIN, *Of Queen's Gardens*, in SESAME AND LILIES 87 (1900 ed.). *See also* J.A. FROUD, THE NEMESIS OF FAITH, 112–13 (1904 ed.).

132. *See generally* J. LEWIS; L. STONE, at 221–480.

133. P. GAY, EDUCATION OF THE SENSES, at 428. *See also* R. GRISWOLD, FAMILY AND DIVORCE IN CALIFORNIA, 1850–1890 5 (1982).

134. *See* I. SINGER, THE NATURE OF LOVE Vol. 2, COURTLY AND ROMANTIC 35 (1984).

135. In fact, there is some evidence that romantic love and marriage had been seen for some time as antithetical. For instance, Andreas Capellanus indicated in his twelfth-century work ART OF COURTLY LOVE, "We declare and hold as firmly established that love cannot exert its power between two people who are married to each other." Quoted in Monter, *The Pedestal and the Stake: Courtly Love and Witchcraft*, in BECOMING VISIBLE: WOMEN IN EUROPEAN HISTORY 123 (R. Bridenthal & C. Koonz eds. 1977). *See also* D. DEROUGEMENT, LOVE IN THE WESTERN WORLD (1956 rev. ed.). From the mid–eighteenth century onward, however, there is evidence of a trend toward a companionate view of marriage. *See, e.g.*, C. DEGLER, AT ODDS: WOMEN AND THE FAMILY IN AMERICA FROM THE REVOLUTION TO THE PRESENT 8–25 (1980); R. GRISWOLD, at 5–17; L. KERN, at 9; S. MINTZ & S. KELLOGG, at 45–49; L. STONE, at 325–404.

136. *See, e.g.*, P. GAY, THE TENDER PASSION (1986); C. DEGLER, at 14; S. MINTZ & S. KELLOGG, at 46; R. GRISWOLD, at 5; M.J. PETERSON, at 84.

137. GOOD HOUSEKEEPING, Feb. 6, 1886, at 190.

138. S. MINTZ & S. KELLOGG, at 48. *See also* C. DEGLER, at 38–41; P. GAY, EDUCATION OF THE SENSES, at 117–18.

139. *Id.*

140. P. GAY, EDUCATION OF THE SENSES, at 443. Suzanne Lebsock has suggested that the companionate ideal also created the potential for frustration because of the imbalance of power between husband and wife in the nineteenth century. The increased "emotional stakes," she contends, meant that "[t]he rewards could be great, but the potential for disappointment had never been greater." S. LEBSOCK, THE FREE WOMEN OF PETERSBURG 28 (1984).

141. *See* J. D'EMILIO & E. FREEDMAN, INTIMATE MATTERS: A HISTORY OF SEXUALITY IN AMERICA 56 (1988); P. GAY, THE TENDER PASSION, at 418–19; P. GAY, EDUCATION OF THE SENSES, at 117–18; C. MOSHER, THE MOSHER SURVEY: SEXUAL ATTITUDES OF FORTY-FIVE VICTORIAN WOMEN (J. MaHood & K. Wenburg eds. 1980); K. LYSTRA, SEARCHING THE HEART (1989).

142. *See, e.g.*, N. HALE, FREUD AND THE AMERICANS 36–37 (1971); S. MARCUS, THE OTHER VICTORIANS (1966).

143. *See* pp.000.

144. *See, e.g.*, W. ACTON, THE FUNCTIONS AND DISORDERS OF THE REPRODUCTIVE ORGANS IN YOUTH, IN ADULT AGE, AND IN ADVANCED LIFE 133 (American ed. 1865). For discussions of this sexual ideology, see Cott, *Passionless: An Interpretation of Victorian Sexual Ideology, 1970–1850,* 4 SIGNS 219 (1978); Degler, *What Ought to Be and What Was: Women's Sexuality in the Nineteenth Century*, in THE AMERICAN FAMILY IN SOCIAL-HISTORICAL PERSPECTIVE 403 (M. Gordon ed. 1978 2d ed.).

145. Degler.

146. *Id.* at 421.

147. C. MOSHER.

148. *See, e.g.*, C. MOSHER, at 176.

149. *See* Degler, at 419. *See also* P. GAY, EDUCATION OF THE SENSES, at 141. For general discussions of the Mosher survey, see *id.* at 135–43; Degler, at 413–21.

150. P. GAY, EDUCATION OF THE SENSES, at 458.

151. Phillipe Aries has suggested that the beginnings of a nurturant attitude toward children can be traced to the seventeenth century. *See* P. ARIES.

152. *See* S. MINTZ & S. KELLOGG, at 47.

153. *See* M. RYAN, CRADLE OF THE MIDDLE CLASS, at 48.

154. *See* S. MINTZ, at 33. For other discussions of shifting attitudes toward children in the eighteenth and nineteenth centuries, see J. FLIEGELMAN, PRODIGALS AND PILGRIMS (1982); P. GREVEN, THE PROTESTANT TEMPERAMENT (1977); B. WISHY, THE CHILD AND THE REPUBLIC (1968).

155. G. BROWN, DOMESTIC INDIVIDUALISM: IMAGINING SELF IN NINE-TEENTH- CENTURY AMERICA 3 (1990).

156. A. DE TOCQUEVILLE, 2 DEMOCRACY IN AMERICA 506–7 (G. Lawrence ed. 1969).

157. *See* M. GROSSBERG, at 87. Some scholars find this shift in orientation attributable to the more egalitarian ideals of republicanism ascendant in the period following the American revolution. *See, e.g.*, J. FLIEGELMAN; M. GROSSBERG, at 17–30; M. YAZAWA, FROM COLONIES TO COMMONWEALTH (1985).

158. C. DEGLER, at 14.

159. *See* M. RYAN, WOMANHOOD IN AMERICA, at 123. *See also* J. FLIEGELMAN, 123–54; S. MINTZ & S. KELLOGG, at 46.

160. M. RYAN, CRADLE OF THE MIDDLE CLASS, at 185.

161. *Id.*

162. *Id.*

163. *See* S. MINTZ, at 38.

164. *Id.* at 33.

165. *See* M. GROSSBERG, at 11.

166. L. KERN, at 30.

167. *Id.* at 23.

168. K. LYSTRA, at 226.

169. *Id.* at 47.

170. *Id.* at 32–33.

171. *Id.* at 225.

172. *See* W.S. JOHNSON, at 257.

173. L. KERN, at 23.

174. *Id.* at 20.

175. *See* P. GAY, EDUCATION OF THE SENSES, at 271–77; L. KERN, at 32.

176. *See* R. ROSEN, THE LOST SISTERHOOD 38–50 (1982); P. GAY, THE TENDER PASSION, at 352–90.

177. *See* A. TENNYSON.

178. *See* P. GAY, EDUCATION OF THE SENSES, at 141; R. GRISWOLD, at 172; E. MAY, at 157.

179. *See* D'EMILIO & E. FREEDMAN, at 68–69; P. GAY, EDUCATION OF THE SENSES, at 295–309.

180. *See* E. MAY, at 16; D. PIVEN, PURITY CRUSADE: SEXUAL MORALITY AND SOCIAL CONTROL, 1868–1900 (1973); Howe, at 17.

181. *See* S. MINTZ, at 31.

182. *See* N. COTT, BONDS OF WOMANHOOD, at 98; S. MINTZ, at 20.
183. R. GRISWOLD, at 172.
184. E. GOFFMAN, at 106.
185. *See* Turner, *The Real Self: From Institution to Impulse*, 81 AM. J. SOC. 989 (1976). By "institution," I mean not only formal organizational structures, but any "system or pattern of positions" (E. GOFFMAN, at 85) that contains relatively well-defined role expectations.
186. *See* Turner, *Real Self* at 991.
187. *See* Dan-Cohen, *Law, Community, and Communication*, 1989 DUKE L. J. 1654, 1655. Role identification has obvious similarities to Goffman's "role embracement," but the latter focuses most explicitly on the *behavior* of the person in a particular context, rather than on the extent to which the person sees the "virtual self" in that context as constitutive of some basic sense of self. For instance, Goffman entertains the possibility that "[a]n individual may affect the embracing of a role in order to conceal a lack of attachment to it" (E. GOFFMAN, at 107), which suggests the possibility of a divergence between behavior and cognition. *Id.* at 89.

Role identification also bears some resemblance to Ralph Turner's concept of "role merger": "When a role is deeply merged with the person, socialization in that role has persuasive effects in personality formation." Turner, *The Role and the Person*, 84 AM J. SOC. 1 (1978). Turner emphasizes, however, that his concept is "behavioral rather than cognitive," which allows for the possibility that "the individual's stated self- conception may be at odds with the behaviorally relevant merger of person and role." *Id.* at 20.

Finally, I should stress that by role identification I intend to refer to a person's *perception* of the significance of a role to her sense of self. I do not mean to convey acceptance of the *actual* ability of a radically autonomous self to pick and choose which roles to integrate into her identity. As Steven Winter has pointed out, "the self cannot be understood apart from its relations to its roles and other learned modes of interaction[.]" Winter, *Contingency and Community in Normative Practice*, 139 U. PA. L. REV. 963, 987 (1991). As I will discuss in chapter 2, one way in which I contend that we differ from the Victorian era is our greater perception of a distance between the self and the roles that it enacts.

188. Turner, *Real Self*, at 992.
189. *Id.* at 993.
190. *Id.* at 993–94.
191. *Id.* at 994.
192. *Id.*
193. *See* E. GOFFMAN, at 101.
194. P. RIEFF, TRIUMPH OF THE THERAPEUTIC: THE USES OF FAITH AFTER FREUD 16 (1966).
195. P. BERGER & T. LUCKMANN, THE SOCIAL CONSTRUCTION OF REALITY 55 (1966). *See also* R. BELLAH, R. MADSDEN, W. SULLIVAN, A. SWIDLER & S. TIPTON, THE GOOD SOCIETY 3–18 (1991).
196. P. BERGER & T. LUCKMANN, at 58.
197. *Id.* (footnote omitted).
198. "Institutions are embodied in individual experiences by means of roles." *Id.* at 74.
199. S. MINTZ, at 13.
200. *See* S. MINTZ & S. KELLOGG, at 48.
201. *Id.*

202. *See* generally C. DEGLER; A. DOUGLAS; N. COTT, BONDS OF WOMANHOOD; M. RYAN, WOMANHOOD IN AMERICA.

203. *Santa Clara Argus*, Sept. 8, 1866 (quoted in R. GRISWOLD, at 130).

204. J.S. MILL, THE SUBJECTION OF WOMEN 94–95 (S. Mansfield ed. 1980).

205. Wohl, *Introduction*, in THE VICTORIAN FAMILY 9 (A. Wohl ed. 1978).

206. Teitlebaum, *Moral Discourse and Family Law*, 84 MICH. L. REV. 430, 432 (1985).

207. *See* P. GAY, EDUCATION OF THE SENSES, at 224–25.

208. *See, e.g.,* F. CANCIAN, LOVE IN AMERICA 15–29 (1987); S. COONTZ, at 210–50; N. COTT, BONDS OF WOMANHOOD, at 63–100; C. DEGLER, at 52–85; A. DOUGLAS, at 44–79; E. MAY, at 15–48; M. RYAN, CRADLE OF THE MIDDLE CLASS, at 186–229; M. RYAN, WOMANHOOD IN AMERICA, at 139–91.

209. E. MAY, at 27.

210. *Id.* at 157.

211. *See, e.g.,* W. ALCOTT, THE YOUNG WIFE (1837); S. ELLIS, THE WIVES OF ENGLAND (1843); O.S. FOWLER, LOVE AND PARENTAGE (1846); A.B. MUZZEY, THE YOUNG MAIDEN (1841 2d ed.). For discussion of the various nineteenth-century literary forms promoting domesticity, see A. DOUGLAS, at 225–56; M. RYAN, WOMANHOOD IN AMERICA, at 143–44.

212. *See* generally R. GRISWOLD; E. MAY.

213. Susman, *"Personality" and the Making of Twentieth- Century Culture*, in NEW DIRECTIONS IN AMERICAN INTELLECTUAL HISTORY 212, 220 (J. Higham & P. Conkin eds. 1979).

214. SMITH-ROSENBERG, at 213. *See also* N. COTT, BONDS OF WOMANHOOD, at 195.

215. R. GRISWOLD, at 101.

216. *See* Minow, *"Forming underneath Everything That Grows".*

217. *See* L. KERN, at 12.

218. E. MAY, at 28–29.

219. *See* L. KERN, at 31.

220. R. GRISWOLD, at 46; E. MAY, at 17; M. RYAN, CRADLE OF THE MIDDLE CLASS, at 196.

221. H.S. CANBY, THE AGE OF CONFIDENCE 50 (1934). *See also* E. MAY, at 47.

222. Howe, at 26. *See also* R. GRISWOLD, at 174; N. COTT, BONDS OF WOMANHOOD; C. DEGLER. *But see* A. DOUGLAS. Suzanne Lebsock is more equivocal, concluding that her study of women in nineteenth- century Petersburg, Virginia, "affirms that the experience of women in the nineteenth century cannot be readily classified as either decline or progress." S. LEBSOCK, at xv.

223. *See* DEGLER, at 17; S. MINTZ & S. KELLOGG, at 55–58.

224. *See* SMITH-ROSENBERG, at 109–28.

225. *See* N. COTT, BONDS OF WOMANHOOD, at 84.

226. *See* S. MINTZ, at 140–45.

227. *See* N. COTT, BONDS OF WOMANHOOD, at 100; C. SMITH-ROSENBURG, at 60.

228. "Nineteenth-century women—even birth control reformers deemed extremists—considered the fate and advancement of women conjoined with those of the home (and necessarily marriage), not opposed to them." N. COTT, BONDS OF WOMANHOOD, at 192 (footnote omitted).

229. This sense of shared experience also was the basis for networks of female friendship

that flourished in the nineteenth century. *See id.* at 160–96; R. GRISWOLD, at 83–87; C. SMITH-ROSENBERG, at 53–76. While these friendships provided a source of emotional intimacy for women in addition to the family, their foundation was to a large extent the common ground of their gender role. As Nancy Cott says of these friendships, "The irony of the situation was that without marriage supplying women with home and children, the central prerequisite of their sex-role disappeared." N. COTT, BONDS OF WOMAN-HOOD, at 192. Thus, even extrafamilial friendships among women reflected to some degree the centrality of the family in the intimate domain of "private" life.

230. M. RYAN, CRADLE OF THE MIDDLE CLASS, at 232–33.

231. K. LYSTRA, at 225–26.

232. S. MINTZ, at 136.

233. *See* R. GRISWOLD, at 92; S. MINTZ, at 138–40; E. MAY, at 157.

234. *See, e.g.,* W. ALCOTT; O.S. FOWLER.

235. S. MINTZ, at 135.

236. *Id.* at 135–36.

237. S. MINTZ, at 126.

238. Evangelicism saw personal choice and decision as necessary for salvation, achieved through "sincerity, earnestness," and renunciation of selfish impulses. *Id.* at 120. This outlook made "the quest to transcend selfishness a constant concern" among Evangelicals. *Id.*

239. S. MINTZ, at 129.

240. S. MINTZ, at 133.

241. *Id.* at 134–36. *See also* K. LYSTRA, at 250.

242. S. MINTZ, at 145. As Karen Lystra has suggested, "Romantic love made inroads in nineteenth-century American cultural life not because it challenged Christianity but because it absorbed its basic functions, used its basic language, and retained its basic structure and world view." K. LYSTRA, at 257.

243. S. MINTZ, at 135.

244. *Id.* at 136–45.

245. *Id.* at 141–42.

246. Harriet Beecher Stowe letter to Calvin Stowe, September 4, 1842 (quoted in S. MINTZ, at 141).

247. S. MINTZ, at 140.

248. *Id.* at 129. Mintz notes that, despite a contrary trend in continental countries, the idea of marriage as "holy matrimony" persisted in the nineteenth century in England and the United States, "the twin archetypes of the emerging market economy." *Id.*

249. Gladstone, *The Bill for Divorce,* QUARTERLY REVIEW 253 (1857).

250. *See* P. GAY, EDUCATION OF THE SENSES, at 442; W. HOUGHTON, at 375. As Karen Lystra has suggested, "[t]he logic of the belief in romantic love was readily ameliorated by competing conceptions of spousal obligations." K. LYSTRA, at 210.

251. E. MAY, at 17.

252. M. RYAN, CRADLE OF THE MIDDLE CLASS, at 154.

253. *Id.*

254. *See* S. COONTZ; A. SKOLNICK, EMBATTLED PARADISE (1991).

255. *See, e.g.,* C. TAYLOR, SOURCES OF THE SELF 456–92 (1989).

256. *See, e.g.,* M. GLENDON, THE NEW FAMILY AND THE NEW PROPERTY (1981).

257. *See, e.g.,* T.J. LEARS, NO PLACE OF GRACE: ANTIMODERNISM AND THE

TRANSFORMATION OF AMERICAN CULTURE, 1880–1920 (1981); Turner, *The Real Self*, at 1002.

258. *See, e.g.,* F. CANCIAN.

2. The Modern Construction of Intimacy

1. The discussion of this topic will draw to varying degrees on the following works: D. BELL, THE CULTURAL CONTRADICTIONS OF CAPITALISM (1976); R. BELLAH, R. MADSEN, W. SULLIVAN, A. SWIDLER, S. TIPTON, HABITS OF THE HEART (1985); F. CANCIAN, LOVE IN AMERICA (1987); R. BOWERS (ed.), PSYCHOLOGICAL MAN (1971); P. CLECAK, AMERICA'S QUEST FOR THE IDEAL SELF (1983); B. EHRENREICH, THE HEARTS OF MEN (1983); A. GIDDENS, MODERNITY AND SELF-IDENTITY (1991); A. GIDDENS, CONSEQUENCES OF MODERNITY (1990); M. GROSS, THE PSYCHOLOGICAL SOCIETY (1978); C. LASCH, THE CULTURE OF NARCISSISM (1979); C. LASCH, THE MINIMAL SELF (1984); R. LIFTON, BOUNDARIES (1970); R. UNGER, PASSION (1984); C. TAYLOR, SOURCES OF THE SELF (1989); P. RIEFF, TRIUMPH OF THE THERAPEUTIC (1966); P. RIEFF, FREUD: MIND OF THE MORALIST (1959); R. SENNETT, THE FALL OF PUBLIC MAN (1977); L. TRILLING, SINCERITY AND AUTHENTICITY (1971); J. VEROFF, E. DOUVAN & R. KULKA, THE INNER AMERICAN (1981); D. YANKELOVICH, NEW RULES: SEARCHING FOR SELF-FULFILLMENT IN A WORLD TURNED UPSIDE DOWN (1981); L. ZURCHER, THE MUTABLE SELF (1977); and on the following influential works in humanistic psychology: A. MASLOW, TOWARD A PSYCHOLOGY OF BEING (1968 2d ed.); C. ROGERS, ON BECOMING A PERSON (1961); S. JOURARD, THE TRANSPARENT SELF (1971).

2. *See* pp. 42–56.

3. For works that sound similar notes of caution, see Schneider, *Moral Discourse and the Transformation of American Family Law,* 83 MICH. L. REV. 1803, 1823–26 (1985); Minow, *"Forming underneath Everything that Grows": Toward a History of Family Law,* 1985 WIS. L. REV. 819.

4. *See, e.g.,* UNIFORM MARRIAGE AND DIVORCE ACT § 307 (West Supp. 1991) (UMDA).

5. *See, e.g., id.* § 402.

6. Bellotti v. Baird, 443 U.S. 622 (1979).

7. *See* Fineman, *Societal Factors Affecting the Creation of Legal Rules for Distribution of Property at Divorce,* in AT THE BOUNDARIES OF THE LAW: FEMINISM AND LEGAL THEORY 265 (M. Fineman & N. Thomadsen eds. 1991); Hafen, *The Family as an Entity,* 22 U.C. DAVIS L. REV. 866, 882–89 (1989); Markovits, *Family Traits* (Book Review), 88 MICH. L. REV. 1734 (1990).

8. Hafen, *Family as Entity,* at 883.

9. Schultz, *Contractual Ordering of Marriage: A New Model for State Policy,* 70 CALIF. L. REV. 204, 291 (1982). *See also* Areen, *Baby M Reconsidered,* 76 GEO L.J. 1741, 1745 (1988). For an excellent overview of this evolution, see Singer, *The Privatization of Family Law,* 1992 WIS. L. REV. –.

10. UMDA § 207.

11. *Id.* § 208, comment to § 201.

12. *Id.* at § 206.

13. *See* Glendon, *Marriage and the State: The Withering Away of Marriage*, 62 VA. L. REV. 663, 681 (1976).

14. Loving v. Virginia, 388 U.S. 1, 12 (1967) (quoting Skinner v. Oklahoma, 316 U.S. 535, 541 [1942]).

15. *Id.*

16. Zablocki v. Redhail, 434 U.S. 374 (1978)

17. Turner v. Safley, 482 U.S. 78 (1987).

18. Zablocki, 434 U.S. at 386.

19. *See, e.g.*, Kirschberg v. Feenstra, 450 U.S. 455 (1981) (management of community property); Wengler v. Druggists Mutual Insurance Co., 446 U.S. 142 (1980) (worker compensation benefits); Califano v. Westcott, 443 U.S. 76 (1979) (welfare benefits); Orr v. Orr, 440 U.S. 268 (1979) (eligibility for alimony).

20. Stanton, 421 U.S. at 14–15.

21. Griswold v. Connecticut, 381 U.S. 499 (1965).

22. Roe v. Wade, 410 U.S. 113 (1973).

23. *See* chapter 1, at 10–11. For twentieth-century examples of this reluctance, see Norris v. Norris, 174 N.W.2d 368 (Iowa 1970); Fincham v. Fincham, 165 P.2d 209 (Kan. 1946).

24. *See, e.g.*, Barnhill v. Barnhill, 386 So. 2d 752 (Ala. 1980); In re Marriage of Dawley, 551 P.2d 323 (Cal. 1976); Marschall v. Marschall, 477 A.2d 833, 839 (N.J. Ch. Div. 1984).

25. UNIF. PREMARITAL AGREEMENT ACT, §§ 3(a)(1)–(6) (West Supp. 1991) (UPAA). Sixteen states have adopted some version of the act.

26. UNIF. MARITAL PROPERTY ACT §§ 3, 10 (1987).

27. *Id.* at § 10.

28. UMDA § 306(b). The comment to section 306 declares that the standard of unconscionability "includes protection against overreaching, concealment of assets, and sharp dealing not consistent with the obligations of marital partners to deal fairly with each other." *See* In re Marriage of Weck, 706 P.2d 436 (Colo. App. 1985).

29. UMDA § 306 (d)(1).

30. *Id.* at Section 306(f). *See, e.g.*, Nakao v. Nakao, 602 S.W.2d 223 (Mo. App. 1980); DeMatteis v. DeMatteis, 582 A.2d 666 (Pa. 1990). Even if an agreement is deemed modifiable with respect to property or maintenance, the UMDA provides that modification is appropriate "only upon a showing of changed circumstances so substantial and continuing as to make the terms unconscionable." UMDA § 316(a).

31. UMDA, comment to § 306. *See also* In re Marriage of Black, 477 N.E.2d 1359 (Ill. App. 1985).

32. *See, e.g.*, Hill v. Hill, 356 N.W.2d 49 (Minn. Ct. App. 1984); Newman v. Newman, 653 P.2d 728 (Colo. 1982).

33. *See, e.g.*, Newman v. Newman, at 734–35; Osborne v. Osborne, 428 N.E.2d 810 (Mass. 1981). Uniform Premarital Agreement Act § 6(b) provides that the court may disregard a provision modifying or eliminating spousal support if as a result of that provision a spouse becomes eligible for assistance at the time of separation or divorce. Section 3(b) of the act also states that "[t]he right of a child to support may not be adversely affected by a premarital agreement."

34. *See, e.g.*, CAL. CIV. CODE § 5202 (West Supp. 1988); DEL. CODE ANN. tit. 13, Secs. 301, 302 (1981).

35. *See, e.g.*, In re Estate of Crawford, 730 P.2d 675 (Wash. 1986) (en banc); CAL. CIV. CODE § 5317 (West Supp. 1988).

36. *See* Oldham, *Premarital Contracts Are Now Enforceable, Unless...*, 21 HOU. L.

REV. 757, 788 (1984) ("vague equitable limits" on enforceability "must be clarified so the spouses can know what types of marital agreements will be enforceable").

37. *See, e.g.,* UPAA § 3(a)(8); L. WEITZMAN, THE MARRIAGE CONTRACT 255–86 (1980); Schultz, *Contractual Ordering,* at 220–23.

38. *See, e.g.,* Younger, *Perspectives on Antenuptial Agreements,* 40 RUTGERS L. REV. 1059, 1072 (1988).

39. L. WEITZMAN, THE MARRIAGE CONTRACT, at 231 (footnote omitted).

40. Walker, *Family Law in the Fifty States: An Overview,* 25 FAM. L. Q. 417, 439–40 (1992).

41. *See* M. GLENDON, ABORTION AND DIVORCE IN WESTERN LAW 68 (1989). For an account of the movement toward no-fault divorce in the United States, see H. JACOB, SILENT REVOLUTION: THE TRANSFORMATION OF DIVORCE LAW IN THE UNITED STATES (1988).

42. 401 U.S. 371 (1971).

43. *See* Hafen, *The Constitutional Status of Marriage, Kinship, and Sexual Privacy— Balancing the Individual and State Interests,* 81 MICH. L. REV. 463, 507–8 (1983); Jones, *The Rights to Marry and Divorce: A New Look at Some Unanswered Questions,* 63 WASH. U. L. Q. 577 (1985).

44. *See* Freed & Walker, *Family Law Overview in the Fifty States: An Overview,* 21 FAM. L. Q. 417, 467 (1988). Eighteen states explicitly prohibit consideration of fault in property allocation decisions, and the Virgin Islands permits it only in awards of the marital home. Walker, at 451–52. *See also* UMDA § 307. Furthermore, many states that permit consideration of fault define it narrowly. *See, e.g.,* Mosbarger v. Mosbarger, 547 So.2d 188 (Fla. Dist. Ct. App. 1989) (conduct that depletes marital assets); Sommers v. Sommers, 792 P.2d 1005 (Kan. 1990) (extreme behavior).

45. *See* Freed & Walker, at 472. Twenty-nine states and the Virgin Islands explicitly exclude fault as a consideration in alimony determinations. Walker, at 462–63. The UMDA does as well. *See* UMDA § 308(b).

46. *See, e.g.,* UMDA comment to § 402; Etheridge v. Etheridge, 375 So.2d 474 (Ala. 1979); Rizzo v. Rizzo, 420 N.E.2d 555 (Ill. App. 1981).

47. *See* H. CLARK, THE LAW OF DOMESTIC RELATIONS IN THE UNITED STATES 590 (1988 2d ed.) (listing state statutes).

48. *See* UMDA § 308. The comment to Section 308 states that the intention of that section and the section relating to property disposition at divorce "is to encourage the court to provide for the financial needs of the spouses by property disposition rather than by an award of maintenance."

49. *See* Kay, *An Appraisal of California's No- Fault Divorce Law,* 75 CAL. L. REV. 291, 313 (1987).

50. Temple, *Freedom of Contract and Intimate Relationships,* 8 HARV. J.L. & PUB. POL. 121, 151 (1985).

51. *Id.*

52. *See* Eisenstadt v. Baird, 405 U.S. 438 (1972) (contraception); Roe v. Wade, 410 U.S. 113 (1973) (abortion).

53. Eisenstadt, 405 U.S. at 453.

54. Planned Parenthood of Central Missouri v. Danforth, 428 U.S. 52 (1976).

55. Bellotti v. Baird, 443 U.S. 622 (1979). The Court held that a state must make available the alternative of demonstrating to a judge that the minor is sufficiently mature or that an abortion would be in her best interests. *Id.* at 643–44. *See also* Hodgson v.

Minnesota, 497 U.S. 417 (1990) (upholding requirement that minor seeking abortion notify both parents, on ground that statute provides for "judicial bypass" option).

56. *See, e.g.,* Karst, *The Freedom of Intimate Association,* 89 YALE L. J. 624 (1980); Richards, *The Individual, the Family, and the Constitution,* 55 N.Y.U. L. REV. 1 (1980). *But see* Hafen, *Marriage, Kinship, and Sexual Privacy.*

57. *See* Fineman, *Law and Changing Patterns of Behavior: Sanctions on Non-Marital Cohabitation,* 1981 WIS. L. REV. 275, 285; Note, *Fornication, Cohabitation, and the Constitution,* 77 MICH. L. REV. (1978).

58. *See, e.g.,* Levar v. Elkins, 604 P.2d 602 (Alk. 1980); Gilbert v. Cliche, 398 A.2d 387 (Me. 1979).

59. *See, e.g.,* Marvin v. Marvin, 557 P.2d 106 (Cal. 1976) (en banc); Poe v. Estate of Levy, 411 So.2d 253 (Fla. Dist. Ct. App. 1982). For a discussion of the evolution of judicial attitudes toward enforcement of domestic contracts between unmarried persons, see Hunter, *An Essay on Contract and Status: Race, Marriage, and the Meretricious Spouse,* 64 VA. L. REV. 1039, 1076–96 (1978); Temple, at 136–39.

60. *See, e.g.,* Green v. Richmond, 337 N.E.2d 691 (Mass. 1975); Humiston v. Bushnell, 394 A.2d 844 (N.H. 1978).

61. *But see* Casad, *Unmarried Couples and Unjust Enrichment: From Status to Contract and Back Again?* 77 MICH. L. REV. 47, 61 (1978) (arguing that acknowledging cohabitant claims creates new status). I discuss in chapter 5, at 122–28, the interplay between contract and status principles in the treatment of claims by unmarried cohabitants against each other.

62. Olsen, *The Family and the Market,* 96 HARV. L. REV. 1496, 1536 n. 51 (1983).

63. *See, e.g.,* Lehr v. Robertson, 463 U.S. 248 (1983); Caban v. Mohammed, 441 U.S. 380 (1979); Stanley v. Illinois, 405 U.S. 645 (1972).

64. *See, eg.,* Cahill v. New Jersey Welfare Rights Organization, 411 U.S. 619 (1973) (welfare eligibility); Gomez v. Perez, 409 U.S. 535 (1973) (right to support); Weber v. Aetna Casualty, 406 U.S. 164 (1972); Glona v. American Casualty Co., 391 U.S. 73 (1968) (parent's right to wrongful death action for death of child). *But see* Labine v. Vincent, 401 U.S. 532 (1971) (state may distinguish between legitimate and illegitimate children with respect to intestate succession).

65. *See, e.g.,* MINN. STAT. § 363.03, subd. 1 (1991); MONT. CODE ANNOT. § 49–2–303(1)(a). 49–3–201(1) (1991).

66. *See e.g.,* Kraft, Inc. v. Minnesota Department of Human Rights, 284 N.W.2d 386 (Minn. 1979); Thompson v. Board of Trustees, School District No. 12, 627 P.2d 1229 (Mont. 1981). *But see* Thomson v. Sanborn's Motor Express, Inc., 382 A.2d 53 (N.J. App. Div. 1977) (antinepotism policy not in violation of prohibition on discrimination by marital status). For a discussion of nepotism prohibitions and a call for their relaxation, see Wexler, *The Uneasy Case for Antinepotism Rules,* 62 B.U.L. REV. 75 (1982).

67. *See* H. CLARK, at 374.

68. *Id.* at 377. Some states have abolished the immunity in general while still preserving some limitations on liability. *See, e.g.,* Holodook v. Spencer, 324 N.E.2d 338 (N.Y.1974) (abolition qualified by holding that parent not liable for negligent supervision of child).

69. M. GLENDON, THE TRANSFORMATION OF FAMILY LAW 284 (1989).

70. *See, e.g.,* Michael H. v. Gerald D., 491 U.S. 110 (1989) (married husband of mother entitled to conclusive presumption that he is father of her child); California v. Boles, 443 U.S. 282 (1979) (denial of survivor's Social Security benefits to surviving unmarried mother of decedent's child); Village of Belle Terre v. Boraas, 416 U.S. 1 (1974) (zoning ordinance

excluding households of more than two unmarried persons). *See also* Blumberg, *Cohabitation without Marriage: A Different Perspective*, 28 U.C.L.A. L. REV. 1125 (1981); Jaff, *Wedding Bell Blues: The Position of Unmarried People in American Law*, 30 ARIZ. L. REV. 207 (1988); Lacey, *The Law of Artificial Insemination and Surrogate Parenthood in Oklahoma: Roadblocks to the Right to Procreate*, 22 TULSA L.J. 281 (1987).

71. Hafen, *Family as Entity*, at 889.

72. M. GLENDON, TRANSFORMATION OF FAMILY LAW, at 284.

73. *See, e.g.*, Norton v. Mathews, 427 U.S. 524 (1976) (Social Security survivors' benefits).

74. *See* Hafen, *Family as Entity*, at 889.

75. *See* M. GLENDON, TRANSFORMATION OF FAMILY LAW, at 292.

76. Hafen, *Family as Entity*, at 899.

77. F. CANCIAN, at 3.

78. *See* P. CLECAK, at 13. As Anthony Giddens puts it, a distinctive feature of modernity is that "[t]he self is a reflexive project, for which the individual is responsible." A. GIDDENS, MODERNITY AND SELF-IDENTITY, at 75.

79. J. VEROFF, *et al.*, at 114.

80. D. YANKELOVICH, at 66.

81. L. ZURCHER, THE MUTABLE SELF (1977).

82. *Id.* at 176.

83. *Id.*

84. *Id.* For a listing of some of the studies that have used the Twenty Statements Test, see *id.* at 60 n. 6. For a review of some of the literature based on the test, see S. SPITZER, C. COUCH & J. STRATTON, THE ASSESSMENT OF THE SELF (1973). A discussion of the scoring protocol generating the categories of self-concept is contained in *id.* at 26–28 and in McPartland, Cumming & Garretson, *Self-Conception and Ward Behavior in Two Psychiatric Hospitals*, 24 SOCIOMETRY 111 (1964).

85. F. CANCIAN, at 30. *See also* W. BENNIS & P. SLATER, THE TEMPORARY SOCIETY 79 (1968).

86. D. YANKELOVICH, at 69. *See also* J. VEROFF, *et al.*, at 17.

87. *See* chapter 1, at 15.

88. See *id.* at 25–32.

89. *See* E. GOFFMAN, *Role Distance*, in E. GOFFMAN, ENCOUNTERS: TWO STUDIES IN THE SOCIOLOGY OF INTERACTION 85 (1961); Dan-Cohen, *Law, Community, and Communication*, 1989 DUKE L. J. 1654, 1655.

90. E. GOFFMAN, at 108. As with his concept of "role embracement," Goffman uses the term "role distance" to refer to behavior, rather than cognition. *See id.* at 107–8. As I indicated earlier, I chose not to use the concept of role embracement to describe Victorian attitudes because Goffman suggests that one might *act* in a way that embraced a role while actually declining to accept the virtual self contained within it. *See* chapter 1, at 25 and note 187. By contrast, most persons who exhibit role distance probably also reject the virtual self characteristic of the role. Because a divergence between behavior and cognition seems less likely in this instance, I use Goffman's term to refer to the perception of a self apart from the roles that it may play.

91. R. UNGER, PASSION 9 (1984).

92. P. BERGER, B. BERGER & H. KELLNER, THE HOMELESS MIND 77 (1974).

93. C. ROGERS, at 122.

94. *See* A. MASLOW, at 71–114. *See also* D. YANKELOVICH, at 10.

95. C. ROGERS, at 122.

96. C. ROGERS, at 119. *See also* R. UNGER, at 8.

97. *See* chapter 1, at 25–32.

98. *See* A. MASLOW, at 10; E. ZARETSKY, CAPITALISM, THE FAMILY, AND PERSONAL LIFE 30 (1986 rev. ed.).

99. P. RIEFF, TRIUMPH OF THE THERAPEUTIC, at 58. *See also* A. GIDDENS, MODERNITY AND SELF-IDENTITY, at 78–79.

100. *See, e.g.,* C. ROGERS, at 119.

101. C. TAYLOR, SOURCES OF THE SELF 368 (1989).

102. *See generally* C. CAMPBELL, THE ROMANTIC ETHIC AND THE SPIRIT OF MODERN CONSUMERISM (1987); C. TAYLOR, at 355–90.

103. C. CAMPBELL, at 180–81; C. TAYLOR, at 382–84.

104. Colin Campbell suggests that belief in the capacity to discern an ultimate reality distinguished Romanticism from the sentimentalism from which it was derived. C. CAMPBELL, at 185.

105. C. CAMPBELL, at 183. *See also* C. TAYLOR, at 368.

106. C. TAYLOR, at 391.

107. R. BELLAH, *et al.*, at 333,

108. C. TAYLOR, at 390.

109. B. BERGER & P. BERGER, THE WAR OVER THE FAMILY 109 (1983).

110. *See* Turner, *The Real Self: From Institution to Impulse*, 81 AM. J. SOC. 989 (1976).

111. *See* chapter 1, at 25–26.

112. Turner, *The Real Self*, at 998.

113. *Id.* at 992.

114. *Id.* at 994.

115. *Id.* at 998.

116. *See* Schneider, *State-Interest Analysis in Fourteenth Amendment Privacy Law: An Essay on the Constitutionalization of Social Issues*, 51 LAW & CONTEMP. PROB. 79, 108–10 (1988).

117. *See, e.g.,* R. BELLAH, *et al.*, HABITS OF THE HEART; M. SANDEL, LIBER-ALISM AND THE LIMITS OF JUSTICE (1982); A. MACINTYRE, BEYOND VIRTUE (1984 2nd ed.); A. MACINTYRE, WHOSE JUSTICE? WHICH RATIONALITY? (1988); C. GILLIGAN, IN A DIFFERENT VOICE (1982); T. SULLIVAN, RECONSTRUCTING PUBLIC PHILOSOPHY (1986).

118. I discuss feminist critiques in chapter 6, at 155–65. Some feminists, however, seem to suggest that greater role distance and commitment to individuality have benefited women, and are, for instance, wary of positing the family as a model of relational identity. *See, e.g.,* S. OKIN, GENDER, JUSTICE, AND THE FAMILY (1989).

119. *See, e.g.,* J. HUNTER, AMERICAN EVANGELICISM: CONSERVATIVE RE-LIGION AND THE QUANDARY OF MODERNITY 73–101 (1983).

120. *See, e.g.,* R. BELLAH, *et al.*, HABITS OF THE HEART, at 275–96.

121. L. FRIEDMAN, THE REPUBLIC OF CHOICE 2 (1990).

122. *See* chapter 1, at 25–32.

123. Thornton, *Changing Attitudes toward Family Issues in the United States*, 51 J. MARR. AND THE FAM. 873, 873 (1989).

124. *See* T. CAPLOW, H. BAHR, B. CHADWICK, R. HILL & M. WILLIAMSON, MIDDLETOWN FAMILIES 295, table 12–3, App. A (1982); Goldschneider & LeBourdais, *The Falling Age at Leaving Home, 1920–1979*, 70 SOCIOLOGY AND SOC. RES. 99 (1986); Pampel, *Changes in the Propensity to Live Alone: Evidence from Consecutive*

Cross-Sectional Surveys, 1960–1976, 20 DEMOG. 433 (1983); Michael, Fuchs & Scott, *Social Changes in the Propensity to Live Alone, 1950–1976*, 17 DEMOG. 39 (1980).

125. *See* Goldschneider & Goldschneider, *Moving Out and Marriage: What Do Young Adults Expect?* 52 AM. SOC. REV. 278 (1987).

126. Goode, *Individual Investments in Family Relationships over the Coming Decades*, 6 TOCQUEVILLE REV. 51, 57 (1984). *See also* Thornton & Freedman, *Changing Attitudes toward Marriage and Single Life*, 14 FAM. PLAN. PERSP. 297, 303 (1982).

127. U.S. DEPARTMENT OF COMMERCE, Current Population Reports, Population Characteristics, Series P–20, No. 450, Marital Status and Living Arrangements: March 1990, at 14. The rate of increase from 1970 to 1982 was an even more dramatic 250 percent. Espenshade, *Marriage Trends in America: Estimates, Implications, and Underlying Causes*, 11 POP. & DEV. REV. 193, 236 (1985).

128. Spanier, *Married and Unmarried Cohabitation in the United States: 1980*, 45 J. MARR. AND THE FAM. 277, 287 (1983). *See also* Thornton, at 887.

129. *See* Espenshade, at 195. *See also* Thornton, at 880 (documenting continuing preference for older age at first marriage).

130. *See* F. FURSTENBERG & G. SPANIER, RECYCLING THE FAMILY 52 (1984); Goode, at 68.

131. *See* DeMaris & Leslie, *Cohabitation with the Future Spouse: Its Influence upon Marital Satisfaction and Communication*, 46 J. MARR. & FAM. 77 (1984).

132. *See* DeMaris & Leslie, at 83.

133. *See* F. FURSTENBERG & G. SPANIER, at 52.

134. *See* Aries, *Two Successive Motivations for the Declining Birthrate in the West*, 6 POP. & DEV. REV. 645 (1980); Lesthaege, *A Century of Demographic and Cultural Change in Western Europe: An Explanation of Underlying Dimensions*, 9 POP. & DEV. REV. 411 (1983); Thornton, at 881.

135. *See* J. SWEET & L. BUMPASS, AMERICAN FAMILIES AND HOUSEHOLDS 397 (1987); Wilkie, *The Trend toward Delayed Parenthood*, 43 J. MARR. & THE FAM. 583 (1981).

136. Taylor, *Nonmarital Births: As Rates Soar, Theories Abound*, WASHINGTON POST, January 22, 1991, at A3. *See also* J. SWEET & L. BUMPASS, at 397.

137. Taylor, at A3. From 1965 to 1988 the rate of increase in black births out of wedlock doubled to 63.5 percent, while the white rate quadrupled to 17.8 percent. *Id.*

138. *Id.*

139. *See* T. CAPLOW, *et al.*, at 131; Thornton, at 880–81.

140. *See* F. FURSTENBERG & G. SPANIER, at 36. For data on the 1980s, see U.S. DEPARTMENT OF COMMERCE, BUREAU OF THE CENSUS, STATISTICAL ABSTRACT OF THE UNITED STATES, table No. 82 (111th ed. 1991), at 62.

141. Martin & Bumpass, *Recent Trends in Marital Disruption*, 26 DEMOG. 49 (1989).

142. Thornton & Freedman, at 8; Espenshade, at 206.

143. J. SWEET & L. BUMPASS, at 400.

144. Eighty-two percent of American women in 1980 disagreed with the proposition that parents who don't get along should stay together if they have children, compared to 51 percent who disagreed with the proposition in 1962. Thornton & Freedman, at 9. *See also* T. CAPLOW, *et al.*, at 131; B. FARBER, THE FAMILY: ORGANIZATION AND INTERACTION 319 (1964); F. FURSTENBERG & G. SPANIER, at 52.

145. *See* F. FURSTENBERG & G. SPANIER, at 44, 92–100.

146. J. VEROFF, *et al.*, at 140 .

147. *See* Martin & Bumpass, at 45–48 (1989); McCarthy, *A Comparison of the Prob-*

ability of the Dissolution of First and Second Marriages, 15 DEMOG. 345 (1978). Martin and Bumpass suggest that the marital disruption rates become comparable once analysis controls for differences in education and age at first marriage. Martin & Bumpass, at 48.

148. In one study, two-thirds of remarriers expressed the view that "remarried couples are far less likely than those in first marriages to stay in an ungratifying marriage." F. FURSTENBERG & G. SPANIER, at 62.

149. *Id.* at 63. *See also* J. SWEET & L. BUMPASS, at 393. A theoretical basis for explaining this behavior is suggested in G. BECKER, A TREATISE ON THE FAMILY 219–36 (1981).

150. Espenshade, at 203. *See also* F. FURSTENBERG & G. SPANIER, at 49; J. SWEET & L. BUMPASS, at 391.

151. J. VEROFF, *et al.,* at 155.

152. Thornton & Freedman, at 299.

153. Watkins, Menker, & Bongaarts, *Demographic Foundations of Family Change* 52 AM. SOC. REV. 346, 354 (1987). *See also* Eggebeen & Uhlenberg, *Changes in the Organization of Men's Lives, 1960–1980,* 34 FAM. REL. 251 (1985); Glenn & Weaver, *The Changing Relationship of Marital Status to Reported Happiness,* 50 J. MARR. & THE FAM. 317 (1988); Goldschneider & Goldschneider, at 278.

154. Waite, Goldschneider, & Witsberger, *Nonfamily Living and the Erosion of Traditional Family Orientations among Young Adults,* 51 AM. SOC. REV. 541, 542 (1986). *Cf.* J. SWEET & L. BUMPASS, at 400 ("Delayed parenthood exposes both men and women to lifestyles that may compete more directly with future childbearing").

155. *See* Norton, *Family Life Cycle: 1980,* 45 J. MARR. AND THE FAM. 267 (1983).

156. For an exploration of the implications of this trend, see F. GOLDSCHNEIDER & L. WAITE, NEW FAMILIES, NO FAMILIES (1991).

157. F. FURSTENBERG & G. SPANIER, at 48.

158. Glenn & Weaver, at 322.

159. Farber, *The Future of the American Family: A Dialectical Account,* 8 J. FAM. ISS. 431, 431 (1987).

160. J. VEROFF, *et al.,* at 19.

161. *See* Farber, at 431–32.

162. *See, e.g.,* J. VEROFF, *et al.,* at 24.

163. Rausch, *Orientations to the Close Relationship,* in CLOSE RELATIONSHIPS: PERSPECTIVES ON THE MEANING OF INTIMACY 163, 182 (G. Levinger & H. Rausch eds. 1977). *See also* Goode, at 98.

164. "The view from the present forward to a long remaining life with a spouse may provoke a revision of what is owed to the spouse, or of what could be gained by a new contract negotiated under new conditions." Watkins, *et al.,* at 355.

165. J. SCANZONI, K. POLONKO, J. TEACHMAN & L. THOMPSON, THE SEXUAL BOND: RETHINKING FAMILIES AND CLOSE RELATIONSHIPS 78 (1989).

166. J. VEROFF, *et al.,* at 22–23.

167. *Id.* at 22. *See also* M. WINN, CHILDREN WITHOUT CHILDHOOD 101 (1983); C. LASCH, HAVEN IN A HEARTLESS WORLD 126 (1979).

168. NATIONAL COMMISSION ON WORKING WOMEN, PRIME TIME KIDS: AN ANALYSIS OF CHILDREN AND FAMILIES ON TELEVISION 5 (1985). *See also* T. CAPLOW, *et al.,* at 149–50; WINN, at 17.

169. *See* R. BELLAH, *et al.,* HABITS OF THE HEART, at 89.

170. *See* A. CHERLIN, MARRIAGE, DIVORCE, REMARRIAGE 86 (1971); F. FURSTENBERG & G. SPANIER, at 117; Hagestad, *Demographic Change and the Life Course:*

Some Emerging Trends in the Family Realm, 37 FAM. REL. 405, 408 (1988); Price-Bonham & Balswick, *The Non-Institutions: Divorce, Desertion, and Remarriage*, 42 J. MARR. AND THE FAM. 225, 233 (1980).

171. F. FURSTENBERG & G. SPANIER, at 125. *See also* Hagestad, at 408.

172. *See, e.g.*, S. JOURARD, at 109; J. MCCARY, FREEDOM AND GROWTH IN MARRIAGE 4 (1975); A. PIETROPINO & J. SIMENAUER, HUSBANDS AND WIVES: A NATIONWIDE SURVEY OF MARRIAGE 406 (1979).

173. F. FURSTENBERG & G. SPANIER, at 74.

174. Aries, at 650.

175. Rausch, at 182.

176. Block, *New Shapes of Family Life*, 28 DISSENT 350, 350 (1981).

177. Schwartz, *The Family as a Changed Institution*, 8 J. FAM. ISS. 455, 458 (1987).

178. R. SENNETT, at 5.

179. *Id.* at 259. Similarly, Ralph Turner suggests that a movement from institution to impulse as the source of self- definition results in heightened value on self-discovery through interpersonal intimacy. Turner, *The Real Self*, at 995.

180. J. VEROFF, *et al.*, at 8.

181. *Id.*

182. D. YANKELOVICH, at 251.

183. On the emergence of sexuality as a topic of discussion, see P. ROBINSON, THE MODERNIZATION OF SEX (1976). For examples of more liberal attitudes toward sexual behavior, see T. CAPLOW, *et al.*, at 161–94; Thornton, at 883–85; Booth, *Sexual Activity of Teenage U.S. Girls Rose in 1980s*, WASHINGTON POST, Nov. 8, 1990, at A1. That sex is firmly entrenched as a subject in mainstream media is illustrated by DeAngelis, *Sex Secrets Women Need to Know*, READER'S DIGEST, March 1991, at 177. Emphasis on sex as a vehicle for self-discovery is discussed in J. D'EMILIO & E. FREEDMAN, at 326–43.

184. "In the vast distance between the protection and the protected, there is space for mirages of pseudo-intimacy. It is in this space that celebrities dance." G. TROW, WITHIN THE CONTEXT OF NO CONTEXT 19 (1978). *See also* R. SCHICKEL, INTIMATE STRANGERS: THE CULTURE OF CELEBRITY (1985).

185. *See* Ablow, *Inevitable Disappointments: Politics Can Mirror the Way People Expect Too Much from Relationships*, WASHINGTON POST, April 14, 1992, at Health p. 29. Illustrative of this phenomenon was a comment by then-Representative Tony Coehlo on National Public Radio during the 1988 presidential campaign. Coehlo said that the election was about whom "we're going to invite into our living rooms each evening for the next four years." An example of the contemporary emphasis on personal qualities in political candidates is G. SHEEHY, CHARACTER (1988).

186. D. BELL, at xii.

187. Bell, *Beyond Modernism, beyond Self*, in ART, POLITICS, AND WILL 213, 216 (Q. Anderson, S. Donadio & S. Marcus eds. 1977).

188. A. GIDDENS, MODERNITY AND SELF-IDENTITY, at 35–69; A. GIDDENS, CONSEQUENCES OF MODERNITY, at 114.

189. A. GIDDENS, CONSEQUENCES OF MODERNITY, at 119.

190. A. GIDDENS, MODERNITY AND SELF-IDENTITY, at 89–98.

191. R. SENNETT, at 7.

192. *Id.* at 8.

193. *See* chapter 1, at 21–25.

194. *See id.* at 28–29.

195. *See id.*

196. *See* DEMOS, A LITTLE COMMONWEALTH: FAMILY LIFE IN PLYMOUTH COLONY 183 (1970).
197. B. ADAMS, THE FAMILY: A SOCIOLOGICAL INTERPRETATION 95 (1975). *See also* E. BURGESS, J. LOCKE & M. THOMAS, THE FAMILY: FROM INSTITUTION TO COMPANIONSHIP (1963).
198. J. VEROFF, at 168. *See also* Farber, at 297.
199. T. CAPLOW, *et al.*, at 128.
200. R. BELLAH, *et al.*, HABITS OF THE HEART, at 108.
201. This vision is expressed, for instance, in Robert Frost's well-known lines: "Home is the place where, when you have to go there / They have to let you in." R. FROST, *Death of the Hired Man*, in R. FROST, NORTH OF BOSTON 53 (1914).
202. R. BELLAH, *et al.*, HABITS OF THE HEART, at 90.
203. B. FARBER, at 301.
204. *See* chapter 1, at 15.
205. *See* chapter 1, at 15–16.
206. A. GIDDENS, CONSEQUENCES OF MODERNITY, at 39.
207. As one scholar puts it, an emphasis on interpersonal relations "removes emotionality from the social context in which it originates and relocates it within the realm of skill." Gadlin, *Private Lives and Public Order: A Critical View of the History of Intimate Relations in the United States*, in CLOSE RELATIONSHIPS: PERSPECTIVES ON THE MEANING OF INTIMACY 33, 66 (G. Levinger & H. Rausch eds. 1977). *See also* C. LASCH, HAVEN IN A HEARTLESS WORLD, at 12–18; M. WINN, at 54–55.
208. J. VEROFF, *et al.*, at 485. *See also* B. BERGER & P. BERGER, at 122.
209. M. WINN, at 140–43.
210. Weiss, *On the Current State of the American Family*, 8 J. FAM. ISS. 464, 467 (1987).
211. *See, e.g.*, J. SCANZONI, *et al.*; Walters, *Are Families Different from Other Groups?* 44 J. MARR. & THE FAM. 841 (1982); Huston & Robins, *Conceptual and Methodological Issues in Studying Close Relationships*, 44 J. MARR. & THE FAM. 901 (1982).
212. Scanzoni, *Families in the 1980s: Time to Refocus Our Thinking*, 8 J. FAM. ISS. 394, 398 (1987).
213. *Id.* at 407.
214. Scanzoni, at 399.
215. *See id.* at 414. On methodological issues that have arisen in family studies due to increased family disruption, see Duncan & Morgan, *The Panel Study of Income Dynamics*, in LIFE COURSE DYNAMICS 50 (G.H. Elder ed. 1985); Norton.
216. Turner, *The Real Self*, at 1004.
217. MASS MUTUAL LIFE INSURANCE CO., FAMILY VALUES 1 (no date; received April 30, 1991). The survey results on this question are set forth in MELMAN & LAZARUS, MASS MUTUAL AMERICAN VALUES STUDY 11–12 (1989).
218. MELMAN & LAZARUS, at 12.
219. A. BORGMANN, CROSSING THE POSTMODERN DIVIDE 43 (1992).
220. This section draws to varying degrees on the following works: R. BOWLBY, JUST LOOKING: CONSUMER CULTURE IN DREISER, GISSING, AND ZOLA (1985); C. CAMPBELL; A. DOUGLAS, THE FEMINIZATION OF AMERICAN CULTURE (1977); S. EWEN, CAPTAINS OF CONSCIOUSNESS (1976); S. EWEN, ALL-CONSUMING IMAGES: THE POLITICS OF STYLE IN CONTEMPORARY CULTURE (1988); S. EWEN & E. EWEN, CHANNELS OF DESIRE (1982); R.W. FOX & T.J. LEARS (eds.),

2. The Modern Construction of Intimacy 213

THE CULTURE OF CONSUMPTION (1983); S. FOX, THE MIRROR MAKERS: A HISTORY OF AMERICAN ADVERTISING AND ITS CREATORS (1984); T.J. LEARS, NO PLACE OF GRACE: ANTIMODERNISM AND THE TRANSFORMATION OF AMERICAN CULTURE, 1880–1920 (1981); W. LEISS, THE LIMITS OF SATISFACTION: AN ESSAY ON THE PROBLEM OF NEEDS AND COMMODITIES (1976); W. LEISS, S. KLINE & S. JHALLY, SOCIAL COMMUNICATION IN ADVERTISING (1986); R. MARCHAND, ADVERTISING THE AMERICAN DREAM (1985); M. SCHUDSON, ADVERTISING: THE UNEASY PROFESSION (1984); T. SCITOVSKY, THE JOYLESS ECONOMY (1976); A. TOMLINSON (ed.), CONSUMPTION, IDENTITY, AND STYLE (1990); ; J. WILLIAMSON, DECODING ADVERTISEMENTS (1978).

221. See M. DOUGLAS & B. ISHERWOOD, THE WORLD OF GOODS (1979); T. VEBLEN, THE THEORY OF THE LEISURE CLASS (1934 ed.).

222. See C. CAMPBELL, at 39; W. LEISS, at 92.

223. See C. CAMPBELL, at 18; N. MCKENDRICK, J. BREWER & J.H. PLUMB (eds.), THE BIRTH OF A CONSUMER SOCIETY: THE COMMERCIALIZATION OF EIGHTEENTH-CENTURY ENGLAND (1982); K. NAIR, BLOSSOMS IN THE DUST: THE HUMAN FACTOR IN INDIAN DEVELOPMENT 56 (1962); H. PERKIN, THE ORIGINS OF MODERN ENGLISH SOCIETY 91 (1969); Hoyt, *The Impact of a Money Economy upon Consumption Patterns*, 305 ANN. AM. ACAD. POL. & SOC. SCI. 12 (1956).

224. R. LIPSEY, G. SPARKS & P. STEINER, ECONOMICS 5 (1973 4th ed.). *See also* W. LEISS, at 24–28; D. LEVINE, ECONOMIC THEORY 299 (1978).

225. See M. SCHUDSON, at 155.

226. W. LEISS, at 92.

227. *Id.* at 19.

228. M. SCHUDSON, at 232.

229. *Id.* at 230.

230. T. LUCKMANN, THE INVISIBLE RELIGION 107–8 (1967). *See also* Stepp, *Many Shun Church for Other Acts of Faith*, WASHINGTON POST, Aug. 4, 1988, at A1, A17.

231. WASHINGTON POST Magazine, Sept. 4, 1988, at 53.

232. Remarks by President Reagan at the Republican National Convention, Session II, Aug. 15, 1988.

233. Randolph, *Study Urges Law Be Changed to Reduce Libel Litigation*, WASHINGTON POST, Oct. 19, 1988, at A2.

234. See G. BECKER, THE ECONOMIC APPROACH TO HUMAN BEHAVIOR (1976); R. POSNER, THE ECONOMICS OF JUSTICE (1981); R. POSNER, AN ECONOMIC ANALYSIS OF LAW (3d ed. 1986); B. SCHWARTZ, THE BATTLE FOR HUMAN NATURE (1986); A. WOLFE, WHOSE KEEPER? SOCIAL SCIENCE AND MORAL OBLIGATION (1989); Brenner, *Economics: An Imperialist Science?*, 9 J. LEG. STUD. 179 (1980); Hirschleifer, *The Expanding Domain of Economics*, 75 AM. ECON. REV. 53 (1985).

235. G. BECKER, ECONOMIC APPROACH, at 14.

236. Landes & Posner, *The Economics of the Baby Shortage*, 7 J. LEG. STUD. 323 (1978).

237. See G. BECKER, THE ECONOMICS OF DISCRIMINATION (1971).

238. See Rubin, *The Economics of Crime*, 28 ATLANTA ECON. REV. 38 (1978).

239. See R. POSNER, SEX AND REASON (1992).

240. A. WOLFE, at 40.
241. *See, e.g.*, Baker, *The Ideology of the Economic Analysis of Law*, 5 PHIL. & PUB. AFF. 3 (1975); Kelman, *Consumption Theory, Production Theory, and Ideology in the Coase Theorem*, 52 S. CAL. L. REV. 669 (1979); Kennedy & Michelman, *Are Property and Contract Efficient?* 8 HOFSTRA L. REV. 711 (1975).
242. *See* C. CAMPBELL, at 158.
243. *See* Lears, *From Salvation to Self-Realization: Advertising and the Roots of Consumer Culture, 1880–1930*, in R.W. Fox & T.J. Lears (eds.), at 4.
244. J.S. DUSENBERRY, INCOME, SAVINGS, AND THE THEORY OF CONSUMER BEHAVIOR 26 (1967).
245. C. LASCH, MINIMAL SELF, at 38.
246. *See* M. FRIEDMAN, FREE TO CHOOSE (1980).
247. *See* W. LEISS, at 27; C. CAMPBELL, at 95.
248. *See* Curti, *The Changing Concept of "Human Nature" in the Literature of American Advertising*, 41 BUS. HIST. REV. 335, 337–38 (1967).
249. C. CAMPBELL, at 48.
250. Lears, at 28.
251. Lears, at 22. *See also* R. BARTHES, CAMERA LUCIDA 119 (1981); H. LEFEBVRE, EVERYDAY LIFE IN THE MODERN WORLD 110–23 (1971); Angus, *Media beyond Representation*, in CULTURAL POLITICS IN CONTEMPORARY AMERICA 333 (I. Angus & S. Jhally eds. 1989).
252. C. CAMPBELL, at 86.
253. W. LEISS, at 93.
254. *See* C. LASCH, MINIMAL SELF, at 30.
255. *See* M. SCHUDSON, at 220.
256. W. LEISS, at 90.
257. *Id.*
258. M. SCHUDSON, at 230.
259. C. CAMPBELL, at 86.
260. *Id.* at 90.
261. *Id.* at 91.
262. *Id.* at 89–90.
263. *See* p. 44.
264. *Id.* at 86–87.
265. D. BELL, at 70.
266. K. GERGEN, THE PSYCHOLOGY OF BEHAVIOR EXCHANGE 36 (1969) (citation omitted).
267. K. GERGEN, THE SATURATED SELF: DILEMMAS OF IDENTITY IN CONTEMPORARY LIFE 217 (1991).
268. B. FARBER, at 33.
269. *Id.* at 365. For support for the permanent availability hypothesis, see Udry, *Marital Alternatives and Marital Disruption*, 43 J. MARR. & THE FAM. 889 (1981); Levinger, *A Social Psychological Perspective on Marital Dissolution*, in DIVORCE AND SEPARATION 37 (G. Levinger & O.C. Moles eds. 1979). For a more theoretical treatment consistent with the concept, see Becker, Landes, & Michael, *An Economic Analysis of Marital Instability*, 85 J. POL. ECON. 1141 (1977).
270. F. FURSTENBERG & G. SPANIER at 52.
271. Goode.
272. *See* pp. 55–56.

273. J. SCANZONI, et al., at 52.

274. G. BECKER, TREATISE, at 38–65 (1981).

275. Id. at 39.

276. Id. See also A. CIGNO, ECONOMICS OF THE FAMILY (1991).

277. Udry, at 889.

278. Hunt & Hunt, Here to Play: From Families to Lifestyles, 8 J. FAM. ISS. 440, 441 (1987).

279. C. ROGERS, at 118.

280. Scanzoni, at 414.

281. F. FURSTENBERG & G. SPANIER, at 192.

282. Scanzoni, at 415.

283. K. GERGEN, SATURATED SELF, at 181.

284. B. BERGER & P. BERGER, at 166.

285. C. LASCH, HAVEN IN A HEARTLESS WORLD, at 116.

286. Brown, Family Intimacy in Magazine Advertising, 1920–1977, 32 J. COMMUNICATION 173, 178 (1982).

287. MELLMAN & LAZARUS, at 10.

288. See M. SCHUDSON, at 220–21.

289. J. VEROFF, et al., at 19. See also F. FURSTENBERG & G. SPANIER, at 92–117; Callan & Gallois, Perceptions about Having Children: Are Daughters Different from Their Mothers? 45 J. MARR. & THE FAM. 607, 611 (1983); Glenn & McLanahan, Children and Marital Happiness: A Further Specification of the Relationship, 44 J. MARR. & THE FAM. 63 (1982).

290. See B. BERGER & P. BERGER, at 166.

291. F. FURSTENBERG & G. SPANIER, at 53. See also J. VEROFF, et al., at 168; T. LUCKMANN, at 106; WINN, at 138; Glenn & Weaver, at 323.

292. C. CAMPBELL, at 93–94. See also S. COONTZ, THE SOCIAL ORIGINS OF PRIVATE LIFE 353 (1988) (suggesting that consumerism introduces "planned obsolescence" into family relationships).

293. R. BELLAH, et al., HABITS OF THE HEART, at 103.

294. Id.

295. See Eagleton, Capitalism, Modernism, and Postmodernism, in T. EAGLETON, AGAINST THE GRAIN: ESSAYS, 1975–1985 131, 145 (1986).

3. Postmodern Personal Life

1. My discussion therefore won't directly touch upon the myriad other aspects of postmodernism. See generally A. BORGMANN, CROSSING THE POSTMODERN DIVIDE (1992); S. CONNOR, POSTMODERNIST CULTURE (1989); D. HARVEY, THE CONDITION OF POSTMODERNITY (1989); F. JAMESON, POSTMODERNISM; OR, THE CULTURAL LOGIC OF LATE CAPITALISM (1991); R. RORTY, PHILOSOPHY AND THE MIRROR OF NATURE (1979).

2. Indeed, some would say that this world is not postmodern at all, but represents "hypermodernity" (A. BORGMANN, at 78–109) or "late" modernity (A. GIDDENS, MODERNITY AND SELF-IDENTITY [1991]).

3. See K. GERGEN, THE SATURATED SELF: DILEMMAS OF IDENTITY IN CONTEMPORARY LIFE (1991).

4. Id. at 55.

5. *Id.* at 71. *See also* R. SCHICKEL, INTIMATE STRANGERS: THE CULTURE OF CELEBRITY (1985).

6. *Id.* at 61.

7. *Id.* at 48–80.

8. *Id.* at 69.

9. *Id.* at 73–74.

10. *Id.* at 73.

11. *Id.* at 6.

12. *Id.* at 138.

13. *Id.* at 203.

14. *Id.* at 150.

15. Markus & Nurius, *Possible Selves*, 41 AM. PSYCHOLOGIST 954 (1986).

16. For scholarship in psychology that indicates the salience of multiple perspectives in the effort to construct a sense of self, see M. WATKINS, INVISIBLE GUESTS: THE DEVELOPMENT OF INTERNAL DIALOGUES (1986); Baldwin & Holmes, *Private Audiences and Awareness of the Self*, 52 J. OF PERS. & SOC. PSYCH. 52 (1987); Markus & Nurius; Rosenblatt & Wright, *Shadow Realities in Close Relationships*, 12 AM. J. OF FAM. THERAPY 45 (1984).

17. *See, e.g.*, Jameson, *Postmodernism and Consumer Society*, in THE ANTI-AESTHETIC: ESSAYS ON POSTMODERN CULTURE 111, 115 (H. Foster ed. 1983).

18. *Id.* at 118.

19. *Id.* at 125.

20. *Id.* Jameson links this to a "crisis in historicity." *See* Jameson, *Postmodernism; or, The Cultural Logic of Late Capitalism*, 146 NEW LEFT REVIEW 53, 71 (1984). According to Jameson, this crisis reflects the fact that we have lost confidence in our ability to understand the past in some unmediated fashion, and are ever more aware of history as a consciously constructed narrative. This heightened self-consciousness, and its skepticism about the existence of historical events that exist independently of our reference to them, shifts our focus from the past to the present—that is, to the internal structure of the narratives that we construct. *Id. See also* Brooke-Rose, *The Dissolution of Character in the Novel*, in RECONSTRUCTING INDIVIDUALISM 184, 187 (T. Heller, M. Sosna & D. Wellbery eds. 1986).

21. *Id.* at 120.

22. *Id.* at 119.

23. Jameson, *Cultural Logic of Late Capitalism*, at 72.

24. Baudrillard, *The Ecstacy of Communication*, in THE ANTI-AESTHETIC: ESSAYS ON POSTMODERN CULTURE 126, 127 (H. Foster ed. 1983).

25. *Id.* at 128.

26. *Id.* at 132. *See, e.g.*, Van Voorst, *The Office Goes Airborne*, TIME, June 8, 1992, at 72.

27. *Id.* at 132.

28. *Id.* at 133.

29. *Id.* at 133.

30. *Id.* at 133.

31. J. LYOTARD, THE POSTMODERN CONDITION (G. Bennington & B. Massumi trans. 1984).

32. The concept is taken from L. WITTGENSTEIN, PHILOSOPHICAL INVESTIGATIONS (G.E.M. Anscombe transl. 3d ed. 1958).

33. J. LYOTARD, at 15. Lyotard hastens to add, "I am not claiming that the *entirety* of social relations is of this nature—that will remain an open question." *Id.*

34. *Id.* at 14–17.

35. *Id.* at 15 (footnote omitted).

36. D. HARVEY, at 291.

37. D. MILLER, THE NEW POLYTHEISM 5 (1973).

38. S. CONNOR, POSTMODERNIST CULTURE 48 (1989).

39. G. VATTIMO, THE END OF MODERNITY: NIHILISM AND HERMENEU-TICS IN POSTMODERN CULTURE 26 (1988).

40. Jameson, *Postmodernism and Consumer Society*, at 115.

41. Brooke-Rose, at 189. Mark Edmundsen depicts the effect of postmodernism on literature differently, arguing that it results in vivid characters who undergo various metamorphoses in a process of perpetual recreations of the self. Edmundsen, *Prophet of a New Postmodernism*, HARPER'S, Dec. 1989, at 62. Thus, he and Brooke-Rose agree on the loss of self as a postmodern literary theme, but differ in their descriptions of the way in which that theme is expressed.

42. I. CALVINO, IF ON A WINTER'S NIGHT A TRAVELER 8 (1981).

43. Grossberg, *MTV: Swinging on the (Postmodern) Star*, in CULTURAL POLITICS IN CONTEMPORARY AMERICA 254, 262 (I. Angus & S. Jhally eds. 1989). *See also* E.A. KAPLAN, ROCKING AROUND THE CLOCK: MUSIC TELEVISION, POSTMOD-ERNISM, AND POPULAR CULTURE (1987).

44. Grossberg, at 265.

45. *Id.*

46. *See* chapter 2, at 42–46.

47. R.J. LIFTON, BOUNDARIES 51 (1970).

48. M. SANDEL, LIBERALISM AND THE LIMITS OF JUSTICE 20 (1982).

49. *Id.*

50. *Id.* at 21 (emphasis omitted).

51. Eagleton, at 144.

52. Jameson, *Postmodernism and Consumer Society*, at 119.

53. *Id.*

54. *Id.* at 119–20. *See also* A. GIDDENS, MODERNITY AND SELF-IDENTITY, at 76.

55. *See* D. HOLLAND & N. QUINN (eds.), CULTURAL MODELS IN LANGUAGE AND THOUGHT (1987); R. SHWEDER, THINKING THROUGH CULTURES (1991).

56. Steven Connor describes metanarratives as "narratives which subordinate, organize, and account for other narratives[.]" S. CONNOR, at 30. On the postmodern rejection of metanarratives, see D. HARVEY, at 9 ; J. LYOTARD, at xxiv.

57. *Cf.* Schlag, *Missing Pieces: A Cognitive Approach to Law*, 67 TEX. L. REV. 1195 (1989) (discussing incommensurability of nonrationalist, rationalist, modernist, and post-modernist modes of legal discourse).

58. *See* L. ZURCHER, THE MUTABLE SELF (1977); chapter 2, at 43.

59. *Id.* at 175–76.

60. *Id.* at 41–59.

61. *Id.* at 205.

62. *Id.* at 181.

63. *Id.* at 213.

64. *Id.* at 182.

65. *Id.* at 216.
66. *Id.* at 46 (quoting T. MCPARTLAND, MANUAL FOR THE TWENTY STATE-MENTS PROBLEM (1959).
67. *Id.* at 176.
68. R.J. LIFTON, BOUNDARIES, at 37–63.
69. *Id.* at 44.
70. *Id.* at 53.
71. *Id.* at 58.
72. Lifton argues that the history of self-concepts reflects an evolution from Freud's model of a relatively fixed character, through Erikson's attempt to introduce more fluidity into a model of identity, to the open-ended conception of Protean man. R. LIFTON, THE FUTURE OF IMMORTALITY 18 (1987).
73. R. LIFTON, BOUNDARIES, at 43.
74. *Id.*
75. *Id.* at 39.
76. *Id.* at 60.
77. *Id.* at 63.
78. *See, e.g.,* E. GOFFMAN, ENCOUNTERS: TWO STUDIES IN THE SOCIOLOGY OF INTERACTION 85 (1961) ("role performance" is the "conduct of a particular person while on duty in his position"); *id.* at 88 (useful "to distinguish between the *regular performance* of a role and a *regular performer* of a role").
79. *See* R. LINTON, THE STUDY OF MAN (1936).
80. E. GOFFMAN, ENCOUNTERS, at 86.
81. *Id.* at 90 (emphasis added).
82. As Alasdair MacIntyre observes, "In Goffman's anecdotal descriptions of the social world there is still discernible that ghostly 'I,' the psychological peg to whom Goffman denies substantial selfhood, flitting evanescently from one solidly role-structured situation to another." A. MACINTYRE, AFTER VIRTUE 32 (1984 2d ed.).
83. *See* chapter 2, at 42–56.
84. E. GOFFMAN, ENCOUNTERS, at 114–33.
85. *Id.* at 122 (footnote omitted).
86. *Id.* at 121.
87. *Id.* at 139.
88. *Id.* at 120.
89. *See* Scott, *Rational Decisionmaking about Marriage and Divorce*, 76 VA. L. REV. 9, 58–62 (1990); Thaler & Shefrin, *An Economic Theory of Self-Control*, 89 J. POL. ECON. 392 (1981).
90. K. GERGEN, SATURATED SELF, at 177.
91. *Id.* at 77.
92. "In the search for committed intimacy the postmodern individual confronts a startling and dismaying contrast between the search for an inner core of being and the scattered multiplicity of the populated self." *Id.* at 176.
93. *Id.* at 137.
94. D. SIPRESS, SEX, LOVE, AND OTHER PROBLEMS 72 (1991).
95. *See* J. MEYEROWITZ, NO SENSE OF PLACE (1985).
96. *Id.* at 116.
97. *Id.* at 36–67.
98. *Id.* at 320.
99. K. GERGEN, SATURATED SELF, at 178.

100. *Id.* at 178.
101. *Id.* at 68.
102. *See, e.g.,* D. HARVEY, at 291; J. LYOTARD, at 66.
103. Eagleton, at 141. *See also* S. CONNOR, at 224; Jameson, *Postmodernism and Consumer Culture,* at 124.
104. Grossberg, at 263.

4. Status and Intimacy

1. *See generally* P.S. ATIYAH, THE RISE AND FALL OF FREEDOM OF CONTRACT (1979); L. FRIEDMAN, CONTRACT LAW IN AMERICA (1965); M. HORWITZ, THE TRANSFORMATION OF AMERICAN LAW, 1780–1860 160–210 (1977); J.W. HURST, LAW AND THE CONDITIONS OF FREEDOM IN THE NINETEENTH-CENTURY UNITED STATES (1956).
2. L. FRIEDMAN, CONTRACT LAW IN AMERICA, at 20–21.
3. R. POUND, INTERPRETATIONS OF LEGAL HISTORY 54–55 (1923).
4. The seminal case in this vein is regarded as Seymour v. Delancey, 3 Cow. 445 (N.Y. 1824). *See also* D. CHIPMAN, AN ESSAY ON THE LAW OF CONTRACTS FOR THE PAYMENT OF SPECIFICK ARTICLES 109–11 (1822).
5. 198 U.S. 45 (1905).
6. *Id.* at 61.
7. L. FRIEDMAN, CONTRACT LAW IN AMERICA, at 20.
8. Peller, *The Metaphysics of American Law,* 73 CAL. L. REV. 1151, 1214 (1985).
9. *Id.* at 1215.
10. *Id.* at 1216.
11. R. POUND, at 60.
12. *See, e.g.,* Cohen, *The Basis of Contract,* 46 HARV. L. REV. 553 (1933); Cohen, *Property and Sovereignty,* 13 CORN. L.Q. 8 (1927); Hale, *Bargaining, Duress, and Economic Liberty,* 43 COLUM. L. REV. 603 (1943); Hale, *Coercion and Distribution in a Supposedly Non-Coercive State,* 38 POL. SCI. Q. 470 (1923).
13. *See* Cohen, *Property and Sovereignty;* Hale, *Coercion and Distribution;* Hale, *Bargaining, Duress, and Economic Liberty.*
14. Cohen, at 569.
15. Sunstein, *Lochner's Legacy,* 87 COLUM. L. REV. 873 (1987).
16. *See generally* UNIF. COMMERCIAL CODE Article 2 (1991). *See also* Danzig, *A Comment on the Jurisprudence of the New Commercial Code,* 27 STAN. L. REV. 621 (1975); Mooney, *Old Kontract Principles and Karl's New Kode: An Essay on the Jurisprudence of Our New Commercial Law,* 11 VILL. L. REV. 213 (1966).
17. 29 U.S.C. §§ 151 *et seq.* (1988).
18. *See, e.g.,* Ludwick v. This Minute of Carolina, 337 S.E.2d 213 (S.C. 1985). *See generally* Linzer, *The Decline of Assent: At-Will Employment as a Case Study of the Breakdown of Private Law Theory,* 20 GA. L. REV. 323 (1986).
19. 29 U.S.C. §§ 1001 *et seq.* (1988).
20. 29 U.S.C. §§ 651 *et seq.* (1988).
21. 29 U.S.C. §§ 201 *et seq.* (1988).
22. *See, e.g.,* Hilder v. St. Peter, 478 A.2d 202 (Vt. 1984) (implied warranty of habitability). *See generally* R. SCHOSHINSKI, AMERICAN LAW OF LANDLORD AND TENANT (1980); Cunningham, *The New Implied and Statutory Warranties of Habitability*

in Residential Leases: From Contract to Status, 16 URB. L. ANN. 3 (1979); Glendon, *The Transformation of American Landlord- Tenant Law*, 23 B.C.L. REV. 503 (1982); Rabin, *The Revolution in Residential Landlord-Tenant Law: Causes and Consequences*, 69 CORN. L. REV. 519 (1984).

23. *See generally* R. ANDERSON & G. COUCH, COUCH'S CYCLOPEDIA OF IN-SURANCE LAW (2d ed. 1982).

24. *See also* Slawson, *The New Meaning of Contract: The Transformation of Contract Law by Standard Forms*, 46 U. PITT. L. REV. 21 (1984).

25. *See* S. MACAULAY, LAW AND THE BALANCE OF POWERS: THE AUTO-MOBILE MANUFACTURERS AND THEIR DEALERS (1966); I. MACNEIL, THE NEW SOCIAL CONTRACT: AN INQUIRY INTO MODERN CONTRACTUAL RELATIONS (1980); Gordon, *Maccauley, Macneil, and the Discovery of Solidarity and Power in Contract Law*, 1985 WIS. L. REV. 565; Macaulay, *Elegant Models, Empirical Pictures, and the Complexities of Contract*, 11 L. & SOC. REV. 507 (1977); Macaulay, *Non- Contractual Relations in Business: A Preliminary Study*, 28 AM. SOC. REV. 55 (1963); Macneil, *Economic Analysis of Contractual Relations: Its Shortfalls and the Need for a "Rich Classificatory Apparatus,"* 75 Nw. L. REV. 1018 (1981).

26. *See, e.g.*, RESTATEMENT (SECOND) OF CONTRACTS § 90 (1981); Bush v. Bush, 177 So.2d 568 (Ala. 1964).

27. *See* Burton, *Breach of Contract and the Common Law Duty to Perform in Good Faith*, 94 HARV. L. REV. 369 (1980).

28. *See* P.S. ATIYAH, RISE AND FALL; P.S. ATIYAH, PROMISES, MORALS, AND THE LAW (1981); G. GILMORE, THE DEATH OF CONTRACT (1976). *But see* C. FRIED, CONTRACT AS PROMISE (1981) (offering a justification of contract law as enforcement of promises).

29. For an examination of the concern for protecting reliance in other areas of the law, see Singer, *The Reliance Interest in Property*, 40 STAN. L. REV. 611, 663–701 (1988).

30. Marjorie Schultz, for instance, argues that contractual ordering of marriage reflects a preference for "private ordering over the intrusion of outside norms as the basis for choices about life-styles." Schultz, *Contractual Ordering of Marriage: A New Model for State Policy* 70 CALIF. L. REV. 258 (1982).

31. Berger & Kellner, *Marriage and the Construction of Reality*, 46 DIOGENES 1, 11 (1964).

32. *Id.* at 1.

33. *Id.* at 9. *See also* P. BERGER & T. LUCKMANN, THE SOCIAL CONSTRUC-TION OF REALITY 47–128 (1966).

34. S. WHITBOURNE & J. EBMEYER, IDENTITY AND INTIMACY IN MAR-RIAGE 127 (1990).

35. Gilligan, *Remapping the Moral Domain: New Images of Self in Relationship*, in MAPPING THE MORAL DOMAIN 9 (C. Gilligan, J. Ward, J. Taylor eds. 1988).

36. *Id.*

37. *See* S. WHITBOURNE & J. EBMEYER, at 127.

38. *See, e.g.*, C. RIESSMAN, DIVORCE TALK 177–82, 198–203 (1990); D. VAUGHAN, UNCOUPLING (1986); J. WALLERSTEIN & S. BLAKESLEE, SECOND CHANCES 52 (1989).

39. H. EBAUGH, BECOMING AN EX (1988).

40. *Id.*

41. R. BELLAH, R. MADSDEN, W. SULLIVAN, A. SWIDLER, S. TIPTON, HABITS OF THE HEART 103 (1985).

42. R. GOODIN, PROTECTING THE VULNERABLE 11 (1985).
43. *See* J. VEROFF, E. DOUVAN & R. KULKA, THE INNER AMERICAN 39 (1981).
44. G.H. MEAD, MIND, SELF, AND SOCIETY (1934).
45. Thus, I don't plan to explore in depth the full implications of the many aspects of Mead's work. For other expressions of Mead's ideas, see, *e.g.*, G.H. MEAD, THE PHILOSOPHY OF THE ACT (1938); G.H. MEAD, THE PHILOSOPHY OF THE PRESENT (1932). Nor do I mean to embrace in full the "symbolic interactionist" school of social psychology that attributes much of its foundation to Mead. For discussions of the many variations of symbolic interactionist thought, see Fine, *Symbolic Interactionism in the Post-Blumerian Age*, in FRONTIERS OF SOCIAL THEORY: THE NEW SYNTHESES 117 (G. Ritzer ed. 1990); Stryker, *Symbolic Interactionism: Themes and Variations*, in SOCIAL PSYCHOLOGY: SOCIOLOGICAL PERSPECTIVES 3 (M. Rosenberg & R. Turner eds. 1981). For a feminist treatment of Mead that is both sympathetic and critical, see K. FERGUSON, SELF, SOCIETY, AND WOMANKIND 23–63 (1980).
46. G.H. MEAD, MIND, SELF, AND SOCIETY, at 138.
47. *Id.* at 172.
48. *Id.*
49. *Id.* at 138.
50. *Id.* at 172.
51. *Id.* at 149.
52. *Id.* at 145. This equivalence of meaning of course depends on the participants' location within a shared culture. This underscores yet again Mead's insistence on the character of the self as fundamentally social. As Mead put it,
The significant gesture of symbol always presupposes for its significance the social process of experience and behavior in which it arises; or, as the logicians say, a universe of discourse is always implied as the context in terms of which, or as the field within which, significant gestures or symbols do in fact have significance. (*Id.* at 89)
53. *Id.* at 139.
54. *Id.* at 89.
55. *Id.* at 175.
56. *See id.* at 196 ("me" is "that self which is able to maintain itself in the community, that is recognized in the community in so far as it recognizes the others").
57. L. ZURCHER, SOCIAL ROLES 31 (1983).
58. *See* chapter 1, at 25–26.
59. G.H. MEAD, MIND, SELF, AND SOCIETY, at 177.
60. "The 'I,' then, in this relation of the 'I' and the 'me,' is something that is, so to speak, responding to a social situation which is within the experience of the individual." *Id.* at 177.
61. "The "I" is "the answer which the individual makes to the attitude which others take toward him when he assumes an attitude toward them." *Id.*
62. *Id.* at 199.
63. *See* chapter 2, at 43. *See also* L. ZURCHER, THE MUTABLE SELF 33 (1977) ("mutable self," characterized by relative independence from social structures, draws on Mead's concept of the "I"). This is not to say that the "I" represents the ability to act in radically autonomous fashion in isolation from the social setting. Rather, the "I" reflects the capacity to achieve some critical distance from that setting even while influenced by it.
64. G.H. MEAD, MIND, SELF AND SOCIETY, at 182.
65. *Id.*

66. "The 'I' is the response of the individual to the attitude of the community as this appears in his own experience. His response to that organized attitude in turn changes it." *Id.* at 196.

67. "There would not be an 'I' in the sense in which we use that term if there were not a 'me'; there would not be a 'me' without a response in the form of the 'I.'" *Id.* at 182.

68. *Id.* at 204.

69. P. BERGER & T. LUCKMANN, at 133. Berger and Luckmann make clear that their conceptualization of identity is "Meadian." *Id.* at n. 9.

70. G.H. MEAD, MIND, SELF, AND SOCIETY, at 209.

71. *Id.* at 194.

72. "It cannot be said that the individuals come first and the community later, for the individuals arise in the very process itself, just as much as the human body or any multicellular form is one in which differentiated cells arise." *Id.* at 189.

73. *Id.* at 158.

74. *Id.* at 158.

75. *Id.*

76. *Id.* at 150.

77. *Id.* at 152.

78. *Id.* at 159.

79. *See generally* chapter 3.

80. Mead does suggest that the attitudes of the particular individuals might be included in one's sense of self (*id.* at 158), but this is true only as long as the person is playing the role in question. In play, the person is free to "pass from one role to another just as a whim takes him." *Id.* at 151. As I've suggested earlier, what I mean by a "constitutive" context is one whose relationship(s) have some influence on the individual in other contexts. *See* chapter 3, at 76–79. From this perspective, the condition in which every context is constitutive is indistinguishable from one in which none is constitutive. *See id.*

81. G.H. MEAD, MIND, SELF, AND SOCIETY, at 152.

82. *Id.* at 159.

83. *See id.* at 151 (in a game, the "different roles must have a definite relationship to each other").

84. *Id.* at 151.

85. *Id.*

86. *Id.* at 154.

87. *Id.*

88. *Id.* at 167.

89. "The individual enters as such into his own experience only as an object, not as a subject; and he can enter as an object only on the basis of social relations and interactions[.]" *Id.* at 225.

90. *Cf.* M. PHILLIPS, THE DILEMMAS OF INDIVIDUALISM 153–78 (1983) (status provides grounded restraints that make possible meaningful exercise of freedom).

91. *See* J. MEYEROWITZ, NO SENSE OF PLACE (1985).

92. *See* chapter 3, at 85.

93. *See id.*

94. *See* chapter 3, at 83.

95. This, of course, is dependent on the understanding within a particular culture that exclusivity of romantic involvement is an expectation of marriage. Different cultures will

generate different understandings; those understandings will filter experience in different ways.

96. N. LUHMANN, TRUST AND POWER 39 (1979).

97. *Id.*

98. *Id.* at 41.

99. *Id.*

100. P. BERGER & T. LUCKMANN, at 72. "Reciprocal" typification comprises what Berger and Luckmann term an "institution." *Id.* at 54.

101. *Id.*

102. *Id.*

103. Schultz, *Contractual Ordering*, at 334 (footnote omitted).

104. Jaff, *Wedding Bell Blues: The Position of Unmarried People in American Law*, 30 ARIZ. L. REV. 207, 209 (1988).

105. G.H. MEAD, MIND, SELF, AND SOCIETY, at 178.

106. "[O]ne is continually affecting society by his own attitude because he does bring up the attitude of the group toward himself, responds to it, and through that response changes the attitude of the group." *Id.* at 180.

107. Minow, *"Forming Underneath Everything That Grows": Toward a History of Family Law*, 1985 WISC. L. REV. 819. *Cf.* Winter, *Contingency and Community in Normative Practice*, 139 U. PA. L. REV. 963, 996–1001 (1991) (discussing concept of "slippage" with respect to roles and other social practices).

108. Olsen, *The Family and the Market*, 96 HARV. L. REV. 1496, 1529 (1983).

109. Areen, *Baby M Reconsidered*, 76 GEO L.J. 1741, 1742 (1988). *See also* Olsen, *Family and Market*, at 1505.

110. *See* chapter 1, at 21–25.

111. N. COTT, THE BONDS OF WOMANHOOD: "WOMAN'S SPHERE" IN NEW ENGLAND, 1780–1835 98 (1977).

112. *See* chapter 1, at 000.

113. W. HOUGHTON, THE VICTORIAN FRAME OF MIND 342 (1957). *See also* Olsen, *Family and Market*, at 1499.

114. *See* A. WOLFE, WHOSE KEEPER? SOCIAL SCIENCE AND MORAL OBLIGATION 52 (1989).

115. *In re* Baby M, 537 A.2d 1227 (N.J. 1988).

116. *Id.* at 1249.

117. *Id.* at 1249.

118. *Id.*

119. *Id.* at 1248.

120. *See* Spann, *Baby M and the Cassandra Problem*, 76 GEO. L.J. 1719, 1730 (1988).

121. *Cf.* Areen, at 1744 (surrogate parenthood issue requires judge to decide "whether the market's ethic of individualism or the family's ethic of altruism will shape the issue of surrogacy") (footnote omitted).

122. *See* chapter 1, at 29–30.

123. S. MINTZ & S. KELLOGG, DOMESTIC REVOLUTIONS: A SOCIAL HISTORY OF AMERICAN FAMILY LIFE 55 (1988).

124. *See* M. RYAN, CRADLE OF THE MIDDLE CLASS 60–104 (1981); C. DEGLER, AT ODDS: WOMEN AND THE FAMILY IN AMERICA FROM THE REVOLUTION TO THE PRESENT 298–303 (1980).

125. *See* M. RYAN, CRADLE OF THE MIDDLE CLASS; M. RYAN, WOMANHOOD IN AMERICA (1975); N. COTT, BONDS OF WOMANHOOD; C. DEGLER;

K. SKLAR, CATHARINE BEECHER: A STUDY IN AMERICAN DOMESTICITY (1981); Minow, *"Forming underneath Everything That Grows"*, at 877–82.

126. *See* Olsen, *Family and Market*, at 1525.

127. C. DEGLER, at 298. *See also* S. COONTZ, at 219–20; Minow, *"Forming underneath Everything That Grows"*, at 885.

128. Minow, *"Forming underneath Everything That Grows."* *See also* T. DUBLIN, WOMEN AT WORK: THE TRANSFORMATION OF WORK AND COMMUNITY IN LOWELL, MASSACHUSETTS, 1826–1860 (1979).

129. Minow, *"Forming underneath Everything That Grows"*, at 871.

130. *Id.*

131. *Id.*

132. These women "inherited the social roles of daughter, wife, and mother even as they invented the post of female factory worker—and dreamed of assuming family roles again." *Id.* at 873–74 (footnote omitted).

133. *Id.* at 838.

134. Cuomo, Excerpts from Keynote Address from Democratic National Convention (July 16, 1984), in FACTS ON FILE, July 20, 1984, at 518 B1, B5.

135. *Id.* at B6.

136. *Id. See also* Gardels, *America as a Family*, New Perspectives Q., Fall 1988, at 21.

137. Minow, *"Forming underneath Everything That Grows"*, at 882.

138. Brown, *Modernization: A Victorian Climax*, in VICTORIAN AMERICA (D.W. Howe ed. 1976), at 42.

139. *See* S. MINTZ, at 197; M. RYAN, CRADLE OF THE MIDDLE CLASS, at 153–54.

140. *See* L. DAVIDOFF & C. HALL, FAMILY FORTUNES: MEN AND WOMEN OF THE ENGLISH MIDDLE CLASS, 1780–1850 (1987); M. RYAN, CRADLE OF THE MIDDLE CLASS, at 165–79.

141. "The ideology of the private family provided reassurance that certain traditional human values would not be lost to society when they were banished from the market." Olsen, *Family and Market*, at 1524.

142. A. DOUGLAS, THE FEMINIZATION OF AMERICAN CULTURE 12 (1977).

143. *Id.*

144. N. COTT, BONDS OF WOMANHOOD, at 69.

145. It may well be that, as Frances Olsen has suggested, we ultimately will be better off by transcending the family/market dichotomy in favor of a more satisfying synthesis. *See* Olsen, *Family and Market*, at 1560–78. In at least a near term characterized by the power of mass consumer culture, however, preserving family as an oppositional discourse may be necessary in order to work toward such a objective.

146. As Marx put it, "[e]xchange value . . . presents itself as a quantitative relation, as the proportion in which values in use of one sort are exchanged for those of another sort[.]" K. MARX, 1 CAPITAL 36 (S. Moore & E. Aveling eds. 3d German ed. 1967).

147. This definition does not follow Marx, who said that "[t]he utility of a thing makes it a use-value," and that "[u]se- values become a reality only by use or consumption[.]" *Id.* (footnote omitted). Rather, it tracks the way in which the term is used by Gianni Vattimo. *See* G. VATTIMO, THE END OF MODERNITY 22–24 (1988).

148. Olsen, *Family and Market*, at 1566.

149. G. VATTIMO, at 23.

150. *See* J. DEWEY, THE QUEST FOR CERTAINTY (1960 ed.); W. JAMES, PRAG-

MATISM (1991 ed.); R. RORTY, *Introduction: Pragmatism and Philosophy*, in CON-
SEQUENCES OF PRAGMATISM xix (1982).

151. R. RORTY, *Introduction*, at xliii.

152. Olsen, *Family and Market*, at 1566.

153. *See* chapter 2, at 56–66.

154. This is not to say that family members will not have the experience of choice;
indeed, many choices in this context may seem excruciating. The different is relative, not
absolute. My point is that family and market depict ideal ways of relating to experience
that differ in their underlying premises about identity. These make choice seem the paradigm
of market action and spontaneity the paradigm of family-oriented activity.

Furthermore, the notion that some process of rational choice occurs does not necessarily
mean that it takes the form of cost-benefit analysis, in which alternatives are treated as
containing commensurable units of gain and loss. More likely the process reflects a more
subtle and flexible form of practical reasoning, which acknowledges plural incommensurable values. *See* Nussbaum, *The Discernment of Perception: An Aristotelian Conception
of Private and Public Rationality*, in M. NUSSBAUM, LOVE'S KNOWLEDGE: ESSAYS
ON PHILOSOPHY AND LITERATURE 54 (1990).

155. Monroe, Barton & Klingemann, *Altruism and the Theory of Rational Action:
Rescuers of Jews in Nazi Europe*, 101 ETHICS 103 (1990).

156. *Id.* at 114.

157. *Id.* at 119.

158. *Id.* at 114.

159. *Id.* at 118.

160. *Id.*

161. *Id.* at 121 (footnote omitted).

162. *Id.* at 122.

163. *Id.* at 117.

164. *Id.*

165. *Id.* at 114.

166. *Id.* at 122. Other evidence that the promotion of a relational identity, not reducible
to egoistic motives, enhances the likelihood of cooperation is described in Dawes, van de
Kragt & Orbell, *Cooperation for the Benefit of Us—Not Me, or My Conscience*, in BE-
YOND SELF-INTEREST 97 (J. Mansbridge ed. 1990). The authors discuss numerous
experiments indicating that the cultivation of "group identity" leads to cooperative behavior
by creating a concern for "group welfare," and that this occurs independently of expectations of future reciprocity, current rewards or punishment, or reputation among group
members. *Id.* at 99. The authors conclude that such research underscores that "*sociality*
is primary for humans[.]" *Id.* at 109.

167. *See* chapter 3, at 85.

168. I'm aware that this is one among many ways that altruism could be described.
Indeed, the literature is voluminous. *See, e.g.*, R. FRANK, PASSIONS WITHIN REASON
(1988); ALTRUISM, MORALITY, AND ECONOMIC THEORY (E. Phelps ed. 1975);
Elster, *Selfishness and Altruism*, in BEYOND SELF-INTEREST 44 (J. Mansbridge ed.
1990); Jencks, *Varieties of Altruism*, in *id.* at 53.

169. M. SANDEL, LIBERALISM AND THE LIMITS OF JUSTICE 180 (1982).

170. *See* p. 103.

171. M. SANDEL, at 179.

172. Hafen, *The Family as an Entity*, 22 U.C. DAVIS L. REV. 866, 892 (1989). For

an account of new "recombinant" family forms, see J. STACEY, BRAVE NEW FAMILIES (1984).

173. Levinson, *Testimonial Privileges and the Preferences of Friendship*, 1984 DUKE L.J. 631, 662.

5. Status, Contract, and Family Law

1. *See, e.g.*, TEX. FAM. CODE ANN. § 1.01 (Vernon 1975).

2. *See, e.g.*, Dean v. District of Columbia, 18 FAM. L. REP. 1141 (D.C. 1991); Jones v. Hallahan, 501 S.W. 2d 588 (Ky. Ct. App. 1973).

3. Singer v. Hara, 522 P.2d 1187, 1196 (Wash. 1974). For thoughtful discussion of the various issues raised by the possibility of same- sex marriage, see Symposium, *The Family in the 1990s: An Exploration of Gay and Lesbian Rights*, 1 LAW & SEXUALITY 1 (1991).

4. *See* S. BUCHANAN, MORALITY, SEX, AND THE CONSTITUTION 127–82 (1985); Buchanan, *Same-Sex Marriage: The Linchpin Issue*, 10 U. DAYTON L. REV. 541 (1985). Richard Posner also has suggested that same-sex marriage may be inappropriate given the current climate of opinion in the United States. R. POSNER, SEX AND REASON 311–13 (1992).

5. Buchanan, at 557–62.

6. *Id.* at 567.

7. *Id.* at 569.

8. On the general possibilities of such reconstructive enterprises, see Cornell, *Institutionalization of Meaning, Recollective Imagination, and the Potential for Transformative Legal Interpretation*, 136 PA. L. REV. 1135 (1988).

9. *See, e.g.*, P. BLUMSTEIN & P. SCHWARTZ, AMERICAN COUPLES 448–545 (1983); D. MCWHIRTER & A. MATTISON, THE MALE COUPLE (1984); M. MENDOLA, THE MENDOLA REPORT (1980); Peplau, *What Homosexuals Want*, PSYCHOLOGY TODAY 28 (March 1981).

10. Peplau, at 28.

11. M. MENDOLA, at 68, 71.

12. Peplau, at 34.

13. M. MENDOLA, at 57.

14. *See, e.g.*, MCWHIRTER & MATTISON, at 249–83; M. MENDOLA, at 68; Harry, *Marriage among Gay Males: The Separation of Intimacy and Sex*, in THE SOCIOLOGICAL PERSPECTIVE 330 (S. McNall ed. 4th ed. 1977); Peplau & Cochran, *Value Orientations in the Intimate Relationships of Gay Men*, in GAY RELATIONSHIPS 195, 212 (J. DeCecco ed. 1988).

15. J. SPADA, THE SPADA REPORT 194 (1979).

16. Harry, at 339.

17. *Id.*

18. *Id.*

19. *Id.*

20. *Id.* at 340.

21. M. MENDOLA, at 4.

22. Singer, *Ellen and Debbie: A Lesbian Couple and Their Commitment*, WASHINGTON POST, May 27, 1991, at C5.

23. *Id.*

24. *See* chapter 2, at 47, 53–54.

25. *See* Shapiro & Schultz, *Single-Sex Families: The Impact of Birth Innovations upon Traditional Family Notions*, 24 J. FAM. L. 271 (1985–86).

26. Current law generally, however, provides neither rights nor responsibilities for a same-sex partner who is not biologically related to a partner's child. *See* Alison D. v. Virginia M., 17 Fam. L. Rep. (BNA) 1319 (N.Y. Ct. App. 1991); Nancy S. v. Michele G., 17 Fam. L. Rep. (BNA) 1263 (Cal. Ct. App. 1st Dist. 1991).

27. For arguments that a right to privacy is the basis for legal protection of homosexual conduct, see Richards, *Constitutional Legitimacy and Constitutional Privacy*, 61 N.Y.U. L. Rev. 800 (1986); Bowers v. Hardwick, 478 U.S. 186, 199 (1986) (Blackmun, J. dissenting).

28. *See* Sandel, *Moral Argument and Liberal Toleration: Abortion and Homosexuality*, 77 CALIF. L. REV. 521, 533–37 (1989).

29. *See* Lewis, *From This Day Forward: A Feminine Moral Discourse on Homosexual Marriage*, 97 YALE L.J. 1783 (1988).

30. For a similar criticism that a privacy-based argument for same-sex marriage fails to confront the extent to which privacy is infused with substantive moral values, see Schwarzchild, *Same- Sex Marriage and Constitutional Privacy: Moral Threat and Legal Anomaly*, 4 BERK. WOMEN'S L.J. 94 (1988–89).

31. Census data indicate an 80 percent increase in the number of opposite-sex couples living together without marriage from 1980 to 1990. U.S. DEPARTMENT OF COMMERCE, Marital Status and Living Arrangements, at 14.

32. *See, e.g.*, Vincent v. Moriarty, 31 App. Div. 484, 52 N.Y.S. 519 (1898).

33. *See, e.g.*, MINN. STAT. §§ 513.075-.076 (1991).

34. *See, e.g.*, Marvin v. Marvin, 557 P.2d 106 (Calif. 1976) (en banc).

35. *See, e.g.*, Eaton v. Johnston, 672 P.2d 10 (Kan. Ct. App. 1984).

36. *But see* Hewitt v. Hewitt, 394 N.Ed. 2d 1204 (Ill. 1979) (denying claim by cohabitant on ground that judicial recognition of property rights between unmarried partners would undermine state promotion of marriage). For an overview of the legal treatment of claims by cohabitants, see Krause, *Legal Position: Unmarried Couples*, in LAW IN THE U.S.A. FACES SOCIAL AND SCIENTIFIC CHANGE (Supplement) 34 AM. J. COMP. L. 533 (J. Hazard and W. Wagner eds. 1986.)

37. *See, e.g.*, Bullock v. New Jersey, 487 F. Supp. 1078 (D. N.J. 1980).

38. *See, e.g.*, Department of Industrial Relations v. Workers' Compensation Appeals Board, 94 Cal. App.3d 72, 156 Cal. Rptr. 183 (1979).

39. *See, e.g.*, Madison, Wis. General Ordinance sections 3.36, 28.03; Sanchez, *D.C. Council Approves Partners Bill*, WASHINGTON POST, April 8, 1992, at B1.

40. *See, e.g.*, 42 U.S.C. § 402(g) (1988)(Social Security mother's benefits); 42 U.S.C. §§ 402(b)–(d) (1988 & Supp. I 1989)(Social Security survivor's benefits); Elden v. Sheldon, 758 P.2d 582 (Calif. 1988) (loss of consortium suit); State Farm Mutual Auto Insurance Co. v. Pizzi, 12 Fam. L. Rep. 1263 (BNA) (N.J. Super Ct. App. Div. 1986) (insurance).

41. *See, e.g.*, Blumberg, *Cohabitation without Marriage: A Different Perspective*, 28 U.C.L.A. L. REV. 1125 (1981); Bruch, *Cohabitation in the Common Law Countries a Decade after Marvin: Settled In or Moving Ahead?* 22 U.C.D. L. REV. 717 (1989); Jaff, *Wedding Bell Blues: The Position of Unmarried People in American Law*, 30 ARIZ. L. REV. 207 (1988).

42. See chapter 4, at 104–5.

43. Bumpass, Sweet & Cherlin, *Cohabitation and the Declining Rates of Marriage*, 53 J. MARR. & FAM. 913, 921 (1991).

44. Bumpass, Sweet & Cherlin, at 919.

45. *See* Blumberg at 1163, 1168–69.

46. *See, e.g.*, Marvin v. Marvin; In the Matter of the Estate of Stettes, 290 N.W.2d 697 (Wis. 1980).

47. An extensive survey of cohabiting couples revealed, for instance, "a surprisingly high level of disagreement between partners about whether they will marry[.]" Bumpass, Sweet & Cherlin, at 926.

48. *See* Blumberg, at 1164.

49. Warden v. Warden, 676 P.2d 1037, 1039 (Wash. 1984).

50. *See* Warden v. Warden; Foster v. Thilges, 812 P.2d 523 (Wash. Ct. App. 1991).

51. *See* Blumberg, at 1164.

52. Radin, *Market-Inalienability*, 100 HARV. L. REV. 1849, 1882 (1987).

53. It's true that status can also be the source of individual rights, which delineate a zone of ostensible freedom from interference, and that contract law on occasion imposes obligations, such as promissory estoppel, not directly attributable to the will of the parties. Yet status rights are consistent with the message of status, since they reflect conscious social determination that certain activity is of such importance that it should be protected. By contrast, contract law's concessions to dependence are seen as anomalies, exceptions to the general rule of "freedom of contract."

54. Bartlett, *Re-expressing Parenthood*, 98 YALE L.J. 293, 315 (1988).

55. *See* 42 U.S.C. §§ 402(b-d), (g) (1988 & Supp. I 1989).

56. *See, e.g.*, Crenshaw v. Indus. Comm'n., 712 P.2d 247 (Utah 1985).

57. *See, e.g.*, Elden v. Sheldon.

58. This suggests that an unmarried cohabitant ought to be able to take her deceased partner's estate through intestacy, which generally is not now the case. *See, e.g.*, N.Y. EST. POWERS & TRUSTS LAW § 4–1.1 note 65 (McKinney 1981) (must be "lawful matrimonial status" for property to pass intestate to cohabitant).

59. *See, e.g.*, ARIZ. REV. STAT. ANN. § 13–1406.01 (1989).

60. *See, e.g.*, CALIF. PENAL CODE § 262 (West 1988); N.H. REV. STAT. ANN. § 632-A:2 (1986 & 1987 Supp.).

61. *See, e.g.*, CALIF. PENAL CODE § 262 (West 1988); IDAHO CODE § 18–6107 (Supp. 1989).

62. *See, e.g.*, ILL. ANN. STAT. ch. 38, para. 12–18(c) (Smith-Hurd 1989) (30 days); VA. CODE ANN. § 18.2–61 (1988) (10 days).

63. *See, e.g.*, MICH. COMP. LAWS ANN. § 750.520b (1991); 18 PA. CONS. STAT. ANN. § 3128 (Supp. 1991).

64. *See, e.g.*, KY. REV. STAT. ANN. § 510.010(3) (Baldwin 1989); 18 PA. CONS. STAT. ANN. § 3103 (Purdon 1983). Some states have also responded to criticism by defining those who are married so as to exclude spouses living apart or those who have begun divorce proceedings. *See, e.g*, TENN. CODE ANN. § 39–2–610 (1982); N.M. STAT. ANN. §§ 30–9–10 to - 11 (1978 & Supp. 1990).

65. *See, e.g.*, Clancy, *Equal Protection Considerations of the Spousal Sexual Assault Exclusion*, 16 NEW ENG. L. REV. 1 (1980); Freeman, *"But If You Can't Rape Your Wife, Who(m) Can You Rape?": The Marital Rape Exemption Re-examined*, 15 FAM. L.Q. 1 (1981); Schwartz, *The Spousal Exemption for Criminal Rape Prosecution*, 7 VT. L. REV. 33 (1982); Note, *To Have and to Hold: The Marital Rape Exemption and the Fourteenth Amendment*, 99 HARV. L. REV. 1255 (1986); Note, *The Marital Rape Exemption*, 52 N.Y.U. L. REV. 306 (1977).

66. Hilf, *Marital Privacy and Spousal Rape*, 16 NEW ENGL. L. REV. 31, 33 n. 11

(1980). *See also* Shearer, "Rape in Marriage," *Parade Special* (April 22, 1979) ("Many U.S. jurists agree that when a husband compels his wife to engage in sex relations, she suffers relatively little of the psychological trauma incurred in rape by a stranger"). These attitudes are reflected in a survey of responses to questions about marital rape. Nearly three-fourths of the respondents expressed opposition to punishing husband-rapists by incarceration in jail or prison. Note, *For Better or for Worse: Marital Rape*, 15 NO. KY. L. REV. 611, 636 (1988). The sanction most favored by respondents was mandatory counseling and/or community service work. *Id.* at 635 n. 166.

67. *See, e.g.*, West, *Equality Theory, Marital Rape, and the Promise of the Fourteenth Amendment*, 42 FLA L. REV. 45 (1990); Note, *The Marital Rape Exemption*; Comment, *Rape Laws, Equal Protection, and Privacy Rights*, 54 TUL. L. REV. 456 (1980).

68. *See* Cover, *Foreword: Nomos and Narrative*, 97 HARV. L. REV. 4 (1983).

69. D. RUSSELL, RAPE IN MARRIAGE 192–93 (1982).

70. D. FINKELHOR & K. YLLO, LICENSE TO RAPE 126 (1985).

71. *Id.*

72. Bart, *Rape Doesn't End with a Kiss*, 2 VIVA 39–42, 100–101 (1975).

73. D. RUSSELL, at 198.

74. *Id.* at 199.

75. *See id.*; Frieze, *Investigating the Causes and Consequences of Marital Rape*, 8 SIGNS 532, 549 (1983).

76. D. FINKELHOR & K. YLLO, at 118.

77. M. HALE, 1 THE HISTORY OF THE PLEAS OF THE CROWN 628 (1st American ed. 1847). The exemption was first accepted in the United States in dictum in Commonwealth v. Fogerty, 74 Mass. 489, 491 (8 Gray) (1857). The defendant in that case cited Hale as authority for the existence of the exemption. *Id.* at 490. One scholar questions whether the exemption was in fact well established at the time of Hale's statement, and suggests that English precedents are more equivocal about the exemption than its supporters contend. *See* Freeman, at 9–14.

78. People v. Liberta, 474 N.E.2d 567, 576 (N.Y. 1984). *See also* State v. Smith, 426 A.2d 38, 38; 2 BURDICK, LAW OF CRIME §§ 471–77 (1946).

79. Frieze, at 553.

80. *See* D. FINKELHOR & K. YLLO, at 122; Frieze, at 545.

81. *See* D. RUSSELL, 225–69.

82. Note, *To Have and to Hold*, at 1266. This author's argument is slightly different from mine, in that her criticism is directed at the failure to emphasize marital rape as an instance of more general gender discrimination and subordination.

83. One defender of the exemption argues, for instance, that there is no compelling need to prosecute the husband because "proceedings for separation or divorce can be instituted soon after a single non-consensual encounter." Hilf, at 42 (footnote omitted).

84. *See* D. RUSSELL, at 206–23.

85. *See, e.g.*, Ex parte Presse, 554 So. 2d 406 (Ala. 1989); In re Paternity of C.A.S., 468 N.W.2d 719 (Wis. 1991). *See also* UNIF. PARENTAGE ACT § 4(a)–(b), 6(a) (West Supp. 1991) (UPA) (putative biological father denied standing to challenge presumption). Some of the eighteen states that have adopted the Uniform Act have modified it so as to authorize a putative biological father to rebut the presumption. *See, e.g.*, WASH. REV. CODE ANN. § 26.26.060 (1986).

86. The UPA, for instance, reflects the influence of Professor Harry Krause, whose scholarship was important in producing a more compassionate climate for the legal treat-

ment of illegitimate children. *See* Krause, *Bringing the Bastard into the Great Society—A Proposed Act on Legitimacy*, 44 TEX. L. REV. 829 (1966).

87. *See, e.g.*, Cahill v. New Jersey Welfare Rights Organization, 411 U.S. 619 (1973) (welfare eligibility of illegitimate children); Levy v. Louisiana, 391 U.S. 68 (1968) (illegitimate child's wrongful death action for loss of parent).

88. 491 U.S. 110 (1989).

89. *See e.g.*, Cox, *Love Makes a Family—Nothing More, Nothing Less*, 8 J. LAW & POLITICS 5, 23–34 (1991); Kisthardt, *Of Fatherhood, Families, and Fantasy: The Legacy of Michael H. v. Gerald D.*, 65 TUL. L. REV. 585 (1991); Schultz, *Reproductive Technology and Intent-Based Parenthood: An Opportunity for Gender Neutrality*, 1990 WIS. L. REV. 297, 392–94. The case also has generated considerable commentary on an exchange between Justice Scalia and Justice Brennan regarding the appropriate level of specificity at which to characterize a constitutionally protected liberty interest. *Compare* 491 U.S. at 127 n. 6 (plurality opinion) *with* 491 U.S. at 139–41 (Brennan dissent). *See, e.g.*, West, *The Ideal of Liberty: A Comment on Michael H. v. Gerald D.*, 139 U. PA. L. REV. 1373 (1991). My discussion here will not directly address this issue.

90. California has since amended its statute to permit the biological father to challenge paternity. *See* CAL. EVID. CODE § 621(c) (West Supp. 1992).

91. 491 U.S. at 117–18.

92. *Id.* at 118–19.

93. *Id.* at 113–14.

94. *Id.* at 114–15.

95. *Id.* at 119–21. Victoria's guardian ad litem also presented a claim by Victoria in support of Michael's right to challenge paternity. The plurality dismissed this claim as either the obverse of Michael's, which it found defective, or as the assertion of a right to multiple fatherhood that is not a constitutionally protected interest. *Id.* at 130–31. My discussion does not focus on Victoria's claim, although I believe that my approach should inform, if it does not wholly govern, consideration of her claim.

96. *Id.* at 119–21.

97. *Id.* at 127.

98. *Id.* at 130.

99. *Id.* at 142.

100. *Id.* at 145.

101. *Id.* at 144.

102. *Id.* at 148–56.

103. *See* Bartlett, *Re-Expressing Parenthood.*

104. Similarly, when a wife has had an affair of which her husband is unaware, and decides to remain with her husband, the law should respect her judgment that the affair was a mistake, and that the marriage best can be sustained by not revealing her infidelity. A paternity challenge thus might also be disruptive by providing notice of infidelity in cases in which this revelation may be particularly harmful.

105. *See id.* at 145–46.

106. *See* Schneider, *Rights Discourse and Neonatal Euthanasia*, 76 CAL. L. REV. 151 (1988). On the limitations of rights analysis generally, see M. GLENDON, RIGHTS TALK (1991).

107. Michelle W. v. Ronald W., 703 P.2d 88 (Cal. 1985) (en banc), for instance, involved a case in which the spouses divorced and the mother married the putative biological father. The court held the presumption applicable only after a close analysis of the relationships between the child and the presumed and putative father, weighing the likelihood

that each would be disrupted by a paternity challenge. As the court observed, "we have declined to interpret [the presumption] as an absolute bar to all suits to establish paternity by either the putative father or the presumed legitimate child." *Id.* at 94. Rather, the court noted, "we have applied [a] balancing test analysis[.]" *Id. See also In re Melissa G.*, 213 Cal. App.3d 1060 (1989).

108. The dissent is able to maintain its acontextual position by characterizing Michael's right as merely the right to a hearing. As we've seen, however, a hearing itself could place considerable strain on the spouses. Furthermore, given the extremely high degree of accuracy of blood tests, the right to a hearing is virtually tantamount to a determination of paternity in favor of the putative father. This in turn triggers additional hearings on custody and visitation, which may result in the putative father's ongoing involvement in the child's life. The notion that Michael's right to a hearing can be vindicated without injury to others is thus illusory.

109. *Id.* at 144.

110. *Id.* at 141.

111. *Id.* at 144.

112. Nagel, *Constitutional Doctrine and Political Direction*, TRIAL, Dec. 1989, at 72, 73.

113. Carl Schneider, for instance, has suggested that family law may serve a "channelling" function that encourages the use of social institutions such as marriage and the family. *See* Schneider, *State Interest Analysis and the Channelling Function in Privacy Law*, 20 HOFSTRA L. REV. (1992). *See also* M. GLENDON, ABORTION AND DIVORCE IN WESTERN LAW (1989); Bartlett, *Re-Expressing Parenthood*; Schneider, *State-Interest Analysis in Fourteenth Amendment "Privacy" Law.*

114. 491 U.S. at 157.

115. *See* Bartlett, *Rethinking Parenthood as an Exclusive Status: The Need for Legal Alternatives When the Premise of the Nuclear Family Has Failed*, 70 VA. L. REV. 879 (1984).

116. This also serves as a response to the claim by the dissent in *Michael H.* that the Court recognized unwed fathers' claims in other cases despite disruption to the family unit of the mother and her new husband. *See* 491 U.S. at 144.

117. *See* chapter 2, at 39.

118. *See* Walker, *Family Law in the Fifty States: An Overview*, 25 FAM. L. Q. 417, 451–52 (property); 462–63 (alimony) (1992).

119. Mosbarger v. Mosbarger, 547 So.2d 188 (Dist. Ct. App. Fla. 1989). *But see* Venkursawmy v. Venkursawmy, 16 Fam. L. Rep. (BNA) 1250 (N.Y. Sup. Ct. 1990) (attempted murder of one spouse by another is act that "shocks the conscience," thereby warranting consideration in equitable distribution of property at divorce).

120. Smith v. Smith, 331 S.E.2d 682 (N.C. 1985).

121. *See, e.g.*, D.H. v. J.H., 418 N.E. 2d 286 (Ind. App. 1981).

122. Cahn, *Civil Images of Battered Women: The Impact of Domestic Violence on Child Custody Decisions*, 44 VAND. L. REV. 1041, 1072 (1991).

123. *See, e.g.*, Ellman, *The Theory of Alimony*, 77 CALIF. L. REV. 1, 13 (1989).

124. *See, e.g.*, Lichtenstein, *Marital Misconduct and the Allocation of Financial Resources at Divorce: A Farewell to Fault*, 54 U.N.K.C. L. REV. 3 (1985).

125. *See generally* D. VAUGHAN, UNCOUPLING (1986).

126. *See, e.g.*, L. WEITZMAN, THE MARRIAGE CONTRACT 24 (1980); Erlanger, Chambliss & Melli, *Participation and Flexibility in Informal Processes: Cautions from the*

Divorce Context, 21 LAW & SOC. REV. 585 (1987); Ingleby, *Matrimonial Breakdown and the Legal Process: The Limitations of No-Fault Divorce*, 11 LAW & POLICY 1 (1989).
127. *See* C. RIESSMAN, DIVORCE TALK (1990).
128. Ingleby, at 14.
129. *See, e.g.*, Bohannon, *Matrimonial Lawyers and the Divorce Industry*, in TAX, FINANCIAL, AND ESTATE PLANNING DEVELOPMENTS IN FAMILY LAW—1981 EDITION 127 (J. DuCanto ed. 1981); Erlanger, Chambliss & Melli at 591; Frank, Berman & Mazur-Hart, *No-Fault Divorce and the Divorce Rate: The Nebraska Experience—An Interrupted Time Series Analysis and Commentary*, 58 NEB. L. REV. 1, 50–52 (1978); Ingleby, at 12–14; Wardle, *No- Fault Divorce and the Divorce Conundrum*, 1991 B.Y.U. L. REV. 79, 99–100.
130. Schneider, *Rethinking Alimony: Marital Decisions and Moral Discourse*, 1991 B.Y.U. L. REV. 197, 243.
131. *See, e.g.*, Muris, *Opportunistic Behavior and the Law of Contracts*, 65 MINN. L. REV. 521 (1981); Scott, *Conflict and Cooperation in Long-Term Contracts*, 75 CALIF. L. REV. 2005 (1987).
132. *See, e.g.*, UNIF. COMMERCIAL CODE § 1–203 (West Supp. 1991).
133. *See* Brinig, Crafton & Levy, *Marriage and Opportunism* (unpublished manuscript); Carbone & Brinig, *The Reliance Interest in Marriage and Divorce*, 62 TUL. L. REV. 855 (1988).
134. *See* Schwartz, *The Serious Marital Offender: Tort Law as a Solution*, 6 FAM. L.Q. 219 (1972).
135. Brinig, Crafton & Levy, at 27.
136. *See* M. GLENDON, RIGHTS TALK.
137. *See* Wels, *New York: The Poor Man's Reno*, 35 CORNELL L. Q. 303 (1950).
138. Wardle, at 103.
139. *See* Cahn; Minow, *Words and the Door to the Land of Change: Law, Language, and Family Violence*, 43 VAND. L. REV. 1665 (1990).
140. *See, e.g.*, Stuart v. Stuart, 421 N.W. 2d 505 (Wis. 1988).
141. *See generally* Schneider, *Rules, Discretion, and Law: Child Custody and the UMDA's Best-Interest Standard*, 89 MICH. L. REV. 2215 (1991).
142. In addition, whatever unpredictability will result may serve as a welcome deterrent to opportunistic behavior.
143. Some states, for instance, require joinder of a tort action with the divorce proceeding. *See, e.g.*, Tevis v. Tevis, 400 A.2d 1189, 1196 (N.J. 1979). This may create a conflict between the right to a jury trial for the tort and the inability of divorce courts in many states to conduct jury trials. For a discussion of this and other complications arising from combining tort suits with divorce proceedings, see Note, *Interspousal Torts and Divorce: Problems, Policies, Procedures*, 27 J. FAM. L. 489 (1988–89).
144. *See, e.g.*, Tevis v. Tevis.
145. *See, e.g.*, M. FINEMAN, THE ILLUSION OF EQUALITY 17–75 (1991); L. WEITZMAN, THE DIVORCE REVOLUTION (1985); Garrison, *The Economics of Divorce: Changing Rules, Changing Results*, in DIVORCE REFORM AT THE CROSSROADS 75 (S. Sugarman & H. Kay eds. 1990); Sugarman, *Dividing Financial Interests at Divorce*, in *id.* at 130,135; Bell, *Alimony and the Financially Dependent Spouse in Montgomery County, Maryland*, 22 FAM. L.Q. 225 (1988); Jacob, *Faulting No-Fault*, 1987 AM. BAR FOUND. RES. J. 773; McLindon, *Separate but Unequal: The Economic Disaster of Divorce for Women and Children*, 21 FAM. L.Q. 351 (1987).

146. *See* H. JACOB, SILENT REVOLUTION: THE TRANSFORMATION OF DI-VORCE LAW IN THE UNITED STATES 113 (1988).

147. *See* L. WEITZMAN, THE DIVORCE REVOLUTION, at 143–45.

148. *See* J. AREEN, FAMILY LAW: CASES AND MATERIALS 591 (2d ed. 1985).

149. *See* Carbone & Brinig, *Rethinking Marriage: Feminist Ideology, Economic Change, and Divorce Reform*, 65 TUL. L. REV. 953 (1991).

150. M. GLENDON, THE TRANSFORMATION OF FAMILY LAW, at 227–28.

151. *Id.*

152. *See, e.g.*, MINN. STAT. § 518.58 (Supp. 1992).

153. *See* Kay, *An Appraisal of California's No-Fault Divorce Law*, 75 CALIF. L. REV. 291, 313 (1987) (describing "the no-fault philosophy that seeks to achieve a clean break between spouses to enable each to begin a new life") (footnote omitted).

154. *See, e.g.*, Price v. Price, 503 N.E.2d 684, 687 (N.Y. 1986).

155. UNIF. MARR. & DIV. ACT (UMDA) § 308 (West Supp. 1991).

156. *See, e.g.*, Talent v. Talent, 334 S.E.2d 256, 263 (N.C. 1985).

157. *See, e.g.*, IND. CODE ANN. §§ 31–1–11.5–11(e), 31–1–11.5–9(c) (Burns Supp. 1986) (two-year limit).

158. Turner v. Turner, 385 A.2d 1280, 1280 (N.J. 1978). *See also* Hunt v. Hunt, 698 P.2d 1168 (Alk. 1985).

159. *See, e.g.*, In re Marriage of Bramson, 427 N.W. 2d 285 (Ill. App. 1981) (wife who was custodian of two children and who earned $7,825 per year awarded $750 per month in alimony and child support despite twenty-year marriage and husband's income of $67,000 per year).

160. *See, e.g.*, In re Marriage of Carney, 462 N.E.2d 596 (Ill. App. 1984).

161. *See, e.g.*, L. WEITZMAN, THE DIVORCE REVOLUTION, at 143–83; Garrison, *Good Intentions Gone Awry: How New York's Equitable Distribution Law Affected Divorce Outcomes*, 57 BROOK. L. REV. 621 (1991); McLindon, at 360–66.

162. *See, e.g.*, L. WEITZMAN, THE DIVORCE REVOLUTION, at 70–109; Garrison, *Good Intentions.*

163. *See* Sugarman, at 149; Garrison, *Good Intentions.*

164. *See, e.g.*, Combs, *The Human Capital Concept as a Basis for Property Settlement at Divorce*, 2 J. DIVORCE 329 (1979); Krauskopf, *Recompense for Financing Spouse's Education: Legal Protection for the Marital Investor in Human Capital*, 28 KAN. L. REV. 379 (1980).

165. *See* O'Brien v. O'Brien, 489 N.E.2d 712 (N.Y. 1985); Thompson v. Thompson, 17 Fam. L. Rep. 1159 (BNA) (Fla. Sup. Ct. 1991).

166. *See, e.g.*, Stevens v. Stevens, 492 N.E.2d 131 (Ohio 1986); Holbrook v. Holbrook, 309 N.W.2d 343 (Wis. Ct. App. 1981).

167. In Maryland, for instance, the professional goodwill of a solo dental practice is treated as marital property (see Hollander v. Hollander, 18 Fam. L. Rep. 1029 [BNA] [Md. Ct. Spec. App. 1991]), while the professional goodwill of a solo law practice is not (see Prahinski v. Prahinski, 582 A.2d 784 [Md. Ct. App. 1990]).

168. Holbrook v. Holbrook, 309 N.W. 2d at 355 (footnote omitted).

169. *See, e.g.*, Haugen v. Haugen, 343 N.W.2d 796 (Wis. 1984); DeLaRosa v. De-LaRosa, 309 N.W.2d 755 (Minn. 1981). Indeed, even some states that classify, for instance, a professional degree as property calculate relief as the amount necessary to reimburse a spouse for her contributions. *See, e.g.*, Postema v. Postema, 17 Fam. L. Rep. 1503 (BNA) (Mich. Ct. App. 1991).

170. Ira Ellman, for example, has argued that reimbursement should be available only

when one spouse suffers a loss in earning capacity motivated by a desire to maximize the couple's total income or to raise children. Ellman, at 53–73.

171. *See, e.g.,* Hubbard v. Hubbard, 603 P.2d 747 (Okla. 1979).

172. *See, e.g.,* Mahoney v. Mahoney, 453 A.2d 527 (N.J. 1982).

173. Such an approach reflects the influence of an economic approach to analysis of the family. *See generally* G. BECKER, A TREATISE ON THE FAMILY (1981).

174. It's true that payments may extend beyond the marriage. This, however, is simply a practical way of compensating for obligations that arose because of benefits received during marriage. It doesn't reflect an understanding that there are any lingering obligations that continue after divorce.

175. *See* Sugarman, at 158–59. Indeed, Scotland's divorce law explicitly reflects a human capital theory, but has operated to disadvantage women. The law directs that financial provision upon divorce take into account any economic advantage gained by a spouse through the contributions of the other, or any economic disadvantage suffered by a spouse in the interests of the other spouse or the family. *See* THE LAWS OF SCOTLAND: STAIR MEMORIAL ENCYCLOPEDIA, vol. 10, ¶ 963 (1990). It also provides that in considering a claim based on this principle a court is to take into account "the extent to which any economic advantages to either party have been balanced by the economic advantages or disadvantages sustained by the other[.]" *Id.* at ¶ 965. The latter provision has been construed to deny a wife's claim for a financial award based on the economic disadvantage principle, on the ground that the husband's support of her during the marriage at a higher standard of living than she had enjoyed as a single worker constituted compensation for her disadvantage. *See* Petrie v. Petrie, 1988 SCLR 390, 394, Sh. Ct.

176. *See* Rhode & Minow, *Reforming the Questions, Questioning the Reforms: Feminist Perspectives on Divorce Law,* in DIVORCE REFORM AT THE CROSSROADS 191, 193 (S. Sugarman & H. Kay eds. 1990).

177. Sugarman, at 159.

178. *See* Singer, *Divorce Reform and Gender Justice,* 67 N.C.L. REV. 1103 (1989); Sugarman, at 159–60. While the length of a marriage is typically taken into account in financial determinations at divorce, it is now only one of several unweighted factors for consideration. *See, e.g.,* UMDA § 307(a), Alternative A (property); § 307(b), Alternative B (property); § 308(b)(4) (maintenance).

179. Scott, *Rational Decisionmaking about Marriage and Divorce,* 76 VA. L. REV. 9, 36 (1990).

180. *See* Mnookin, *Divorce Bargaining: The Limits on Private Ordering,* 18 U. MICH. J. LAW REF. 1015, 1016 (1985). The Uniform Premarital Agreement Act, for instance, provides that "the right of a child to support may not be adversely affected by a premarital agreement." UNIF. PREMAR. AGREEMENT ACT, § 3(b) (1987) (UPAA).

181. Schultz, *Contractual Ordering of Marriage: A New Model for State Policy,* 70 CALIF. L. REV. 204, 258 (1982).

182. *See, e.g.,* Newman v. Newman, 653 P.2d 728 (Colo. 1982) (en banc).

183. *Id.*

184. *See, e.g.,* Osborne v. Osborne, 428 N.E.2d 810 (Mass. 1981). Some courts will use this standard only to review agreements relating to property. *See, e.g.,* Gooch v. Gooch, 664 S.W.2d 900 (Ark. 1984). Other courts will review provisions relating to alimony, but not property, for their conscionability at the time of divorce. *See, e.g.,* Newman v. Newman, 653 P.2d at 733.

185. *See, e.g.,* Burtoff v. Burtoff, 418 A.2d 1085 (D.C. 1980).

186. *See* Scott, *Rational Decisionmaking*, at 80 ("the current trend is toward more routine judicial enforcement" of marital contracts) (footnote omitted).

187. *See, e,g,,* Newman v. Newman, 653 P.2d at 735; Osborne v. Osborne, 428 N.E.2d at 816.

188. *See, e.g.,* Re Marriage of Burgess, 485 N.E. 2d 504 (Ill. 3d Dist. 1985); Matlock v. Matlock, 576 P.2d 629 (Kan. 1978).

189. UPAA § 6(a).

190. Chiles v. Chiles, 779 S.W.2d 127, 129 (Dist. Ct. App. Tex. 1989). *See also* chapter 2, at 37–38 for a discussion of the UPAA.

191. UNIF. MARR. AND DIVORCE ACT § 306(b) (1987).

192. *See generally* Myers, Gallas, Hanson & Keilitz, *Divorce Mediation in the States: Institutionalization, Use, and Assessment,* 12 STATE COURT J. 17 (1988).

193. *See generally* Eisenberg, *The Bargain Principle and Its Limits,* 95 HARV. L. REV. 741 (1982).

194. *See, e.g.,* Bruch, *And How Are the Children?* 2 INT'L. J. LAW & FAM. 106, 120 (1988). For disagreement with the assertion that husbands typically have greater bargaining leverage than wives in mediation, see L. MARLOW & S. SAUBER, THE HAND-BOOK OF DIVORCE MEDIATION 104 (1990).

195. *See, e.g.,* Klaff, *The Tender Years Doctrine: A Defense,* 70 CALIF. L. REV. 335 (1982); Neely, *The Primary Caretaker Parent Rule: Child Custody and the Dynamics of Greed,* 3 YALE L. & POL'Y. REV. 168 (1984).

196. For instance, in Karkaria v. Karkaria, 17 Fam. L. Rep. 1404 (BNA) (Pa. Super. Ct. 1991), an appellate court reversed a lower court's refusal to enforce an antenuptial agreement under which a wife waived all rights to property or support to which she otherwise would be entitled under state law. The appellate court declared that deference to the agreement was based on the principle that "both parties to a premarital agreement, regardless of gender, stand on equal ground in the bargaining posture." *Id.* at 1405.

197. "Persons contemplating marriage are unlikely to view the prospective partner objectively and may not measure the potential costs and benefits of the marital state accurately." Scott, *Rational Decisionmaking,* at 63. For empirical evidence on this point, see Baker & Emery, *When Every Relationship Is above Average: Perceptions and Expectations of Divorce at the Time of Marriage* (unpublished manuscript).

198. Some observers claim that the failure to take account of changed circumstances is a particularly serious defect of the UPAA. *See* Ladden & Franco, *The Uniform Premarital Agreement Act: An Ill-Reasoned Retreat from the Unconscionability Analysis,* 4 AM. J. FAM. L. 267 (1990); Oldham, *Premarital Contracts Are Now Enforceable, Unless . . . ,* 21 HOU. L. REV. 757, 775–77 (1984).

199. Sharp, *Fairness Standards and Separation Agreements: A Word of Caution on Contractual Freedom,* 132 U. PA. L. REV. 1399 (1984).

200. *See, e.g.,* In re Marriage of Connolly, 591 P.2d 911 (Cal. 1979) (en banc).

201. *See, e.g.,* Zakoor v. Zakoor, 240 So.2d 193 (Fla Dist. Ct. App. 1970).

202. *See, e.g.,* Applebaum v. Applebaum, 566 P.2d 85 (Nev. 1977).

203. *See, e.g.,* Reynolds v. Reynolds, 415 A.2d 535 (D.C. 1980) (reconciliation promise); Zeeb v. Zeeb, 395 N.E. 2d 660 (Ill. 1979) (custody challenge).

204. *See* L. WEITZMAN, THE MARRIAGE CONTRACT; Hartog, *Marital Exits and Marital Expectations in Nineteenth-Century America* 80 GEO. L.J. 95, 107–8 (1991).

205. *See* Schultz, *Contractual Ordering,* at 258.

6. Objections

1. Victor Fuchs's study of women's economic inequality concludes, for instance, that "the biggest source of women's economic disadvantage" is women's "greater desire for and concern about children[.]" V. FUCHS, WOMEN'S QUEST FOR ECONOMIC EQUALITY 140 (1988). Large portions of the labor market are organized around this assumption about women's preferences. *See* Schultz, *Telling Stories about Women and Work: Judicial Interpretations of Sex Segregation in the Workplace in Title VII Cases Raising the Lack of Interest Argument*, 103 HARV. L. REV. 1749 (1990). An insightful account of the ways in which women's choices about work and family are affected both by socialization and the opportunities that they encounter is contained in K. GERSON, HARD CHOICES (1985).

2. *See* A. HOCHSCHILD (WITH A. MACHUNG), SECOND SHIFT (1989); Heath & Ciscel, *Patriarchy, Family Structure, and the Exploitation of Women's Labor*, 22 J. ECON. ISSUES 781 (1988).

3. Schwartz, *A Liberal Model for the Family?* 2 THE RESPONSIVE COMMUNITY 86 (1991). Schwartz's comments are a reaction to Galston, *A Liberal Democratic Case for the Two-Parent Family*, 1 THE RESPONSIVE COMMUNITY 14 (1991).

4. *See* Offen, *Defining Feminism: A Comparative Historical Approach*, 14 SIGNS 119, 135 (1988). This corresponds to what Robin West has called "cultural" feminism. *See* West, *Jurisprudence and Gender*, 55 U. CHI. L. REV. 1, 13 (1988).

5. My use of the term "women" in this section as a category of analysis isn't meant to suggest that there is a universal women's experience. Feminist theory has become increasingly sensitive to the fact that there are "myriads of women living in elaborate historical complexes of class, race, and culture." Harding, *The Instability of the Analytical Categories of Feminist Theory*, 11 SIGNS 645, 647 (1986). *See, e.g.,* B. HOOKS, AIN'T I A WOMAN (1981); A. LORDE, SISTER OUTSIDER (1984); E. SPELMAN, INESSENTIAL WOMAN (1988); Harris, *Race and Essentialism in Feminist Legal Theory*, 42 STAN. L. REV. 581 (1990). At the same time, the concept of gender does illuminate some aspects of women's shared experience for which the use of status in family law has particular salience. It thus seems reasonable to anticipate that one response to my call for a new model of status will be framed in terms of gender.

6. *See, e.g.,* J. ELSHTAIN, PUBLIC MAN, PRIVATE WOMAN (1981); C. GILLIGAN, IN A DIFFERENT VOICE (1982); J. MILLER, TOWARD A NEW PSYCHOLOGY OF WOMEN (1976); N. NODDINGS, CARING (1974); S. RUDDICK, MATERNAL THINKING (1989); Menkel-Meadow, *Portia in a Different Voice: Speculations on a Women's Lawyering Process*, 1 BERK. WOMEN'S L. J. 39 (1989); Sherry, *The Feminine Voice in Constitutional Adjudication*, 72 VA. L. REV. 543 (1986); West, *Jurisprudence and Gender*. Some theorists seem to suggest that this orientation is primarily the result of socialization (*see, e.g.,* M. MINOW, MAKING ALL THE DIFFERENCE 194 [1991]), while others focus more on biology (*see, e.g.,* Rossi, *Gender and Parenthood*, 49 AM. SOC. REV. 1 [1984]).

7. *See* C. GILLIGAN; Gilligan, *Remapping the Moral Domain: New Images of Self in Relationship*, in MAPPING THE MORAL DOMAIN 9 (C. Gilligan, J. Ward, J. Taylor eds. 1988).

8. C. GILLIGAN, at 159.

9. *Id.*

10. *Id.* at 30.

11. *Id.* at 32.

12. *See generally id.* at 24–63.

13. *Id.* at 26.

14. *Id.* at 29.

15. *Id.* at 26–27.

16. *Id.* at 28.

17. *Id.* at 29.

18. *Id.* at 29.

19. *See* L. KOHLBERG, THE PHILOSOPHY OF MORAL DEVELOPMENT (1981).

20. For commentary on the resulting conflict between work and family life, *see, e.g.*, Dowd, *Work and Family: Restructuring the Workplace*, 32 ARIZ. L. REV. 431 (1990); Symposium, *Legislative Approaches to Work and the Family*, 26 HARV. J. LEGIS. 295 (1989); Williams, *Sameness Feminism, and the Work/Family Conflict*, 35 N.Y.L. SCH. L. REV. 347 (1990).

21. *Rising Proportion of American Workers Holds More Than One Job*, Daily Labor Rep. (BNA) no. 153, at B–1 (Aug. 8, 1986).

22. *BLS Day Care Survey Shows Eleven Percent of Employers Offer Benefits or Services*, Daily Lab. Rep. (BNA) No. 10, at B–1 (Jan. 15, 1988).

23. *One-Third of Employees Covered by Maternity Leave Policies, BLS Says*, Daily Lab. Rep. (BNA) No. 64, at B–1 (Apr. 5, 1989).

24. Finley, *Transcending Equality Theory: A Way out of the Maternity and the Workplace Debate*, 86 COLUM. L. REV. 1118, 1176 (1986).

25. BUREAU OF LABOR STATISTICS, EMPLOYEE BENEFITS IN MEDIUM AND LARGE FIRMS, 1986, at 2 (June 1987).

26. *Id.* at 5.

27. *See* ME. REV. STAT. ANN. tit. 26, §§ 843–49 (1988); WIS. STAT. ANN. § 103.10 (West Supp. 1988).

28. For a description of various federal legislative proposals, see Lenhoff & Becker, *Family and Medical Leave Legislation in the States: Toward a Comprehensive Approach*, 26 HARV. J. LEGIS. 403, 412–15 (1989).

29. K. GERSON, at 163. One study of college students over the past several years, for instance, revealed that more than 60 percent of the women but less than 10 percent of the men said that they would substantially reduce work hours or quit work for awhile if they had young children. V. FUCHS, at 47. Similarly, a survey of law students indicated that 50 percent of the women but virtually none of the men expected to have half or more of the child-care responsibility if they had children. *Project: Law Firms and Lawyers with Children: An Empirical Analysis of the Work/Family Conflict*, 34 STAN. L. REV. 1263, 1281 (1982).

30. A recent survey indicates, for instance, that only 35 percent of women in management positions have children, compared to 95 percent of their male counterparts. Williams, *Sameness Feminism*, at 352.

31. *See* W. GELLHORN, J. HYMAN & S. ASCH, CHILDREN AND FAMILIES IN THE COURTS OF NEW YORK CITY 340–43 (1953); Weitzman & Dixon, *The Alimony Myth: Does No-Fault Make a Difference?* 14 FAM. L. Q. 141 (1980).

32. See chapter 5, at 144–45.

33. *See, e.g.*, B. BAKER, FAMILY EQUITY AT ISSUE (1981); L. WEITZMAN, THE DIVORCE REVOLUTION (1985); McLindon, *Separate but Unequal: The Economic Disaster of Divorce for Women and Children*, 21 FAM. L. Q. 351 (1987); Wishik, *Economics of Divorce: An Exploratory Study*, 20 FAM. L. Q. 79 (1986).

Weitzman's study has received the most attention; for critiques of it, see Hoffman & Duncan, *What Are the Economic Consequences of Divorce?* 25 DEMOG. 641 (1988); *Review Symposium on Weitzman's Divorce Revolution,* 1987 AM. BAR. FOUND. RES. J. 759. As Joan Krauskopf observes, "Even those who criticize Weitzman's figures differ on amount, not on significant disparity in standard of living between ex-husbands and ex-wives." Krauskopf, *Theories of Property Division/Spousal Support: Searching for Solutions to the Mystery,* 23 FAM. L. Q. 253 (1988).

34. *See* discussion in chapter 5, at 144.

35. M. FINEMAN, THE ILLUSION OF EQUALITY 149 (1991). *See also* N. COTT, THE GROUNDING OF MODERN FEMINISM 6 (1987) ("as many have argued, feminism can be seen as a demand to extend to women the individualistic premises of the political theory of liberalism").

36. *See* P. BLUMSTEIN & P. SCHWARTZ, AMERICAN FAMILIES 53–56 (1983).

37. *See, e.g.,* Auerbach, Blum, Smith, & Williams, *Commentary on Gilligan's "In a Different Voice,"* 11 FEM. STUD. 149 (1985); James McCormick Mitchell Lecture, *Feminist Discourse, Moral Values, and the Law—A Conversation,* 34 BUFF. L. REV. 11, 59 (1985) (hereinafter Mitchell Lecture); Nails, *Social-Scientific Sexism: Gilligan's Mismeasure of Man,* 50 SOC. RES. 643 (1983).

38. *See, e.g.,* Williams, *Deconstructing Gender,* 87 MICH. L. REV. 797 (1989).

39. Mitchell Lecture, at 27.

40. 628 F. Supp. 1264 (N.D. Ill.), *aff'd.,* 839 F.2d 302 (7th Cir. 1988).

41. 628 F. Supp. at 1308.

42. *Id.* at 1305.

43. Williams, *Deconstructing Gender,* 87 MICH. L. REV. 797, 816 (1989). For other discussion of the case, see Milkman, *Women's History and the Sears Case,* 12 FEM. STUD. 375 (1986); Scott, *Deconstructing Equality-Versus Difference: Or, the Uses of Poststructural Theory for Feminism,* 14 FEM. STUD. 33, 38–47 (1988).

44. 479 U.S. 272 (1987). The law gave pregnant women an advantage over other workers in that these women (1) could take unpaid leave even during the first three months of employment and (2) were entitled to reinstatement upon return, unless their position was unavailable due to business necessity and the employer could not find a substantially similar position. *Id.* at 275–76. The issue before the Court was whether this provision violated Title VII's prohibition on sex discrimination, which includes discrimination on the basis of pregnancy. *See* 42 U.S.C. § 2000e(k) (1981).

45. *See* Brief Amici Curiae of Coalition for Reproductive Equality in the Workplace, *et al.,* No. 85–494 (June 11, 1986).

46. *See* Brief Amici Curiae of the National Organization for Women, *et al.,* No. 85–494 (April 4, 1986).

47. These organizations urged the Court to hold that if the requirement of pregnancy leave benefits conflicted with Title VII, the inconsistency should be reconciled by the extension of comparable benefits to other disabled employees, rather than elimination of pregnancy leave. *Id.* at 17–24.

48. *See* Harris, at 585.

49. Mitchell Lecture, at 57.

50. Joan Williams describes this as the potential of relational feminism to serve as a critique of "possessive individualism." Williams, *Deconstructing Gender,* at 813.

51. As Albert Borgmann puts it, Gilligan's work is an important critique of modernism because it "has shown the universal to be particular." A. BORGMANN, CROSSING THE POSTMODERN DIVIDE 54 (1992).

52. *See, e.g.*, West, *Jurisprudence and Gender*; West, *The Difference in Women's He-donic Lives: A Phenomenological Critique of Feminist Legal Theory*, 3 WIS. WOMEN'S LAW J. 81 (1987).

53. *See, e.g.*, Schepple, *The Reasonable Woman*, 1 THE RESPONSIVE COMMUNITY 36 (1991); West, *The Difference in Women's Hedonic Lives*.

54. *See, e.g.*, Frug, *Re-Reading Contracts: A Feminist Analysis of a Contracts Casebook*, 34 AMER. U. L. REV. 1065 (1985).

55. *See, e.g.*, Lahey, *Reasonable Women and the Law*, in AT THE BOUNDARIES OF LAW: FEMINISM AND LEGAL THEORY 3 (M. Fineman & M. Thomadsen eds. 1991).

56. *See, e.g.*, Finley, *A Break in the Silence: Including Women's Issues in a Torts Course*, 1 YALE J. LAW & FEM. 41 (1989); Howe, *The Problem of Privatized Injuries: Feminist Strategies for Litigation*, in AT THE BOUNDARIES OF LAW, at 148.

57. *See, e.g.*, Sherry.

58. *See, e.g.*, Menkel-Meadow.

59. *See, e.g.*, Resnik, *On the Bias: Feminist Reconsiderations of the Aspirations for Our Judges*, 61 S. CAL. L. REV. 1877 (1988).

60. *See, e.g.*, COTT, THE BONDS OF WOMANHOOD: "WOMAN'S SPHERE" IN NEW ENGLAND, 1780–1835 (1977); M. RYAN, CRADLE OF THE MIDDLE CLASS: THE FAMILY IN ONEIDA COUNTY, NEW YORK, 1790–1865 (1981); A. SCOTT, MAKING THE INVISIBLE WOMAN VISIBLE (1984). For an overview of recent trends in women's history, see E. FOX- GENOVESE, FEMINISM WITHOUT ILLUSIONS 113–65 (1991).

61. *See* C. GILLIGAN; Gilligan, *Remapping the Moral Domain*.

62. Pateman, *Feminist Critiques of the Public/Private Dichotomy*, in FEMINISM AND EQUALITY 103, 122 (A. Phillips ed. 1987). As Gilligan herself says of the values of care and relationship, "it is important to use them as a way of reconstructing all the institutions in which we live at the same time that we reconstruct ourselves." Mitchell Lecture, at 304.

63. Nedelsky, *Reconceiving Autonomy: Sources, Thoughts, and Possibilities*, 1 YALE J. LAW & FEM. 7 (1989).

64. *Id.* at 30.

65. *Id.* at 12.

66. *Id.* at 12. *See also* J. NEDELSKY, PRIVATE PROPERTY AND THE LIMITS OF AMERICAN CONSTITUTIONALISM (1991).

67. *See* Nedelsky, at 15–26.

68. *Id.* at 12.

69. *Id.*

70. *Id.*

71. Finley, at 1171.

72. *See* M. MINOW, at 87–88.

73. 479 U.S. at 289.

74. M. MINOW, at 88.

75. Schultz, *Telling Stories*, at 1804.

76. *Id.* at 1804 n. 28. *See* S. BENSON, COUNTER CULTURES: SALESWOMEN, MANAGERS, AND CUSTOMERS IN AMERICAN DEPARTMENT STORES, 1890–1940 130–31 (1986).

77. Littleton, *Reconstructing Sexual Equality*, 75 CALIF. L. REV. 1279, 1284 (1987).

78. *Id.* at 1297. *See also* D. RHODE, JUSTICE AND GENDER 317 (1989).

79. Becker, *Prince Charming: Abstract Equality*, 1987 SUP. CT. REV. 201, 208–9.

80. *See* chapter 2, at 44–45.

81. Averill, *A Constructivist View of Emotion*, in EMOTION: THEORY, RE-SEARCH, AND EXPERIENCE. Vol. 1, THEORIES OF EMOTION 305, 305 (R. Plutchik & H. Kellerman eds. 1980).

82. Averill, *The Social Construction of Emotion: With Special Reference to Love*, in THE SOCIAL CONSTRUCTION OF THE PERSON 89, 89 (K. Gergen & K. Davis eds. 1985).

83. Sarbin, *Emotion and Act: Roles and Rhetoric*, in THE SOCIAL CONSTRUC-TION OF EMOTION 83, 84 (R. Harre ed. 1986).

84. Coulter, *Affect and Social Context: Emotion Definition as a Social Task*, in *id.* at 120, 120.

85. Gordon, *The Sociology of Sentiments and Emotion*, in SOCIAL PSYCHOLOGY: SOCIOLOGICAL PERSPECTIVES 562, 562 (M. Rosenberg & R. Turner eds. 1981).

86. Coulter, at 120.

87. Sarbin, at 84. *See also* Harre, *An Outline of the Social Constructionist Viewpoint*, in THE SOCIAL CONSTRUCTION OF EMOTION, at 2, 4 (R. Harre ed. 1986) ("There has been a tendency among both philosophers and psychologists to abstract an entity—call it 'anger,' 'love,' 'grief' or 'anxiety'—and to try to study it").

88. J. AVERILL, ANGER AND AGGRESSION: AN ESSAY ON EMOTION 13 (1982).

89. Sarbin, at 84. *See also* J. AVERILL, at 13.

90. *Id.*

91. J. AVERILL, at 13.

92. *Id.*

93. *Id.* at 15.

94. Averill, *Social Construction of Emotion*, at 94.

95. Silver & Sabini, *Sincerity: Feelings and Constructions in Making a Self*, in THE SOCIAL CONSTRUCTION OF THE PERSON, at 199.

96. Averill, *Social Construction of Emotion*, at 90.

97. Gordon, at 562.

98. *See, e.g.*, Ekman & Oster, *Facial Expressions of Emotion*, 30 ANN. REV. PSYCH. 527 (1979).

99. Gordon, at 573.

100. J. AVERILL, at 43.

101. *Id.* at 52.

102. *Id. See also* Schachter & Singer, *Cognitive, Social, and Psychological Determinants of Emotional State*, 1962 PSYCHOL. REV. 69.

103. Coulter, at 125.

104. Gordon, at 574.

105. *See, e.g.*, Zborowski, *Cultural Components in Responses to Pain*, 4 J. SOC. ISS. 16 (1952).

106. *See, e.g.*, S. SCHACHTER, EMOTION, OBESITY, AND CRIME (1967); Schach-ter, *Cognitive Effects on Bodily Functioning: Studies of Obesity and Eating*, in NEURO-PHYSIOLOGY AND EMOTION 117 (D.C. Glass ed. 1967).

107. *See, e.g.*, A.C. KERCKHOFF & K.W. BACK, THE JUNE BUG: A STUDY OF HYSTERICAL CONTAGION (1968); Mechanic, *Social Psychological Factors Affecting the Presentation of Bodily Complaints*, 286 NEW ENG. J. MED. 1132 (1972).

108. Storms, *Sexual Orientation and Self-Perception*, in PERCEPTION OF EMOTION IN SELF AND OTHERS 165 (P. Pliner, K.R. Blankstein & I.M. Spiegel eds. 1979).

109. Storms & Nisbett, *Insomnia and the Attribution Process*, 16 J. PERS. & SOC. PSYCH. 319 (1970).

110. C. MACANDREW & R. EDGERTON, DRUNKEN COMPORTMENT (1969); Becker, *History, Culture, and Subjective Experience*, 8 J. HEALTH & SOC. BEH. 163 (1967).

111. Gordon, at 574. *See also* H. GERTH & C.W. MILLS, CHARACTER AND SOCIAL STRUCTURE: THE PSYCHOLOGY OF SOCIAL INSTITUTIONS 20 (1953).

112. Coulter, at 121 (emphasis in original). *See also* Sarbin, at 87.

113. *See* J. AVERILL, at 25 ("The experience of emotion is reflective, an interpretation of events").

114. Coulter, at 121.

115. Harre, at 4.

116. *See* Geertz, *The Growth of Culture and the Evolution of Mind*, in C. GEERTZ, THE INTERPRETATION OF CULTURES 55, 80 (1973).

117. *See* J.L. BRIGGS, NEVER IN ANGER: PORTRAIT OF AN ESKIMO FAMILY (1970).

118. H. GEERTZ, THE VOCABULARY OF EMOTION 233 (1959).

119. Gordon, at 578.

120. M. KUNDERA, THE BOOK OF LAUGHTER AND FORGETTING 121 (M.H. Heim transl. 1980).

121. *Id.*

122. *Id.* at 150.

123. Averill, *Social Construction of Emotion*, at 93.

124. Gordon, at 577.

125. *See* P. BERGER & T. LUCKMANN, THE SOCIAL CONSTRUCTION OF REALITY 47–128 (1966).

126. Gordon, at 583.

127. *See* J. AVERILL, at 151, 159–208; 341–54.

128. *See id.* at 151–52; 209–28; 355–68.

129. *See id.* at 152–53; 229–52.

130. *See id.* at 153, 253–79.

131. *See id.* at 153–54, 281–316.

132. *Id.* at 324–25.

133. *Id.* at 324.

134. *Id.* at 327.

135. *Id.* at 171.

136. *Id.* at 172.

137. *Id.* at 172.

138. *Id.*

139. *Id.* at 7.

140. *See* Averill, *A Constructivist View*, at 315 ("In the case of social roles, the plot is the cultural system").

141. *See* Sarbin. *See also* De Souza, *The Rationality of Emotions*, in EXPLAINING EMOTIONS 285 (A. Rorty ed. 1980) (arguing that a person's "emotional repertoire" is learned in the context of "paradigm scenarios").

142. J. AVERILL, at 321.

143. Gordon, at 574.

144. *Id.* (citation omitted). *See also* Candland, *The Persistent Problems of Emotion*, in EMOTION 1, 65–71 (D.K. Candland, J. Fell, E. Keen, A. Leshner & R. Tarpy eds.

1977); Lewis and Rosenblum, *Introduction: Issues in Affect Development*, in THE DE-VELOPMENT OF AFFECT 1 (M. Lewis & L. Rosenblum eds. 1978).

145. Gordon at 585.

146. Averill, *Social Construction of Emotion*, at 91–94. *See also* Averill & Boothroyd, *On Falling in Love in Conformance with the Romantic Ideal*, 1 MOTIVATION & EMOTION 235 (1977).

147. Sunstein, *Legal Interference with Private Preferences*, 53 U. CHI. L. REV. 1129, 1170 (1986).

148. *See, e.g.*, Olsen, *The Myth of State Intervention within the Family*, 18 MICH. J. L. REF. 835 (1985).

149. *See, e.g.*, J. ELSTER, SOUR GRAPES: STUDIES IN THE SUBVERSION OF RATIONALITY (1983). Elster notes that "[i]n the standard theory of individual or social choice, preferences are taken as *given* independently of the choice situation." *Id.* at 121. By contrast, Elster provides support for a perspective that enables us "to see preferences as causally shaped by the situation." *Id. See also* Sunstein, *Neutrality in Constitutional Law (with Special Reference to Pornography, Abortion, and Surrogacy)*, 92 COLUM. L. REV. 1 (1992).

150. This ability to choose, of course, is not unbounded, but must be exercised in light of the constraints and opportunities that we all face as "situated" subjects. *See* Winter, *Indeterminacy and Incommensurability in Constitutional Law*, 78 CALIF. L. REV. 1441 (1990).

151. *See* In re Baby M, 537 A.2d 1227 (N.J.1988). *See also* Olsen, *Myth of State Intervention*; Cohen, *The Basis of Contract*, 46 HARV. L. REV. 553 (1933); chapter 1, at 10–11 (discussing refusal of Victorian law to enforce most contracts between spouses).

152. *See* Seidman, *Baby M and the Problem of Unstable Preferences*, 76 GEO. L.J. 1829, 1836 (1988) ("Revolutions in birth technology have made it plain that what was once thought of as 'natural' or inevitable is now within our control").

153. Scott, *Rational Decisionmaking*.

154. *Id.* at 79–87.

155. *Id.* at 91.

156. *Id.* at 11.

157. *Id.* at 12–13.

158. As Scott observes,

[A] marriage that is intrinsically satisfactory may be vulnerable if few barriers reinforce the relationship or if alternate attractions are powerful. Alternatively, a marriage with few intrinsic rewards may be relatively stable if the barriers to exit are substantial or if the unmarried status has little appeal.

Id. at 46. *See also* Levinger, *A Social Psychological Perspective on Marital Dissolution*, in DIVORCE AND SEPARATION: CONTEXT, CAUSES, AND CONSEQUENCES 37–60 (G. Levinger & O. Moles eds. 1979).

159. Turner, *The Real Self: From Institution to Impulse*, 81 AM. J. SOC. 989, 1011 (1976).

160. For diverse discussions of this approach, see M. GLENDON, ABORTION AND DIVORCE IN WESTERN LAW (1989); Geertz, *Fact and Law in Comparative Perspective*, in C. GEERTZ, LOCAL KNOWLEDGE 167 (1983); Melton & Saks, *The Law as an Instrument of Socialization and Social Structure*, in THE LAW AS A BEHAVIORAL INSTRUMENT 235 (G. Melton ed. 1986); LAW AND THE ORDER OF CULTURE (R. Post ed. 1991); J.B. WHITE, JUSTICE AS TRANSLATION (1990); J.B. WHITE, HER-ACLES' BOW: ESSAYS ON THE RHETORIC AND POETICS OF THE LAW (1985); J.B. WHITE, WHEN WORDS LOSE THEIR MEANING (1984); Bartlett, *Re- Expressing*

Parenthood, 98 YALE L. J. 293 (1988); Bartlett & Stack, *Joint Custody, Feminism, and the Dependency Dilemma*, 2 BERKELEY WOMEN'S L.J. 9 (1986); Schneider, *State-Interest Analysis in Fourteenth Amendment "Privacy" Law*; Schneider, *State Interest Analysis and the Channelling Function in Privacy Law*, 20 HOFSTRA L. REV. – (1992); Weisbrod, *On the Expressive Functions of Family Law*, 22 U.C. DAVIS L. REV. 991 (1989).

161. O.W. HOLMES, *The Path of the Law*, in COLLECTED LEGAL PAPERS 171 (1920).

162. *Id.*

163. G. GILMORE, THE AGES OF AMERICAN LAW 110–11 (1977).

164. One study indicates, for instance, that even applicants for marriage licenses are relatively uninformed about the legal consequences should they decide to divorce. *See* Baker & Emery, *When Every Relationship Is above Average: Perceptions and Expectations of Divorce at the Time of Marriage* (unpublished manuscript).

165. M. GLENDON, ABORTION AND DIVORCE, at 138.

166. White, *Rhetoric and Law: The Arts of Cultural and Communal Life*, in J.B. WHITE, HERACLES' BOW, at 29, 36.

167. Other areas of the law feature standards as well; indeed, all contain a combination of rules and standards. *See, e.g.*, Rose, *Crystals and Mud in Property Law*, 40 STAN. L. REV. 577 (1988). My contention is simply that family law is characterized by a particularly high proportion of standards to rules.

168. Kennedy, *Form and Substance in Private Law Adjudication*, 89 HARV. L. REV. 1685, 1688–89 (1976).

169. *Id.* at 1688.

170. *Id.* (footnote omitted).

171. As Kennedy observes, case law relating to standards "gradually fills in the area with rules so closely bound to particular facts that they have little or no precedential value." *Id.*, at 1690 (footnote omitted).

172. C. GEERTZ, *Thick Description: Toward an Interpretive Theory of Culture*, in C. GEERTZ, THE INTERPRETATION OF CULTURES, at 3.

173. *Id.* at 18.

174. For varied discussions of practical reasoning, see ARISTOTLE, NICOMACHEAN ETHICS, book 6, chs. 5–11 (J.E.C. Welldon transl. 1987); R. BERNSTEIN, BEYOND OBJECTIVISM AND RELATIVISM (1983); R. POSNER, THE PROBLEMS OF JURIS-PRUDENCE (1990); S. SALKEVER, FINDING THE MEAN (1990); Eskridge & Frickey, *Statutory Interpretation as Practical Reasoning*, 42 STAN. L. REV. 321 (1990); Farber & Frickey, *Practical Reasoning and the First Amendment*, 34 U.C.L.A. L. REV. 1615 (1987); Michelman, *Takings, 1987*, 88 COLUM. L. REV. 1600 (1988); Nussbaum, *The Discernment of Perception: An Aristotelian Conception of Private and Public Rationality*, in M. NUSSBAUM, LOVE'S KNOWLEDGE: ESSAYS ON PHILOSOPHY AND LITERATURE 54 (1990); Radin, *The Liberal Conception of Property: Cross- Currents in the Jurisprudence of Takings*, 88 COLUM. 1667 (1988).

175. ARISTOTLE, book 6, ch. 5, at 191.

176. A. MACINTYRE, AFTER VIRTUE 223 (1984 2d ed.).

177. *Id.*

178. C. TAYLOR, SOURCES OF THE SELF 25 (1989).

179. *Id.* at 27.

180. On the significance and ubiquity of narrative in human experience, see J. BRUNER, ACTS OF MEANING (1990); J. BRUNER, ACTUAL MINDS, POSSIBLE WORLDS (1986); D. POLKINGHORNE, NARRATIVE KNOWING AND THE HUMAN SCI-

ENCES (1988); Gergen & Gergen, *Narrative and the Self as Relationship*, 21 ADV. EX-PERIMENTAL PSYCH. 17 (1988).

181. A. MACINTYRE, AFTER VIRTUE, at 222. This is of course the same as seeing oneself as a participant in an ongoing "game," to use Mead's concept. *See* chapter 4, at 101–2.

182. Geertz, *Fact and Law*, at 215.

183. *See* Weisbrod. This uncertainty is not confined to family law. *See, e.g.*, M. KAMMEN, A MACHINE THAT WOULD GO OF ITSELF (1986) (discussing various meanings attributed by popular culture to the Constitution).

184. M. GLENDON, ABORTION AND DIVORCE, at 138.

185. *See, e.g.*, M. GLENDON, RIGHTS TALK (1991); M. KAMMEN.

186. A. MACINTYRE, AFTER VIRTUE, at 222.

187. *See* chapter 4, at 106–17.

188. *See* chapter 2, at 59–62.

189. C. CAMPBELL, THE ROMANTIC ETHIC AND THE SPIRIT OF MODERN CONSUMERISM 213 (1987).

190. *Id.* at 214.

191. *Id.*

192. *Id.*

193. *See* A. DOUGLAS, THE FEMINIZATION OF AMERICAN CULTURE (1977).

194. *See* Introduction, at 1.

195. MELLMAN & LAZARUS, MASS MUTUAL AMERICAN VALUES STUDY 14 (1989).

196. *See* M. GLENDON, RIGHTS TALK.

7. Conclusion

1. Hafen, *The Family as an Entity*, 22 U.C. DAVIS L. REV. 866, 914 (1989).

2. Advertisement, *Rent a Father's Day Convertible*, BETHESDA–CHEVY CHASE ALMANAC, June 13, 1991, at 10.

3. *Id.*

4. *Id.*

5. Hafen, *The Constitutional Status of Marriage, Kinship, and Sexual Privacy—Balancing the Individual and Social Interests*, 81 MICH. L. REV. 463, 476 (1983).

6. *See* Subcommittee on Human Resources of the Committee on Ways and Means, U.S. House of Representatives, *Child Support Enforcement Report Card* (1991); Taylor, *Life without Father*, WASHINGTON POST, June 7, 1992, at C1. For an overview of recent efforts to improve enforcement of child support obligations, see Krause, *Child Support Reassessed: Limits of Private Responsibility and the Public Interest*, in DIVORCE REFORM AT THE CROSSROADS 166, 169–74 (S. Sugarman & H. Kay eds. 1990). Professor Krause's essay provides a useful discussion of the complexities we must confront in attempting to fashion a response to the needs of the children of divorce.

7. F. FURSTENBERG & A. CHERLIN, DIVIDED FAMILIES 119 (1991).

8. *Id. See also* N. CHODOROW, THE REPRODUCTION OF MOTHERING (1978); D. DINNERSTEIN, THE MERMAID AND THE MINOTAUR (1976).

9. Sennett, *Fragments against the Ruin: Coping with an Unbounded Present*, TIMES LITERARY SUPPLEMENT, Feb. 8, 1991, at 6.

10. *Id.*

11. Meyer, *American Intellectuals and the Victorian Crisis of Faith*, in VICTORIAN AMERICA 77 (D.W. Howe ed. 1976).

Bibliography

Ablow, *Inevitable Disappointments: Politics Can Mirror the Way People Expect Too Much from Relationships*, WASHINGTON POST, April 14, 1992, at Health p. 29.

ACTON, W., THE FUNCTIONS AND DISORDERS OF THE REPRODUCTIVE ORGANS IN YOUTH, IN ADULT AGE, AND IN ADVANCED LIFE (American ed. 1865).

ADAMS, B., THE FAMILY: A SOCIOLOGICAL INTERPRETATION (1975).

Advertisement, *Rent a Father's Day Convertible*, BETHESDA–CHEVY CHASE ALMANAC, June 13, 1991, at 10.

ALCOTT, W., THE YOUNG WIFE (1837).

ANDERSON, R. & G. COUCH, COUCH'S CYCLOPEDIA OF INSURANCE LAW (2d ed. 1982).

Angus, *Media beyond Representation*, in CULTURAL POLITICS IN CONTEMPORARY AMERICA (I. Angus & S. Jhally eds. 1989).

Appleby, *Value and Society*, in COLONIAL BRITISH AMERICA: ESSAYS IN THE NEW HISTORY OF THE EARLY MODERN ERA (J. Greene & J.R. Pole 1984).

Areen, *Baby M Reconsidered*, 76 GEO L.J. 1741 (1988).

AREEN, J., FAMILY LAW: CASES AND MATERIALS (2d ed. 1985).

Aries, *Two Successive Motivations for the Declining Birthrate in the West*, 6 POP. & DEV. REV. 645 (1980).

ARIES, P., CENTURIES OF CHILDHOOD (1962).

ARISTOTLE, NICOMACHEAN ETHICS (J.E.C. Welldon transl. 1987).

ATIYAH, P.S., PROMISES, MORALS, AND THE LAW (1981).

ATIYAH, P.S., THE RISE AND FALL OF FREEDOM OF CONTRACT (1979).

Auerbach, Blum, Smith & Williams, *Commentary on Gilligan's "In a Different Voice,"* 11 FEM. STUD. 149 (1985).

Averill & Boothroyd, *On Falling in Love in Conformance with the Romantic Ideal*, 1 MOTIVATION & EMOTION 235 (1977).

Averill, *A Constructivist View of Emotion*, in EMOTION: THEORY, RESEARCH AND EXPERIENCE. Vol. 1, THEORIES OF EMOTION (R. Plutchik & H. Kellerman eds. 1980).

Averill, *The Social Construction of Emotion: With Special Reference to Love*, in THE SOCIAL CONSTRUCTION OF THE PERSON (K. Gergen & K. Davis eds. 1985).

AVERILL, J., ANGER AND AGGRESSION: AN ESSAY ON EMOTION (1982).

Baker & Emery, *When Every Relationship is above Average: Perceptions and Expectations of Divorce at the Time of Marriage* (unpublished manuscript).

Baker, *The Ideology of the Economic Analysis of Law*, 5 PHIL. & PUB. AFF. 3 (1975).

BAKER, B., FAMILY EQUITY AT ISSUE (1981).

Baldwin & Holmes, *Private Audiences and Awareness of the Self*, 52 J. OF PERS. & SOC. PSYCH. 52 (1987).

Bart, *Rape Doesn't End with a Kiss*, 2 VIVA 39 (1975).

BARTHES, R., CAMERA LUCIDA (1981).

Bartlett & Stack, *Joint Custody, Feminism, and the Dependency Dilemma*, 2 BERKELEY WOMEN'S L.J. 9 (1986).

Bartlett, *Re-expressing Parenthood*, 98 YALE L.J. 293 (1988).

Bartlett, *Rethinking Parenthood as an Exclusive Status: The Need for Legal Alternatives When the Premise of the Nuclear Family Has Failed*, 70 VA. L. REV. 879 (1984).

BASCH, N., IN THE EYES OF THE LAW: WOMEN, MARRIAGE, AND PROPERTY IN NINETEENTH-CENTURY NEW YORK (1982).

Baudrillard, *The Ecstacy of Communication*, in THE ANTI- AESTHETIC: ESSAYS ON POSTMODERN CULTURE (H. Foster ed. 1983).

Becker, Landes & Michael, *An Economic Analysis of Marital Instability*, 85 J. POL. ECON. 1141 (1977).

Becker, *History, Culture, and Subjective Experience*, 8 J. HEALTH & SOC. BEH. 163 (1967).

Becker, *Prince Charming: Abstract Equality*, 1987 SUP. CT. REV. 201.

BECKER, G., A TREATISE ON THE FAMILY (1981).

BECKER, G., THE ECONOMIC APPROACH TO HUMAN BEHAVIOR (1976).

BECKER, G., THE ECONOMICS OF DISCRIMINATION (1971).

Bell, *Alimony and the Financially Dependent Spouse in Montgomery County, Maryland*, 22 FAM. L.Q. 225 (1988).

Bell, *Beyond Modernism, beyond Self*, in ART, POLITICS, AND WILL (Q. Anderson, S. Donadio & S. Marcus eds. 1977).

BELLAH, R., R. MADSEN, W. SULLIVAN, A. SWIDLER & S. TIPTON, HABITS OF THE HEART (1985).

BENNIS, W. & P. SLATER, THE TEMPORARY SOCIETY (1968).

BENSON, S., COUNTER CULTURES: SALESWOMEN, MANAGERS, AND CUS-TOMERS IN AMERICAN DEPARTMENT STORES, 1890–1940 (1986).

Berger & Kellner, *Marriage and the Construction of Reality*, 46 DIOGENES 1 (1964).

BERGER, B. & P. BERGER, THE WAR OVER THE FAMILY (1983).

BERGER, P. & T. LUCKMANN, THE SOCIAL CONSTRUCTION OF REALITY (1966).

BERGER, P., B. BERGER & H. KELLNER, THE HOMELESS MIND (1974).

BERMAN, M., ALL THAT IS SOLID MELTS INTO AIR: THE EXPERIENCE OF MODERNITY (1982).

BERNSTEIN, R., BEYOND OBJECTIVISM AND RELATIVISM (1983).

BIDDLE, B., ROLE THEORY: EXPECTATIONS, IDENTITIES, AND BEHAVIORS (1979).

BISHOP, J., NEW COMMENTARIES ON MARRIAGE, DIVORCE, AND SEPARATION (1891) (2 Vols.).

BLAKE, N., THE ROAD TO RENO (1962).

Block, *New Shapes of Family Life*, 28 DISSENT 350 (1981).

BLS Day Care Survey Shows Eleven Percent of Employers Offer Benefits or Services, Daily Lab. Rep. (BNA) No. 10, at B–1 (Jan. 15, 1988).

Blumberg, *Cohabitation without Marriage: A Different Perspective*, 28 U.C.L.A. L. REV. 1125 (1981).

BLUMSTEIN, P. & P. SCHWARTZ, AMERICAN FAMILIES (1983).

Bohannon, *Matrimonial Lawyers and the Divorce Industry*, in TAX, FINANCIAL, AND ESTATE PLANNING DEVELOPMENTS IN FAMILY LAW— 1981 EDITION (J. DuCanto ed. 1981).

Booth, *Sexual Activity of Teenage U.S. Girls Rose in 1980s*, WASHINGTON POST, Nov. 8, 1990, at A1.

BORGMANN, A., CROSSING THE POSTMODERN DIVIDE (1992).

BOWERS, R. (ed.), PSYCHOLOGICAL MAN (1971).

BOWLBY, R., JUST LOOKING: CONSUMER CULTURE IN DREISER, GISSING, AND ZOLA (1985).

Brenner, *Economics: An Imperialist Science?*, 9 J. LEG. STUD. 179 (1980).

BRIGGS, J.L., NEVER IN ANGER: PORTRAIT OF AN ESKIMO FAMILY (1970).

Brinig, Crafton & Levy, *Marriage and Opportunism* (unpublished manuscript).

Brooke-Rose, *The Dissolution of Character in the Novel*, in RECONSTRUCTING IN-DIVIDUALISM (T. Heller, M. Sosna & D. Wellbery eds. 1986).

Brown, *Family Intimacy in Magazine Advertising, 1920–1977*, 32 J. COMMUNICATION 173 (1982).

Brown, *Modernization: A Victorian Climax*, in VICTORIAN AMERICA 42 (D.W. Howe ed. 1976).

BROWN, G., DOMESTIC INDIVIDUALISM: IMAGINING SELF IN NINETEENTH-CENTURY AMERICA (1990).

BROWN, R., MODERNIZATION: THE TRANSFORMATION OF AMERICAN LIFE, 1600–1865 (1976).

Bruch, *And How Are the Children?* 2 INT'L. J. LAW & FAM. 106 (1988).

Bruch, *Cohabitation in the Common Law Countries a Decade after Marvin: Settled In or Moving Ahead?* 22 U.C.D. L. REV. 717 (1989).

BRUCHEY, S., THE ROOTS OF AMERICAN ECONOMIC GROWTH, 1607–1861 (1968).

BRUNER, J., ACTS OF MEANING (1990).

BRUNER, J., ACTUAL MINDS, POSSIBLE WORLDS (1986).

Buchanan, *Same-Sex Marriage: The Linchpin Issue*, 10 U. DAYTON L. REV. 541 (1985).

BUCHANAN, G.S., MORALITY, SEX, AND THE CONSTITUTION (1985).

BULLOCK, W., A TREATISE ON THE LAW OF HUSBAND AND WIFE IN THE STATE OF NEW YORK (1897).

Bumpass, Sweet & Cherlin, *Cohabitation and the Declining Rates of Marriage*, 53 J. MARR. & FAM. 913 (1991).

BUREAU OF LABOR STATISTICS, EMPLOYEE BENEFITS IN MEDIUM AND LARGE FIRMS, 1986, at 2 (June 1987).

BURGESS, E., J. LOCKE & M. THOMAS, THE FAMILY: FROM INSTITUTION TO COMPANIONSHIP (1963).

Burton, *Breach of Contract and the Common Law Duty to Perform in Good Faith*, 94 HARV. L. REV. 369 (1980).

Cahn, *Civil Images of Battered Women: The Impact of Domestic Violence on Child Custody Decisions*, 44 VAND. L. REV. 1041 (1991).

Callan & Gallois, *Perceptions about Having Children: Are Daughters Different from Their Mothers?* 45 J. MARR. & FAM. 607 (1983).

CALVINO, I., IF ON A WINTER'S NIGHT A TRAVELER (1981).

CAMPBELL, C., THE ROMANTIC ETHIC AND THE SPIRIT OF MODERN CONSUMERISM (1987).

CANBY, H.S., THE AGE OF CONFIDENCE (1934).

CANCIAN, F., LOVE IN AMERICA (1987).

Candland, *The Persistent Problems of Emotion*, in EMOTION (D.K. Candland, J. Fell, E. Keen, A. Leshner & R. Tarpy eds. 1977).

CAPLOW, T., H. BAHR, B. CHADWICK, R. HILL & M. WILLIAMSON, MIDDLETOWN FAMILIES (1983).

Carbone & Brinig, *Rethinking Marriage: Feminist Ideology, Economic Change, and Divorce Reform*, 65 TUL. L. REV. 953 (1991).

Carbone & Brinig, *The Reliance Interest in Marriage and Divorce*, 62 TUL. L. REV. 855 (1988).

CARLYLE, T., *Characteristics*, in 3 CRITICAL AND MISCELLANEOUS ESSAYS (Centenary ed. of CARLYLE'S WORKS H.D. Traill ed. 1896–1901).

Casad, *Unmarried Couples and Unjust Enrichment: From Status to Contract and Back Again?* 77 MICH. L. REV. 47 (1978).

CASSIRER, E., THE PHILOSOPHY OF THE ENLIGHTENMENT (1951).

CHERLIN, A., MARRIAGE, DIVORCE, REMARRIAGE (1971).

CHESTERTON, G.K., THE AUTOBIOGRAPHY OF G.K. CHESTERTON (1936).

CHIPMAN, D., AN ESSAY ON THE LAW OF CONTRACTS FOR THE PAYMENT OF SPECIFICK ARTICLES (1822).

CHODOROW, N., THE REPRODUCTION OF MOTHERING (1978).

Chused, *Married Women's Property Law: 1800–1850*, 71 GEO. L.J. 1359 (1983).

CIGNO, A., ECONOMICS OF THE FAMILY (1991).

Clancy, *Equal Protection Considerations of the Spousal Sexual Assault Exclusion*, 16 NEW ENG. L. REV. 1 (1980).

CLARK, H., THE LAW OF DOMESTIC RELATIONS IN THE UNITED STATES (1988 2d ed.).

CLECAK, P., AMERICA'S QUEST FOR THE IDEAL SELF (1983).

Cohen, *Property as Sovereignty*, 13 CORN. L.Q. 8 (1927).

Cohen, *The Basis of Contract*, 46 HARV. L. REV. 553 (1933).

Combs, *The Human Capital Concept as a Basis for Property Settlement at Divorce*, 2 J. DIVORCE 329 (1979).

Comment, *Marriage as Contract: Towards a Functional Redefinition of the Marital Status*, 9 COLUM. J.L. & SOC. PROBS. 607 (1973).

Comment, *Rape Laws, Equal Protection, and Privacy Rights*, 54 TUL. L. REV. 456 (1980).

CONNOR, S., POSTMODERNIST CULTURE (1989).

COONTZ, S., THE SOCIAL ORIGINS OF PRIVATE LIFE (1988).

Cornell, *Institutionalization of Meaning, Recollective Imagination, and the Potential for Transformative Legal Interpretation*, 136 U. PA. L. REV. 1135 (1988).

Cott, *Passionless: An Interpretation of Victorian Sexual Ideology, 1790–1850*, 4 SIGNS 219 (1978).

COTT, N., THE BONDS OF WOMANHOOD: "WOMAN'S SPHERE" IN NEW ENGLAND, 1780–1835 (1977).

COTT, N., THE GROUNDING OF MODERN FEMINISM (1987).

Coulter, *Affect and Social Context: Emotion Definition as a Social Task*, in THE SOCIAL CONSTRUCTION OF EMOTION (R. Harre ed. 1986).

Cover, *Foreword: Nomos and Narrative*, 97 HARV. L. REV. 4 (1983).

Cox, *Love Makes a Family—Nothing More, Nothing Less*, 8 J. LAW & POLITICS 5 (1991).

CROW, D., THE VICTORIAN WOMAN (1971).

Cunningham, *The New Implied and Statutory Warranties of Habitability in Residential Leases: From Contract to Status*, 16 URB. L. ANN. 3 (1979).

Curti, *The Changing Concept of "Human Nature" in the Literature of American Advertising*, 41 BUS. HIST. REV. 335 (1967).

D'EMILIO, J. & E. FREEDMAN, INTIMATE MATTERS: A HISTORY OF SEXUALITY IN AMERICA (1988).

Dan-Cohen, *Law, Community, and Communication*, 1989 DUKE L. J. 1654.

Danzig, *A Comment on the Jurisprudence of the New Commercial Code*, 27 STAN. L. REV. 621 (1975).

DAVIDOFF, L. & C. HALL, FAMILY FORTUNES: MEN AND WOMEN OF THE ENGLISH MIDDLE CLASS, 1780–1850 (1987).

Dawes, van der Kragt & Orbell, *Cooperation for the Benefit of Us—Not Me, or My Conscience*, in BEYOND SELF-INTEREST (J. Mansbridge ed. 1990).

De Souza, *The Rationality of Emotions*, in EXPLAINING EMOTIONS (A. Rorty ed. 1980).

DeAngelis, *Sex Secrets Women Need to Know*, READER'S DIGEST, March 1991, at 177.

Degler, *What Ought to Be and What Was: Women's Sexuality in the Nineteenth Century*, in THE AMERICAN FAMILY IN SOCIAL- HISTORICAL PERSPECTIVE (M. Gordon ed. 1978 2d ed.).

DEGLER, C., AT ODDS: WOMEN AND THE FAMILY IN AMERICA FROM THE REVOLUTION TO THE PRESENT (1980).

DeMaris & Leslie, *Cohabitation with the Future Spouse: Its Influence upon Marital Satisfaction and Communication*, 46 J. MARR. & FAM. 77 (1984).

Demos, *Images of the Family Then and Now*, in CHANGING IMAGES OF THE FAMILY (B. Meyerhoff & V. Tuft eds. 1979).

DEMOS, J., A LITTLE COMMONWEALTH: FAMILY LIFE IN PLYMOUTH COLONY (1970).

DEROUGEMENT, D., LOVE IN THE WESTERN WORLD (1956 rev. ed.).

DETOCQUEVILLE, A., 2 DEMOCRACY IN AMERICA (G. Lawrence ed. 1969).

DEWEY, J., THE QUEST FOR CERTAINTY (1960 ed.).

DINNERSTEIN, D., THE MERMAID AND THE MINOTAUR (1976).

DOUGLAS, A., THE FEMINIZATION OF AMERICAN CULTURE (1977).

DOUGLAS, M. & B. ISHERWOOD, THE WORLD OF GOODS (1979).

Dowd, *Work and Family: Restructuring the Workplace*, 32 ARIZ. L. REV. 431 (1990).

DUBLIN, T., WOMEN AT WORK: THE TRANSFORMATION OF WORK AND COMMUNITY IN LOWELL, MASSACHUSETTS, 1826–1860 (1979).

Duncan & Morgan, *The Panel Study of Income Dynamics*, in LIFE COURSE DYNAMICS (G.H. Elder ed. 1985).

DUSENBERRY, J.S., INCOME, SAVINGS, AND THE THEORY OF CONSUMER BEHAVIOR (1967).

Eagleton, *Capitalism, Modernism, and Postmodernism*, in T. EAGLETON, AGAINST THE GRAIN: ESSAYS, 1975–1985 (1986).

EBAUGH, H., BECOMING AN EX (1988).

Edmundsen, *Prophet of a New Postmodernism*, HARPER'S, Dec. 1989, at 62.

Eggebeen & Uhlenberg, *Changes in the Organization of Men's Lives: 1960–1980*, 34 FAM. REL. 251 (1985).

EHRENREICH, B., THE HEARTS OF MEN (1983).

Eisenberg, *The Bargain Principle and Its Limits*, 95 HARV. L. REV. 741 (1982).

Ekman & Oster, *Facial Expressions of Emotion*, 30 ANN. REV. PSYCH. 527 (1979).

ELLIS, S., THE WIVES OF ENGLAND (1843).

Ellman, *The Theory of Alimony*, 77 CALIF. L. REV. 1 (1989).

ELSHTAIN, J., PUBLIC MAN, PRIVATE WOMAN (1981).

Elster, *Selfishness and Altruism*, in BEYOND SELF-INTEREST (J. Mansbridge ed. 1990).

ELSTER, J., SOUR GRAPES: STUDIES IN THE SUBVERSION OF RATIONALITY (1983).

Erlanger, Chambliss & Melli, *Participation and Flexibility in Informal Processes: Cautions from the Divorce Context*, 21 LAW & SOC. REV. 585 (1987).

Eskridge & Frickey, *Statutory Interpretation as Practical Reasoning*, 42 STAN. L. REV. 321 (1990).

Espenshade, *Marriage Trends in American: Estimates, Implications, and Underlying Causes*, 11 POP. & DEV. REV. 193 (1985).

EWEN, S. & E. EWEN, CHANNELS OF DESIRE (1982).

EWEN, S., ALL-CONSUMING IMAGES: THE POLITICS OF STYLE IN CONTEMPORARY CULTURE (1988).

EWEN, S., CAPTAINS OF CONSCIOUSNESS (1976).

Farber & Frickey, *Practical Reasoning and the First Amendment*, 34 U.C.L.A. L. REV. 1615 (1987).

Farber, *The Future of the American Family: A Dialectical Account*, 8 J. FAM. ISS. 431 (1987).

FARBER, B., THE FAMILY: ORGANIZATION AND INTERACTION (1964).

FERGUSON, K., SELF, SOCIETY, AND WOMANKIND (1980).

Fine, *Symbolic Interactionism in the Post-Blumerian Age*, in FRONTIERS OF SOCIAL THEORY: THE NEW SYNTHESES (G. Ritzer ed. 1990).

Fineman, *Law and Changing Patterns of Behavior: Sanctions on Non-Marital Cohabitation*, 1981 WIS. L. REV. 275.

Fineman, *Societal Factors Affecting the Creation of Legal Rules for Distribution of Property at Divorce*, in AT THE BOUNDARIES OF LAW: FEMINISM AND LEGAL THEORY (M. Fineman & N. Thomadsen (1991).

FINEMAN, M., THE ILLUSION OF EQUALITY (1991).

FINKELHOR, D. & K. YLLO, LICENSE TO RAPE (1985).

Finley, *A Break in the Silence: Including Women's Issues in a Torts Course*, 1 YALE J. LAW & FEM. 41 (1989).

Finley, *Transcending Equality Theory: A Way Out of the Maternity and the Workplace Debate*, 86 COLUM. L. REV. 1118 (1986).

FLIEGELMAN, J., PRODIGALS AND PILGRIMS (1982).

FOWLER, O.S., LOVE AND PARENTAGE (1846).

FOX, R.W. & T.J. LEARS (eds.), THE CULTURE OF CONSUMPTION (1983).

FOX, S., THE MIRROR MAKERS: A HISTORY OF AMERICAN ADVERTISING AND ITS CREATORS (1984).

FOX-GENOVESE, E., FEMINISM WITHOUT ILLUSIONS (1991).

Frank, Berman & Mazur-Hart, *No-Fault Divorce and the Divorce Rate: The Nebraska Experience—An Interrupted Time Series Analysis and Commentary*, 58 NEB. L. REV. 1 (1978).

FRANK, R., PASSIONS WITHIN REASON (1988).
Freed & Walker, *Family Law in the Fifty States: An Overview*, 21 FAM. L. Q. 417 (1988).
Freeman, *"But If You Can't Rape Your Wife, Who(m) Can You Rape?": The Marital Rape Exemption Re-examined*, 15 FAM. L.Q. 1 (1981).
FRIED, C., CONTRACT AS PROMISE (1981).
FRIEDMAN, L., A HISTORY OF AMERICAN LAW (1973).
FRIEDMAN, L., CONTRACT LAW IN AMERICA (1965).
FRIEDMAN, L., THE REPUBLIC OF CHOICE (1990).
FRIEDMAN, M., FREE TO CHOOSE (1980).
Friedmann, *Some Reflections on Status and Freedom*, in ESSAYS IN JURISPRUDENCE IN HONOR OF ROSCOE POUND (R. Newman ed. 1962).
Frieze, *Investigating the Causes and Consequences of Marital Rape*, 8 SIGNS 532 (1983).
FROST, R., *Death of the Hired Man*, in NORTH OF BOSTON (1914).
FROUD, J.A., THE NEMESIS OF FAITH (1904 ed.).
Frug, *Re-Reading Contracts: A Feminist Analysis of a Contracts Casebook*, 34 AMER. U. L. REV. 1065 (1985).
FUCHS, V., WOMEN'S QUEST FOR ECONOMIC EQUALITY (1988).
FURSTENBERG, F. & A. CHERLIN, DIVIDED FAMILIES (1991).
FURSTENBERG, F. & G. SPANIER, RECYCLING THE FAMILY (1984).
Gadlin, *Private Lives and Public Order: A Critical View of the History of Intimate Relations in the United States*, in CLOSE RELATIONSHIPS: PERSPECTIVES ON THE MEANING OF INTIMACY (G. Levinger & H. Rausch eds. 1977).
Galston, *A Liberal Democratic Case for the Two-Parent Family*, 1 THE RESPONSIVE COMMUNITY 14 (1991).
Gamble, *The Antenuptial Contract*, 26 U. MIAMI L. REV. 692 (1972).
Gardels, *America as a Family*, NEW PERSPECTIVES Q., Fall 1988, at 21.
Garrison, *Good Intentions Gone Awry: How New York's Equitable Distribution Law Affected Divorce Outcomes*, 57 BROOKLYN L. REV. 621 (1991).
Garrison, *The Economics of Divorce: Changing Rules, Changing Results*, in DIVORCE REFORM AT THE CROSSROADS (S. Sugarman & H. Kay eds. 1990).
GAY, P., EDUCATION OF THE SENSES (1984).
GAY, P., THE SCIENCE OF FREEDOM (1969).
GAY, P., THE TENDER PASSION (1986).
Geertz, *Fact and Law in Comparative Perspective*, in C. GEERTZ, LOCAL KNOWLEDGE (1983).
Geertz, *The Growth of Culture and the Evolution of Mind*, in C. GEERTZ, THE INTERPRETATION OF CULTURES (1973).
Geertz, *Thick Description: Toward an Interpretive Theory of Culture*, in C. GEERTZ, THE INTERPRETATION OF CULTURES (1973).
GEERTZ, H., THE VOCABULARY OF EMOTION (1959).
GELLHORN, W., J. HYMAN & S. ASCH, CHILDREN AND FAMILIES IN THE COURTS OF NEW YORK CITY (1953).
Gergen & Gergen, *Narrative and the Self as Relationship*, 21 ADV. EXPERIMENTAL PSYCH. 17 (1988).
GERGEN, K., THE PSYCHOLOGY OF BEHAVIOR EXCHANGE (1969).
GERGEN, K., THE SATURATED SELF: DILEMMAS OF IDENTITY IN CONTEMPORARY LIFE (1991).
GERSON, K., HARD CHOICES (1985).

GERTH, H. & C.W. MILLS, CHARACTER AND SOCIAL STRUCTURE: THE PSY-
CHOLOGY OF SOCIAL INSTITUTIONS (1953).
GIDDENS, A., THE CONSEQUENCES OF MODERNITY (1990).
GIDDENS, A., MODERNITY AND SELF-IDENTITY (1991).
Gilligan, Remapping the Moral Domain: New Images of Self in Relationship, in MAPPING
THE MORAL DOMAIN (C. Gilligan, J. Ward, J. Taylor eds. 1988).
GILLIGAN, C., IN A DIFFERENT VOICE (1982).
GILMORE, G., THE AGES OF AMERICAN LAW (1977).
GILMORE, G., THE DEATH OF CONTRACT (1976).
Gladstone, The Bill for Divorce, QUARTERLY REVIEW 253 (1857).
Glendon, Marriage and the State: The Withering Away of Marriage, 62 VA. L. REV. 663
(1976).
Glendon, The Transformation of American Landlord-Tenant Law, 23 B.C.L. REV. 503
(1982).
GLENDON, M., ABORTION AND DIVORCE IN WESTERN LAW (1989).
GLENDON, M., RIGHTS TALK (1991).
GLENDON, M., THE NEW FAMILY AND THE NEW PROPERTY (1981).
GLENDON, M., THE TRANSFORMATION OF FAMILY LAW (1989).
Glenn & McLanahan, Children and Marital Happiness: A Further Specification of the
Relationship, 44 J. MARR. & THE FAM. 63 (1982).
Glenn & Weaver, The Changing Relationship of Marital Status to Reported Happiness,
50 J. MARR. & THE FAM. 317 (1988).
Goffman, E., Role Distance, in E. GOFFMAN, ENCOUNTERS: TWO STUDIES IN THE
SOCIOLOGY OF INTERACTION (1961).
Goldschneider & Goldschneider, Moving Out and Marriage: What Do Young Adults
Expect? 52 AM. SOC. REV. 278 (1987).
Goldschneider & LeBourdais, The Falling Age at Leaving Home, 1920–1979, 70 SOCI-
OLOGY AND SOC. RES. 99 (1986).
GOLDSCHNEIDER, F. & L. WAITE, NEW FAMILIES, NO FAMILIES (1991).
GOOD HOUSEKEEPING, Feb. 6, 1886, at 190.
Goode, Individual Investments in Family Relationships over the Coming Decades, 6
TOCQUEVILLE REV. 51 (1984).
GOODIN, R., PROTECTING THE VULNERABLE (1985).
Gordon, Maccauley, Macneil, and the Discovery of Solidarity and Power in Contract Law,
1985 WIS. L. REV. 565.
Gordon, The Sociology of Sentiments and Emotion, in SOCIAL PSYCHOLOGY: SOCI-
OLOGICAL PERSPECTIVES (M. Rosenberg & R. Turner eds. 1981).
GREVEN, P., THE PROTESTANT TEMPERAMENT (1977).
GRISWOLD, R., FAMILY AND DIVORCE IN CALIFORNIA, 1850–1890 (1982).
GROSS, M., THE PSYCHOLOGICAL SOCIETY (1978).
Grossberg, MTV: Swinging on the (Postmodern) Star, in CULTURAL POLITICS IN CON-
TEMPORARY AMERICA (I. Angus & S. Jhally eds. 1989).
GROSSBERG, M., GOVERNING THE HEARTH (1985).
Habermas, Modernity—An Incomplete Project, in THE ANTI-AESTHETIC: ESSAYS ON
POSTMODERN CULTURE (H. Foster ed. 1983).
Hafen, The Constitutional Status of Marriage, Kinship, and Sexual Privacy—Balancing the
Individual and Social Interests, 81 MICH. L. REV. 463 (1983).
Hafen, The Family as an Entity, 22 U.C. DAVIS L. REV. 866 (1989).

Hagestad, *Demographic Change and the Life Course: Some Emerging Trends in the Family Realm*, 37 FAM. REL. 405 (1988).

Hale, *Bargaining, Duress, and Economic Liberty*, 43 COLUM. L. REV. 603 (1943).

Hale, *Coercion and Distribution in a Supposedly Non- Coercive State*, 38 POL. SCI. Q. 470 (1923).

HALE, M., 1 THE HISTORY OF THE PLEAS OF THE CROWN (1st American ed. 1847).

HALE, N., FREUD AND THE AMERICANS (1971).

Harding, *The Instability of the Analytical Categories of Feminist Theory*, 11 SIGNS 645 (1986).

Harre, *An Outline of the Social Constructionist Viewpoint*, in THE SOCIAL CONSTRUCTION OF EMOTION (R. Harre ed. 1986).

Harris, *Race and Essentialism in Feminist Legal Theory*, 42 STAN. L. REV. 581 (1990).

Harry, *Marriage among Gay Males: The Separation of Intimacy and Sex*, in THE SOCIOLOGICAL PERSPECTIVE (S. McNall ed. 4th ed. 1977).

Hartog, *Marital Exits and Marital Expectations in Nineteenth- Century America* 80 GEO. L.J. 95 (1991).

HARVEY, D., THE CONDITION OF POSTMODERNITY (1989).

Heath & Ciscel, *Patriarchy, Family Structure, and the Exploitation of Women's Labor*, 22 J. ECON. ISSUES 781 (1988).

Heiss, *Social Roles*, in SOCIAL PSYCHOLOGY: SOCIOLOGICAL PERSPECTIVES (M. Rosenberg & R.H. Turner ed. 1981).

Hilf, *Marital Privacy and Spousal Rape*, 16 NEW ENGL. L. REV. 31 (1980).

Hirschleifer, *The Expanding Domain of Economics*, 75 AM. ECON. REV. 53 (1985).

HOCHSCHILD, A. (WITH A. MACHUNG), SECOND SHIFT (1989).

Hoffman & Duncan, *What Are the Economic Consequences of Divorce?* 25 DEMOG. 641 (1988).

HOLLAND, D. & N. QUINN, CULTURAL MODELS IN LANGUAGE AND THOUGHT (1987).

HOLMES, O.W., *The Path of the Law*, in COLLECTED LEGAL PAPERS 171 (1920).

HOOKS, B., AIN'T I A WOMAN (1981).

HORWITZ, M., THE TRANSFORMATION OF AMERICAN LAW, 1780–1860 (1977).

HOUGHTON, W., THE VICTORIAN FRAME OF MIND (1957).

Howe, *The Problem of Privatized Injuries: Feminist Strategies for Litigation*, in AT THE BOUNDARIES OF LAW: FEMINISM AND LEGAL THEORY (M. Fineman & M. Thomadsen eds. 1991).

Howe, *Victorian Culture in America*, in VICTORIAN AMERICA (D.W. Howe ed. 1976).

Hoyt, *The Impact of a Money Economy upon Consumption Patterns*, 305 ANN. AM. ACAD. POL. & SOC. SCI. 12 (1956).

Hunt & Hunt, *Here to Play: From Families to Lifestyles*, 8 J. FAM. ISS. 440 (1987).

Hunter, *An Essay on Contract and Status: Race, Marriage, and the Meretricious Spouse*, 64 VA. L. REV. 1039 (1978).

HUNTER, J., AMERICAN EVANGELICISM: CONSERVATIVE RELIGION AND THE QUANDARY OF MODERNITY (1983).

HURST, J.W., LAW AND THE CONDITIONS OF FREEDOM IN THE NINETEENTH-CENTURY UNITED STATES (1956).

Huston & Robins, *Conceptual and Methodological Issues in Studying Close Relationships*, 44 J. MARR. & THE FAM. 901 (1982).

Ingleby, *Matrimonial Breakdown and the Legal Process: The Limitations of No-Fault Divorce*, 11 LAW & POLICY 1 (1989).

INKELES, A. & D. SMITH, BECOMING MODERN: INDIVIDUAL CHANGE IN SIX DEVELOPING COUNTRIES (1974).

Jacob, *Faulting No-Fault*, 1987 AM. BAR FOUND. RES. J. 773.

JACOB, H., SILENT REVOLUTION: THE TRANSFORMATION OF DIVORCE LAW IN THE UNITED STATES (1988).

Jaff, *Wedding Bell Blues: The Position of Unmarried People in American Law*, 30 ARIZ. L. REV. 207 (1988).

James McCormick Mitchell Lecture, *Feminist Discourse, Moral Values, and the Law—A Conversation*, 34 BUFF. L. REV. 11 (1985).

JAMES, W., PRAGMATISM (1991 ed.).

Jameson, *Postmodernism and Consumer Society*, in THE ANTI-AESTHETIC: ESSAYS ON POSTMODERN CULTURE (H. Foster ed. 1983).

Jameson, *Postmodernism; or, The Cultural Logic of Late Capitalism*, 146 NEW LEFT REVIEW 53 (1984).

JAMESON, F., POSTMODERNISM; OR, THE CULTURAL LOGIC OF LATE CAPITALISM (1991).

Jencks, *Varieties of Altruism*, in BEYOND SELF- INTEREST (J. Mansbridge ed. 1990).

JOHNSON, W.S., SEX AND MARRIAGE IN VICTORIAN POETRY (1975).

Jones, *The Rights to Marry and Divorce: A New Look at Some Unanswered Questions*, 63 WASH. U. L. Q. 577 (1985).

JOURARD, S., THE TRANSPARENT SELF (1971).

KAMMEN, M., A MACHINE THAT WOULD GO OF ITSELF (1986).

KAPLAN, E.A., ROCKING AROUND THE CLOCK: MUSIC TELEVISION, POST-MODERNISM, AND POPULAR CULTURE (1987).

Karst, *The Freedom of Intimate Association*, 89 YALE L. J. 624 (1980).

Kay, *An Appraisal of California's No-Fault Divorce Law*, 75 CALIF. L. REV. 291 (1987).

Kelman, *Consumption Theory, Production Theory, and Ideology in the Coase Theorem*, 52 S. CAL. L. REV. 669 (1979).

Kennedy & Michelman, *Are Property and Contract Efficient?* 8 HOFSTRA L. REV. 711 (1975).

Kennedy, *Form and Substance in Private Law Adjudication*, 89 HARV. L. REV. 1685 (1976).

Kerber, *Making Republicanism Useful*, 97 YALE L. J. 1663 (1988).

KERCKHOFF, A.C. & K.W. BACK, THE JUNE BUG: A STUDY OF HYSTERICAL CONTAGION (1968).

KERN, L., AN ORDERED LOVE (1981).

Kisthardt, *Of Fatherhood, Families, and Fantasy: The Legacy of Michael H. v. Gerald D.*, 65 TUL. L. REV. 585 (1991).

Klaff, *The Tender Years Doctrine: A Defense*, 70 CALIF. L. REV. 335 (1982).

Klarman, *Marital Agreements in Contemplation of Divorce*, 10 U. MICH. J.L. REF. 397 (1977).

KOHLBERG, L., THE PHILOSOPHY OF MORAL DEVELOPMENT (1981).

Krause, *Bringing the Bastard into the Great Society— A Proposed Act on Legitimacy*, 44 TEX. L. REV. 829 (1967).

Krause, *Child Support Reassessed: Limits of Private Responsibility and the Public Interest*, in DIVORCE REFORM AT THE CROSSROADS (S. Sugarman & H. Kay eds. 1990).

Krause, *Legal Position: Unmarried Couples*, in LAW IN THE U.S.A. FACES SOCIAL AND SCIENTIFIC CHANGE (Supplement) 34 AM. J. COMP. L. 533 (J. Hazard & W. Wagner eds. 1986).

Krauskopf & Thomas, *Partnership Marriage: The Solution to an Ineffective and Inequitable Law of Support*, 35 OHIO ST. L.J. 558 (1974).

Krauskopf, *Recompense for Financing Spouse's Education: Legal Protection for the Marital Investor in Human Capital*, 28 KAN. L. REV. 379 (1980).

Krauskopf, *Theories of Property Division/Spousal Support: Searching for Solutions to the Mystery*, 23 FAM. L. Q. 253 (1988).

KUNDERA, M., THE BOOK OF LAUGHTER AND FORGETTING (M.H. Heim transl. 1980).

Lacey, *The Law of Artificial Insemination and Surrogate Parenthood in Oklahoma: Roadblocks to the Right to Procreate*, 22 TULSA L.J. 281 (1987).

Ladden & Franco, *The Uniform Premarital Agreement Act: An Ill-Reasoned Retreat from the Unconscionability Analysis*, 4 AM. J. FAM. L. 267 (1990).

Lahey, *Reasonable Women and the Law*, in AT THE BOUNDARIES OF LAW: FEMINISM AND LEGAL THEORY (M. Fineman & M. Thomadsen eds. 1991).

Landes & Posner, *The Economics of the Baby Shortage*, 7 J. LEG. STUD. 323 (1978).

LASCH, C., HAVEN IN A HEARTLESS WORLD (1979).

LASCH, C., THE CULTURE OF NARCISSISM (1979).

LASCH, C., THE MINIMAL SELF (1984).

Lears, *From Salvation to Self-Realization: Advertising and the Roots of Consumer Culture, 1880–1930*, in THE CULTURE OF CONSUMPTION (R.W. Fox & T.J. Lears eds. 1983).

LEARS, T.J., NO PLACE OF GRACE: ANTIMODERNISM AND THE TRANSFORMATION OF AMERICAN CULTURE, 1880–1920 (1981).

LEBSOCK, S., THE FREE WOMEN OF PETERSBURG (1984).

LEFEBVRE, H., EVERYDAY LIFE IN THE MODERN WORLD (1971).

LEISS, W. & S. JHALLY, SOCIAL COMMUNICATION IN ADVERTISING (1986).

LEISS, W., THE LIMITS OF SATISFACTION: AN ESSAY ON THE PROBLEM OF NEEDS AND COMMODITIES (1976).

Lenhoff & Becker, *Family and Medical Leave Legislation in the States: Toward a Comprehensive Approach*, 26 HARV. J. LEGIS. 403 (1989).

Lesthaege, *A Century of Demographic and Cultural Change in Western Europe: An Explanation of Underlying Dimensions*, 9 POP. & DEV. REV. 411 (1983).

LEVINE, D., ECONOMIC THEORY (1978).

LEVINE, D., FAMILY FORMATION IN AN AGE OF NASCENT CAPITALISM (1977).

Levinger, *A Social Psychological Perspective on Marital Dissolution*, in DIVORCE AND SEPARATION: CONTEXT, CAUSES, AND CONSEQUENCES (G. Levinger & O. Moles eds. 1979).

Levinson, *Testimonial Privileges and the Preferences of Friendship*, 1984 DUKE L.J. 631.

Lewis and Rosenblum, *Introduction: Issues in Affect Development*, in THE DEVELOPMENT OF AFFECT (M. Lewis & L. Rosenblum eds. 1978).

Lewis, *From This Day Forward: A Feminine Moral Discourse on Homosexual Marriage*, 97 YALE L.J. 1783 (1988).

LEWIS, J., THE PURSUIT OF HAPPINESS (1983).

Lichtenstein, *Marital Misconduct and the Allocation of Financial Resources at Divorce: A Farewell to Fault*, 54 U.M.K.C. L. REV. 3 (1985).

LIFTON, R., BOUNDARIES (1970).

LIFTON, R., THE FUTURE OF IMMORTALITY (1987).

LINTON, R., THE STUDY OF MAN (1936).

Linzer, *The Decline of Assent: At-Will Employment as a Case Study of the Breakdown of Private Law Theory*, 20 GA. L. REV. 323 (1986).

LIPSEY, R., G. SPARKS & P. STEINER, ECONOMICS (1973 4th ed.).

Littleton, *Reconstructing Sexual Equality*, 75 CALIF. L. REV. 1279 (1987).

Lopata, *Role Theory*, in SOCIAL ROLES AND SOCIAL INSTITUTIONS (J. Blau & N. Goodman eds. 1991).

LORDE, A., SISTER OUTSIDER (1984).

LUCKMANN, T., THE INVISIBLE RELIGION (1967).

LUHMANN, N., TRUST AND POWER (1979).

LYOTARD, THE POSTMODERN CONDITION (G. Bennington & B. Massumi trans. 1984).

LYSTRA, K., SEARCHING THE HEART (1989).

MACANDREW, C. & R. EDGERTON, DRUNKEN COMPORTMENT (1969).

Macaulay, *Elegant Models, Empirical Pictures, and the Complexities of Contract*, 11 L. & SOC. REV. 507 (1977).

Macaulay, *Non-Contractual Relations in Business: A Preliminary Study*, 28 AM. SOC. REV. 55 (1963).

MACAULAY, S., LAW AND THE BALANCE OF POWERS: THE AUTOMOBILE MANUFACTURERS AND THEIR DEALERS (1966).

MACFARLANE, A., THE ORIGINS OF ENGLISH INDIVIDUALISM: THE FAMILY, PROPERTY, AND SOCIAL TRANSFORMATION (1978).

MACINTYRE, A., AFTER VIRTUE (1984 2d ed.).

MACINTYRE, A., WHOSE JUSTICE? WHICH RATIONALITY? (1988).

Macneil, *Economic Analysis of Contractual Relations: Its Shortfalls and the Need for A "Rich Classificatory Apparatus,"* 75 Nw. L. REV. 1018 (1981).

MACNEIL, I., THE NEW SOCIAL CONTRACT: AN INQUIRY INTO MODERN CONTRACTUAL RELATIONS (1980).

MAINE, H., ANCIENT LAW (2d ed. 1864).

MALLOCK, W.H., THE NEW REPUBLIC; OR, CULTURE, FAITH, AND PHILOSOPHY IN AN ENGLISH COUNTRY HOUSE (1877).

MARCHAND, R., ADVERTISING THE AMERICAN DREAM (1985).

MARCUS, S., THE OTHER VICTORIANS (1966).

Markovits, *Family Traits* (Book Review), 88 MICH. L. REV. 1734 (1990).

Markus & Nurius, *Possible Selves*, 41 AM. PSYCHOLOGIST 954 (1986).

MARLOW, L. & S. SAUBER, THE HANDBOOK OF DIVORCE MEDIATION (1990).

Martin & Bumpass, *Recent Trends in Marital Disruption*, 26 DEMOG. 37 (1989).

MARX, K., 1 CAPITAL (S. Moore & E. Aveling eds. 3d German ed. 1967).

MASLOW, A., TOWARD A PSYCHOLOGY OF BEING (1968 2d ed.).

MASS MUTUAL LIFE INSURANCE CO., FAMILY VALUES 1 (no date; received April 30, 1991).

MAY, E., GREAT EXPECTATIONS: MARRIAGE AND DIVORCE IN POST-VICTORIAN AMERICA (1980).

McCarthy, *A Comparison of the Probability of the Dissolution of First and Second Marriages*, 15 DEMOG. 345 (1978).

MCCARY, J., FREEDOM AND GROWTH IN MARRIAGE (1975).

MCKENDRICK, N., J. BREWER & J.H. PLUMB (eds.), THE BIRTH OF A CONSUMER SOCIETY: THE COMMERCIALIZATION OF EIGHTEENTH-CENTURY ENGLAND (1982).

McLindon, *Separate but Unequal: The Economic Disaster of Divorce for Women and Children*, 21 FAM. L.Q. 351 (1987).

McPartland, Cumming & Garretson, *Self-Conception and Ward Behavior in Two Psychiatric Hospitals*, 24 SOCIOMETRY 111 (1964).

MCWHIRTER, D. & A. MATTISON, THE MALE COUPLE (1984).

MEAD, G.H., MIND, SELF, AND SOCIETY (1934).

MEAD, G.H., THE PHILOSOPHY OF THE ACT (1938).

MEAD, G.H., THE PHILOSOPHY OF THE PRESENT (1932).

Mechanic, *Social Psychological Factors Affecting the Presentation of Bodily Complaints*, 286 NEW ENG. J. MED. 1132 (1972).

MELLMAN & LAZARUS, MASS MUTUAL AMERICAN VALUES STUDY (1989).

Melton & Saks, *The Law as an Instrument of Socialization and Social Structure*, in THE LAW AS A BEHAVIORAL INSTRUMENT (G. Melton ed. 1986).

MENDOLA, M., THE MENDOLA REPORT (1980).

Menkel-Meadow, *Portia in a Different Voice: Speculations on a Women's Lawyering Process*, 1 BERK. WOMEN'S L. J. 39 (1989).

Meyer, *American Intellectuals and the Victorian Crisis of Faith*, in VICTORIAN AMERICA (D.W. Howe ed. 1976).

MEYEROWITZ, J., NO SENSE OF PLACE (1985).

Michael, Fuchs & Scott, *Social Changes in the Propensity to Live Alone: 1950–1976*, 17 DEMOGRAPHY 39 (1980).

Michelman, *Foreword: Traces of Self-Government*, 100 HARV. L. REV. 4 (1986).

Michelman, *Takings, 1987* 88 COLUM. L. REV. 1600 (1988).

Milkman, *Women's History and the Sears Case*, 12 FEM. STUD. 375 (1986).

MILL, J.S., 2 LETTERS (H.S.R. Elliot ed. 1910).

MILL, J.S., THE SPIRIT OF THE AGE (F.A. von Hayek ed. 1942).

MILL, J.S., THE SUBJECTION OF WOMEN (S. Mansfield ed. 1980).

MILLER, D., THE NEW POLYTHEISM (1973).

MILLER, J., TOWARD A NEW PSYCHOLOGY OF WOMEN (1976).

Minow, *"Forming underneath Everything that Grows": Toward a History of Family Law*, 1985 WIS. L. REV. 819.

Minow, *Words and the Door to the Land of Change: Law, Language, and Family Violence*, 43 VAND. L. REV. 1665 (1990).

MINOW, M., MAKING ALL THE DIFFERENCE (1991).

MINTZ, S. & S. KELLOGG, DOMESTIC REVOLUTIONS: A SOCIAL HISTORY OF AMERICAN FAMILY LIFE (1988).

MINTZ, S., A PRISON OF EXPECTATIONS: THE FAMILY IN VICTORIAN CULTURE (1983).

Mnookin & Kornhauser, *Bargaining in the Shadow of the Law: The Case of Divorce*, 88 YALE L.J. 950 (1979).

Mnookin, *Divorce Bargaining: The Limits on Private Ordering*, 18 U. MICH. J. LAW REF. 1015 (1985).

Monroe, Barton & Klingemann, *Altruism and the Theory of Rational Action: Rescuers of Jews in Nazi Europe*, 101 ETHICS 103 (1990).

Monter, *The Pedestal and the Stake: Courtly Love and Witchcraft*, in BECOMING VISIBLE: WOMEN IN EUROPEAN HISTORY (R. Bridenthal & C. Koonz eds. 1977).

Mooney, *Old Kontract Principles and Karl's New Kode: An Essay on the Jurisprudence of Our New Commercial Law*, 11 VILL. L. REV. 213 (1966).

MORGAN, E., THE PURITAN FAMILY (1966).

MOSHER, C., THE MOSHER SURVEY: SEXUAL ATTITUDES OF FORTY- FIVE VIC-
TORIAN WOMEN (J. MaHood & K. Wenburg eds. 1980).

Muris, *Opportunistic Behavior and the Law of Contracts*, 65 MINN. L. REV. 521 (1981).

Myers, Gallas, Hanson & Keilitz, *Divorce Mediation in the States: Institutionalization,
Use, and Assessment*, 12 STATE COURT J. 17 (1988).

Nagel, *Constitutional Doctrine and Political Direction*, TRIAL, Dec. 1989, at 72.

Nails, *Social-Scientific Sexism: Gilligan's Mismeasure of Man*, 50 SOC. RES. 643 (1983).

NAIR, K., BLOSSOMS IN THE DUST: THE HUMAN FACTOR IN INDIAN DEVEL-
OPMENT (1962).

NATIONAL COMMISSION ON WORKING WOMEN, PRIME TIME KIDS: AN ANAL-
YSIS OF CHILDREN AND FAMILIES ON TELEVISION (1985).

Nedelsky, *Reconceiving Autonomy: Sources, Thoughts, and Possibilities*, 1 YALE J. LAW
& FEM. 7 (1989).

NEDELSKY, J., PRIVATE PROPERTY AND THE LIMITS OF AMERICAN CONSTI-
TUTIONALISM (1991).

Neely, *The Primary Caretaker Parent Rule: Child Custody and the Dynamics of Greed*, 3
YALE L. & POL'Y. REV. 168 (1984).

NODDINGS, N., CARING (1974).

NORTH, D., THE ECONOMIC GROWTH OF THE UNITED STATES, 1780–1860
(1966).

Norton, *Family Life Cycle: 1980*, 45 J. MARR. AND THE FAM. 267 (1983).

Note, *Fornication, Cohabitation, and the Constitution*, 77 MICH. L. REV. (1978).

Note, *Interspousal Torts and Divorce: Problems, Policies, Procedures*, 27 J. FAM. L. 489
(1988–89).

Note, *The Marital Rape Exemption*, 52 N.Y.U. L. REV. 306 (1977).

Note, *To Have and to Hold: The Marital Rape Exemption and the Fourteenth Amendment*,
99 HARV. L. REV. 1255 (1986).

Nussbaum, *The Discernment of Perception: An Aristotelian Conception of Private and
Public Rationality*, in M. NUSSBAUM, LOVE'S KNOWLEDGE: ESSAYS ON PHI-
LOSOPHY AND LITERATURE (1990).

O'NEILL, W., DIVORCE IN THE PROGRESSIVE ERA (1967).

Offen, *Defining Feminism: A Comparative Historical Approach*, 14 SIGNS 119 (1988).

OKIN, S., GENDER, JUSTICE, AND THE FAMILY (1989).

Oldham, *Premarital Contracts Are Now Enforceable, Unless...*, 21 HOU. L. REV. 757
(1984).

Olsen, *The Family and Market*, 96 HARV. L. REV. 1496 (1983).

Olsen, *The Myth of State Intervention within the Family*, 18 MICH. J. L. REF. 835 (1985).

One-Third of Employees Covered by Maternity Leave Policies, BLS Says, Daily Lab. Rep.
(BNA) No. 64, at B–1 (Apr. 5, 1989).

Pampel, *Changes in the Propensity to Live Alone: Evidence from Consecutive Cross-
Sectional Surveys, 1960–1976*, 20 DEMOGRAPHY 433 (1983).

Pateman, *Feminist Critiques of the Public/Private Dichotomy*, in FEMINISM AND
EQUALITY (A. Phillips ed. 1987).

PATMORE, C., *The Wedding Song*, in THE POEMS OF COVENTRY PATMORE (F.
Page ed. 1949).

Peller, *The Metaphysics of American Law*, 73 CALIF. L. REV. 1151 (1985).

Peplau & Cochran, *Value Orientations in the Intimate Relationships of Gay Men*, in GAY
RELATIONSHIPS (J. DeCecco ed. 1988).

Peplau, *What Homosexuals Want*, PSYCHOLOGY TODAY, March 1981, at 28.

PERKIN, H., THE ORIGINS OF MODERN ENGLISH SOCIETY (1969).

PETERSON, M.J., FAMILY, LOVE, AND WORK IN THE LIVES OF VICTORIAN GENTLEWOMEN (1989).

PHELPS, E. (ed.), ALTRUISM, MORALITY, AND ECONOMIC THEORY (1975).

PHILLIPS, M., THE DILEMMAS OF INDIVIDUALISM (1983).

PIETROPINO, A. & J. SIMENAUER, HUSBANDS AND WIVES: A NATIONWIDE SURVEY OF MARRIAGE (1979).

PIVEN, D., PURITY CRUSADE: SEXUAL MORALITY AND SOCIAL CONTROL, 1868–1900 (1973).

PLATO, THE REPUBLIC (B. Jowett tr. 1986).

POLKINGHORNE, D., NARRATIVE KNOWING AND THE HUMAN SCIENCES (1988).

POSNER, R., AN ECONOMIC ANALYSIS OF LAW (3d ed. 1986).

POSNER, R., SEX AND REASON (1992).

POSNER, R., THE ECONOMICS OF JUSTICE (1981).

POSNER, R., THE PROBLEMS OF JURISPRUDENCE (1990).

POST, R. (ed.), LAW AND THE ORDER OF CULTURE (1991).

POUND, R., INTERPRETATIONS OF LEGAL HISTORY (1923).

Price-Bonham & Balswick, *The Non-Institutions: Divorce, Desertion, and Remarriage*, 42 J. MARR. AND THE FAM. 225 (1980).

Project: Law Firms and Lawyers with Children: An Empirical Analysis of the Work/Family Conflict, 34 STAN. L. REV. 1263 (1982).

Rabin, *The Revolution in Residential Landlord-Tenant Law: Causes and Consequences*, 69 CORN. L. REV. 519 (1984).

Radin, *Market-Inalienability*, 100 HARV. L. REV. 1849 (1987).

Radin, *The Liberal Conception of Property: Cross-Currents in the Jurisprudence of Takings*, 88 COLUM. 1667 (1988).

Randolph, *Study Urges Law Be Changed to Reduce Libel Litigation*, WASHINGTON POST, Oct. 19, 1988, at p. A2.

Rausch, *Orientations to the Close Relationship*, in CLOSE RELATIONSHIPS: PERSPECTIVES ON THE MEANING OF INTIMACY (G. Levinger & H. Rausch eds. 1977).

Rehbinder, *Status, Contract, and the Welfare State*, 23 STAN. L. REV. 941 (1971).

Resnik, *On the Bias: Feminist Reconsiderations of the Aspirations for Our Judges*, 61 S. CAL. L. REV. 1877 (1988).

Review Symposium on Weitzman's Divorce Revolution, 1987 AM. BAR. FOUND. RES. J. 759.

Rhode & Minow, *Reforming the Questions, Questioning the Reforms: Feminist Perspectives on Divorce Law*, in DIVORCE REFORM AT THE CROSSROADS (S. Sugarman & H. Kay eds. 1990).

RHODE, D., JUSTICE AND GENDER (1989).

Richards, *Constitutional Legitimacy and Constitutional Privacy*, 61 N.Y.U. L. Rev. 800 (1986).

Richards, *The Individual, the Family, and the Constitution*, 55 N.Y.U. L. REV. 1 (1980).

RIEFF, P., FREUD: MIND OF THE MORALIST (1959).

RIEFF, P., TRIUMPH OF THE THERAPEUTIC: THE USES OF FAITH AFTER FREUD (1966).

RIESSMAN, C., DIVORCE TALK (1990).

Rising Proportion of American Workers Holds More Than One Job, Daily Labor Rep. (BNA) no. 153, at B–1 (Aug. 8, 1986).

ROBINSON, P., THE MODERNIZATION OF SEX (1976).
ROGERS, C., ON BECOMING A PERSON (1961).
RORTY, R., CONSEQUENCES OF PRAGMATISM (1982).
RORTY, R., PHILOSOPHY AND THE MIRROR OF NATURE (1979).
Rose, *Crystals and Mud in Property Law*, 40 STAN. L. REV. 577 (1988).
ROSEN, R., THE LOST SISTERHOOD (1982).
Rosenblatt & Wright, *Shadow Realities in Close Relationships*, 12 AM. J. OF FAM. THERAPY 45 (1984).
Rossi, *Gender and Parenthood*, 49 AM. SOC. REV. 1 (1984).
Rubin, *The Economics of Crime*, 28 ATLANTA ECON. REV. 38 (1978).
RUDDICK, S., MATERNAL THINKING (1989).
RUSKIN, J., *Of Queen's Gardens*, in SESAME AND LILIES (1900 ed.).
RUSSELL, D., RAPE IN MARRIAGE (1982).
RYAN, M., CRADLE OF THE MIDDLE CLASS: THE FAMILY IN ONEIDA COUNTY, NEW YORK, 1790–1865 (1981).
RYAN, M., WOMANHOOD IN AMERICA (1975).
SALKEVER, S., FINDING THE MEAN (1990).
Sanchez, *D.C. Council Approves Partners Bill*, WASH. POST, April 8, 1992, at B1.
Sandel, *Moral Argument and Liberal Toleration: Abortion and Homosexuality*, 77 CALIF. L. REV. 521 (1989).
SANDEL, M., LIBERALISM AND THE LIMITS OF JUSTICE (1982).
Sarbin, *Emotion and Act: Roles and Rhetoric*, in THE SOCIAL CONSTRUCTION OF EMOTION (R. Harre ed. 1986).
Scanzoni, *Families in the 1980s: Time to Refocus Our Thinking*, 8 J. FAM. ISS. 394 (1987).
SCANZONI, J., K. POLONKO, J. TEACHMAN & L. THOMPSON, THE SEXUAL BOND: RETHINKING FAMILIES AND CLOSE RELATIONSHIPS (1989).
Schachter & Singer, *Cognitive, Social, and Psychological Determinants of Emotional State*, 1962 PSYCHOL. REV. 69.
Schachter, *Cognitive Effects on Bodily Functioning: Studies of Obesity and Eating*, in NEUROPHYSIOLOGY AND EMOTION (D.C. Glass ed. 1967).
SCHACHTER, S., EMOTION, OBESITY, AND CRIME (1967).
Schepple, *The Reasonable Woman*, 1 THE RESPONSIVE COMMUNITY 36 (1991).
SCHICKEL, R., INTIMATE STRANGERS: THE CULTURE OF CELEBRITY (1985).
Schlag, *Missing Pieces: A Cognitive Approach to Law*, 67 TEX. L. REV. 1195 (1989).
Schneider, *Moral Discourse and the Transformation of American Family Law*, 83 MICH. L. REV. 1803 (1985).
Schneider, *Rethinking Alimony: Marital Decisions and Moral Discourse*, 1991 B.Y.U. L. REV. 197.
Schneider, *Rights Discourse and Neonatal Euthanasia*, 76 CALIF. L. REV. 151 (1988).
Schneider, *Rules, Discretion, and Law: Child Custody and the UMDA's Best-Interest Standard*, 89 MICH. L. REV. 2215 (1991).
Schneider, *State-Interest Analysis and the Channelling Function in Privacy Law*, 20 HOFSTRA L. REV. – (1992).
Schneider, *State-Interest Analysis in Fourteenth Amendment "Privacy" Law: An Essay on the Constitutionalization of Social Issues*, 51 LAW & CONTEMP. PROB. 79 (1988).
SCHOSHINSKI, R., AMERICAN LAW OF LANDLORD AND TENANT (1980).
SCHOULER, J., A TREATISE ON THE LAW OF DOMESTIC RELATIONS (1870).
SCHUDSON, M., ADVERTISING: THE UNEASY PROFESSION (1984).

Schultz, *Contractual Ordering of Marriage: A New Model for State Policy*, 70 CALIF. L. REV. 204 (1982).

Schultz, *Reproductive Technology and Intent-Based Parenthood: An Opportunity for Gender Neutrality*, 1990 WIS. L. REV. 297.

Schultz, *Telling Stories about Women and Work: Judicial Interpretations of Sex Segregation in the Workplace in Title VII Cases Raising the Lack of Interest Argument*, 103 HARV. L. REV. 1749 (1990).

Schwartz, *A Liberal Model for the Family?* 2 THE RESPONSIVE COMMUNITY 86 (1991).

Schwartz, *The Family as a Changed Institution*, 8 J. FAM. ISS. 455 (1987).

Schwartz, *The Serious Marital Offender: Tort Law as a Solution*, 6 FAM. L.Q. 219 (1972).

Schwartz, *The Spousal Exemption for Criminal Rape Prosecution*, 7 VT. L. REV. 33 (1982).

SCHWARTZ, B., THE BATTLE FOR HUMAN NATURE (1986).

Schwarzchild, *Same-Sex Marriage and Constitutional Privacy: Moral Threat and Legal Anomaly*, 4 BERK. WOMEN'S L.J. 94 (1988–89).

SCITOVSKY, T., THE JOYLESS ECONOMY (1976).

Scott, *Conflict and Cooperation in Long-Term Contracts*, 75 CALIF. L. REV. 2005 (1987).

Scott, *Deconstructing Equality-Versus Difference; or, The Uses of Poststructural Theory for Feminism*, 14 FEM. STUD. 33 (1988).

Scott, *Rational Decisionmaking about Marriage and Divorce*, 76 VA. L. REV. 9 (1990).

Seidman, *Baby M and the Problem of Unstable Preferences*, 76 GEO. L.J. 1829 (1988).

Sennett, *Fragments against the Ruin: Coping with an Unbounded Present*, TIMES LITERARY SUPPLEMENT, Feb. 8, 1991, at 6.

SENNETT, R., THE FALL OF PUBLIC MAN (1977).

Shapiro & Schultz, *Single-Sex Families: The Impact of Birth Innovations upon Traditional Family Notions*, 24 J. FAM. L. 271 (1985–86).

Sharp, *Fairness Standards and Separation Agreements: A Word of Caution on Contractual Freedom*, 132 U. PA. L. REV. 1399 (1984).

Shearer, "Rape in Marriage," *Parade Special* (April 22, 1979).

SHEEHY, G., CHARACTER (1988).

SHELLEY, P., COMPLETE POETICAL WORKS (T. Hutchinson ed. 1933).

Sherry, *The Feminine Voice in Constitutional Adjudication*, 72 VA. L. REV. 543 (1986).

SHORTER, E., THE MAKING OF THE MODERN FAMILY (1975).

SHWEDER, R., THINKING THROUGH CULTURES (1991).

Silver & Sabini, *Sincerity: Feelings and Constructions in Making a Self*, in THE SOCIAL CONSTRUCTION OF THE PERSON (K. Gergen & K. Davis eds. 1985).

Singer, *Divorce Reform and Gender Justice*, 67 N.C.L. REV. 1103 (1989).

Singer, *Ellen and Debbie: A Lesbian Couple and Their Commitment*, WASHINGTON POST, May 27, 1991, at C5.

Singer, *The Privatization of Family Law*, 1992 WIS. L. REV. –.

Singer, *The Reliance Interest in Property*, 40 STAN. L. REV. 611 (1988).

SINGER, I., THE NATURE OF LOVE. Vol. 2, COURTLY AND ROMANTIC (1984).

SIPRESS, D., SEX, LOVE, AND OTHER PROBLEMS (1991).

SKLAR, K., CATHARINE BEECHER: A STUDY IN AMERICAN DOMESTICITY (1981).

SKOLNICK, A., EMBATTLED PARADISE (1991).

Slawson, *The New Meaning of Contract: The Transformation of Contract Law by Standard Forms*, 46 U. PITT. L. REV. 21 (1984).

Smith, *The Study of the Family in Colonial America: Trends, Problems, and Prospects*, WM. & MARY Q., 3rd ser., 39 (1982).

SMITH-ROSENBERG, C., DISORDERLY CONDUCT: VISIONS OF GENDER IN VIC-
TORIAN AMERICA (1985).

SPADA, J., THE SPADA REPORT (1979).

Spanier, *Married and Unmarried Cohabitation in the United States: 1980*, 45 J. MARR.
AND THE FAM. 277 (1983).

Spann, *Baby M and the Cassandra Problem*, 76 GEO. L.J. 1719 (1988).

SPELMAN, E., INESSENTIAL WOMAN (1988).

SPITZER, S., C. COUCH & J. STRATTON, THE ASSESSMENT OF THE SELF (1973).

STACEY, J., BRAVE NEW FAMILIES (1984).

Stepp, *Many Shun Church for Other Acts of Faith*, WASHINGTON POST, Aug. 4, 1988,
at A1.

STONE, L., THE FAMILY, SEX, AND MARRIAGE IN ENGLAND, 1500–1800 (1977).

Storms & Nisbett, *Insomnia and the Attribution Process*, 16 J. PERS. & SOC. PSYCH.
319 (1970).

Storms, *Sexual Orientation and Self-Perception*, in PERCEPTION OF EMOTION IN SELF
AND OTHERS 165 (P. Pliner, K.R. Blankstein & I.M. Spiegel eds. 1979).

STORY, J., COMMENTARIES ON THE CONFLICTS OF LAW (1834 ed.).

STRACHEY, L., EMINENT VICTORIANS (1918).

STRASSER, S., SATISFACTION GUARANTEED (1991).

Stryker, *Symbolic Interactionism: Themes and Variations*, in SOCIAL PSYCHOLOGY:
SOCIOLOGICAL PERSPECTIVES (M. Rosenberg & R. Turner eds. 1981).

Subcommittee on Human Resources of the Committee on Ways and Means, U.S. House
of Representatives, *Child Support Enforcement Report Card* (1991).

Sugarman, *Dividing Financial Interests at Divorce*, in DIVORCE REFORM AT THE
CROSSROADS (S. Sugarman and H. Kay eds. 1990).

SULLIVAN, W., RECONSTRUCTING PUBLIC PHILOSOPHY (1986).

Sunstein, *Beyond the Republican Revival*, 97 YALE L. J. 1539 (1988).

Sunstein, *Legal Interference with Private Preferences*, 53 U. CHI. L. REV. 1129 (1986).

Sunstein, *Lochner's Legacy*, 87 COLUM. L. REV. 873 (1987).

Sunstein, *Neutrality in Constitutional Law (with Special Reference to Pornography, Abortion,
and Surrogacy)*, 92 COLUM. L. REV. 1 (1992).

Susman, *"Personality" and the Making of Twentieth-Century Culture*, in NEW DIREC-
TIONS IN AMERICAN INTELLECTUAL HISTORY (J. Higham & P. Conkin eds.
1979).

SWEET, J. & L. BUMPASS, AMERICAN FAMILIES AND HOUSEHOLDS (1987).

Symposium, *Legislative Approaches to Work and the Family*, 26 HARV. J. LEGIS. 295
(1989).

Symposium, *The Family in the 1990s: An Exploration of Gay and Lesbian Rights*, 1 LAW
& SEXUALITY 1 (1991).

Symposium, *The Republican Civic Tradition*, 97 YALE L. J. 1493 (1988).

Taylor, *Life without Father*, WASHINGTON POST, June 7, 1992, at C1.

Taylor, *Nonmarital Births: As Rates Soar, Theories Abound*, WASHINGTON POST, Jan.
22, 1991, at A3.

TAYLOR, C., HEGEL (1975).

TAYLOR, C., SOURCES OF THE SELF (1989).

Teitlebaum, *Family History and Family Law*, 1985 WIS. L. REV. 1135.

Teitlebaum, *Moral Discourse and Family Law*, 84 MICH. L. REV. 430 (1985).

Temple, *Freedom of Contract and Intimate Relationships*, 8 HARV. J.L. & PUB. POL.
121 (1985).

TENNYSON, A., IDYLLS OF THE KING (J.M. Gray ed. 1983).

Thaler & Shefrin, *An Economic Theory of Self-Control*, 89 J. POL. ECON. 392 (1981).

Thornton & Freedman, *Changing Attitudes toward Marriage and Single Life*, 14 FAM. PLAN. PERSP. 297 (1982).

Thornton, *Changing Attitudes toward Family Issues in the United States*, 51 J. MARR. AND THE FAM. 873 (1989).

TOMLINSON, A. (ed.), CONSUMPTION, IDENTITY, AND STYLE (1990).

TRILLING, L., SINCERITY AND AUTHENTICITY (1971).

TROW, G., WITHIN THE CONTEXT OF NO CONTEXT (1978).

Turner, *The Real Self: From Institution to Impulse*, 81 AM. J. SOC. 989 (1976).

Turner, *The Role and the Person*, 84 AM J. SOC. 1 (1978).

Udry, *Marital Alternatives and Marital Disruption*, 43 J. MARR. & THE FAM. 889 (1981).

UNGER, R., PASSION (1984).

U.S. DEPARTMENT OF COMMERCE, BUREAU OF THE CENSUS, STATISTICAL ABSTRACT OF THE UNITED STATES (111th ed. 1991).

Van Voorst, *The Office Goes Airborne*, TIME, June 8, 1992, at 72.

VATTIMO, G., THE END OF MODERNITY (1988).

VAUGHAN, D., UNCOUPLING (1986).

VEBLEN, T., THE THEORY OF THE LEISURE CLASS (1934 ed.).

VEROFF, J., E. DOUVAN & R. KULKA, THE INNER AMERICAN (1981).

Waite, Goldschneider & Witsberger, *Nonfamily Living and the Erosion of Traditional Family Orientations among Young Adults*, 51 AM. SOC. REV. 541 (1986).

Walker, *Family Law in the Fifty States: An Overview*, 25 FAM. L. Q. 417 (1992).

Walters, *Are Families Different from Other Groups?* 44 J. MARR. & THE FAM. 841 (1982).

Wardle, *No-Fault Divorce and the Divorce Conundrum*, 1991 B.Y.U. L. REV. 79.

WASHINGTON POST Magazine, Sept. 4, 1988, at 53.

Watkins, Menker & Bongaarts, *Demographic Foundations of Family Change*, 52 AM. SOC. REV. 346 (1987).

WATKINS, M., INVISIBLE GUESTS: THE DEVELOPMENT OF IMAGINAL DIALOGUES (1986).

Weinrib, *Enduring Passion* (Book Review), 94 YALE L.J. 1825 (1985).

WEINSTEIN, F. & G. PLATT, THE WISH TO BE FREE: SOCIETY, PSYCHE, AND VALUE CHANGE (1969).

Weisbrod, *On the Expressive Functions of Family Law*, 22 U.C. DAVIS L. REV. 991 (1989).

Weiss, *On the Current State of the American Family*, 8 J. FAM. ISS. 464 (1987).

Weitzman & Dixon, *The Alimony Myth: Does No-Fault Make a Difference?* 14 FAM. L. Q. 141 (1980).

WEITZMAN, L., THE DIVORCE REVOLUTION (1985).

WEITZMAN, L., THE MARRIAGE CONTRACT (1980).

Wels, *New York: The Poor Man's Reno*, 35 CORNELL L. Q. 303 (1950).

West, *Equality Theory, Marital Rape, and the Promise of the Fourteenth Amendment*, 42 FLA. L. REV. 45 (1990).

West, *Jurisprudence and Gender*, 55 U. CHI. L. REV. 1 (1988).

West, *The Difference in Women's Hedonic Lives: A Phenomenological Critique of Feminist Legal Theory*, 3 WIS. WOMEN'S LAW J. 81 (1987).

West, *The Ideal of Liberty: A Comment on Michael H. v. Gerald D.*, 139 U. PA. L. REV. 1373 (1991).

Wexler, *The Uneasy Case for Antinepotism Rules*, 62 B.U.L. REV. 75 (1982).

WHITBOURNE, S. & J. EBMEYER, IDENTITY AND INTIMACY IN MARRIAGE (1990).

WHITE, J.B., HERACLES' BOW: ESSAYS ON THE RHETORIC AND POETICS OF THE LAW (1985).

WHITE, J.B., JUSTICE AS TRANSLATION (1990).

WHITE, J.B., WHEN WORDS LOSE THEIR MEANING (1984).

Wilkie, *The Trend toward Delayed Parenthood*, 43 J. MARR. & THE FAM. 583 (1981).

Williams, *Deconstructing Gender*, 87 MICH. L. REV. 797 (1989).

Williams, *Sameness Feminism, and the Work/Family Conflict*, 35 N.Y.L. SCH. L. REV. 347 (1990).

WILLIAMSON, J., DECODING ADVERTISEMENTS (1978).

WINN, M., CHILDREN WITHOUT CHILDHOOD (1983).

Winter, *Contingency and Community in Normative Practice*, 139 U. PA. L. REV. 963 (1991).

Winter, *Indeterminacy and Incommensurability in Constitutional Law*, 78 CALIF. L. REV. 1441 (1990).

Wishik, *Economics of Divorce: An Exploratory Study*, 20 FAM. L. Q. 79 (1986).

WISHY, B., THE CHILD AND THE REPUBLIC (1968).

WITTGENSTEIN, L., PHILOSOPHICAL INVESTIGATIONS (G.E.M. Anscombe transl. 3d ed. 1958).

Wohl, *Introduction,* in THE VICTORIAN FAMILY (A. Wohl ed. 1978).

WOLFE, A., WHOSE KEEPER? SOCIAL SCIENCE AND MORAL OBLIGATION (1989).

YANKELOVICH, D., NEW RULES: SEARCHING FOR SELF-FULFILLMENT IN A WORLD TURNED UPSIDE DOWN (1981).

YAZAWA, M., FROM COLONIES TO COMMONWEALTH (1985).

Younger, *Perspectives on Antenuptial Agreements*, 40 RUTGERS L. REV. 1059 (1988).

Zainaldin, *The Emergence of A Modern American Family Law: Child Custody, Adoption, and the Courts, 1796–1851*, 73 Nw. U.L. REV. 1038 (1979).

ZARETSKY, E., CAPITALISM, THE FAMILY, AND PERSONAL LIFE (1986 rev. ed.).

Zborowski, *Cultural Components in Responses to Pain*, 4 J. SOC. ISS. 16 (1952).

Zuckerman, *The Fabrication of Identity in Early America*, 34 WM. & MARY Q. 183, 185 (1977).

ZURCHER, L., SOCIAL ROLES (1983).

ZURCHER, L., THE MUTABLE SELF (1977).

Index